ANGELINA MORETTI

BEARDIE
BOOKS

CRITTER HAVEN

BEARDIE BOOKS
Arizona

Printed in the U.S.A.
ISBN: 978-0-578-44141-2

For Sully and Koda,
my little adventurers.

And for Sydney,
who finds great interest in spying on me.

CONTENTS

Sydney cautions you not to use this book
as a care guide for any animal. Syrian hamsters
are solitary rodents and should not be paired
together in case of serious injury.

PART I
THE GIANT WORLD

PROLOGUE

A WARM GLOW of light cast on a small, sleeping dragon. Outside her vivarium, red and green twinkles floated amongst the dark. Lids flicking open (she only *appeared* to be asleep), her eyes dilated—the colors were very distracting upon the glass. She gazed past them to a furry ball on the carpet, and her eyes dilated a little more.

Sydney was a bearded dragon. Her sandstone-colored body blended perfectly on the wooden perch, so the rodent hadn't seen her. *Brainless pests don't even know what is going on half the time,* Sydney thought. Pointed teeth gleamed within her reflection.

She crept down slowly, her belly warm on the driftwood. Mashed crickets and worms shifted inside, but she could hunt them on any given day. The prey she hunted now was bigger, fatter. A rodent. It wasn't wild, it was a *pet!* And Insect-Giver wouldn't let her have it, nor the smaller, thinner one. They were forbidden prey, and that made them more enticing.

Quietly Sydney leered at the front of the vivarium. She was aware of a ruckus in the room—possibly danger—but ignored it as her eyes stilled on the rodent inches from her face. He shrieked when he saw her, legs sprawling out, and those stupid beady eyes shone with alarm. How fearsome she must look to him. How

3

frighteningly beautiful. Curious, she looked to see her reflection again and glimpsed a dark shape swelling above it.

Sydney had only to wait until she could finally get her claws on the two rodents who Insect-Giver lovingly called "Sully" and "Koda."

1
BROTHERS

KODA BARED his sharp rodent teeth. His left paw clenched where he felt the nub between his fingers. Cringing, black-pebbled eyes opened, and, letting terror fade from an old memory, he closed his mouth.

It was warm, though not as warm as it could have been inside the ceramic house. Koda had made his burrow there. His hoard of seeds lay in the corner, a prized cheese slice leaned against it, and bedding covered the floor. One tiny window, which he had once made the mistake of shoving his head through, gaped darkness.

A noise came in sporadic leaps. Thump. Shuffle. Thump. Shuffle.

It's too late in the night for this.

He shoveled past the doorway plugged with bedding and peeked out. Not much to see. By memory he knew Sully's glass home was opposite to his, level on a dresser, but he couldn't tell the distance (he was nearsighted, as well as colorblind), and the shape was blurred. Movement drew his attention to the front. A small, leaping shape danced on the glass.

Koda called out in a tired whisper, "It's going to be morning soon. Didn't anyone tell you that hamsters are nocturnal?"

The little body flopped onto the bedding. Sully replied cheerfully, "Oh, you're awake."

"Of course. You're making a racket," Koda said.

"Sorry. I'll be out soon."

"Giant isn't awake yet." Koda glanced to his left. A wide shape spread along the wall: Giant's bed. *She's under the covers. Good. It's too near winter rain.* The thought sent a shiver through him.

Sully shuffled away. The exercise wheel standing close to the back of the home turned. After several clear, audible grunts, he reappeared on top of the wheel and stood unsteadily before launching over the wall.

Koda heard the thud and leaped out of his burrow. "Sully!"

Somewhere on the floor Sully cried, "I did it!"

Koda jumped as a sudden light glared by the bedroom door. A timer set it off every day close to dawn. He knew when that part of the room turned aglow, the dragon would soon be watching. He had seen it up close only once. The lizard was mean, and it had over three hundred teeth. He heard a shifting noise: the sound of it leaning forward.

Koda pressed his paws on the glass. "It's seen you!"

"The door's locked," Sully said without a care in the world.

Koda recalled that while feeding the dragon, Giant had left the heat lamp on the plastic above the cage door. It was now warped and didn't always close properly.

"Hide! I'm coming down."

He weaved through the obstacles in his home: ceramic hides, a chewed parsley treat, various cardboard tubes. Giant hadn't changed the setup in about two weeks, and though he couldn't see well, he knew the path from physical memory. He halted at one of the taller play gyms, a series of flat plastic squares that interlocked together. Finally, Koda stood huffing at the top and reached for the wall edge. He hoisted his body upwards, legs dangling awkwardly, and down he fell to the ground with a jolt.

He shook off the impact and looked around, listening. Cricket noise hummed farther off. The furniture shadows stretched long. They confused him. He thought if they needed to run, the door was beside the dresser. But tonight, it was closed.

There came a scratching sound. Koda stood up on his hind legs, paws curved in to his chest. The glare was in his eyes. Behind it, as if in a fog, was the dragon's cage. The dragon was sliding across the glass, scratching insistently.

"Told you the door was locked."

Startled, Koda whirled around and in the next instant felt anger at the anxious flutter in his chest. He quickly drew back his raised paws.

Since he didn't lower to the floor, Sully was forced to stand with him. A friendly, chubby face, masked dark gray around the eyes, smiled reassuringly. The ears were spotted—what Giant liked to call "cow ears." Light-gray fur—shaggy and long, unlike Koda's—draped into a skirt at his bottom. Also unlike Koda, he had no missing fingers. Sully had all four on his left paw. He was bigger, too.

Koda hurriedly nudged Sully under the bed. The blanket hanging over the side blocked out some of the glare. He chittered. "I've told you not to jump out at me like that," he scolded in a low voice.

"Sorry," Sully said.

"You shouldn't be out here."

"The door's locked," Sully repeated. "The dragon would've been out already." He gave his cheek a quick prod. The fur spread out slightly around a bulge. *Again, pouching. I always tell him he's going to get booty sneezes eating giant food.* To which Sully always laughed and ate it anyway.

Koda glanced at the glare leaking from underneath the

blanket. "I still don't like being out here," he said. He sniffed for the dragon's scent in case it had escaped but instead sniffed butter on Sully's paws. Giant had watched a horror movie before going to sleep. "That's popcorn, isn't it?"

"Ahuh," Sully said, smiling. "Want some?"

"You chanced a run-in with the dragon for food?" Koda said, exasperated.

"I also wanted you to smell something."

"Smell?"

"Yeah. It's new."

Koda darkened. "Probably a cat." He could feel another pair of eyes watching them, somewhere he couldn't see. There could be more out there. Anywhere. Waiting to toss them around before tearing them open. He turned slowly away from the light, staring into the darkness.

"Not a cat," Sully said. "This is different. I'll show you."

Koda continued to stare.

"Koda?"

He forced himself to breathe normally and returned his attention to Sully. "It's not in the walls, is it?" he asked. "You go in those holes again, Giant's going to keep a lid on your home for sure." *And, maybe, that'd be a good thing.* Except Sully hadn't taken it well, and it seemed moving everything forward from the walls except the wheel hadn't been enough to keep him in.

Sully's lips pulled back over his teeth in disgust. "Not if she loves me, she won't." He started for the end of the bed. "The smell isn't in the walls. Let's go," he said eagerly.

"Sully, you have the energy of a dwarf hamster." Dwarf hamsters could spin right out of their exercise wheels.

"You always say that." Koda's view of Sully blurred.

They scampered out into the open. Almost immediately the scratches returned with startling speed. Koda froze.

Sully passed him and said loudly, "Come get us, dragon!"

"Stop it!"

"She's not going to get out of there," Sully dismissed him.

Koda ducked his head lower to the carpet. "Why do you always need me to go with you?"

"It wouldn't be any fun without you," Sully said.

This, but likely also because if Koda really were to make a fuss over it, Sully wouldn't go. It had happened before. Blaming the nightmare (he still had chills), Koda didn't have the strength to disagree tonight. Not that Sully would fight with him about it. He was a sensitive hamster, and, in the end, he was really only bold when Koda was around.

He followed Sully onto a kind of thick blanket that glittered and flashed. Koda's nose bumped a box. A painted snowman smiled at him.

"What gift do you think Giant got you?" Sully asked. "I hope I get yogurt drops." He moved to the box and started to dance. The scratches returned on the other side of the tree.

Koda stiffened. "Don't move around so much. You'll make it angry."

"Almost got it," Sully huffed.

His bottom slid up onto the box. Koda stood to see him. He could just see the large bauble to Sully's side and the flickering light creating strange glows on his fur.

"Let's climb the tree. We can get up to the window that way," Sully said.

"Keep away from the windows," Koda warned. "It's winter. Your fur isn't thick enough."

"It hasn't snowed here in a long time, Koda. I won't stay for long."

The tree jingled. On the floor, round shadows bobbed in a slight shimmer. "You're going to break her ornaments and get cut,"

9

Koda scolded.

The jingles continued. Koda jumped onto the box and sniffed the air for Sully. A strand of tinsel tickled his ear.

"I'm gonna beat you!" Sully teased.

"It's not a game!"

Climbing onto the first branch, Koda groaned. *The play gym and now this.* He was grateful if only for the fact the tree was significantly shorter than the one in the living room. His weight shifted as the branch bounced under him. He climbed very slowly, but his feet still often slipped. He could tell the branches were getting smaller as, all the while, the cool breeze blew in stronger gusts. Finally, he neared the tree's peak and cut through to the other side.

Sully's huffing had long since quieted. "Reach up, Koda," he encouraged from the top. "It's not far."

Koda raised on his feet, being very careful as the branch dipped. He found a ledge in the wall and pulled himself up onto the window sill. Outside it was still dark, though possibly lightening to gray. Soon the crickets would be silent.

He combed his nose. He smelled a murkiness in the breeze whistling through the window mesh—not like rain or snow at all. It smelled ugly.

Sully zoomed in Koda's face. He back-stepped. "It's scary, huh?" Sully said, not a smidge of fright in him at all.

"It smells like sickness."

"It's not an animal, right?" Sully asked, though he sounded sure enough already. "What do you think it is?"

When he had been near the dragon's cage that one occasion, Koda had smelled the collard greens in its dish. They had been dragged in by the dragon and left overnight. It wanted meat, not greens. Imagining it feasting on prey gave him another guess. A stain on his mind insisted it was the scent of death.

Koda chose not to say so to Sully, not because he didn't want to frighten him, but because he was afraid of saying it out loud, as if he would be tempting something dangerous. "It's like… rotten plants."

"The trees are wilting in the backyard?" Sully asked.

"I don't know."

"It's weird," said Sully. "Giant mentioned the national forest was dying in some areas but that's, like, very far from here."

Koda walked to where the breeze slackened. Cold glass shocked him on the nose. "Let's get down. I hate the way it lingers."

"I'm worried about the Critters. I hope they'll be okay."

"The wild animals choose to live out there. They would be glad to kill Critters like you and me."

"Yeah, but…"

This time Koda zoomed in *Sully's* face. "You remember what they're like. You know, the drowning lizard in the bucket outside?"

"Oh, yeah! The one Giant put in the dragon's cage, so he could get warm," Sully said. "I didn't know lizards could burrow under bedding so fast."

"It just goes to show a Hunter will eat even their own kind. 'Cause that's exactly what would have happened to that lizard if the dragon would've run faster," Koda said. "When Giant let that lizard go it raced off into the woods without a 'thank you.' If they were smart, they would live with giants where they could be taken care of like us."

"But he was so small, smaller than us, and we get afraid, too," Sully said. "I was really shocked when you first came here, and you bit Giant's finger."

"That was different." Koda turned away. He became very aware of the gap between his fingers. An image of blood gushing down Giant's hand flashed in his mind, and he blocked it out. "The

11

thing is, those animals had rather be in the wild. And whatever's out there isn't locked up like the dragon. Doesn't matter whether they're Hunter or Critter. Both are dangerous if they're our size or bigger."

Sully gazed dreamily beyond the mesh. "I've never been in a forest. I'd like to see what it's like."

"I think you cause enough mischief inside."

"But think of what I could do *outside*," Sully said with a grin.

"I try not to." Koda returned to the meshed section of the window to begin the climb down the tree.

Sully bumped his nose on his backside. "How about we go in the walls?" he asked energetically.

"How about we go to the attic instead?" Koda teased, knowing the effect this would have.

"Pantry pooper."

"I think Giant calls it '*party* pooper.' And you *did* go in a pantry once."

"I couldn't help it! I forgot to go before escaping. Are there really bats in the attic like you said?"

"Maybe," said Koda. He put a paw forward on the nearest branch and could already feel it dipping. He prepared himself for the descent and having to chew on Giant's furniture. It would wake her then she would put them in their homes. "Come on, let's head back. I really wish you would stop escaping. Giant just went to sleep a few hours ago."

"She should be nocturnal. Besides, it's not every night Giant watches scary movies," Sully said brightly. "There's popcorn." He prodded his cheek again. "And she thinks it's cute when I watch."

As they stepped up to the edge of the windowsill, Koda heard a distant noise almost like a whisper. He paused, thinking it had merely been a tree branch swaying in the wind.

Just then the spoiled scent flushed in. There was an earsplitting crash and Sully squeaked. Koda lost sight of him as he fell through the branches, barely catching himself on the way down. The window's mesh shook, rattled, then clattered against the outside wall. Dazed from the fall, he vaguely heard Giant scream.

Tinsel flew, blinding Koda with silvery shimmers. Ornaments whacked him as he heard a spectacular *CRUNCH*. Suddenly, he fell on his side and the branches above him were snapping open. Something jabbed down an inch from his head. Squeaking, Koda bound out of the tree. It had fallen pointed toward his cage and he ran to it.

He felt a wave of air. The thing that had come in screeched and flapped around. Koda darted under the dresser and to its farthest corner. He stared out, terrified at the frantic shadows just visible in the light cast low to the floor. Giant had gotten up from her bed. She jerked to the side, most likely ducking as the flying creature seemed to follow her above. Koda's view across to Sully's dresser became clear. The tree lay halfway in front.

"Sully! Where are you?"

"Help me!"

Did that come from the dresser? His sides beating fast, Koda left the corner to approach the band of light but recoiled as a large shape swiped past him. There was the sound of drawers sliding out (Giant had struck one of the dressers), and she stepped on a remote which had fallen on the floor. Music blared, dulling Koda's squeak and Giant's scream.

"Leave her alone!" Koda yelled.

The bedroom door slammed; Giant's shadow was gone. On Koda's right, a lamp knocked into his glass home then slid along it to the ground. It fell on the tree, shattering. A light flared with a great *WHOOSH*. The tree was on fire.

Heat and smoke quickly engulfed him. Koda dashed to the bed and for one terrifying second, he was uncovered. His heart surged, the light dimmed, the hanging blanket cloaked him in shadow, and he was under the bed.

There was a nook between the end of the bed and the wall that had suitcases and bags he could hide in. He stopped at a bed leg, barely hidden, so close to a tote bag lying open on its side. But Koda didn't dare run into it—the part of the blanket that was hanging down waved slightly. The sound of flapping wings had disappeared.

"I know where you are," said a low, growling voice.

Koda's breath caught in his chest. He hadn't heard Hunters speak very often, though he found most spoke similarly from what he had heard. They were obnoxious, bad-tempered, and usually showed glee when bullying a rodent. Except for the one hunting him. It exceeded deviousness, it was malevolent, and there was no hunger about it. Koda swallowed his breaths and shut his eyes as he heard it speak again.

"A vermin's heartbeat is very quick, very loud. I can hear you."

The Hunter went silent. The radio blared on, an oldies song Giant liked. Crackling sounds came from the tree and rug. The blanket was already catching fire.

Koda heard a clack like the snap of a beak. The bird spoke again, this time on the verge of shouting. "THERE YOU ARE."

He gaped in horror, but instead of his own squeak he heard Sully's. The blanket billowed upward in a harsh whack. By the light of the heat lamp he saw the owl as a black figure, wings extended and sharp talons in tow. Nothing so obscure looking had ever chilled him in the way it did. He watched as it chased Sully behind the dragon's cage, praying it would protect him.

Koda darted into the tote bag. The fabric caught the shadows in terrifying shapes. Everywhere it seemed the owl's wings were dancing on him and suddenly enlarged. A moment later Sully entered. They tumbled into each other as the bag lifted off the floor. The owl's stench was strong.

The crickets droned as the wind brought in the rotted stench. Out the window they flew and into the night.

2
OUTSIDE GIANT'S NEST

T HE BAG ROCKED like a playground swing twisting out of control. Sully bowled into Koda as he rolled from one end to the other. His brother was on his back with his legs and arms up in the air, shuddering like an overturned bug.

"*Koda! What do we do?*" Sully screamed.

All through their flight the owl had been silent. Now it gave several flaps of its wings before a shrill cry that wasn't its own soared over the wind. Sully ducked his head as something large and heavy whacked the bag. Koda screamed, a prolonged, fur-raising wail so loud Sully thought there must not be any air left in him. The owl rivaled it with a strident screech. Sully's stomach surged, built up to a high that seized control of his legs and drove him up the bag in a squirming panic. Wind rushed at the cloth at an incredible speed.

He bounced midair, fell into a fold and pulled it down as if the bag had caught on something. Far below him he heard a splash. He jumped, catching his claws deep into the cloth. It gave under his feet. His stomach plunged again, and he landed with a jarring thud.

Sully breathed raggedly and listened. Splashing. Warring bird cries. Large wings beat violently in the sky. He crawled out from the bag and leaves crunched under his feet. For a few precious

16

seconds, he was lost amongst them as soft light shone through thick lines banding the outside world.

Koda screamed, "Sully, to the tree! There's a hollow in its roots!"

Sully chased Koda's voice. He bumped his nose on tree bark and found him. He bolted into the hollow. As he turned, the owl's talon pushed into the opening. Sully lunged back into Koda. He watched, eyes wide, his heart beating hard enough to hurt, as the talon twisted inside the little space, raking the rooted walls in deep, jagged scars. A hair's breadth between them, the end wall at their backs, he could see the leathery underside of the blood-stained foot. The owl screeched.

"GO AWAY!" Koda shrieked.

The talon yanked out of the hole, plowing a cluster of leaves backward. A minute passed. The squeaks in Sully's throat quieted. At his side, Koda trembled. He was unusually cold.

Sully took a step forward but stopped as Koda pawed him hard on the shoulder.

Owls don't stay on the ground. It's not safe for them because of other Hunters, Sully thought.

In a rush of crackling leaves and grating dirt, Sully glimpsed the talon shoving in. He cringed against Koda, whimpering under his brother's chin with his eyes shut. The scrapes of the talon gouging the hole sounded shriller, causing a stabbing pain in his ear drum as if it were a pin cushion. His whole body clenched as he imagined the talon reaching farther—inch by inch—to his face.

The talon withdrew. A wrathful screech stretched into the quiet, broken only by the sound of Sully's heartbeat in his ears. He waited for a long while until he was absolutely sure the owl wasn't coming back.

He swallowed. "That's not an ordinary owl," Sully said. "Do you— Do you think he'll be back...?"

Turning around, he gasped. Mud and water clung to Koda's fur. He shivered and appeared to have shrunken half his size. He looked the tiniest he had ever been, even for Koda.

Sully pulled his paws in to his chest. They weren't quite steady. "Koda… You got wet."

Koda spoke haltingly in a hoarse whisper. "We fell from a tree. I th-think I landed in a pond."

"You always say we can't get wet!"

"I'll… be okay."

Sully examined the dirt, trying to think of other things besides the trembling of Koda's ears. "I heard an eagle. That's what attacked the owl."

"We— we might be in a forest."

"*A forest?*"

"This is not a good thing! We're not at Giant's nest anymore. W-we're lost."

Giant's not here, Sully thought. What did that mean for them? They had never been on their own since they were adopted and even then, there had been other giants taking care of them.

"There's usually giants in a forest, right?" Sully said. "We could be in a park. I'll go find someone who can help—"

"Don't leave the hollow!" Koda snapped. "No one's going to help us. We have to find our w-way home on our—" A violent shiver interrupted him. He rubbed his face on the dirt wall and shook once more. "—own. When I'm feeling warmer, I'll t-t-take the first look. Then we'll go together."

Sully faced the outside. A breeze shook the moss overhanging the hole. Koda sat on his haunches and licked his fur. As Sully watched him, his tongue dragged slower and slower. He blinked, blinked again and didn't open his eyes.

Sully felt a tremble within himself. He pawed Koda on the forehead. "Why are you falling asleep?"

18

"I d-didn't get to s-sleep that long, remember? You were—You were m-making... noise..."

"I'm sorry. I don't want you to go to sleep."

"I w-won't," Koda said. He took a deep breath and was soon asleep.

Sully fought the urge to cry. He lingered, looking at Koda, and when he didn't stir, he looked tentatively at the entrance. He crept up to the hole, waited, listened, and peered out. Bits of blackness speckled the sky: the top leaves in a canopy. There were no owl shapes in sight. After a few more minutes of hesitation he left the hollow. Almost immediately a sudden breeze startled him back in. He gathered his courage, and as quick as he could, he stuffed leaves and moss into the hollow. Then he blocked the entrance with rocks.

Sully blanketed Koda with the brush. Still, he shivered continually. Sully was relieved when he spoke again.

"In Giant's r-room, you distracted the owl, so I c-could try to escape," Koda said weakly. "Thank you."

Feeling a pang of guilt, Sully licked the mud off his fur. He did so until his tongue went numb. Then he sulked.

Sully could sleep anywhere. He once slept in an envelope box, using the flap like a blanket, and another time behind the water heater. And with all the brush in the hollow he could ignore some of the cold still in the tree's bark. He had time to think over their situation before he fell asleep, and he convinced himself that Koda would be alright. Sully had had a little of a bad moment, but Koda had stopped shaking and their lives were too happy for anything really bad to happen. He just kept saying that over and over. In a way, the owl taking them could be a good thing. They were finally outside!

A while later he woke to an irregular clicking sound. Under him the leaves brought up the hollow's scent of dirt, mud, and moss. The smell of illness clouding it caused him to start.

Koda was curled tight on his side in the faint sunlight shining through the brush, eyes closed. His nose glistened wet, and his body lurched with each breath. The clicks, Sully realized, came from his lungs.

Frantically, he pawed Koda's face. The fur was like ice. "Koda!" Sully hesitated then pushed him with all his might. Koda didn't blink or make any sign he had felt it.

Sully pressed his cheek against Koda's side. He sobbed. "You weren't supposed to go to sleep."

Scuttling sounded outside the hollow. Sully released a choked squeak.

"Koda… there's someone there."

The scuttling picked up again, grew more excited. The leaves shook.

Sully screamed. *"Koda!"*

A lizard, one so small it could sit on his nose, poked out low to the ground. It bobbed at him and retreated.

Sully sat, stunned. He lowered his head and cried harder. Koda was sick. Giant was very far away.

I'm alone.

For a while he let himself cry. He listened to Koda's breaths, longing for the small chance he would wake up. It dawned on him it was getting later in the day. He stood up, his whole body feeling weak, and pushed the brush to the outside. The trees stood bolder against the sky. By their stark white sides, the nearly transparent leaves in the sun, and the heat on his fur, it ought to be afternoon.

Koda had once warned that Hunters were awake day and night. "You can't be oblivious. Most hamsters are. They don't even know what a Hunter *looks like*. They'll stare one right in the face before they're killed by one. So, you need to be aware."

Sully believed everything Koda said. But it was the owl he was most worried about, mostly because he had seen it. He had one thought: *Owls come out at night.*

He bunched up what shrubbery he could and brought it inside the hollow. As he remolded the brush to block the opening, he looked inside at Koda. "I'll come back, Koda. I'll find someone to make you better."

He left quickly, venturing into a forest a lot bigger than he expected. It was understandable to think from a pet hamster's perspective that the sky was at most eight feet and ended in plaster. It also came as a surprise that the forest floor was so dirty! Ants crawled everywhere, and dead bugs littered the dirt. At Giant's nest the carpet was clean apart from the occasional popcorn kernel, and it was clear, so he could see far ahead. No giant had trimmed this grass for some time.

He stood prairie-dog fashion, using all his senses to figure out where he was. With the forest air in his fur—morning mist, silver firs, and alpine flowers truer than any giant-made perfume— Sully smelled more all at once than he had in his whole life. It may have excited him if Koda weren't sick. Sully wandered alone, hungry, and sad.

He became aware around evening that his cover was dwindling, as the air had chilled and the shadows darkened. The grass shortened to stubs. The long bars against the sky he thought were probably trees thinned and shortened. Sludge coated the flowers, which had wilted and dried out. He sniffed the rotten plant smell, the one he had smelled at Giant's window. It suffocated the land. Without any real destination, Sully had been drawn to it.

This is the national forest, he realized.

The forest was silent for over half an hour. At no point had Sully heard birds chirping despite finding their odd white pee. Or at least, that is what he thought it was. He paused at the sound of logs knocking on a bank.

It had been hours since he drank or napped. He followed the broken trees onto where the land, wide, muddy, and threaded bare of grass, flowed into glistening ground as dark as the mud between his toes. Sully collapsed on the bank and hesitated. At Giant's nest water always came from a water bottle spout. He drank it from the air, not at his feet. Literally testing the waters, he dunked his mouth, but he did it a little too much, and the water rushed into his nose. Sully sneezed, grimacing. *It tastes awful!*

The water rippled in front of him. Sully inched closer and cringed as it splashed in his eyes. Something tiny with webbed feet jumped out onto his head and landed on the ground behind him.

"Hey!" He spun, seeing a spotted frog hopping away. Sully chased him into a patch of dying heather where the frog sat on one of the drooping blades. It was odd. The frog was the only animal he had seen so far.

"Hello," Sully said timidly. "I really need your help. My brother is very sick. A Hunter got into our house and took us, so we don't know where we are."

The frog's lower jaw pulsed. His bulging eyes stared.

The frog should be able to understand. Sully understood the owl clearly enough when it had spoken to Koda, and the owl was a Hunter. This meant it didn't matter if an animal was a different species or a Critter or a Hunter. They should be able to understand each other. Right?

"Is there, um, someone, a Critter like me, who knows where giants are?"

Still staring.

"Do you speak hamster?"

"*RIBBIT.*"

"Can you… ribbit… help… ribbit… my brother… ribbit?"

"*RIBBIT.*"

22

Maybe I'm wrong. Maybe I can't speak frog.

The heather stems snapped in Sully's face. Beyond them the frog was jumping away.

"Wait!"

He ran past the heather to the other side. The frog skipped like a pebble on water. Soon it was too tiny for him to spot.

Sully cried pitifully as his legs gave out under him. Long ago he had emptied his cheek pouches—he hadn't ever thought to do that before unless he was dropping off forage in his hideaway, but some instinct told him it was safer this way, just in case he needed to be lighter to run. No chance of that now. His mud-soaked belly growled. Pollen and other forest litter stuck in his fur. He didn't brush it away. He didn't even have the energy to speak.

Could he really do this without Koda? What would it be like without him?

The dropping sun lingered high enough in the sky for Sully to see the lake several feet out bordered by a few lighter trees standing amongst the blacker shapes. Gazing at them made his eyelids heavy. *I want to sleep.* He might have been able to see the landscape more clearly during the afternoon since there would have been more contrast then, but it had been hours since he left Koda.

Koda's depending on me. Sully let the image of him struggling to breathe, cold and alone, lead him off the bank.

His vision darkened as time passed. So overwhelming was the rotten plant stink it seemed as if it were pushing him back, and Sully could hardly stand to keep walking forward. He stood staring at a black belt of dead trees spanning widely across the landscape. Curious, he withstood the smell and ventured inside.

A sea of decomposing foliage plagued the ground. The plants wilted low to the dirt, plastered in sludge. Sully's paws immediately stuck. He pulled them up, taking several tries to do so. The trees thinned as he walked. Their gnarled, bare branches draped

23

the floor in barbed shapes. Peeled bark cluttered the floor like blackened pencil shavings, rocking in the wind and smelling like oil and pill bugs. The only bugs living there, as far as Sully could see, were gnats. They zipped around him and the plants and the trees. They became so many, it was like looking into a black cloud.

Sully gazed at the scene in sadness. "What's going on?"

By now he could tell what was sky and what were large bunches of leaves by their star-shaped shadows. Somewhere beyond the snags were healthy trees.

"Hello! Anyone?" Sully called.

The gnats buzzed in reply. He paced a little, annoyed.

"Hello?"

A breeze perforated the gnat cloud. The bugs returned to fly at Sully, and he began to cry again. He had traveled too far. How was he going to get back? And before Koda... Before Koda... He wanted to say goodbye.

A branch snapped. Sully's ears pointed straight in the air.

Someone called beyond the snags, "Who's there?"

Sully sprang to his feet. He called back, "You speak hamster?"

"What?" They sounded confused. "You don't want to be out at night. It's almost sunset."

"My brother is sick! Can you help?"

"Cross the big trees!"

"He's dying!"

A pause.

"Where is he?"

For one terrible second Sully couldn't speak past the knot in his throat. "Under a tree by a pond! I'll show you!"

A small shadow he hadn't seen scuttled down a tree and disappeared. He heard hushed voices. Two branches moved oddly in a way Sully had never seen on a tree. As he realized they weren't branches, a large Critter walked out from the fir and turned its horned head in Sully's direction. Not even once did Sully stop to think it could be a Hunter. He simply assumed he was friendly.

The horned animal trotted toward him. Each stomp coursed straight under Sully's paws. *He weighs like a giant!* Sully thought, amazed. Another smaller Critter rushed ahead. For the first time other than Koda he saw a rodent like himself (though a family or two apart on the animal tree). The gray squirrel met him face on, twitching constantly every which way. Sully sniffed pinenuts on him. His companion, a billy goat, was a silhouette next to him. They looked Sully over.

The goat said, "Show us where your brother is."

3
POACHER

S YDNEY HEARD Insect-Giver talking on the phone in the living room. She was talking fast but not fast enough. Sydney grumbled her impatience, wondering when she would be able to get a better look at the aftermath.

Insect-Giver opened the door and shrieked at the flames climbing the doorframe. She ran away and returned with a fire extinguisher. Foam jetted out in a flying spray. After many, many shouts and jets of foam, Insect-Giver set the extinguisher down, panting, with a look of shock and worry at the rodents' cages. She thrust her torn up arm inside, searching for them frantically.

Pulling her arm out of the cage, Insect-Giver leaned against the scorched wall. Her eyes turned pink, scanning the room—the Christmas tree nothing but blackened wire, the lamp fallen over it with the shade dissolved, the rug like newspaper ashes—and she sobbed.

Her hands and legs trembled as she walked around. Sydney thought she was going to collapse or faint. Instead, she unlocked Sydney's door. Smoke instantly filled the terrarium. Sydney tilted her head up at her, lingering for a few seconds to let Insect-Giver know she would leave when *she* was ready. Then she climbed onto her arm, licked it, and received a chin pet.

Sydney did her usual panning of the head as they went to the living room. Insect-Giver placed her on the couch and left to search more for the rodents. They were gone for good, so she returned, disinfected her arm, wrapped it in gauze, and lit several gingerbread-scented candles to rid the house of smoke.

Ten minutes later someone knocked on the door. Insect-Giver opened it.

A stocky male scaleless entered. He looked like a cop with the tucked in shirt, badges, and walkie talkie on his belt. Sydney was well aware of cops from the action shows. Rodents weren't the only ones who liked to watch TV. He held an empty pet carrier she assumed was for animal criminals. The lucky owl had escaped. Scratching his comb-over, the scaleless saw Sydney reclining on the couch. He frowned slightly.

Sydney presented him her widest, glaring eye. "I'm looking at you, fat human. You wish you were attractive like me."

Giving her one last glance, he turned to Insect-Giver. His eyes glazed stupidly then refocused as he saw the gauzed arm. "Hi. What happened here?" he asked in a high, concerned tone.

Insect-Giver wiped her eyes. "The owl came in when I was asleep. I kinda panicked and got in the way."

Did someone call the cops? Sydney wondered, amused. While there was a certain enjoyment in insulting scaleless when they weren't aware of it, Sydney couldn't understand them, either, besides what little words she had picked up. She had to be careful when speaking scaleless speak around non-animals.

We don't want them wizening up. There's more mischief to get away with when they think they know everything. Sydney smiled innocently.

"Real glad the guy didn't get at your face. He came right through the window?" The scaleless headed toward the hallway. Peering around the corner, he leaned awkwardly. Sydney could hear his weight shifting as the objects on his belt knocked together.

"Yes. He tore right through the mesh," Insect-Giver said timidly. "He's not here anymore. I'm sorry I didn't call to tell you he was gone."

An analyzing look appeared on the scaleless's face, whether from realizing he had made the trip for nothing or from what Insect-Giver had said. "You say he *tore* through it?"

Tears instantly fell on her cheeks. "I think the owl took my pets when I ran out of the room. Maybe that's why he was trying to come in so badly."

Whatever Insect-Giver was saying, the scaleless seemed skeptical but soon changed his expression to sympathy.

Insect-Giver wiped her face. "I'm very sorry for wasting your time."

"No problem. Sorry I didn't make it here fast enough." The scaleless walked back to the door. "You be careful. I'd have that checked out." He indicated her gauzed arm. "Not that you need to worry about rabies—that's a mammal thing—but it'd be a good idea," he said. "And keep looking for your pets. They might still be around here somewheres."

"Thank you." Insect-Giver opened the door. After the scaleless had walked out, she left it open a crack with her hand still on it as if she were afraid the owl would come flying in. "Could I ask you a question?"

"Yes, ma'am."

"How big are horned owls?"

"Around two feet in height. With their wings outstretched it's about five."

"Oh, I mean the adults."

"Those *are* the adults."

Insect-Giver stammered. "It had to at least been double that! I saw it flying right in front of the wall and both wings practically took up the whole thing."

"That'd be your average Andean condor—the largest bird of prey in the world! And we don't get those around here. Great horned owls just don't get that big," said the scaleless.

"Owl's not here anymore, bub!" Sydney was getting bored, especially since the scaleless was out of sight and taking the joy away from her taunting. *How long does it take to say goodbye? Does he need a police sketch of the bird or what?*

Sydney jumped off the couch. Without either scaleless noticing, she slipped into the space between Insect-Giver's shoes and the doorframe.

"If I were coming to catch an Andean condor, I'd need a bigger carrier! Probably looked that big 'cause you were inside."

A pause from Insect-Giver made Sydney assume she wanted to insist on something but perhaps didn't have the strength for it.

Sydney understood by their tone and the closing of the door that the two were saying goodbye. On a whim, she snuck outside, thinking Insect-Giver would see and snatch her. She didn't. The door closed.

The scaleless walked down the steps to a SUV parked to the side of the road. Sydney trailed him in the grass like a lioness.

A cellphone chimed. He set the carrier on the ground, opened the rear hatch, and answered it. "Hey, the house call was a no-show."

He turned sideways to the car, his back to Sydney. She made her move to the carrier.

"Pretty odd. I'll talk to you about it later. I've got two all fixed up and ready to be released." He paused, listening. "Nope. Not around here. It's worth a drive on up to the reserve instead. Some idiot shot them in the legs with a BB gun, and I wanna make sure he doesn't get at them again."

Sydney climbed the metal cage door, rattling it a little, onto the top of the carrier. The scaleless stood right above her, his back still turned. She made the leap toward the inside of the car but only scratched the car, sliding down the outside when she didn't make it. Jumping again, she made a louder screech with her claws. Sydney lifted her weight and, darting around metal equipment, hid behind more carriers. Two of them were occupied.

The scaleless mistook the scratching sound for a pair of ugly-looking badgers. "Settle down, guys. You're on your way to freedom."

Sydney grinned as he placed the empty carrier in the SUV. Completely clueless.

I'd never get a chance like this again. Who knows? There might be some prey in it for me.

The hatch slammed closed. The scaleless sat in the front seat and drove off, unaware of the hitch-hiking bearded dragon inside.

Sydney didn't expect a long road trip. She had wanted to break the rules a little, prove she was smarter than any copper (bonus if she could get a bite to eat), then be back in fifteen minutes. But the cop wasn't taking advantage of his job by driving fast. He drove as if he were behind the reins of a stagecoach.

The car ride wasn't as she had expected, either. It had been a while since her last. Sydney knew about cars and had guessed how they worked when she had escaped in the car one time. Insect-Giver had almost stepped on her while on their way back from the pet store, so Sydney wasn't ignorant about the mechanics of driving. It was the *outside* of the car that was a nuisance. A window revealed pastel clouds underlined by racing trees. They were the color of evergreens, frosted in a mist that faded the orange sky to peach. Unlike rodents, Sydney could see every color a scaleless could. Any number of birds could be nesting in those trees. The day was anew with unruly bird song. Her beard (the scales beneath her head) flared, and her body inflated in a pancake shape. Not that Sydney was scared.

Hiding bored her very quickly, and the scaleless had been singing along awfully to the same Elvis song since leaving the house. Once she had deflated some, Sydney crawled out in view of the badgers. Their glinted stares weren't the kind she gave to prey when she was about to eat them, which was unfortunate as she had hoped to tease them. All their staring was doing, instead of pleasing her, was irritating her.

"I'm not a TV screen. Mind your own business." Sydney waved a claw in the air, meaning to swat their faces. *Like* rodents, her depth perception was lacking.

One of the badgers, a male, asked, "Why'd ya jump in? Ya dumb or something?"

"Says the idiot that got caught," said Sydney.

"Psh." The badger turned his head, smirking humorlessly.

"What you in for?" If Sydney could rub it in more, she would.

"We didn't do *nooothing.*"

"Uh huh. So, you *did* do something."

"Seriously. Ya don't have to give the humans a reason for them to get mad at ya."

"I guess it's badger jail for you."

"What you mean?"

"Don't cops usually take you to jail?" Sydney said in a superior tone as she lifted a claw in the scaleless's direction.

"That ain't no cop!" the female badger spoke up. Sydney doubted they even knew what she was talking about. "He's a poacher!"

Poacher? Sydney tried not to show her surprise.

"They're *all* poachers. Look at what they did to us." The badgers turned to show Sydney the scars on their back legs.

31

Did poachers wear uniforms? "Okay, turn around. I don't want to see your butts all day," said Sydney.

The badgers faced her.

"I say you refused to be arrested, and the cop tased you or something."

"Cops don't capture animals!" the male badger said. "So, what do ya think he brought the cage for?"

"He's going to kill us!" the other badger said.

"Ya let us out, and we'll all get out of here."

"*I'm* not trapped in a cage. All I have to do is wait for the scaleless to unlock the doors," said Sydney.

"Wherever he's taking us is bad news. Probably to where he's got his gun." A sly expression came over the male badger's face. "Ya worried about us eating you? A tough girl like you?"

Sydney grinned. "Don't try to bait me. It doesn't work."

"We're not interested in eating right now," said the other badger. "We're being kidnapped! You let us out, we're bigger than you."

"That's right. We can cause a *ruckus*."

Sydney had already made up her mind. "Hmmm…" She tapped her nails, drawing out her response. The badgers glanced nervously at the front seat as the poacher cranked up the music, humming.

"I like the sound of that," Sydney said.

"Then help us get out of these cages."

Sydney lingered until she saw the frightened doubt in his face, then leisurely walked to the other badger's metal door.

"Why does she get to go first?" the male badger complained.

"You called me dumb, remember?"

Unlocking the latch was Hunter's play. The cage door swung open in Sydney's face. She opened her mouth, ready to bite the badger as it shoved out of the carrier and walked over her. Sydney flicked her head at its belly to get it moving. The badger then shuffled off and wobbled stupidly in place as if unsure where to go next. It decided on the console. Sydney avidly watched the poacher hum, unaware that beside him the badger was snarling at him, looking every bit like an angry chihuahua.

The other metal door shook. "Me next! What're ya doing just gawking about?"

"Shh. I don't want to miss this."

It took one bite at the poacher for him to take his eyes away from the road and to the badger. He yelped in surprise. Sydney couldn't have *hoped* for a more humiliating response. The badger latched onto his arm, tearing at the sleeve and into the skin beneath. Screeching, the car lurched to a stop. Sydney, the carriers, and the equipment slid.

"I'm sooorry! I'm sorry for calling you dumb," the male badger pleaded. "Get me out of here!"

"Oh, alright. You'd think you were going to be killed or something." Sydney unlocked his cage. This time she was prepared and slipped quickly to the side.

The female badger refused to release the poacher. Grunting in fear, he tugged his arm—a large red spot soaked through the tear in his sleeve—while she continued to play tug of war with it, making screaming, chirping sounds. He grabbed her by the back of the head, and she let go to snatch at his hand. He pushed her over the console onto the passenger seat. *Ding! Ding!* The driver door opened, and the poacher stumbled outside.

This seemed to be the female badger's goal as the anger immediately went out of her. She ran to the driver's side and apparently made her escape since through the window the poacher could be seen running after her, shouting, "Wait!"

He reappeared, looking all sorts of sweaty with his frazzled comb-over. He was further shocked when he saw the male badger climbing the console. The poacher slammed the door shut. His agitated voice came muffled on the other side. "How'd you get out?"

Scratching his head, he walked to the back. He was going to open the hatch to get his equipment. Once Sydney or the badger ran there, he would either close the hatch or grab them now that they no longer had the element of surprise.

Thinking fast, Sydney raced to the driver seat. The male badger was whining and running back and forth over the seats. Sydney ignored him, taking the time to turn off the Elvis song—*what a relief*—before jumping to the floor where she found the pedals. Which one was it? She chose one and pressed all her weight on it. It was no good. She had been monitoring her weight too well apparently, and she wasn't heavy enough to make it budge.

The car beeped. She heard the hiss and pop of the rear hatch opening. Metal clinked as the poacher—who was apparently unaware that the car was beginning to roll—rummaged through the equipment. The badger started for the trunk.

"No, you get over here," Sydney commanded. "I've got a better idea."

The badger must have realized what she had already figured out and climbed down beside her.

"Press here."

The badger thrust his paws onto the pedal. The car lurched. In the back the poacher cried, "What the heck?"

"Wrong one," said Sydney. "Try the middle."

The badger pressed on the pedal, really gunning it as the car accelerated. Sydney could feel the wind racing underneath the floor. It felt particularly dangerous yet exhilarating. Some of the equipment fell out of the trunk and clunked onto the pavement. The poacher shouted, but the sounds lessened as they moved away. Silly scaleless was trying to catch up to them.

"Now don't take your paws off that. Not until we get a big head start," Sydney said, feeling awfully cheery.

Just as the car was really gaining speed it threw them hard over the pedals. Plastic screeched, glass cracked, and there was the sound of various metal objects dropping and spinning. The car bounced back and whined as its wheels spun. The badger had landed back on the pedal.

Sydney looked out the broken window at leaves. A large branch had fallen on the top of the car.

"Nice going. You crashed it." Sydney was genuinely pleased.

The badger climbed onto the seat. The rear hatch was still open. "See ya, lizard!" he called.

Sydney glared. "I'm a bearded dragon!"

The badger fled. Grumbling, Sydney jumped at the seat and slipped. "Not this again!" She tried again, fell.

Stomping and various curses rapidly approached the car. The driver door opened. Sweat dripped from the poacher's face and his comb-over waved at the sky in the breeze. He saw her, those obnoxious globes widening in surprise. "You! You're from the house!"

Sydney jumped down and thwacked the asphalt beside his shoe. As he bent to grab her, she spun and zipped underneath the car toward the forest.

"Hey! Come back!"

The stomping followed her into the underbrush. When she could hardly hear them, she walked back out of the forest onto a large plain of grass off the side of the road. Farther down the poacher walked around in the trees, searching for her. The front of his car was bent around a tree at the edge of a curve in the road. Too bad they were hours away from a tow service.

Sydney grinned widely, feeling smug. The sun beat soothingly on her scales. It felt different compared to the heat lamp at home. More… satisfying.

Heat caressing her shoulders, she hiked onward. When the chaos died down, she would retrace her steps for home on foot. The trip had coursed one long, winding road, and she was confident she could find her way. In the meantime, she would enjoy herself.

An hour later, Sydney sat with a most agreeable mix of crickets, ants, and grasshoppers in her belly. Licking an antenna from her jaw, she basked on a boulder concealed in an outcrop. Sydney watched the sky carefully. At home, the ceiling fan looked suspicious, but there could be real birds flying around. She hadn't heard a peep from any since earlier in the car. They wouldn't fool her though. She kept watch.

The sky had turned a solid, pale blue. Her outlook was of an oily lake which widened for miles between two lines of balding trees. Far out on the lake she heard logs knocking against each other and a plop of water. Sydney tilted her head. There continued to be more plops. Something was alive down there, and by the sound of it, it was bite size.

Sydney climbed down from the outcrop. Because the grass was almost nonexistent, she crawled low, rounding the lake inside the tree line. Mud oozed under her belly.

The last plop sounded close. One leap away on the lake's bank sat a tiny red frog.

Sydney closed in. She could see the spots on his red skin. Out of hunger, wanting to taste it, she stuck her tongue out in the air.

At that very instant, her pupils dilated. She had smelled it. *That rodent! It was here!*

She sensed fear. Sydney had been seen and her prey refused to move. The frog was hoping she hadn't seen him and was staying still so she might lose him in the mud. *Nice try. I look like a dinosaur, but I'm no T-Rex.*

She lunged for the catch…

… and missed!

The harsh color skipping across the ground brought her veering left. *I've made it panic,* Sydney thought gleefully. *You're not smart, otherwise you would have run for the water.*

Manipulating his movements from the side, she chased the frog to the bottom of the outcrop. He made the foolish mistake of jumping into a small cave formed by the boulders in which the single exit was blocked by Sydney. He sat like a pebble, looking somewhat out of breath by the quick movement of his jaw. He stared at her with frightened bulbous eyes.

"Weird little thing, aren't you?" Sydney said. "I'm searching for two rodents. Have you seen them?"

"*RIBBIT.*"

Sydney darted into the cave. The frog tried to hop around her. She caught him under her claw, pinning him into the dirt. "I could gobble you down right now."

"Please don't!" the frog begged, kicking his webbed feet.

"So, you *can* talk! Tell me where the rodents went, and today's lunch won't be frog legs."

The frog whimpered. "The rodent went up the lake."

"And the other?"

"There was only one!"

Sydney pressed her claw down harder. "You lying to me?"

"*No, I swear!*"

Sydney sneered into the frog's face, really letting him see her pointed teeth. Then she released him and watched him run for his life out of the boulders and into the sun.

"I hate red."

4
THE MOUNTAIN PASS

THE STRANGERS wasted no time in finding Koda. As three, their heavy hooves and tail swishes shook the underbrush. The vegetation grew alarmingly fast once they distanced themselves some miles from the snags. Sully would have been lost in the ferns. He found himself so overwhelmed with relief that he had rubbed his scent. The squirrel, who introduced himself as Twiggy, learned to recognize his scent and tracked it. Rowan, the goat, carried Sully like a kitten by the scruff. A good thing, too, for his tired feet. He watched as the white highlights on the trees melted to gray and a deep black crept in among the plants. A cold breeze swept the warmth off his fur. They were losing daylight fast.

Twiggy pulled them along in his haste. "Not good," he muttered. Sully recognized his voice as the Critter in the trees. "I don't know how much you know, small guy, but you *do not* want to be out at night."

A break in the trees lighted the dense growth. Rowan trailed the path festooned in grape plants to an awkward leaning tree. A gentle swoosh of water alerted Sully they had arrived.

Twiggy was already at the bole of the tree. "Watch the sky for me," he said to Rowan and began to dig at the brush in its roots.

As soon as the goat set Sully down, he scurried up behind Twiggy.

The last of the brush caved. Despite Sully's efforts to keep the burrow warm, he felt a chill released from the darkness inside as if someone had opened an old coffin. Sully covered his eyes.

He heard Twiggy poke into the hollow. "Strong little guy. He's freezing, but he's alive."

"Bring him out quickly then," Rowan said.

Sully uncovered his eyes and sobbed at the sight of Twiggy dragging Koda's limp body out of the hollow. Barely breathing, his eyes were closed, and his left paw was curled around a ball of dirt.

Rowan's muzzle loomed in, and he lifted Koda by the scruff. Twiggy waved at him impatiently. "Hurry! I don't want to get eaten today!"

Sully's new friends became blended shadows moving fast ahead of him. Less light fell on the ground, and his vision worsened. Trees turned into tall creatures with stilted legs. Boulders were large heads half buried in the ground. This wasn't his home, he didn't have it memorized, and he hesitated. It was like running blindfolded. Dusk had fled the forest. The sun had set.

"Run, small guy! Oh, this isn't good." Twiggy slowed a little, looking at the sky. Sully slowed, too, to see what that strange shadow was passing over the moon.

Twiggy gave a loud barking sound. "He's here!"

In a flicker of light, the owl rammed Rowan on his side. Sully heard a sound like a carpet beater whacking a rug. Rowan bleated as huge, thrashing wings overtook most of his body.

"Keep under Rowan!" Twiggy yelled, pushing Sully at the goat's beating hooves, and barked *KUK KUK KUK!* like a petrified bird. He continued to scream it as they ran under Rowan, whose hooves kicked in a rapid blur to the sides of Sully's vision. He squeaked as one smashed down near his face.

The owl's thrashing shape flew over Rowan. His wings

hovered back, flapped, and returned, the owl raking down his talons repeatedly. "Give... me... THE VERMIN!" Rowan reared up, and Sully and Twiggy ran out from under him. The owl held onto his horns, lifting him higher and higher.

Rowan twisted. One of his horns must have stabbed or cut the owl, who released his hold with a screech. Rowan fell upright. His front legs bowed a bit as he landed with a grinded scratch of his hooves. They started running again, and Twiggy urged Sully back under him as they steered hard into a curve.

"Too fast!" Sully cried, beginning to lose his nerve.

"There! Just ahead!" shouted Twiggy.

An enormous cracking echoed through the forest, and thousands of leaves rustled. Though it was dark, to Sully's eyes there was no missing a massive winding shape behind the snags.

"What is that?" Sully yelled.

The owl's screech rose as if in frustration. Coming up fast, the winding shape, which had seemed to be broken up with lighted crevasses like a huge willow ball in silhouette, was now becoming solid. As they came close, Sully could see a hole in it, close to the ground, that was rapidly sealing up.

They charged toward it.

Sully left Rowan's protective cover. A blurred wall of wooden limbs and leaves zoomed overhead. There was a final snapping and rustling as all light was cast out of the area. It didn't feel as if Sully were outside at all. It was like he was inside a house, hearing the wind muffled by its walls. The owl's muted cry hung outside the wall of trees. His talons clawed them like someone scratching the wood on the other side of a bedroom door. Sully was inside. He had been trapped in.

The owl flew away, screaming his rage. The monstrous cracking resumed and the blackness largely over Sully's head shattered in moonlight. He could see the dome, massive and enshrouding silhouetted woodland. The trees had grown to where their branches tapered into whips, twisting around each other like snakes, and now unwound. The dense brush which had sealed the dome parted.

Critters blackened by the moonlight's glimmer reacted to the sound with their own unusual calls. They could be seen as bustling shapes in the trees within the dome and crowding the forest floor. So many of them. Some came up to Sully. Their new scents and loud sniffs in his ears drove him to his feet.

Beside Sully, Twiggy's bark quieted to strange croaky purring. "*Quuaaa.* Stop crowding!" He shouted above the noise, "I hope you got in a good head-butt."

Rowan talked around Koda's scruff. "Darn tootin'," he said. He leaned prominently forward like it might hurt to stand.

Sully stared at the dome, feeling flighty in his legs. "What is that?"

"The trees are opening up," Twiggy said, as if it were obvious.

"We have to run! The owl will get in!" Sully exclaimed.

"The owl *can't* get in," Twiggy said. "Where've you been living, small guy? Under a tree?"

"He's not from the forest. Look at him," said Rowan.

"I'm not! And I—"

"Then there's a *huge* problem coming at you in a bit," Twiggy said.

Sully was about to say he didn't want any more problems when someone called Rowan's name.

Long ears cut a line into the crowd. Most of the Critters were oblivious and continued to stare, transfixed, at the dome as it settled to stillness. Others watched the ears, including a mouse who had been gawking at Koda and Sully and now stood up, balancing on its tail, to see a jackrabbit hop up in front of them. The hare leaned his long and serious face toward Koda and sniffed.

"Come to the burrows," he said and hopped back into the crowd.

Sully asked no one in particular, "Is Koda going to get better? Why can't the owl attack us?"

"You're safe. Trust me, you're both in good paws." The goat lowered his head to Sully so he could see him smiling warmly above Koda. His eyes were as mysterious as an insect's, but Sully thought he looked at him fondly. A wet gash cut vertically into one of two white streaks that lined his face.

Sully and his group quested through the crowd. By now he could see everything a lot clearer. The crowd dispersed, their path open apart from a few darting squirrels pausing to bark and crow at Twiggy.

"You'd think they didn't know there was a totem outside," Twiggy said.

Totem?

On either side of Twiggy's bobbing tail, Sully saw sleepy porcupines wandering out of logs, mice scurrying across the sand, marmots sitting on rocks, and rabbits grazing on flowers. All kinds of animals. He couldn't look anywhere without seeing them. Sully walked around a pit in the lower grass where a gopher popped out soon afterwards. The above-ground scars they trailed edged close to the outer ring of trees. The tall trees that made up the dome dwarfed the pines and firs to florets in comparison. Inside the smaller trees, the bigger shapes bucked antlers. The clack bore in Sully's chest like thunder.

"No wonder I couldn't find anyone. They're all right here!" Sully said.

"Of course, pika," said Twiggy.

"What's a pika?"

"A pika is you and one of those over there." He pointed to

a small, furry creature about Sully's size peeking between two slated rocks. It quickly hid.

Sully said timidly, "I'm a hamster."

"Hamster? You sure about that? You look like a pika to me." Sully later realized Twiggy was trying to cheer him up.

They arrived in a small clearing where a series of holes in the dirt teemed with kangaroo rats. The bigger ones carried leaf bushels. Koda was gently set down, and as a flowing stream, they took him into the underground burrow. Sully paced around it, unsure of how to get past. He could see Koda below since they had not taken him in very deep. Two kangaroo rats fanned him with the leaves. Sully was eased a little; it appeared Koda was being pampered. But it seemed even more than that—like the Critters were performing a ceremony.

This idea was further strengthened by a song resonating in the trees and burrows. The Critters of the mountain pass were singing. In giant words! Not English, but a more exotic kind that made Sully think of tipis and dreamcatchers. It was a powerful hum in his paws.

Rowan and the hare were singing, too. The only Critters that weren't were Sully and Twiggy. The squirrel helped the kangaroo rats dab the leaves on Rowan's wounds as he sat with his hooves under him.

Stopping mid-song, the hare said, "We didn't know what Critter you were, so we've had to do this in a hurry." He regarded Sully with eyes that seemed in a constant state of frozen startlement and contrasted with his clear, calm voice. Like the song, his voice comforted Sully, a tone clear and soft that suggested he was older than the others.

"You speak giant really good. I wish I could do that," said Sully.

"We believe it aids in the healing process."

A pika passed by Sully with a large bundle in her mouth and handed it to one of the kangaroo rats. They carried it down into the burrow. Sully moved out of the way, close to Rowan's hoof. "What is that they're taking into the burrow?" he asked.

"Thyme," the hare said.

"Time? No, I mean those leaves."

"Thyme is a medicinal herb. Your brother is suffering from a respiratory infection. With blessing, the leaves will clear his lungs."

"What happened out there?" Rowan cut in before he resumed singing.

"The owl attacked us, and Koda fell into a pond," said Sully.

Twiggy paused in applying the leaves to Rowan's skin. "You escaped Hototo? *On your own?*"

Another giant word. Hototo. Sully made sure to pronounce it correctly. "I guess so. If Hototo's the owl," he said.

"How did you even get out here?"

"The owl—uh, Hototo—saw me and Koda at Giant's nest. He was able to get in and... took us here." Sully drifted, remembering. Koda thought he had squeaked on purpose to rescue him when in fact it was an accident caused by the dragon. Privately Sully promised he would tell Koda the truth when he woke up.

Twiggy said, confused, "A giant nest?"

"It's his human home," Rowan said with some amusement.

A sudden change came over the squirrel's face, one very similar to how Koda looked whenever a Critter or Hunter was mentioned. Sully shrank a little.

"I knew I smelled a human on you. I thought maybe one had attacked you. But you're a house rodent. You live with *humans*." The word seemed to stain Twiggy's tongue like a bad word.

"Him and a hundred others here," Rowan said jokingly. "I lived on a farm, Twiggy. In the South." He sounded very proud of that. Sully had picked up on the dialect ("darn tootin'" kind of gave it away), but Rowan didn't have the accent. That was unique to giants.

"It's just— It's just a surprise, that's all," Twiggy said.

"Hototo is expanding his territory. He's exhausted everything within the forest borders, therefore he's searching for more prey. That is the reason why he found you," said the hare. "Most of us have fled from different areas of the world. You are welcome here."

"Where are we?" Sully asked.

"We are on a special piece of land located on a reserve. I can't tell you using human measurements, though it expands between two mountains and just as long. We're protected from the owl within these borders."

"Don't you ever leave?" Though the mountain pass was certainly bigger than Sully's glass home, he couldn't imagine wanting to be cooped up anywhere.

"A select few of us do when it's necessary, but that's not often," said the hare.

"For good reason," Rowan said. "You hear of eagles snatchin' up cats. Hototo's bigger than 'em. He'd kill a cougar if there were any of 'em left." He bleated as one of the kangaroo rats swiped the thyme too roughly over his wounds.

"An eagle attacked the owl!" Sully exclaimed. "I heard it fly into him while he was carrying us inside the bag. We fell into a tree, and that's how Koda dropped to the pond."

"Eagle, hawk, vulture. You're a lucky Critter. Any of those are easy pickins for Hototo," Rowan said. "I reckon it was a vulture, a pretty desperate one to try to steal prey from *him*."

"Most Hunters fled at the first sign of the forest deteriorating," said the hare. Sully wondered why the Critters hadn't done so, too. "Any that choose to stay here—stubborn territorial

Hunters—must be willing to fight a dangerous game."

Rowan nodded emphatically. "Fact of the matter is, Hototo's not any ordinary owl, and when your brother is feeling right better, with good luck and no problems, we'll give you an idea of why that is."

Sully began to ask anyway but stopped as the hare said to Rowan, "You are fortunate as well. The cuts don't appear to be too deep."

"At the end of the day, my horns are sharper than his talons," Rowan said.

Sully was almost sure that wasn't true. "Twiggy said the word 'totem' earlier. What was that about?"

The song's volume dropped several levels. All the kangaroo rats, those carrying in the thyme leaves for Koda and those caring for Rowan, scurried to their burrows. A few glanced at Sully with strange looks. Suddenly, he felt self-conscious and unnerved.

The hare trailed off his singing. "That," he said, "is for a longer talk. Tomorrow is best. I'm sure the kangaroo rats have unoccupied burrows you can nest in when you're ready. Twiggy will take you to the stream to get cleaned if he's free."

Sully felt a twinge of embarrassment. Covered in mud, he must resemble a dung beetle ball.

"Thank you," he said.

"What is your name, tx'utho bicho?" the hare asked.

I wonder what that means. "Sully," he answered, not successfully hiding his pride.

His name, as well as Koda's, were the only words in giant language they spoke regularly—without her in the room, of course, or when they were positive she was asleep. After a while of hearing Giant say them so often, usually whenever she wanted their attention or took them out of their homes, they assumed "Sully" and "Koda" were their names. Sully wanted to show he could speak giant, too.

The hare bowed his head. "Welcome, Sully. My name is Jack." He said goodnight to Rowan and Twiggy and hopped out of the clearing.

A jackrabbit named Jack. Under different circumstances, Sully would have giggled.

Twiggy started for the bushes. "Come on. I'll get you something to eat, too."

"Wait. What did I say that made the kangaroo rats go away?" Sully asked.

"They're just sensitive," Twiggy said. "Hurry. Gray squirrels aren't nocturnal."

Sully halted at a burrow. "I hope your wounds heal," he said to Rowan.

Rowan raised his head from licking the wounds on his legs. "They will. Go eat. I recommend the blackberries."

Sully scurried into the bushes after Twiggy but started as a strong gust of air blew on his fur. He looked up into very large nostrils. He smelled carrots.

"Is that a horse?" Sully exclaimed.

"Yep," said Twiggy.

Sully walked past the sitting horse. He wondered what pattern she had on her face, but she was holding her head up now, too high for him to see.

The trip to the stream was short, but Sully marveled at the surroundings the whole way, and Twiggy made use of the time to ramble on about nuts. Hickory nuts, beechnuts, pinenuts, walnuts, chestnuts. Sully would have never known there were so many. He spoke rapidly and was always hyper as far as Sully had heard so far. He was glad Twiggy had apparently gotten over the fact that he was a house rodent.

At the stream, which poured in down from the shoulder of

the mountain, Twiggy aided Sully in licking off most of the mud. He encouraged him to drink. Leery, for the lake water was still fresh in Sully's memory, it took persistent prodding from Twiggy before he gave in. It was the freshest water Sully had ever drunk. That, with the blackberries Rowan recommended, and his belly was finally satisfied.

Already cold from the bath, Sully went quickly with the squirrel to a rodent hole hidden in higher grass. "This connects to the burrows we were just at. You'll get to your brother from here," Twiggy said.

Sully said thank you and started to lower inside.

"Pika."

Sully looked up.

"When your brother wakes up—'cause he will—call me. I'll hear you."

Twiggy disappeared into the grass. Sully thought he had sounded a little embarrassed.

Alone, he entered the burrows. There were countless tunnels, so he let the kangaroo rats guide him to the one holding Koda. They had laid him on a bed of thyme leaves and cleaned him; his fur stuck up in places. Sully rested beside him. He wasn't nearly as cold. Deep underground, the air trapped in warmth and the smell of strange animals.

"You're okay now, Koda," Sully said and fell asleep.

5

LEGENDS

A STRONG HERBAL fragrance flooded Koda's senses. He was sure he had woken before while his lungs strained against the heaviness in his chest. Then all feeling changed to dreams of Giant's nest, off and on, to be brought back to consciousness when he remembered where he was last.

It was the scent that followed that shocked him completely awake. A jumping creature was encircling him, touching him. Koda kicked it and sent it sprawling somewhere in the dark. It squeaked.

"GET OUT!" Koda screamed.

The hurried pawsteps faded. Koda slipped on something leathery scattered on the floor. Striking a wall, he left it and bolted into a pulsing mass of bodies.

The rodent scent flared just as a rising fire blazed in Koda's heart. He wheezed, a rattled breath that shook his entire body. He could feel himself tipping, beginning to fall onto his back and freeze with his mouth agape.

But Koda wouldn't let himself be vulnerable again. He flung his claws out blindly, letting terror and anger take control, in every direction he heard a sniff, a squeal. Rodent cries echoed. It was still dark. No way for him to see. He couldn't think clearly, couldn't find his way out.

THEY'RE EVERYWHERE! SULLY! SULLY, WHERE ARE YOU?

"Koda!" Sully's voice. "You're— What's the matter?"

"WHERE'S THE EXIT?"

"The left tunnel—"

His claw snagged in someone's cheek, and Koda couldn't yank it out. His instincts were moving faster than his brain now; they reacted instantly, and with his other claw he sliced their ear. The movement of their head released his paw. He fell, feeling a bite to his arm and tail. Koda spun left, hit a wall, and, skidding off it, kept running.

Sully's shout echoed close by then zoomed away from him. "Wait!"

"*Run!*"

More animals confronted Koda once he ran out of the tunnels. They were like specters, racing backward in his vision, as he charged in a blind panic toward the dark massive shapes writhing and twisting together outside the tree line. They bounced in tune to his tortured breath and heartbeat.

"Koda, stop! You'll leave the barrier!" Sully cried.

A large shadow swooped down, rapidly enlarging. Pain seared Koda's neck. He lifted in the air. It happened so fast that for several seconds he surrendered completely to fear and squealed like a pup.

Koda dropped to the ground and saw the animal bobbing its face at him. Ears pointed to the moon behind. Even though the screeches faded with the sound of grinding branches, he expected to feel a blow to the head, as he would have felt when the owl's beak had jabbed at him through Giant's tree.

Whiskers twitched on a small beakless nose. A hare, instead of an owl, loomed over him.

Sully ran up alongside it. "Go away! Run!" Koda shouted.

His brother looked at him, shocked. "It's okay. The owl's gone."

Koda darted between them, blocking Sully.

"That's Jack! He won't hurt us!" Sully insisted.

The scene was nightmarish. A large murmuring shadow formed on the grass. The wild animals were rallying. Koda backed away, pushing Sully as he went. He clenched his paws to his chest. His heart beat too powerfully for a fragile Critter like him. At any second, he would lay gasping upon the ground. And no one would be there to help Sully.

Koda bared his teeth as a squirrel hurried to the hare's side. "He's awake? What's he doing?"

"Everyone, go to your dens," the hare said, speaking above them before lowering his voice. "I'll leave you and your brother to talk." He turned, gave a look to the squirrel who seemed hesitant, and took the crowd with him as he left. Koda held his stance until every one of them disappeared.

"What's wrong? You were bumping into everybody." Sully saw Koda's bleeding arm and tail. "Are you okay?"

Koda pushed him. "Let's go before they come back."

"We can't!"

"Hurry! They'll kill us!"

Sully spoke fast. "Didn't you see it? The trees create a dome when the owl gets too close. You almost left the barrier. Jack saved you!"

Koda couldn't believe it. "You know its name?"

"I found Critters who could help you. It was amazing! They have these leaves and—"

"What have you *done?*"

Sully looked stunned. "I—"

"You've woken me to an infestation!"

"They won't hurt you," Sully said quietly. "They fixed you.

You were so weak…"

Koda ran.

"Where are you going?" Sully called after him. "Don't forget the barrier…"

"Come with me." The anger boiling inside him almost prevented Koda from speaking. He trailed the larger trees and chose a dense fern growth by the inner edge. Small spirals, which he mistook for snails, tipped their vines low to the dirt. Some had been chewed off and scattered among various animal pellets. He scrunched his lips in frightened revulsion. Their foreign scents were everywhere, though none of the beasts thrust their heads from the shade. He began to uproot the ferns.

Sully entered the umbrellaed space and asked timidly, "What are you doing?"

"I'm making us a burrow to hide in. The owl should be gone by morning, and we can go home," Koda said icily.

"There's a flood coming tonight."

Koda spun to face Sully. "What?"

"The Critters sense it. I can, too. Something big's gonna happen. When you hear it, you won't believe it!"

A kangaroo rat jumped out of the ferns. Koda squeaked. The rat gave him a curious look then retreated. Quickly, Koda moved to a darker area and dug fiercely.

Sully followed him. "Koda, what's the matter? You're scaring me! You've never been like this."

"We could be stuck here *forever* waiting for the ground to dry if there's a flood. Giant always takes us out of our homes in the afternoon," Koda said frantically.

"Then… she'd already know we're missing."

Koda stopped digging. "Why?"

"There's a lot to tell you," Sully said wearily. "You were asleep for four nights."

Four nights? The news hit him like a bite to the face.

"Me and the kangaroo rats checked on you every day. Like I was trying to tell you, they made you better again with special leaves."

"Sully, they're animals! Only Giant and other giants know how to cure a sickness. It's a miracle I'm even alive at all without her!"

"I know. It's amazing," Sully said. "Jack, Rowan, and Twiggy are so smart—"

"Don't call them by their names!" Koda shrieked. He extended his bleeding arm and showed Sully his tail. "This! This is what they did to me! I told you what they are, and you had me trapped down there with them! Like throwing meat to wolves! Trapped... while I was asleep..."

Koda broke into sobs. He heard only silence from Sully then careful sniffing at his arm.

"I'm sorry. I didn't know what to do," Sully said.

Koda shoved the roots and stumbled onto his side. Tiredness stole into his body.

Sully lunged for him. "Koda!" He cried beside him.

The soil couldn't be molded into a burrow. The dirt only collapsed, so they were stuck huddling beneath the ferns. Koda felt he shouldn't have to fight, that the forest should just leave them alone. He jumped at every shift in the vegetation, gnawing noise, or branch snap. There were also whispers, mentions of Sully's name, and "the house rodent suffered shock." Yet he heard none of the noises he expected to. No crickets. No giant speak. No cars honking.

This nightmare place... It's nowhere near Giant's nest. How are we going to make it back? You can bet there's more than just the owl waiting for us out there. And I can feel it is going to rain. Is there no way to escape?!

"Koda?" Sully said tentatively. "Koda, I need to show you

something."

"We're not going with those animals out there. At the earliest opportunity, we're leaving."

"It's winter. You said so."

The chill hovered over Koda's fur, though it wasn't cold enough to penetrate. He would have to find them a warmer place soon.

"Ja— The hare knows where Giant's nest is. He'll get us there faster," Sully said.

Koda frowned out of anger and fear. *Why is he always so trusting?* He answered himself. *Because nothing bad has ever happened to him. And so help me, no one's going to hurt him.*

Sully waited. After a minute of no response, he exited the ferns.

Koda shouted, "Sully!"

I can't believe this! What's he doing?

He abandoned the ferns to find Sully waiting, shamefaced. "I won't take you to the burrows, I promise," Sully said.

He knows I won't let him go by himself.

Koda raced to him. He stood and looked in all directions. Glaring, he said tightly, "Stay close to me."

Sully nodded, probably because he knew anything else would upset Koda further.

Ferns behind them. Tussocks, paw prints, and pellets cluttered the land. How could anyone stand living in such a disorganized and unclean place? Leaves rustled, and the wind howled softly. Koda wished it would be quiet so he could hear if someone was sneaking up to them. He flinched as a group of heavy animals galloped at a distance. Somewhere else other animals chewed loudly on forage.

"Twiggy?" Sully called and threw Koda a careful glance. He had forgotten not to speak names.

Perking his ears at a shrill wine, Sully took them to a fir. Koda pressed himself to Sully as the squirrel jotted up the outstretched roots. He carried a wriggling baby squirrel.

The scrappy thing wasn't yet old enough to open her eyes, and still, those claws and teeth looked menacing to Koda. A great fear overwhelmed him. It came like the smoke that had mushroomed under the dresser and became so dark inside him, he felt as if he had blacked out. He wanted to flee.

Remember Sully. Koda willed himself. *You left him in those burrows. How could you do that?! I'm not doing it again. The forest is a wide, open space. You can run if you have to.*

He had clenched his paws. Koda relaxed them, remaining fully alert to both squirrels, and sensed Sully letting go of some tension in reaction.

"Koda's ready to hear about the totems," Sully said.

The squirrel gawked at Koda. He blinked at Sully as if to agree to his request, and they waited for him as he scaled the tree. Koda recoiled when he returned, taken aback by the speed with which he landed. The squirrel stared at him, then led them at a quick pace.

Sully glanced nervously at Koda. He asked the squirrel, "She fell again?"

"Yeah, she's a clumsy pup," he answered. "So, what's with your brother?"

"Umm…"

"Where are you taking us?" Koda demanded.

Sounding somewhat annoyed, the squirrel replied, "You don't have to be paranoid. There's a lot going on where you are. Jack will help you understand some of it."

"Have you harmed Sully?"

Koda stumbled as the squirrel spun around. "No, why would I?"

"Twiggy's my friend, Koda," Sully said.

"They're strangers," Koda snarled.

"I was, too, when you came to Giant's nest. You trusted *me.*"

The squirrel lowered to Koda's face. A growling buzz loudened from his mouth. "Rowan and I risked our lives to rescue you. We were almost ripped apart, and this is how you—"

"Twiggy."

The squirrel pulled up onto his haunches. Koda had been seconds away from biting him. He took note of where Sully was, as well as the hare seated at the bole of a tree. The one Sully called "Jack."

Koda called to him, "We aren't wild animals. Tell us where Giant's nest is. That's where we belong."

"You want to go back?" The squirrel frowned. "What's so great about being caged?"

"I'm not harassed by owls or Critters in a giant's home," Koda retorted.

"Your brother told us Hototo attacked you at your 'Giant's nest.'"

"Calm yourselves," said the hare. "The human houses are south of us. Once the flood passes, I will gladly take you myself. I don't recommend you go alone considering your condition."

South. That's if the animal isn't lying.

"Jack, you're not really going to stay here, are you?" the squirrel asked. "You shouldn't have to take him back! He looks at you and all of us like we're Hunters!"

"I will assist our kind whenever needed."

"And he won't appreciate it! That's the truth!" The squirrel scurried up a tree. Koda's adrenaline dropped a tad.

Sully had been watching uncomfortably. "Can Koda see the poles?"

The hare still seemed distracted by the argument. "Very well," he said. "Though why don't we take a small detour for your brother to forage? The weather is not too bitter tonight."

"Yes, please," Sully said.

The hare left the bole to disappear into the background. Why did Sully care about anything these wild animals were doing? For the time being Koda had no choice but to tie himself to him. He followed with a knot in his stomach and the hare's thumping feet way in front.

Branches snapped. Koda stopped and stood to see small shapes leaping from tree to tree. On the ground, a pup whined where a falling shape was coming to carry them up the tree.

"What are they doing?" Koda asked, tense.

"It is the squirrel's task to ensure the young are safe off the ground. Arboreal Critters do this typically, though it's enforced in flood season," answered the hare.

Koda lost sight of the squirrels as the canopies threaded together. He heard clamors of wood against wood. They were nearing the antlered animals. He could smell them, as if he were sniffing smoke before seeing flames. Koda flattened himself to the ground.

"It's *okay*, Koda." Sully shoveled his nose under him. When that didn't work, he walked a little ahead to the hare who was waiting and turned to look back at him. Koda could feel himself growing angrier at his brother.

Slowly, cautiously, he walked with Sully into a crowded clearing. Grunting silhouettes wandered, looking for someone to touch muzzles with, bite, neigh at, or kick. The hare caused a small stir among the more skittish of them. Otherwise, they were oblivious to their group. At Koda's height, with the horses' and deer's bellies above him, it was like seeing a land of dinosaurs. He feared their teeth. The sound of munched grass was all around him.

There was little of that for him to hide in—the animals seemed to have eaten most of it—and Koda was all the more distressed.

Haphazard clomping came from Koda's right. The hare darted sideways as two bucks with antlers tangled together staggered onto the path.

Koda clamored backward as one of their hooves stomped too close to them. He shouted, "Sully, run to the—!"

The bucks were already dragging each other into the bushes. Small birds took flight, disrupting the thinner tree branches. The neighing of fleeing horses didn't stop until the vegetation stilled once again.

Koda tried to calm himself. The squeaks of unsettled animals made him want to grind his teeth.

The hare straightened from his kneel to the ground. "No matter how often that happens," he said, slightly shaken, "I'm always spooked."

He continued to lead them. "Fights are bound to occur. We're tremendously overcrowded, more so at night. Few stray to the path we're on since many of the smaller Critters tend to avoid the barrier."

"*I'm* not afraid," said Sully, who had been frozen to the spot.

"We've instructed the few brave ones to remain underground."

"Why?" Sully asked.

"For your brother's comfort."

"I'd be comfortable at home," Koda said grudgingly.

"What I say is true, Nahiossi. We care for our own."

That's giant speak, Koda thought, alarmed. *What's it doing speaking giant?*

Sully asked, "What does 'Nahiossi' mean?"

"The name is Cheyenne, meaning 'has three fingers,'" said

the hare.

"Neat!"

Koda was unnerved. *Has it been spying on me?* "Why do you keep speaking giant?" he asked.

"We have a strong connection with Native American culture."

What kind of animals are these?

Koda's whiskers fluttered from an enticing smell. The hare hopped up to a particularly large grouping of tussocks and parted the grass to reveal various berries, seeds, nuts, and greens. The urge to pouch tugged like an itch. Koda was quickly distracted by a squirrel standing on top of the pile with something in his paws. Seeing them, he shoved the object in his mouth and retreated.

The hare sighed. "They don't listen."

"What giant gave you this?" Koda asked. It was a small chance that a giant other than his would be helpful to them, but amid the animals scattered about, any giant would be a blessing.

The squirrel called down from the trees. Koda had been unaware he was following them. "Since when do humans give Critters forage? Other than the kind that is poisoned or in mouse traps?"

Koda glowered. He had never heard of such things.

"We gathered this forage," said the hare. "It is easier to keep track of it when grouped in one area."

"I didn't save the forage in my pouch, Koda," Sully said. Hearing the sadness in his voice gave Koda a strange feeling. "I wish I did, then there'd be more for the Critters to eat. Even if it was just a little bit."

"The forest is dying all the way to the human camping grounds southeast of here," said the hare.

Camping grounds? That means there's a road, and that road could take us to Giant's nest, Koda thought.

"I've eaten the blackberries, Koda. They're good," said Sully.

Koda's stomach whined, so he grudgingly reached for a berry.

When Koda had eaten his fill, the hare led them outward from the clearing. Soon they walked along a tall shadow. It appeared to cut into the dirt like a chasm. Koda got a terrible feeling looking at it. The longer he stared, the more he thought that if he were to step into the shadow, he would fall and never be found again. It couldn't be a tree; its form gave no impression of branches. Standing, he saw a bold shape, almost black, on the edge of the firs. It seemed to stare at him threateningly.

The animals were silent in this area, the whines and dashing of squirrels now absent. Sully stood so perfectly still, staring at the shape, that Koda felt strongly unnerved.

As his brother stepped toward it, Koda hesitated. "Sully, no."

"Do not be afraid. Any danger is sound asleep," the hare said.

What does that mean? "Where are we?" Koda asked, ready to tow Sully to the ferns.

"We're on the edge of the mountain pass's limits. We'll be safe within the barrier."

"I don't believe this about a magical barrier," Koda retorted.

"I won't force you."

Sully poked Koda's arm. "It's cool."

The hare stepped aside. Koda stepped up to the shape, aware that what he was doing was stupid and unnecessary. He shouldn't have been surprised by the horror he saw.

He gasped, and as he tried to flee, he became trapped inside the hare's arms. Sully was there, insisting that what Koda was seeing wasn't what it looked like.

A creature with wide, sunken eyes. Shadows in the shape of half-moons fell on its angular cheekbones. In some features it resembled an ape, and in others a demon, like the way that its mouth gaped and stared like nothing alive on Earth. It took Koda a moment to realize it wasn't alive. Its blocked face was expertly carved in the wooden pole. Faded paint pleated in the wrinkles and resembled infected wounds, tarnished by years of rainfall.

It was the ugliest thing Koda had ever seen.

"What is it?" he asked softly.

The hare said, "A totem."

Koda rushed out from his arms and reflexively opened his mouth to bite when he saw a hurrying movement on a nearby fir.

The squirrel gave Koda an unfriendly look. "There's another face above the one you saw," he said. Koda could see that the pole continued up from the face. His bad vision kept him from seeing any details. "It's not Native American, either."

"Four totem poles circle the mountain pass," said the hare. "Each totem head is a mythical creature. Hunter totems. There are eleven, ranging from Native American to Japanese. Greek. Even Egyptian. Ironically, they avert any predators of our kind from crossing the barrier."

Sully whispered to Koda, "I think we're on an Indian burial ground."

"Huh?" the squirrel said.

"Sully's a fan of horror movies."

Koda stiffened at the new voice. Another stranger, a goat, cut through the bushes and stood in front of the pole. "Sully and I talked about our favorite things to watch on TV. Mine are the recyclin' shows with tin cans."

This is what he does? Converses about movies while I'm on my deathnest?

"You *would* know about that stuff," said the squirrel.

Noticing Koda, the goat smiled. "Hey, you're awake. You had us worried there for a while."

"Jack knighted him 'Nahiossi,'" Sully said cheerfully.

"He has a good eye for small details."

Koda pawed Sully in the shoulder, not hard, but forceful enough to emphasize his point. "Don't say that word." It was common for Sully to repeat phrases off the television without having any idea what they meant, but repeating what some wild animal was saying... That it should even know a giant word was disturbing enough.

"Rowan fought the owl," Sully said. Koda cringed at the devotion in his voice. *He's not even trying to avoid their names.*

"Don't be fooled by the battle scars. I got the better of it," said the goat with some humor.

"I should tell you Twiggy had a difficult time retrieving Sully from the burrows while you were ill," the hare said. "He and Rowan occupied him, so he would have other things to think about."

The goat bleated as if in awkwardness. Koda was finding more and more that the hare was too observant. It disconcerted him.

There were three animals in the group now. Feeling cornered, Koda nudged Sully to the end of the totem pole's shadow. It was jagged, as if a chunk had been bitten out of it.

"Should I leave?" the goat asked. "I seemed to've frightened him."

"You and everyone else in the pass," said the squirrel.

The hare saw Koda staring at the shadow. "You see that it's different," he said. "There are only two totem heads on this pole instead of three. Judging by how this pole ends, we can assume that the twelfth totem is missing."

"What is it?" Koda asked.

"You've met him," the goat said plainly.

Koda blinked. "The owl?"

"Where else could he have come from?" the squirrel said brusquely.

"You're saying these things are real," Koda said, skeptical.

"Each totem was alive in some respect, yes, prior to being trapped in wood," the hare explained. "The tales tell us so. How it was done, I do not know, but given how they influence the larger trees, I have no doubt something unimaginably powerful confined these creatures."

"If you're wonderin' how the owl escaped, we can't say," said the goat. "We're talkin' 'bout myths. Legends. Stories that have existed since... forever. No one knows how long these have been here."

Koda said grudgingly, "A legend has never tried to eat me."

"This one can," the squirrel was quick to reply.

The hare observed the pole. "Totems loath Critters. Hototo, the owl who captured you, is a powerful spirit. Our forest has seen much destruction; thus, he worsens it and all bad situations. He will remain here in the mountain pass, draining the forest and waiting for any one of us to make a mistake—as he's done with others, as with *you* tonight when you tried to leave—and succeed in killing them. The only consolations are that Hototo cannot fly during daylight, and the barrier protects us."

"The poles aren't visible from the outside," the goat cut in. "Sully will tell you he didn't see anythin' but trees when he approached the barrier."

"Uh huh," Sully confirmed.

"It's a nice touch. And if humans do wander this far and aren't chased away by the rottin' plants, I'm here to say stink worse than a skunk's rear—"

Sully giggled.

"They can't enter. Only Critters allowed. I myself don't mind goin' out. When it's daylight, that is."

"I don't recommend Critters leave the mountain pass," said the hare. "Rowan, however, does encourage scavenging. What he's brought back has helped us tremendously."

"I also bring back lost Critters if Twiggy doesn't beat me to it." The goat smiled at Sully and Koda.

"We get new arrivals every now and then," the hare said. "And there's the pups. We couldn't stop the rodents from pairing, however crowded we are."

"You could say they're growin' on trees," said the goat. "Fallin' out of 'em, that is. The parents claim clumsiness. Askin' me, I'd bet they're impatient."

"Impatient for what?" Koda asked, suspicious.

The goat considered him as if confused, then said to the hare, "You haven't told him yet?"

"I have not."

"Tell him about the flood," Sully insisted.

Koda sensed that something heavy, and of some importance, had passed between his brother and the animals. *Where is this going?*

After a meaningful pause, the hare spoke purposefully to Koda, as if every word counted. "You might question our reasons for staying. The thought has crossed everyone's minds to leave for another preserve, I'm sure, especially since we've never actually seen what the flood brings. But tonight it comes after years of waiting."

"How could you possibly think a flood is a good thing?" Koda demanded.

"It needs the flood to open."

"What needs the flood to open?" Koda couldn't keep up with this.

The hare's startled look bore into him. "We stay for our passage into another world. A haven for Critters and Critters alone. It will open in this pass, and we will never again worry of Hunters."

They've lost their minds, Koda thought. *They've caught a disease in their heads!*

"Stay close to the barrier. You will be safe there for the duration of the event."

The hare stood. An unexpected flicker of lightning and a rumble of distant thunder set him down. "I suggest you stay where you are. It's starting."

6

THE FLOOD

L IGHTNING FLICKERED eerily across the Critters' faces. Brightened flashes of the forest jumped out at Sully. He looked to the canopy where, in sporadic flashes of light, he could see the squirrels hastening toward them. Thunder roared like the deepest rifle blast, seeming to ignite from clouds the color of gun powder.

"I want to leave! *Now!*" Koda shouted.

"Haven't you learned anything?" Twiggy said, annoyed.

Rowan ducked his head so it was level to Twiggy's ear. "Give the Critter some understandin'. He's as nervous as a long-tailed cat in a roomful of rockin' chairs," he said quietly. Sully wouldn't have heard over the shouts of the arriving animals if he weren't right beside him.

Kangaroo rats, mice, and pikas jostled Sully. The smaller Critters ping-ponged amongst the elk, deer, and caribou, who were mindful of the placement of their hooves as they crashed through the bushes. Disoriented by the storm, horses trotted in fast and struck a line of caribou, both neighing and screaming whistled calls as they trotted around each other. Jack called for peace. Rabbits and hares gravitated to him. There were so many and yet they could all disappear in an instant in the pauses of lightning. Whenever the thunder came, Sully seemed to go deaf for all but its voice. He pawed his head. Rain droplets sprinkled him.

"We'll get rained on!"

At the panic in Koda's voice, Sully spun to find him. Koda was quivering against the inner part of one of Rowan's legs. Once again, the expression of sheer terror on his brother's face stunned Sully; he didn't understand it.

Rowan lowered his head to Koda. "No worry here," he said. "I'll keep you covered. Just in case."

Sully threaded through the crowd to join Koda. He knew Rowan was just being nice. He didn't have to cover them. Not with the dome.

The enormous cracking of thunder sounded again. With the Critters in front, their heads highlighted by the lightning, Sully felt as if he was in the back row of a theater. He moved closer to the front. The massive trees formed the dome around and above. Sully couldn't fathom the sound they made, those crushing branches. Rain poured. Koda shouted but the words were almost completely drowned out.

"YOU HEAR THAT, HOTOTO?" Twiggy bellowed. "WE'RE LEAVIN' TONIGHT AND THERE ISN'T ANYTHING YOU CAN DO ABOUT IT!"

The crowd cheered. To Sully, it was like the Critters in the whole world had spoken. Rowan nodded his head repeatedly in approval.

"Is it safe for you to do that?" Sully said loudly. He thought Koda nudged him again, but when he turned, he saw it was a baby tree vole wandering from his mother. She yanked him back.

"It's questionable," yelled Rowan. "Hototo's always out there, ready to shut us down."

"Spoilsport!" someone called out. Rowan made a weird babbling noise in response.

"You said he couldn't get past the trees!" Sully said, suddenly worried.

"He can't, but he isn't going to stand by and watch the Haven open," Rowan said.

"Best not to provoke him," said Jack.

Twiggy smirked. He glanced behind him and dropped to his paws. "Woah, hey, stop!"

Sully realized his view of Koda had been blocked by Critters. Fretting, he searched through them and found Koda forced onto his hind feet, squeaking. Some of the Critters had distanced themselves, while others paced around him as if to fight.

Twiggy inserted himself between Koda and the crowd. They retreated. He leaned right into Koda's face. "What's the matter with you?"

"*Get away!*" Koda lunged forward with his teeth bared. Twiggy scurried back.

"Stop it, Koda!" All Sully could think to do was walk over and try to comfort him.

Jack hopped away from the rabbits and hares up to Rowan. "Pick him up, please."

"Pardon."

As Rowan took Koda by the scruff, another thunder boom muted Koda's cry. During a flash, he twisted at the top of Rowan's leg.

"Me, too," Sully said. Rowan lifted him up to his side, and Sully climbed the rest of the way onto his back.

Something was terribly wrong with Koda. He trembled all over. Why? It had been shocking to see him respond to the Critters the way that he had. *They aren't like Hunters at all,* Sully thought, confused. *Koda said they were. He can't be afraid of them* now.

He didn't like seeing Koda that way, so he looked to a bit of moonlight shining close to the totem pole. Beside it was what must have been one of the larger trees' roots curling up out of the ground.

It writhed. And pulsed. It grew thicker and thicker. Sully heard an immense body of water on the other side of the dome wall. It was like they were inside a fish bowl but with the water outside. The ground glistened wetly where the light shone beside the totem pole, with the tree root poking up through the soaked grass.

The water was helping it grow.

The cracking sound ceased. The dome had sealed. Moonlight and lightning now gone, Sully had only his hearing to rely on. He huddled with Koda, alert to the rain splashing on the roof of the dome and the wind howling as if the clouds were rushing to earth.

***

Water poured into Sydney's nostrils. She jerked awake, bloating at the sight of her drowned den, and guardedly crawled out from the boulder. Rain teemed onto her face. "Water! Water everywhere!"

She felt a strong pull on her legs gliding her backwards. Sydney climbed atop the boulder and blinked at a gloomy woodland terrain over the cliff and now whitened by lightning.

Water ravaged the earth. An oceanic current flowed through the trees, splashing and churning behind a curtain of rain. Spraying mist dispersed a deadened lake smell into the air. The waves before her darkened black until she couldn't see the grass underneath, only the debris it carried in over top.

It had been a longer day out than Sydney predicted. She hadn't anticipated the rodents to be alive, either. *Scaredy rat and Roly-Poly were supposed to be owl food, unless they're haunting me with their stink.* And theirs wasn't the only stink. She had sensed something was off in the four days she had been heading northwest, like a spoiled cricket or a dead mouse in the room.

The sound of an explosion—without lightning—took her by surprise. Sydney jolted. "Shut up, thunder!"

Mouth agape, she tilted her head toward the current swishing about her small island.

Speaking of dead things.

Salmon, with dead eyes staring up at the clouds, floated by the side of the boulder. They filled the entire clearing like one slimy slip and slide. It coursed down to the cliff where they plummeted like flying fish in a waterfall created by the flood and into the black lake.

"Someone call Fish and Wildlife," Sydney remarked.

The salmon hadn't been dead long considering rot had just begun to overtake their gills. Sydney tasted the reek in the air and quickly closed her mouth.

"I'm not eating that."

Sydney shifted back from her view of the waterfall. A sound—undoubtedly loud from afar—rose in pitch. Something like a tree falling. Or several. Maybe it was just thunder. She tilted her head at the sky and saw a large, swooping shape.

Her claws scraped over the side of the boulder. Instead of falling, she hovered upside down. She splayed her claws across the sky, flying higher and higher, where the lightning bolts seemed close enough to scorch her finger tips. Sydney twisted to look above.

SCREECH!

The owl—the same owl who had carried off the rodents—had a hold of her tail. A horrendous fear Sydney had never known coursed through her.

She was a predator! She couldn't be the prey!

But she was now.

***

70

"What's that sound?" Sully shouted.

The earth groaned. He was unsure if he was hearing rain pummeling the dome or rocks vibrating on its surface. At some point the Critters had become abnormally quiet. Sully sensed everyone moving backward except for Rowan, whose shoulders were rigid. There was an immense sound like crumbling dirt. Sully clenched Rowan tighter.

"This is it. We finally get to see it!" Twiggy said.

Sully cowered from the reverberated tremble and tear of something like constricted rope moving inside the dirt. Before then, he had never wished so badly to see like a giant.

The sound exploded like the breaking of a continent. He was blinded. A magnificent light shot out of the ground, as if the sun had been reborn in the void. It faded some, though it widened as a strip. As it cut across the forest—an aurora borealis without color—it took most of the trees with it. The firs snapped and plummeted into the light. The dome's roots knotted in and out of the ground. They stretched to the lighted abyss, stretching it wider and wider, too, until there was a gigantic hole in the center of the mountain pass.

To Sully's amazement, the Haven had opened.

The Critters were a way back from the abyss. Rowan faltered, jostling Sully and Koda, as a stampede of excited small Critters streamed by his hooves. Twiggy yelled for help. Rowan plucked him up.

"What's going on? What happened?" Koda shouted.

"The Haven! It opened!" Sully exclaimed. "Koda... Koda, I think we should go."

"*What?*"

"If we don't go now, we'll never get to," Sully said.

"Why wouldn't you want to go home?" Koda yelled.

Sully tightly gripped Rowan's fur. "You're always saying we

need to be safe! It's the safest place where they're going!"

"Rowan?" Twiggy said from Rowan's mouth. He sounded frightened all of a sudden. "Rowan? Where's my pup?"

"I don't know," Rowan said. He turned in search of her, but the crowd prevented him from moving more than a few steps.

"She was just here! I saw one of the squirrels bring her," Twiggy said. "Rowan, I need to look for her before we enter the opening!"

"I'm not going anywhere!" Koda shrieked.

Jack said, "Rowan, give me Nahiossi and Sull—"

The cracking release of tree branches jerked his head up at the dome. *BOOOOMMM!* It was the loudest thunder roar yet, and somehow Sully could hear every Critter in the mountain pass. Squeaking, barking, up at the sky that was visible again through the unraveling branches. A large shape hovered up there. The closer it got to the dome, the wider the opening.

"HOTOTO!" the Critters screamed.

"STUPID VERMIN." That terrible voice. Sully could picture the owl sneering. "LOOK AT YOUR DOOM… BEFORE YOU *DIE.*"

Hototo carried something in his talon. From between the frame of Rowan's horns, Sully saw whatever it was drop into the abyss.

There was an earsplitting sound and the sweet smell of burnt wood as if lightning had struck a tree. Someone shouted, "The totem's released!"

A blast like a tornado shredding apart a house hit Sully's small, rapidly beating heart. The dome ruptured. Thousands of branches savagely unfurled at breakneck speed and plummeted as broken bits. Rain poured in.

Cast in the abyssal glow, the squealing horses raced to the opening. Sully shuddered and cried from such an unexpected terror.

The Critters screamed, not just from fright, but also from pain as they were trampled.

Twiggy screamed, "*Stop it! Stop it! Jack, what is happ—*"

A violent, hollering wave shoved Rowan forward. Wide-eyed, Sully fell off his back. The body of water, which had been kept at bay by the dome, flooded in. Sully was swept far away from Rowan along with many of the Critters—first with the water pushing at his throat, and then it tossed him head over feet. Sully choked and paddled with all his might. Very quickly he sank.

And the water sank, too. He heard it gurgling like a sink when it's been unplugged. He looked up to see the water draining into the abyss, but then he saw the flash of a rabbit's face. Sully squeaked as it hit his side and toppled him into the path of the tree voles. The baby that had wandered from his mother was water-logged and shivering. Running to them, Twiggy's pup was crying, probably for him to find her.

In the next instant, she was gone. Sully flinched hard as Hototo's haunted shape dove not a foot away from his face and snatched her and the tree voles up into the air.

Landing, his raised talons glinted by the dying abyssal light. He sliced them down, flew up, tucked his wings, and dove again.

Sully couldn't move. He cowered to the ground, crying. A pinch on the back of his neck twanged in his skin. He was lifted. In front of his swinging legs pumped Rowan's hooves.

"Where's Koda?" Sully sobbed as he bounced against Rowan's chin. They ran toward the scene of melted glow, of bodies lain on the grass, of a landscape bombed by branches.

"Sully!" Koda shrieked.

On the wave of jumbled Critters, Sully glimpsed two more. Jack, hopping and falling, carried Koda. They disappeared behind them for a moment before they were suddenly there again, racing alongside Rowan. Twiggy appeared between them. They ran with the flow of the crowd to the abyss. The dome had nearly disappeared. The magical trees had shriveled so much, Sully could barely see them. It was as if they had dissolved into the gray sky. Upon the edges of the abyss, their dead roots lay like the rays of an Aztec sun.

A wing flapped in Sully's face. He gasped, trying to scream, and felt Rowan duck his head. Hototo screeched. Soaked by thumping water, wind sweeping across his hide, Rowan dug in his hooves and ran faster. Jack and Twiggy stayed right with him. They tore up the earth under their feet at a speed Sully thought incapable.

They fell. Darkness swallowed them whole.

PART II
THE TRICKSTER WORLD

7

SHADOWS

ODA LIVED by darkness—he was accustomed to it his whole life—but this felt like he was nowhere. No scents. No sense of touch. Nothing but a mat of inky darkness and a tingling sensation in his eye sockets.

The familiar ache of fear persisted somewhere under the confusion, distant yet present, like a nightmare you couldn't piece together. As when waking from a deep sleep, he didn't remember when the feeling of nowhere lifted and spread a coolness beneath him.

Pouring rain and bloodied images projected in Koda's mind. He started at the memory and looked to the sky. It was as dark as ever, without wind, rain, or the sound of leaves rustling. He wondered if there was a sky up there at all. There had to be an opening. What had they fallen into? Maybe the hole had collapsed. How was he not buried in dirt then? So many questions. At least the owl's screeches were absent for now.

He remembered the cold under his feet. The floor was ridged and gritty. When he moved, little granules stuck in between his toes. Water droplets wet his feet. Rain. Rain! He had gotten wet! He licked his fur.

"Sully!" His brother had been drenched. He had flopped

like a wet rag from the goat's mouth. And where had the animal taken him?

Koda pawed his way across the floor and squeaked as someone bumped him.

"Koda?" His name was a haunting echo.

Koda sniffed a shambled scent of wet fur, earth, and blackberries. His paws shook as he pulled them away from Sully. "It's me."

Sully sniffled.

Koda forgot about the nervous energy in his paws. Where a second before they had been aching to claw into someone's skin, he now placed them with care on Sully's face. His brother was shivering.

"Don't fall asleep! I'll get you warm and we'll—"

"It's not that."

The sadness in Sully's voice stopped him. He reflected on what had just happened, and to Sully specifically. Sully had never seen someone die before.

"You're not cold?" Koda asked.

"No."

Koda pawed him again to make sure and realized there was only a slight coolness to his fur. "The air isn't cold here. You should be fine but dry yourself anyway."

Sully mumbled as if agreeing.

There was a sound like a struck match and something flared, transforming the darkness into light. It faded to a glow, but not before suggesting a wall to their left. Koda could see Sully now, and he huddled close to him. "What was that?" His trembling voice echoed. Given the ringing of their voices, the space seemed to be a generous size. Plenty of room for hungry things.

Sully walked toward the light. Koda was too shaken to stop him, so he followed.

They came upon a slowly rotating lantern about three feet wide, Koda guessed after he had counted his steps alongside it. He couldn't tell how tall it was or what exactly the lighted holes above were, but there appeared to be several of them. They grouped tightly together like fireflies at the top, shrunken by perspective. A series of flickering, lopsided lines could clearly be seen on the bottom. As the lantern rotated, the glowing shapes glided across the space like spirits trapped in a never-ending carousel.

Sully asked fearfully, "Who lit the lantern?"

They detected movement behind the light. Koda squeaked again. "Who's there?" Sully whined.

They heard a scratching sound, like someone pushing themselves off the floor. Sully took a few steps forward and, suddenly running, exclaimed, "Rowan! Jack!"

In a far corner, the goat and hare lifted groggily. In his haste to catch up to Sully, Koda stopped close to them. Blood dripped from the goat's horns from having stabbed the owl in the chest.

Sully slowed. "Where's...?"

The squirrel dragged himself out from between the two. He seemed lost as he looked around at the Critters with a wretched expression on his face. Slumping forward onto his arms, his claws pushed across the floor.

"They're all gone," he said softly.

The goat lowered his head. The hare seemed lost in thought in the light of the lantern.

"*They're all dead?*"

Sully uttered a choked sob. As if released from a trance, the hare leaned in to the squirrel. "Twiggy—"

"We're the only ones left!"

"Not everyone is dead," the hare said. "Some escaped to the opening."

The squirrel's expression turned desperate. "What about my

pup? Did she make it?"

Koda had seen the baby squirrels killed by the owl. One had been the crying pup with large claws. He thought that must be the pup the squirrel was worried about. He felt a twinge of sympathy.

The goat stomped, startling him, and turned away.

"She's alive," Sully said.

The Critters looked at him.

"I— I saw her escape to the opening."

Five months may not be very long to a giant, but to Koda that was a quarter of his life he knew Sully and he knew he tended to stutter or repeat things when he lied.

The squirrel grasped at the floor. "Where is she? Where did they all go?"

"It's Hototo. He's done somethin'," the goat said. The squirrel made an angry choking sound as if he were holding back tears.

The hare stepped toward the lantern, his back facing them. After a long silence, he ducked his head, and Koda heard a small noise in his throat. The hare stiffened and did not move. When he spoke again, it was almost as if Koda had never heard that noise. He spoke quietly and with a steady hold on his voice.

"He used a Hunter to get in."

"I thought they couldn't!" Sully exclaimed.

"The dome was trying to close. It had without failure all these years whenever Hototo tried to enter. The only thing different this time was that he had someone with him," the hare said. "It should have been impossible, yet somehow Hototo used a Hunter to break the barrier."

Koda's temporary loss of anxiety from having survived the flood was beginning to wear off. They didn't have time to speak nonsense. He and Sully needed an open place where they wouldn't be trapped in with these animals. Koda groomed himself anxiously.

"Why do you reckon it was a Hunter?" the goat asked.

"I didn't get a good look at it, but a Critter wouldn't have caused that disaster. The barrier *protected* Critters. It allowed them in," the hare said.

"Right."

"The Hunter is unique in some way. Otherwise it *wouldn't* have gotten past. And neither would have Hototo."

Sully wiped his tears. "I'm glad I didn't see it that well." He turned. "It's— It's not in here with us, right?"

Everyone straightened, listening to their shallow breaths.

"Could it be with the others? Wherever they ended up?" asked the goat.

"It better not," the squirrel said, rising. "It'd better be dead."

"It survived," said the hare. "I doubt Hototo killed it. I imagine it will only harm the Haven further. He will keep it alive for that reason."

A loud scraping sound drew everyone's attention to the goat. He shifted his legs on the floor and stood.

"You should rest," the hare cautioned.

"Sir, pardon if it sounds rude, but I'd *welcome* a fight right now."

The hare said nothing.

"I doubt the Hunter is in here with us. It didn't look very large. For the nearsighted folks, we're in a cave. What I want to see is if there are any tunnels or another route to an exit." The goat wandered into the dark. Koda continued to hear his hooves clomp and echo. They sounded especially violent.

A cave. That's right. We fell into a hole, Koda thought.

Sully asked the hare, "What's going to happen now with the trees destroyed? Are other Critters going to be able to come to the

Haven?" He waited anxiously as the hare looked down at his paws. There was a reluctance to it, a frustrated weariness and sadness, as if he didn't want to say what had to be said.

"Without the trees, the Haven cannot be opened again."

"That isn't fair!" Sully exclaimed, on the verge of crying again.

Koda's ears twitched at a violent scratch.

"He's right. They deserved to come with us," the squirrel said in a dangerous, low voice. "I swear on my tail I'm going to make that totem blind."

"You will do so carelessly," scolded the hare. It was the harshest Koda had heard him. "And you will be killed in the process."

"How's that going to happen if I'm trapped in this cave?"

"We'll find a way out."

The squirrel sighed. "There's not going to be an exit."

Why are they so hung up on this? It's common sense. We dropped, so the exit is right above us. It has to be! I don't care if I can't feel any wind. There was probably a cave in like I thought, and the hole is just small now.

"I'd hate to confirm it…" The goat returned to them. "You won't believe this. Nothin'. I scanned every wall."

"That's impossible!" Koda saw Sully flinch as his voice exploded in the cave. "Did you check the top?"

"Yes, I did," the goat said. "No exits. The cave is fairly small, so I'm positive I didn't miss anythin'."

"We fell into a *hole!* It doesn't make sense!"

"Not just any ordinary hole." The squirrel stared at Koda, full of resentment, as if he were the one to blame for everything. "Forget the nearsightedness," he said. "Are you also hard of hearing? Did you not hear the *entire forest* collapse into the ground?"

"Enough, Twiggy." The hare looked to Koda. "We are now in another world, Nahiossi. There's more than dirt between us and up there." He gestured at the cave's ceiling. "We are literally worlds apart."

"I told you I don't believe in this magic stuff!" Koda snapped.

"Don't despair. The tales handed down to us don't mention an exit from this world, though the trees may not have been our only option."

"If there is a way back, it wouldn't have been necessary to tell us about it," the goat said. "The important thing has always been about *gettin' here*."

"It's a necessity *now!*" Koda shouted. He felt as if the cave was shrinking, that the animals were moving closer to him. *The goat's lying. It wants to keep Sully and me in here so that it can stomp on us. So the hare can chew us like hay. Or the squirrel, just like a rodent, to—*

"Calm yourself, Nahiossi," the hare commanded. Koda jolted. "Reflect for a moment that we are all in an unfamiliar place. Everything has been turned upside down. What possible good could it do to see more violence tonight?"

Koda's heart pumped at the sudden raised voice. He glared. It was then Koda decided he distrusted the hare most.

The animal said more calmly, "Trust us. Those before us wouldn't have had any reason to leave—"

"*Somebody had to!*" Koda shrieked. "Saying this really is all true, that the owl really is a totem, how else would you hear the stories unless someone escaped? How do you know it wasn't always like this? That every time this thing opens, it dooms everyone who enters?"

He inhaled deeply, aware that the squirrel and goat were staring at him.

Sully said tentatively, "I don't want to be stuck."

"As you say, someone must have escaped. My guess is during a flood or by another exit," the hare said. "I hold true to my promise. We'll do our best to find one. Stay with us until then."

"What choice does he have?" said the squirrel. "Sorry, Jack, but that's the whole problem!"

"Everyone hold your horses," said the goat. "I'm not ready to give up. As far as I'm able to tell, there aren't any exits, but I didn't say anythin' about weak spots." He stomped the ground twice and rammed the wall with his head.

BANG!

The tingling sensation behind Koda's eyes returned. His vision worsened. He squinted and pawed his forehead.

"Don't be upset, Koda," Sully said pleadingly.

Hearing the tears in Sully's voice, Koda forced his anger down. *I'm going to get you back home. I don't care what they say*, he thought. "I'm not upset anymore. I just have a headache."

BANG!

"You have one, too?"

"What do you mean?" Koda asked, concerned.

"I mean— it's not that bad."

Koda's sight refocused. Sully was still dripping. "Keep licking your fur," Koda said.

"Okay."

Koda followed cautiously as Sully walked to the hare. "How about we burrow out of the cave?" Sully offered as he dried his face. He began to shake a little again, as if he were uncomfortable crying in front of the other animals. Koda could see it by how he hid his eyes from them.

The hare was staring at the lantern intensely. "The soil is dense. We won't dig far through it."

BANG! "My horns aren't even makin' a dent!"

"Rowan, stop," the squirrel said. "You'll make the whole thing cave in on us more likely. Then where would we be?" He scoffed. "You know, worse off than we already are."

The hare bobbed his head at the lantern. "Whatever rules applied up there, don't down here. We might be approaching this from the wrong angle," he said distantly.

What's with the lantern? The hare stares at it like it's important.

"It's a shadow lantern. I saw one in a Tim Burton movie." Sully paced around it several turns and declared, "It looks like grass."

The hare looked at the lopsided lines at the bottom. Sounding bemused, he said, "Sully, you're right."

"What?" the squirrel asked, suddenly interested.

"The lantern. Look here."

The banging stopped. Koda pushed Sully farther to the side as the goat and squirrel joined them. "What have you found?" the goat asked.

The hare pressed his paw on the lantern to restrict its motion. The lights froze on the cave walls. "They're aligned in a group of eight." He pointed to the circles. "Notice how each gets increasingly bigger starting from the left. Then here in the middle, a full circle. After it, they reverse and shrink to the right with a gap between the next set."

Koda stood. Holding very still so the shapes wouldn't warp, he saw most resembled crescents.

The hare said, "It's depicting the phases of the moon. The full moon, the crescents and half-moons, and the gap, the new moon," he said, pointing to each accordingly. "All above the horizon line, which I would have failed to notice if not for Sully's help."

A bit of sadness lessened from Sully's eyes. Koda was glad that the lantern had taken his mind off the massacre, even if for just a little while.

"I see. Great work," said the goat. "How does it help us, though?"

The hare removed his paw and waited for the lantern to revolve another foot. Then he replaced it. "The pattern continues, except here. This set has the moon completely disappear where it isn't supposed to."

"I don't understand," Sully said.

"Have you ever seen the moon blink out of the sky?" said the squirrel.

The hare tapped the error in the metal. Light filled the space, and something clunked to the bottom. The high contrast of the flame blackened it in shadow.

The squirrel reached through a half-moon and brought out a crude rectangle with a groove running across it. Koda smelled soot. "It's just a piece of wood," the squirrel said.

The wall behind them quaked. Koda spun around to see the beginnings of a fissure cracking it open and something large pushing through the rock. Then nothing. Everything had gone black, as if someone had blown out the lantern. It was soon obvious to Koda that the light was still on in the cave; he had simply stopped seeing. The tingling sensation became an excruciating burn, as though his eyes were balls of fire. Screaming, Koda reeled onto his back. Through his pain he could hear Sully do the same. And there was nothing he could do. Not with the pain stabbing his eyes like fireplace pokers. Koda screamed again, thrusting the back of his paws into his eyes. Someone grabbed his arms.

The pain stopped completely, as if it had never been there. It took Koda a minute to realize it wasn't coming back. Slowly, he sat up and opened his tearing eyes. Out of a smeared image gradually becoming clearer, the squirrel hovered in his face. The goat and hare gathered behind, shouting.

They were all in color.

"Hey, answer me!"

Koda pulled his arms out of the squirrel's paws, noticing

with amazement that his own fur was a light ivory-cream color. Blinking incessantly, he searched for Sully. He was cowered in a ball at least a foot away (he could now tell the distance between things), and yet Koda could see every hair in detail. He stumbled onto his haunches, almost falling again. The squirrel moved to catch him, and for the first time, Koda ignored how close an animal was to him. It seemed irrelevant when all the world in its vividness was grabbing his attention.

Past Sully, the wall had parted around a grinning pumpkin. A dust cloud floated out of the fissure. As he had never seen the color of a candle's light, Koda didn't think it strange that the pumpkin glowed an eerie seafoam green instead of orange. He, himself, didn't know the color's name.

"Would somebody answer!" said the squirrel. "Look! They're just ignoring me!"

Gaping, Sully stood and blinked. "I can see like a giant!"

The squirrel quieted.

"Is that… normal?" the goat asked the hare. His burly hide was brown and coarse like a brush. The blood on his head had dried. What an ugly, disturbing color.

"I can't begin to explain what may happen now that Hototo has disturbed things," said the hare. Both he and the squirrel were mostly gray with patches of darker brown. His wide amber gaze settled on Sully and Koda. "Are you feeling alright?"

"It's amazing!" Sully exclaimed.

"I think he's okay," the squirrel said, eyes lingering on him with a look of unease before turning to the glowing thing in the wall.

"Jack, do you know what it is?" the goat asked.

"Aren't you the one who lived with humans?" the squirrel said.

"The old man on our farm was too busy to celebrate

holidays," said the goat. "It's a Halloween decoration. I know that."

"Giant calls it a Cracker Jack, I think." Sully went to investigate its mouth. Absorbed with his newfound sight, Koda didn't warn him not to.

"It's missing a candle," Sully observed.

Hamsters and lizards weren't often compared by Koda, but as the dragon licked things to test its environment, a hamster nibbled to accomplish much of the same thing. Sully couldn't resist giving the pumpkin a bite.

"OUCH!"

Sully squeaked. Tripping twice, he ran to Koda as the Cracker Jack laughed hysterically. The wall trembled, coughing up more dirt.

"TRICK OR TREAT!"

"Did the Cracker Jacks at your Giant's nest talk?" the squirrel asked in a trembled voice.

"No!" Sully quivered behind the goat's legs.

It must be animatronic, Koda thought. He huddled beside Sully.

The hare stood on all four feet, ears straight. He stared pensively at the laughing pumpkin. "Trickster."

The laughs lowered to giggles. "You have a relic?" asked the Cracker Jack. Its eyes, pushed up in half arcs, sunk lower on the face to look at the piece of wood on the ground. The squirrel had dropped it. "Yes, I see that you do. Throw it into my mouth."

"Move!" the squirrel commanded. "There's an exit behind you, isn't there? You're in the way!"

"You won't miss the relic. There are three more just like it."

The goat whispered in the hare's ear, "What's this about a relic?" The Cracker Jack's eyes shifted to him. "The piece of wood we found in the lantern?"

"It seems so," said the hare.

"Can't we dig around it? It's loosened up the wall a ton."

The hare said loudly, "Where did you come from?"

"What does it matter?" the Cracker Jack said playfully.

"We want to exit this cave."

"I'll let you out if you give me the relic. Just step inside my mouth. But you throw it in first."

"Fat chance!" the squirrel exclaimed.

"What should we do?" the goat asked the hare.

"Tricksters are chronic liars. There's some value in this relic," said the hare. "I agree, we'll not be double-crossed."

Chittering, the squirrel bounded for the Cracker Jack. As he was about to jump in, the mouth clamped shut. *"KUK KUK KUK!"*

The goat frowned. "Well, how do you like that?"

Koda moved away as the squirrel ran back. Instinctively he reached for Sully and found him creeping up toward the Cracker Jack who was tauntingly opening and closing its mouth. Sully started nibbling on its chin.

"OUCH! Hey! Critter!"

Sully backed away, but then he hesitantly resumed nibbling.

"What are you doing?" Koda asked.

Catching on, the hare said, "Let us through."

The Cracker Jack's eyes narrowed.

"You will let us?" the hare asked.

No reply.

"We will go in then." The hare hopped up to the piece of wood, carried it back and dropped it. "It won't do to carry it like that," he said.

"Koda can carry it," said Sully. "I still have some, um, things in my pouch."

The hare turned to Koda. *Sometimes, Sully, you really grind my teeth.* Reluctantly, as he didn't want to anger him, Koda stepped up to the hare and noticed the slivers of green light on his nails. He snatched the relic and scurried back to pouch it.

"I'm glad it won't be a tight fit." The goat wedged his horn under a gap in the Cracker Jack's teeth. "Insurance," he said.

The squirrel jumped in. The hare followed, but he returned over the side to take up Sully and Koda.

It was almost certainly a death wish for them to climb in there with those animals. Was there any other choice? Koda's anxiety ballooned inside him. No, not really. He didn't know where they were anymore. When he heard those sounds during the flood, he had thought a tornado had blown through. Anything, as long as it wasn't magical. What he wasn't sure of was whether the goat was lying about the lack of an exit. If there was still a hole above them, rain would be pouring in. Lightning. At least a breeze if the flash flood had passed. So, what was there to do except follow them into the Cracker Jack?

Koda wouldn't let the hare lift them. The Cracker Jack's mouth was a good deal off the ground, and it was difficult, but he and Sully climbed in. Inside there were no speakers or a glass bulb from which the Cracker Jack could talk or glow. *It's got to be fiber optic or something. The speakers are probably hidden.*

The goat joined them. "Now what?" the squirrel said.

The mouth clamped shut with a loud crunch.

"What's going on?" the squirrel cried. Koda shouted as he bumped into him.

That feeling of nowhere crept in again as the pumpkin scent and green glow faded. Koda was about to panic when instead of hitting a wall, he walked out onto something like dirt. The rest of the world appeared afterward.

8

TOURIST TRAP

E VER SINCE SULLY'S first movie night at Giant's nest, he'd had dreams of fantasy worlds, hoping and wishing they were real places. They weren't always horror movies, but sometimes "science fiction" and adventures that took place in castle-marked landscapes overrun by dragons and other alien creatures. Though nothing magical had ever happened at home, he thought such ideas were too beautiful not to be true. And so, as he viewed the world in front of him, happy, elated, Sully wasn't at all surprised it existed.

A carnival was encompassed by a moonless sky of other-worldly constellations. Green stars which formed troll-like faces shot down to a sand-covered horizon, as if they wanted to get a better view of the Critters. Sully thought one of the faces winked at him. The face hovered like a smiling moon above a Ferris wheel and swing ride. He also spotted a roller coaster twisting into the heart of the carnival. Ghostly, circus-esque music played in the distance. Cantaloupe music? No, calliope music. Instead of fruit, he sniffed a cotton candied breeze.

"We're underground! This can't be here!" Koda ran for the Cracker Jack behind them and gasped. It wasn't there—there was just an endless indigo gloom.

Twiggy flicked his tail like a kazoo, and his body twitched up and down like one of those tiny lizards Sully sometimes saw doing pushups at the window. Twiggy made a squawking, buzzing sound. "That's human made!"

"It's a carnival," said Sully.

"What's it doing in the Haven?!"

Sully hadn't thought it possible for Jack's nose to wiggle so fast. He hopped forward, almost gliding onto the sparkling sand. Luckily, Sully had dried himself enough that hardly any of the tiny granules stuck to him. "We aren't in the Haven," Jack said.

"We aren't?" Sully asked, disappointed.

"This is the Trickster world. I was told we would pass right through."

"By whom?" Sully asked.

"It's spoken of in the tales."

You didn't answer my question, Sully thought. "What are Tricksters? Are they like totems?" He began to tremble at the thought.

"They are magical beings that are neither Critter nor Hunter, though some appear so. They aren't anything to worry about as far as them harming you, but you shouldn't be caught in a room with one, either. They are prone to mischief."

Rowan pointed his hoof at the carnival. It fell back down very quickly, as if he could hardly focus on anything other than his astonishment. "That's 'em over there?" he asked. Seafoam green auras dominated the rides and buildings. Jack nodded.

Koda mumbled to himself. "How? I'm awake!"

"When we reach the carnival, do not remove the relic," Jack told Koda. "We don't want them aware that we have it or the other three if we should find them."

"You want to go into that human thing?" Twiggy whined.

"The Cracker Jack appeared when we retrieved the relic.

Unless it's a strong coincidence, I think we may need to find the other three relics for more Cracker Jacks to show."

Sully asked, "Where did the first Cracker Jack go?"

"I'm not sure. It did seem to appear out of nowhere. Now that I see this," Jack motioned at the carnival and the sky, "I don't think there was anything outside that cave."

"What do you mean?" Rowan asked.

"This world doesn't seem to function the same as the Haven or the human world. I've been told there are several places within this one, and not like cities or forests where you can travel by simply walking long enough. It's difficult to explain."

Sully had heard about this type of thing before. "Is it like... multi...verses?"

"I reckon Sully's got it figured out for you," Rowan said. "Sounds familiar. I used to watch some shows back in the day..."

"Can we stop talking about this?" Twiggy interrupted. "We're stuck here! We're not supposed to be here!"

"This is important. Assuming everything happens as before, we'll need the relics and Cracker Jacks to progress from one location to the next," Jack said. "If we've arrived in a location that has a relic, it's likely to be found in those buildings."

"And if not, we're stranded?" Twiggy grabbed his tail and held it close.

Jack glanced at him. His chest rose from a deep breath, taking in the severity of the situation. He turned back toward the carnival.

"I reckon that goes without sayin', Twiggy," Rowan said, looking supportively at Jack. He, too, kept gazing at the carnival as if to check that it would still be there. Sully watched the green lights with dismay.

"I doubt there's anything else but wasteland except where we are," Jack said. "Eventually—probably after we've gathered all four relics—we might arrive at the Haven."

"And our families? My pup?" Twiggy asked.

Sully tried to conceal his remorse. He hadn't meant to lie. The way Twiggy had looked, though, Sully had wanted to take his sadness away.

Twiggy said, "What if they're in some other location in the Trickster world? How will *they* get to the Haven?"

"My hope is that they're already there," Jack said quietly.

Rowan stepped forward, purposefully snapping the group out of their silence. "I'm on board. The sooner the better." Koda and Twiggy shifted nervously.

"One more thing," Jack said. "I'm sure you haven't forgotten what happened during the disaster."

A grim shadow crossed over Rowan's and Twiggy's faces.

"A totem head has broken."

Sully remembered the terrifying sound of wood bits flying into the air—the sound he had mistaken for lightning. Somewhere, a world apart, a second pole in the mountain pass was missing a totem head.

Sully wished his tail was long enough to hug like Twiggy's. "Which one escaped?" he asked.

"It was far too dark and chaotic to tell," Jack said.

Rowan asked, "Do you reckon the relics could be the pieces that shattered from the totem head?"

"They could be. There's incredible power in the them. Be on your guard."

Jack took the lead with Rowan at his shoulder. As the more hesitant of the Critters, Twiggy, Sully, and Koda stayed in the back of the group. Ominous laughter and the erratic music loudened. *Da da daadadada daaa!* Like a circus. The carnival loomed closer, and with it came both dread and excitement. Sully wasn't always able to figure out what the giants were saying or doing in movies; he didn't need to. He watched them because he loved to see the outside world he was missing, as well as the fantastical creatures they made on their "computers." What would it be like to see a creature in real life? He had always imagined he would be brave.

Sully realized he hadn't relieved himself in a while. Suddenly, with a feeling of turmoil in his stomach, he needed to go very badly—and there wasn't the special corner of his home or a pantry available.

A great arch stood high overhead at the entrance. CARNIVALE. The sand below it shimmered like the morning sun over the ocean. Inside, red and gold lights lit food stands, tents, and all the rides. The buildings seemed to open to the Critters, inviting them in with sweet scents as thick as butter in the air. It was the most beautiful thing Sully had ever seen, that is, until he saw the grisly creatures populating it.

Tricksters roamed the carnival, each possessing a seafoam green aura glowing as a ball in its midsection. These Halloween-like creatures, things with bruise-colored skin and multiple eyes in one socket, were more than just ghouls and goblins. They lurked in alleyways, cluttered popcorn stands, fought over carnival prizes and jumped atop buildings. At a carousel, furry beasts without heads rode on phantom horses and a shambling crowd of conjoined goo-bodied creatures caused passersby to get stuck in the slime they trailed. It was as if the Tricksters had been born of the most twisted fairy tale imaginable.

Twiggy made his buzzing sound and started up with his pushups again. At any second, he might *KUK*. Sully looked to Jack and Rowan for help but couldn't catch their eye. Rowan turned his head as something creaked loudly at the carousel. One of the headless beasts riding the horses had leaned out of its seat, facing their way. Sully nearly jumped out of his fur.

Headless poked a rider in front of it, then pointed at Sully's group. "CRITTERS!" it shouted, though out of what mouth Sully had no idea.

The carousel slowed to a stop. All the riders, and even the horses, gawked at them. Every Trickster in the carnival as well. The popping of popcorn, the fighting over prizes, and every other sound either stopped or quieted.

The Tricksters grinned devilishly. Sully expected them to dance, to crook their arms and scuff left to right. Rowan and Jack tensed, Twiggy *KUK*ed, and Koda's cheek pouches puffed up.

Snickering, the Tricksters waved and continued with their night.

Jack had been up on his back feet the entire time. Even *he* had wanted to run. Sully and the others entered with extreme caution.

"This is interestin'," Rowan said, observing a dunk tank with a small shark swimming in the water. A Trickster who reminded Sully of the Creature from the Black Lagoon sat on the plank in a one-piece swimsuit, laughing at them. "You'd reckon we were doin' somethin' funny."

Jack turned to Sully and Koda. "You recognized that this is a carnival. Do you know what humans do here?"

"They go on rides," Sully said and went off on a tangent of all the information he knew, including the purchasing of tickets. He hadn't seen a ticket booth at this carnival, though.

Rowan asked Jack, "How are we gonna find anythin' in this mess?"

"I think we should separate."

"We'll get lost!" Twiggy protested.

"That's, like, the number one rule not to break in horror movies," Sully warned.

"Unfortunately, it can't be helped," said Rowan. "Where do we start?"

"Check the rides," Jack said.

"You want us to *play* on these things?" Twiggy whined.

"If it helps you find a relic, yes."

Rowan frowned at the Trickster in the dunk tank. Its laugh had turned into high-pitched heaving. "Where will you be in case we do?"

"I'm going to have a look at that tent." Jack motioned between two widely spaced buildings, one titled HAUNTED HOUSE and the other SPOOK SHOW in flashing lights. Unfortunately, Sully couldn't read either one. Far away on the carnival's outskirts, connected by a path of lanterns, there was indeed a red tent. It sat on the indigo sand as if on the end of a dock over a lake. It gave Sully the creeps.

"Feelin' dangerous?" Rowan gave a short, nervous laugh. "I'd feel better if I went with you."

"I'll be perfectly fine," Jack said. "Do you mind taking Sully and Nahiossi?"

"Not at all," Rowan said.

Twiggy asked, "And me?"

"We'll cover more ground if you go alone," Jack said.

"Are you sure that's— I mean, I—"

"You'll be fine, my friend. Be cautious, and you'll be fine." Jack regarded Rowan, Sully, and Koda before hopping past the two buildings.

Rowan asked Twiggy, "Where will you go?"

"I don't want to go anywhere!" He hesitated, flicking his tail, before releasing a sigh. "I guess I should get this over with."

Twiggy ran through an array of concession stands. The dunk tank creature pointed at him mockingly. Challengers had gathered around. One of them hit the target with a ball, and Sully closed his eyes upon the splash. Disturbingly, the creature continued to laugh over the sounds the shark made.

Rowan shook his head as if to make sure he was awake. He looked down at Koda. "You've been quiet…"

Koda was hunched over his stomach. "Whatever's going on, I'll go along with it in order to get home," he said tensely.

Rowan nodded. "You comin', Sully?"

Sully jerked away from what he was doing. He kicked some sand with his back leg to cover what he buried. "Y-yeah, I'm ready." His ears felt hot with embarrassment.

Rowan let Sully and Koda walk ahead so he could see them, which was a little scary at first. Sully made sure to see if the dunk tank creature was still alive. It was climbing back onto the plank, miraculously unharmed and with damage only to its torn swimsuit.

Unlike Koda, who watched his surroundings guardedly, Sully gazed at everything with amazement. His one experience of a carnival was a blurry scene from a movie reflected onto his glass home. Now all of it was clear, nothing was missed—at least, not until it became so crowded amongst the creatures' feet that Sully couldn't see ahead. As he was jumping to see past them, one Trickster tried to pick him up. It turned out alright once Rowan butted his horns to chase the Trickster off. Sully trusted Jack, and he didn't think they would get hurt, so his focus returned to the attractions. Sully pointed out a pendulum ride to Koda and was a little discouraged to see his brother with his eyes closed.

"How does Giant see it all? My eyes are hurting," said Koda.

The paths throughout the carnival were named like streets. A wooden post on a corner declared their location: BUBBLE BUBBLE and the cross street TOIL AND TROUBLE. "Tricksters know Macbeth, apparently," Rowan said. Here, the gloomy buildings weren't even three feet taller than Rowan. The Tricksters were extremely short, pixie-like with villainous faces, and carried plastic bags. They had found the shopping section of the carnival. Sully wasn't sure if there were shops at carnivals in the giant world.

"How does the hare think we're going to find anything in this?" Koda asked, his voice on the verge of cracking.

Sully sniffed benevolently at Koda to calm him. One building on TOIL AND TROUBLE snatched his interest. A monster Venus flytrap grew out of the side like a chimney, large gemstone pipes supported the building's overhang above the porch, and a sign hung in its dark window.

INCENSE, MINERALS, AND OTHER SPIRITUAL GOODS

"How about that shop?" Sully asked. To be honest, he just liked the look of it.

Koda's eyes widened. "*That* shop?"

"Mmhmm."

"Anythin' to get off the street," Rowan said, stepping back as a forty-foot tarantula turned the corner. The scarecrow riding it tipped his straw hat at him. After seeing that, Sully practically ran off without them.

The door to the shop opened, ringing bell chimes, and a ghost exited carrying a bag marked THANK YOU FOR HAUNT-ING. Rowan caught the door with his horn. As they entered, Sully sniffed a sweet smoky fragrance.

Once inside, they took in the store's dramatic lighting. Hanging crystals replaced traditional overhead lights, casting rainbows on the ceiling. It was like viewing reflected water at the bottom of a swimming pool. In the corners of the shop, Buddha statues rested proudly on floating shelves. Below those, luminescent Himalayan rocks set the mood on glass shelves. They were lined up in rows reaching far into the back like a geologist's library, giving the space an earthy, cavernous feel.

"Good place to find a relic," said Rowan. His hooves

clomped on the tile floor.

"There's no one in here," Koda said. Many Critters have excellent hearing. If there was anyone in the shop, one of them would have heard.

"Better for us, isn't it?" Rowan said.

Koda grunted softly.

They wandered down the center aisle that separated the shelves. Sully stopped, letting Rowan and Koda walk ahead. Slowly, Sully looked to the top of the shelves.

There was something up there hiding in a dark spot. Sully wouldn't have seen it if it weren't for its bright red eyes. The large reptilian shape leaned over the edge of the shelf like a cat about to jump.

Sully shrieked. "It's a totem! It's up *there!*"

Rowan trotted back, followed by Koda. Taking one look upward into the aisle, he stopped Sully as he was running by holding out his hoof.

He smiled. "Wait a minute, Sully. That's a Chinese New Year dragon. It's used in a dance at festivals."

Sully hid behind Rowan's hoof, hugging it. "Are you sure?" he asked.

"Positive. Originally, they were used in rain dances. The sign outside did say 'spiritual goods.' I can read a little."

Koda looked at the Chinese dragon with as much fear as Sully. "If this isn't the giant world, why does everything look the same?"

"Besides the Tricksters," Sully reminded. He let go of Rowan's hoof, embarrassed.

"They're imaginary," Koda said dismissively, "just like this carnival. I hit my head too hard when we fell underground."

"You're worse than the giants!" Sully cried.

"Tricksters used to live on Earth." Walking again, Rowan

stepped over the flytrap's stem. Several spread into the shop from the wall where it grew outside. He turned his head at every aisle. "They got into too much mischief and were banned here by some magical event or other, or so it's said in the tales. They're very well known in Native American culture."

"Why the talking in giant speak?" Koda asked. "Why are you pretending to be giants?"

"Oh, well, we're not pretendin' to be human. It's just somethin' Jack picked up," Rowan said.

"From who?" Sully asked.

"His brother."

"Jack has a brother? Where is he? Did he make it into the opening?"

Rowan stopped to rub the wounds around his horns on a shelf. The older wounds from when he had rescued Koda had already begun to heal.

"Are you hurting, Rowan?" Sully asked.

"Itches a bit. I wonder if Hototo cleans his talons."

Sully sped ahead and found an aisle which contained mixing bowls and sticks trailing wisps of smoke on gold plates. A stone dragon sitting on the floor puffed mist from its nose. After confirming it wasn't alive, Sully moved on to see two glass frogs performing yoga. Fibrous leaves filled a brass bowl between them. They were larger and less soft than the thyme leaves. Still, Sully thought they could work.

Koda and Rowan entered the aisle.

"Eat these, Rowan. Maybe they'll help," Sully said.

"Do it quickly if you're going to," Koda whispered hastily, "so we can leave."

Rowan walked over to the bowl and munched.

Koda scolded Sully, "Stay close to me. We don't know what's in here."

"A lot of cool things." Sully turned to one of the shelves that displayed geodes and gemstones. They were an assortment of colors: red, white, crystal blue, amethyst. The orange ones glimmered like lava. For every geode displaying its crystals there were two disguised as round rocks with sparkling holes. "They're like meteors!"

"Dark places like this have bats," Koda said.

Sully felt a twinge of fright then ignored it. The world outside was too exciting, and he was tired of being afraid. He touched one of the rock geodes with blue holes (blue, as it was turning out, was his favorite color), rocking it slightly.

Koda asked Rowan, "Are you done yet?"

Rowan swallowed the last leaf. "Let's go."

On their way out of the aisle, Sully paused and turned back. The geode he had touched was still rocking on the shelf.

Not only that, the crystals were expanding, pulsing outward in hexagonal shards.

"Why's it doing that?" Sully asked, transfixed. The rocking intensified.

Koda shoved him under the shelf as the geode detonated. Rowan backed up, knocking mixing bowls and gold plates onto the floor with a loud clatter. The breathing dragon shattered. Rowan ducked, jolting several times, as the shop filled with the sound of rocking geodes and bursting crystals.

Blue sparkles floated down into Sully's view and to the floor. The blue geode swung under the bottom shelf, hanging onto it with newly formed crystalized limbs. Two yellow spots beneath the glass surface stared right at the brothers. With most of the outer rock shell gone, Sully could now see that the geode glowed the Trickster green. "THIEVES!" it shrieked.

Squeaking, they ran out into the center aisle and the downpour of glass. They paced, not sure what to do. Rowan raced up from behind and snatched them up, but he tripped on the flytrap stem a little way down. Sully felt him losing balance. Rowan was going to fall head first right on top of them! Half running, half stumbling, he got control of his legs and, with a burst of speed, fled for the exit.

Rowan had grabbed Sully backwards, so he faced the glittering swarm of geode Tricksters chasing after them. It was as if a giant treasure chest had opened and spilled them into the shop.

"Criiitters! Criiters, thieves!" the geodes shrieked. Their voices were like knives on glass.

Rowan rammed the front door, and the aftershock threw them back. He dropped Sully and Koda and tried twisting the doorknob with his mouth. Hiding under him, Sully heard it rattle then wrench back into place.

"Hurry!" Koda screamed.

"I can't open it!" Rowan exclaimed.

At the sound of cascading glass, Sully and Koda shrank against the door. The geode Tricksters flowed out from the shelves as a shuddering body of quartz. Rowan turned to face them, kneeling over Sully and Koda with his horns thrust forward. There was silence but for the slight scrape of crystal along the floor. Sully winced at the sound, like nails on a chalkboard.

An amethyst geode approached them in small, wobbly movements. Crystals jutted out all over the Trickster's body, even as spikes through the rock shell on its back. The crystals grated together as it spoke in a sharp, grainy voice.

"You eat it, you buy."

"We don't have money," Sully said, fearing the worst.

"Trade."

Sully waited tensely to see whether Koda or Rowan would offer the relic. They didn't.

The amethyst geode shuddered as if from anger. The yellow

spots shifted to Koda. "We'll take the Critter."

Koda gasped. Rowan bent to grab him, but he was too far back to reach. The geodes swarmed from all sides. One wrangled Koda's head, trying to pull him into the swarm. Squealing, Koda bit it on the face. He may as well have bitten stone.

"Leave him alone!" The Tricksters herded Sully, and he couldn't reach Koda. Rowan repositioned himself to knock Koda's attackers away. They skidded across the floor, making more of the horrible noise, but more kept coming. At no point did Sully want or expect Rowan to stomp on them. They were Critters, and Critters wouldn't do such a thing.

"You can have the Critter when you pay for him and what you stole," said the amethyst.

Sully pawed a geode in the face—or the mouth, but he wasn't sure they had a mouth. Any harder and he would have sliced his paw open. "Wait! We have—!"

"Don't!" Koda yelled. "I won't let go of home." The geodes dragged him out from under Rowan and pulled him farther into the shop.

Sully frantically searched for options. He thought he was going to have to leave Koda to find an object outside somehow. A leaf from the Venus flytrap or a piece of candy or—

He remembered something.

"I'll trade!" Sully shouted.

The swarm came to a standstill.

Sully unpouched as fast as he could. He wasn't supposed to have done this, and he felt ashamed, but he was relieved he had saved some forage from the mountain pass.

The geodes snatched the bits of nuts and seeds off the floor and handled it as if measuring its worth. Sully, Rowan, and Koda, who was still struggling, watched them anxiously.

Koda was released. He knocked over three geodes on his

way to hide behind Rowan's leg. The geode Tricksters returned to their shelves, leaving just the amethyst to stare at them with its shifty eyes. Slowly, it turned and joined its geode-folk.

Bells chimed. The door opened, bumping Rowan on his bottom. A hairless elf-eared creature bent its head into the shop. "Excuse me," it said and hobbled inside. Rowan hurriedly caught the door.

Once outside, Sully apologized to Koda. "I forgot I had the forage in my pouch," he said, embarrassed.

Koda, out of breath, just looked at him.

Rowan chuckled.

"It's not funny," Koda said. He sounded more frightened than upset.

"I apologize." Rowan's chuckle soured. He bent his head. The crystal shards from the geode explosion were deep in his wounds and flank.

Sully cried out. "I'm sorry! I made it worse!"

"Don't worry about it. I'll tough it out." Rowan put on a smile that looked more like a grimace.

"We can try another shop. We can find something to trade with," Sully urged.

"No sense in that."

"Why not?"

"'Cause of what I was laughin' at. We could've been spared that fiasco if we'd known it was just across the street." Rowan laughed hoarsely again.

Confused, Sully followed his gaze to a building on the edge of BUBBLE BUBBLE. Below a sign that said BALLOON RACE, a pink elephant Trickster that looked like a stitched-together stuffed animal was hanging a plush toy bear under a sunshade. There was a small piece of wood in the pocket of its overalls.

A relic.

9

FUN AND GAMES

SHRIEKING LAUGHTER rose from flying carts twisting high above the fun house. Twiggy gripped the railing three stories high as he waited for the vibration to pass.

He had taken Jack's advice to investigate the rides, but nearly every one had a line as long as an express train. He had waited in line at House of Creeps for all of ten minutes until he realized someone was always cutting ahead. Grumpily, he left and discovered the fun house. The faded candy-striped wallpaper and large blinking sign leaning precariously above him suggested it was abandoned.

Twiggy jumped onto the plank balcony. A huge puppet head covered in peeling paint stuck out from the wall, appearing to have melted under the intense neon lights. One bulbous eye drooped to the floor while the other stared at him. Twiggy looked at the fake human head with repulsion. It wasn't glowing like the Tricksters, so he walked by it unhindered to a gaping hole in the planks. Sparkling dust from a collapsed section of the ceiling circulated to a twisting slide below. Twiggy considered leaving back down it. He hadn't found a way into the building on the lower levels, either.

"Does this thing even have an entrance?" he complained.

Something scraped and clunked on the floor behind him.

Twiggy jumped. The puppet's jaw rested open on the planks. "Who did that?" he yelled. Twiggy raced to the opening. Someone inside ran across before stopping directly ahead in the dark.

"You Tricksters need to stop bothering me! Go stare at someone else!"

The figure remained motionless.

Twiggy squinted. He realized it wasn't glowing. This was not a Trickster.

"Who are you?" Twiggy felt hot under the neon lights.

He heard a short buzzing sound. Twiggy took an involuntary step back as florescent ceiling lights flickered on. They did hardly anything to brighten the room, and they continued to buzz and flicker dull light. He could tell it was a large room, though, empty except for a small squirrel near the back wall.

"Pup?"

Her expression reflected Twiggy's overwhelming joy. As they ran to each other memories of the baby squirrel came to him.

She wasn't his pup biologically. On the day the little one had been given to him, her mother had arrived at the mountain pass with a lame leg. It was autumn, when many of the trees were overgrown from spring. The tree the mother and her pups lived in had begun to scrape the nearby human house. It was common for squirrels to live close to humans for easy access to forage. They foolishly pranced around in the human-grown gardens, stealing seeds from bird houses, coming over like they were neighbors. Well, they were *not* neighbors to the humans. They were considered *pests*, as the pup's mother had learned quickly.

Twiggy remembered her speaking to him, lethargic and clinging to consciousness. "I was gone. For foraging. When I got back to the nest, the humans were cutting down our tree. And they were— Oh, they were destroying the nest, and I heard my babies crying for me. I tried to rescue them, and the humans threw rocks at me! They were *laughing!*"

After she had told him this, Twiggy had every intention of sabotaging the humans. Anything could happen at a construction site. If he ran around their feet, maybe they would fall onto something dangerous. Everything the humans carried around with them was dangerous. Poisons. Weapons. The noisy contraption that ran over countless Critters on the road while the humans hid cowardly inside. Nothing could touch them.

Jack hadn't let Twiggy avenge the squirrels. "Critters don't act that way," he had said, which was precisely the reason why Twiggy thought so many of them died.

Sometimes he resented Jack. After all that had happened to them both, it was incredibly foolish to turn the other cheek. It downright infuriated him. And Jack would take the two brothers to their human, knowing how they were. Jack was even going to betray his brother's wishes by refusing to enter the Haven.

Twiggy hoped they wouldn't find a way back to the human world. He didn't think he could handle finding the brothers thrown out in the trash somewhere, dead. Just like he had found the other pups.

"I knew I would get hurt if I tried to fight." The mother looked at her pup, clasping her like she was her last hold on life. Twiggy realized that this was true. "She was the only one left. As I was running away, they continued to throw rocks at me.

"I had heard about this place. I don't know if it's true. It's too late for my other babies, but if you could... if you could take her there, to this Haven..."

She had taken her paw away from the pup in offering her to Twiggy. He had always despised humans, but the anger he had felt then was more than he'd ever been able to stand. Ten grueling days of travel, and she had hardly made it to the barrier before dying on its border.

Twiggy took the pup.

He looked at her now and saw that she had grown. But then he realized this squirrel didn't have a pup's face. The squirrel was an adult, and male. Sorrow squeezed his heart, taking his breath away. He had been so happy a moment ago only to fall into a depression now.

It's still a squirrel. And my pup is still out there.

"Are you from the mountain pass?" Twiggy couldn't identify him. He couldn't even *smell* him.

The squirrel's lips moved soundlessly.

"What was that?"

Another reply without voice. As they moved closer toward each other Twiggy's eyes drifted behind the squirrel to another doorway opened to the carnival backdrop: Ferris wheel, swing ride, and... *another House of Creeps? They have two of everything?*

More than one thing isn't right here, Twiggy thought. *The twisted road with the carts is right behind this building. I should see part of it.*

Distracted by his thoughts, Twiggy had been looking at the squirrel without really seeing it. Its eyes had widened.

"What's—? I can't hear what you're..."

He trailed off as the squirrel moved his lips.

"Hello?"

Inaudibly, the squirrel replied, "hello."

He had a thought. Speaking slowly, Twiggy read the other squirrel's lips. "My name is..."

My name is... Twiggy.

Chills flowed into his tail. "Why are you copying me?" After the phrase was thrown back at him, he walked the rest of the way to meet paws but touched a flat, slippery surface instead.

Twiggy recoiled. So did the squirrel. "What? Where are

you?" He gathered his courage and investigated. He finally recognized the squirrel. It was him, his reflection, but he usually only saw that in water. He angled his head and found that the room and his reflection were flattened on a tall, rectangular object.

Both Twiggys tapped their nails on the strange surface. "What is this?"

"HAHA."

Twiggy flinched and his claws screeched off the surface to the floor. "Who's that?"

"HAHA*haaaaaa!*"

The laughter came from the wall to his left, but it sounded like it was right in the room. As Twiggy paced back and forth in front of it, he saw there were two walls: one closer to him, and the other pushed farther back. The walls were painted to appear as though they were level with each other. Another room was cloaked at the front by black sheets and was hidden between them.

The drapery billowed.

"Ha... ha..."

"Go find someone else to play your s-sick games!"

A loud thwack spun him in the direction of the entrance. The puppet's mouth had sealed.

Twiggy flicked his tail. The wall was otherwise bare, with no doorknob or other means of an exit. He was forced to keep moving forward.

He darted into the drapery before he could lose his nerve, but another sheet soon blocked his way. Twiggy ducked under it and was blocked by yet a third sheet. The pattering of footsteps was at first loud as if someone had been standing directly on the other side. The pace increased to a run, moving away from him. Twiggy chased the footsteps through the labyrinth of sheets, but just when he was sure he was gaining on them, they stopped. He had been so caught up in the chase that he was breathing too loudly, and he

110

hadn't kept track of the footsteps.

"Hello, Critter," said a creepy voice.

The nearest sheet rippled, and a grinning creature peeked under it. Giggling, the creature slipped away.

***

With Jack's speed and agility, even on the unstable sand, he arrived at the tent within seconds.

Lonely. Foreboding. He saw the tent as gray—that special gray the humans called "red." It was like a surreal hole against the bluish environment and the green glow of the face constellations.

His ears twitched. Wind chimes sang at a hanging post. Bursts of laughter turned his gaze to the carnival.

He was confident Rowan had assumed his protective role over the brothers and Twiggy... Twiggy would make it through this. Jack had thought it best considering he and Nahiossi weren't getting along. Twiggy was going to suggest he come with Jack, he'd felt it coming, and he was glad he had made a quick getaway. Jack had always felt alone, even in a group, so why should it be any different by himself? He wanted to be alone right now to think over everything that had happened. To grieve, and that wasn't something he wished the others to see.

He turned back to the tent and saw a claw folded over the outside edge. The claw slipped under the cloth.

Jack stood still for a moment, listening to the chimes and the whistling current that carried them.

He then entered the tent.

Hanging beads knocked softly over his face. Once past the curtain, he felt like the grayness was drawing him in. The entire space bled beyond his sight. Red leather-bound books and glass bottles stacked on red bookcases, and a round table, complete with a ruby-colored fitted cloth and two velvet king chairs, complemented the center. Even the shag carpet he walked on was red. Peculiarly, as he hadn't heard it outside, a gramophone played guitar and violin music.

"Do you like my music?"

Up until he heard the voice, Jack's ears had been pointed forward, tilting his whole body into the scene before him. Now he pulled back, tightening every limb to his body. He felt himself readying to flee as a figure stepped out from behind one of the bookcases. Its core glowed like a will-o'-the-wisp. A Trickster, and yet its stature was human-like, clothed in a red dress beneath a short red cloak. A hood masked its face in darkness.

"Come closer. It wouldn't do to greet you at this distance." The female voice was cool and purring.

Jack stayed where he was.

"You're searching for something. I can tell you where to look." The Trickster motioned to one of the chairs with a long, furry arm. "Fortunes are free for Critters."

Should he refuse? She was baiting him and likely had no information to give. Or perhaps she was deflecting him from finding a relic in the tent. He'd already had a suspicious feeling about this place. Or maybe he was mistaking suspicion for intuition. If he stuck with it, he thought he would find answers to *something*.

Jack cautiously hopped to the chair. His ears peeked above the table.

"One more step up, please. I like to see my visitors."

Jack hopped onto the table.

The Trickster sauntered along the bookcase. She moved her arm behind her and grabbed something that clinked.

Jack's pulse quickened. He realized he had made a mistake and bolted.

He underestimated her swiftness. The table jerked, beginning to tip him off the side, and his claws snagged in the table cloth. He felt the weight of her sliding over to him. She wrenched him forward by his paws, righting the table back onto its feet, and clamped rings over his wrists.

The hood fell back onto her shoulders.

A fox grinned in his face.

Jack jerked his wrists within the clamps. He thumped, scratching the cloth and swishing it about the table as it bounced.

The fox Trickster moved away. "You'll have to stop that," she admonished. Her tone held no merit. It seemed, Jack thought, she was stifling a giggle.

"What is it you told your friends?" She crooked her neck to look up at the ceiling. One large cloudy eye swiveled. "'They aren't really anything to worry about as far as them harming you...'"

Jack gave a violent thump and stopped.

"'...but you shouldn't be caught in—' Oh..." Her teeth shone like daggers as she reached for his paw.

Jack threw himself away from her as hard as he could. His legs slipped under him and pulled his chin to the table.

The Trickster frowned. "Relax, dear. You'll be leaving today with all your body parts accounted for. Well... most of them."

Jack noted her outward-facing ears, the not too close position on the skull—the sign of a fox who is playing a game. *Calm yourself. She's teasing you.*

He lifted himself onto his feet and brought his ears forward. He managed to make himself appear relatively calm after practicing this repeatedly over the years in front of others.

"That was unnecessary," Jack said.

"But fun." She gave him an appraising look and sat in the chair opposite him. Leaning forward, she held his paw.

Jack saw her as an arctic fox (orange was another color he couldn't see). She was like snow shining in a glacier's light from the glow in her chest. Her head was three times larger than it should be compared to her body. It would have to be bigger than usual to support the cataract eye which was like a globe in her skull. The other, clear eye gleamed intelligently.

I've broken my own rule, Jack thought with some bemusement.

She flipped his paw over and traced it with a spider-legged finger. "I'm not that bad, actually. A Trickster's life is to trick. Makes perfect sense."

"What are you doing?"

"Reading your paw. But mostly I just want to hold paws," said the fox.

She released him. Jack pulled his paw back, his wrist catching in the clamp. The fox's teeth appeared smaller in her jaw, at least for the moment. She gently smoothed the table cloth. Casually, she said, "Look at the mess you've made of my furniture."

Jack worked on calming his breathing. "I'm not used to such unusual conditions."

The Trickster laughed. "I'm more informal than most. Though you and your friends are on quite the unusual adventure. Wouldn't you like my assistance, Jack? After all, there are more powerful beings than Tricksters."

He chose not to comment on how she knew his name. His focus drew away from his fear. "You're speaking of the totems."

She looked up from the cloth, smirking, then down again.

"*Is* there one down here?" asked Jack.

"Enough serious talk," the fox said cheerfully. "I know your name. I suppose you'd like to know mine. I'm Shebari, and I'll be your fortune teller. But first...."

She planted her claw on the table and, with the other, began to pluck out her left eye.

Jack stared, unable to look away.

POP.

114

Shebari rotated the eye in the palm of her claw. Something like clear, thick slime dribbled onto the table. She watched Jack for a reaction, the hollow eye socket sunken in her face. Apparently satisfied with what she saw, she grabbed a vintage stand and deck of cards from the bookcase. She set them on the table and placed the eye on the stand. It stuck there.

"Not the traditional type of crystal ball, but here, we're all about the unconventional as you've so boldly stated."

Shebari fanned the cards and held them to her face. "Tarot cards have many meanings. They're unique to each individual, so they aren't always easy to interpret. My eye, ironically, will make things clearer."

Humming along with the gramophone, she shuffled the cards. "Tell me, handsome dear. Can you read?"

"Unfortunately, no."

"Fine. Fine!" she said contentedly. "I'll do it for you."

She slipped the first card in front of him. It portrayed three skulls, all with a wedge-shaped head—Jack couldn't name the species—stacked on top of each other like a totem pole of their own. The skull on top had a large hole on either side. He could only guess that with skin the animal had very large eyes. It had many tiny teeth.

Muscle covered the middle skull. The last, a silhouette, seemed to be of the same animal but with skin. Areas on the head appeared to be more fleshed out and spikes detailed the back of the head. Jack glanced at the foiled letters at the bottom of the card and was irritated with himself that he couldn't make the least bit of sense out of them.

"Deception. You won't find it in any other deck," Shebari bragged. "It's the hiding of things in plain sight, the alteration of truth."

At this point in the conversation, Jack took what the fox

Trickster said with a grain of salt, to use a human phrase. So, it came as a surprise when transparent images like reflections materialized on the cataract eye. Jack recognized them as Twiggy, Rowan, and the two brothers.

Shebari's attention remained on him, her arms folded. She hadn't looked down at the eye. "Ah. Your friends are keeping the truth from you. Not all, but a few."

Jack was stone faced.

"Oh, though it may not be intentional. These things are hard to tell. Maybe it's something you overlooked. Something that will improve your situation."

Shebari plucked another card and the Critters vanished from the eye.

A horned red creature sitting on a throne glared at Jack.

"Mmmm… the Devil. Don't worry, it's not literal. At least, not in your case." Constant slyness in her voice.

The eye displayed another image. Rowan appeared, running with Sully, then came the rain and Hototo. The owl lifted him by his horns.

"One of your friends battled with a powerful spirit. A totem. They're often called devils," Shebari said with a smile. "Psychologically it means your struggles. Your inner demons, so to speak."

The smile fell. Jack thought it could be from sympathy and was angered by it.

Shebari continued, "What is this? Grief? Oh, no. I do not speak of the ones you lost in the disaster."

Jack made every pain to keep his uncertainty hidden. Nothing in the eyes, his ears relaxed. It was important not to indicate anything.

"Yes, I know. I do. You're afraid for the others. Afraid that you won't be able to help them, like *before*."

"You told me you would find the object I'm seeking," Jack said. "If I am to be held against my will, it isn't to listen to information I'm capable of remembering myself."

Shebari eased back in her chair. "How about this then, Jack? I'll avoid your past since it is a touchy subject for you. Presently, the relic has already been found. Cast it from your mind. It's not imperative to what I must tell you. You see, each tarot card gives an individual reading, but as a whole, they connect to a bigger picture, one outcome. While these insights mean a lot to most anyone, they could very well mean a higher consequence to someone like you."

Jack would no longer acknowledge the cards. "Tricksters do well with lies," he said.

"You're also aware that I'm capable of the truth. More than I can say of your party."

Jack let the gramophone fill in their silence. On the cataract eye, Rowan fought Hototo on repeat. "Are we finished?"

"Not quite." Relishing his expression, Shebari plucked a card from the deck but didn't look to see what it was.

"One more left," she teased.

"More bad news, I suspect."

"Ah, but I always save the best for last. I have a good feeling about this one. Though everything comes with a price, don't you think?"

***

Sully and his group hasted to the balloon race building. "That was fast. I thought it would take us longer to find the relic," Sully said.

"Don't bet on it happenin' again," said Rowan.

The bear hung with the other carnival prizes, the relic

peeking out teasingly from its pocket. It was difficult to focus on it in the sea of color. A row of water guns pointed to plastic toad heads that seemed oddly cheerful, given the situation. *At least they're not clowns.* Sully shivered. *That's what they usually are, and I don't like them at all.*

A goblin-like creature wearing patchwork gnome clothes and a pointed hat sat at the counter. The Critters arrived at the building just as a balloon popped. The pink elephant reached for a carnival prize. Sully's heart leaped as it grabbed the bear and handed it to the Trickster.

"Hey! Stop!" Rowan shouted.

The goblin-gnome turned around, smiled widely, and ran out into the street.

Koda chased him. Before the Trickster could disappear in the crowd, he sped up to its bare foot. The Trickster shrieked but kept running. Koda tried to follow but the traffic blocked him.

Sully glanced behind him, wondering why Rowan hadn't raced ahead. He stopped running when he saw he was limping. Trying to catch up, the next step Rowan took landed him in the sand.

"Rowan!"

Rowan tipped over onto his side. His stomach rose and fell. With each breath, the shards in his wounds expanded, and smaller crystals spread over his body. Sully could still see Rowan's fur at first, but then the crystal flattened and thickened like marble. Sully had no doubt that in a short amount of time, Rowan would be trapped within a block of geode.

Koda ran back to them, and Sully exclaimed at the blood wetting his brother's fur. "You're bleeding!"

"It's not mine," Koda said. He stared, disturbed, at the crystals. "If you want to save him, we have to go."

Sully hesitated.

"I'll come out of this alright, Sully. You go find Jack," Rowan rasped. He made an extreme effort to smile.

Feeling yet again that this was all his fault, Sully let Koda weave them through the street.

***

After running past the last of the sheets, Twiggy entered a long, dark hallway. He was only able to see the Trickster by its glow. It had pointed ears like an elf but a gruesome face with overly large features: large nose, large eyes. It wore patchy clothes and a triangle-shaped hat.

Unnerved, Twiggy demanded, "What do you want?"

Still grinning, the Trickster thrust its hand into the air, presenting a small object.

A relic!

Twiggy darted forward. The Trickster leaped into the wall, tearing through the wallpaper.

Crazy psycho!

He thought he heard the Trickster move something inside the wall. A yank, then the pattering of footsteps.

Twiggy considered turning around and leaving through the sheets—the puppet's mouth might be open now—but he was too confused and ticked off.

The wallpaper covered the entire wall. No plaster here. Through the tear was a room decorated in drab browns. A human room, with wooden furniture and wooden frames holding pictures of forest animals on the walls. The entire room was made of wood like he was inside a square tree. The one non-wooden object was a silver gun displayed on a shelf. It had a pale glowing look as if in moonlight, yet there were no windows.

A feeling of dread drove Twiggy back toward the tear in the

wallpaper. As he turned, a *KUK* stuck in his throat and faded to little less than a croak.

On a slanted, looming wall, covering nearly every inch of it, were the heads of moose, deer, and smaller Critters.

Twiggy sprang into a fit of *KUK*s.

"Twiggy…"

He froze. That was Jack's voice. It couldn't be him! Not only had the voice come from in front of him, it had come from *above* him.

A head on the wall clattered onto the floor. Twiggy stumbled, not yet able to scream, as he stared, terror-stricken, into the eyes of Jack's decapitated head.

10

THE FUN HOUSE

E VERY SANE PART of Koda screamed for him to chase after the relic. He shouldn't be on a rescue mission for an animal, but could he have refused finding the hare in front of Sully? Sully would have gone without him.

Koda tried not to think about anything more than protecting him as they hastened to the red tent. Not about almost being kidnapped by geodes. Not about the Tricksters who had tried to harass them on their way here. *Tricksters. Totems. Maybe I've got a disease in my head, too.* He couldn't think about how crazy this was. It didn't matter, though. Not as long as the relic did what it was supposed to and got them home. He wouldn't admit it to Sully, but he believed it would.

Sully took them under the tarp. Suddenly, there was music. "Jack, Rowan's—!" he began and seemed torn about whether he should go in or run away.

Koda saw the fox. A hollow eye socket, looking like a black hole in the scarlet room, studied them from a chair at a table. Koda immediately tensed. So far, he had only seen Tricksters who were more unusual in their appearance. While still fantastical, the fox was a Hunter from the look of everything above her shoulders.

"Are you enjoying our carnival?" she said.

Koda heard the hare's voice behind the other chair. "Is Rowan injured?"

Sully stammered. "He— Rowan's—"

"Yes," said Koda. "And the relic was stolen."

The humanoid fox reached across the table to where the chair blocked Koda's view. The movement looked sneaky. He heard a clink, and the hare hopped quickly to the floor. Koda stiffened as he came running to them with nervous eyes and an overall nervous posture. He thought something unpleasant must have occurred before he and Sully had entered.

Folding his ears down to appear calm, the hare guided them back to the tarp.

"Wait a moment."

The fox stood from the table. She grabbed an item off one of the bookshelves and walked over to them. Koda noted with great fear the bare werewolf-like feet dressed in jeweled ribbons. As she bent down to them, Sully backed halfway under the tarp. Koda prepared to flee.

A werewolf claw offered a small bottle. "For your company."

"What is it?" asked the hare.

"A healing potion. Give it to your injured friend."

The hare reached to take it but froze, sniffing defensively, as the fox plucked it to her shoulder.

A shark-like smile. "We have time for one more card."

"I'm afraid we don't."

What's this about a card? Koda thought. *We're loitering here!*

The claw stretched out. "Very well. And Jack?"

They held each other's gaze.

"Memories have a way of coming back to us. Make sure you are ready."

What's that supposed to mean?

As if uncertain the fox really meant to relinquish it, the hare snatched the bottle.

While exiting the tent, Sully whispered, "Be careful it isn't Love Potion No. 9," sounding quite serious.

Koda paused under the tarp to see the fox return to the table. She seemed cunning. Satisfied in some eerie way. Humming to the strange music, she tucked two cards into the deck and shuffled it. Upon the third, she let her claw hover for a moment before flipping the final card.

The fox Trickster grinned over it. "Well... Isn't that interesting."

Koda remained under the tarp, thinking he might be able to see the image on the card, until he sensed the fox was aware of him. The music stopped as he slipped outside.

Sully was updating the hare. "—growing on him! It's my fault. I shouldn't have told him to shoplift."

"It isn't your fault, Sully," the hare said. "Who will take the potion?"

"I've got room." Sully took the small bottle and pouched it.

As they hurried to the carnival, Koda noticed that the hare was slowing his pace, if just a little, for them. He had taken off much faster than this when they had separated. They ran under the swing ride whirling around in a colorful blur. Koda ducked as several Tricksters flew off it, laughing. They passed the ride as quickly as they could and made it back to the street TOIL AND TROUBLE where they had left the goat.

On the other end of traffic, they spotted him lying on his side. A gang of winged imps pranced around him, hollering like monkeys. Two had the goat by the horns.

"Stop that!" Sully cried.

Koda jumped as the hare stormed off. Tricksters who hadn't been standing in his path went out of their way to block him, but the hare didn't slow. A look of surprise crossed their faces as he ran up to them. A few dove sideways at the last minute, and the rest fell in a jumble of plastic shopping bags and limbs.

Seeing the hare charging in, the imps scattered. He went directly for the two holding the goat's horns. As they rushed to escape, one of them tripped over the other and was left behind. The hare jumped onto its chest, and while the imp frantically waved its arms and threw sand, he drove his paws at the imp's face, pulled back, then dove right back in. Squealing, the imp swiped its hands over its eyes and shoved the hare. It continued to squeal as it flew away over the buildings. Koda was surprised and disturbed by the hare's display of temper.

Crossing the street, Sully and Koda ran up to the goat. It was as if they were watching him thaw from ice but in the reverse. The crystals encased his entire lower torso, and they continued to grow while grating and pulsing. Already his legs and tail were transformed into sharp picks. The skin beneath was pure geode. Sully made a pained noise and swiftly prodded the bottle out of his cheek.

The goat's eyes focused on them. "I'm not havin' a very good day, am I?"

The hare took the bottle from Sully and offered it to the goat. "Drink this," he said.

Without stopping to question it, the goat drank the concoction. Dropping the empty bottle on the sand, increasing discomfort strained his face. The Critters and nearby Tricksters watched the crystals emit a powerful light and, in a terrible shatter, combust in on themselves. The goat couldn't restrain a loud bleat, and Sully lent him his paw for comfort. Koda was about to warn him that shards might burst when they suddenly melted and pooled onto the sand. His fur was again visible.

"The Critters make magic!" a Trickster cried.

It is *magic*, Koda thought.

"Can you stand?" the hare asked.

The goat stood carefully with an air of confusion about him.

Amazed, Sully said quietly, "Your cuts are gone, too."

"Where'd ya'll get that bottle anyway?" the goat asked.

"A Trickster gifted it to us," said the hare.

"*A Trickster?*"

Looking out at the streets, the hare asked, "Where did the thief go?"

The goat seemed embarrassed. "He went that way." He gestured to the intersection of BUBBLE BUBBLE and TOIL AND TROUBLE.

"Let me know if I need to slow down," the hare said to the goat before he took off so fast, the Critters struggled to catch up. Tricksters were quick to get out of his way.

"Shouldn't we find Twiggy first?" Sully asked.

"I'm hoping to find him on the way," the hare said. "I'll need all three of you to track the thief's scent. One of you didn't offer to chase him?"

Sully visibly shrank. "I didn't think of that," he said, sheepish.

"It's alright. It's best you stay together," the hare said.

Koda felt that Sully shouldn't say much. Judging by his manner and tone, the hare was still on edge from the fight. I *did think of splitting up—for a second. But as much as I want that relic, Sully's not going anywhere without me.* Koda had a terrible thought. *The first relic made a Cracker Jack appear. What if the Trickster finds it and uses it before we do?*

Mostly they relied on the goat to do the tracking. Koda and Sully tried their best to sniff for the thief, but hamsters weren't blood hounds. Eventually, they picked up on a trail. It started at the end of the street SOMETHING WICKED, then continued to THIS WAY CRAWLS where, as the name implied, the Critters were subjected to crawly things. It wasn't until they were at the far side of the carnival that the Tricksters disappeared from the streets. The streets were no longer marked here, and they became more like long alleyways. Close by, Koda heard the rapid *clink clink clink* of a roller coaster.

By now the group had found the squirrel's scent. They sped down the street kicking up popcorn bags and shredded balloons as they went.

It wasn't far before they were welcomed by a fun house sitting in the middle of two empty lots. A large shadow cast on it, which was a strange effect since the sky was cloudless. Loose wallpaper flapped wildly on the outside as the roller coaster ribboned above. Sweeping high into the sky, it wound back to disappear over a sudden dip on the horizon. Small world, indeed.

Standing amongst the area's unexpected shadows and silence, Sully held his paws together. "Why would Twiggy pick this place? It looks like a haunted mansion."

"Probably wanted to go where there weren't many Tricksters," said the goat.

"Anything could be in that building," the hare said. "I hesitate to ask you to fight, Rowan…"

"Don't. I've got a hankerin' to butt heads with somebody."

They waited for the roller coaster to make another turn above the fun house and walked onto its "doorstep." The hare sniffed a slide curling to the highest level. "He climbed this."

"Too slippery for my hooves," said the goat.

Sully pointed out a fallen metal railing that could act as a ladder to the second-floor balcony. Koda couldn't argue against the hare carrying them this time. The bars were too widely spaced apart for him and Sully to climb. *It's for the relic*, he told himself. When the animal released him, his heart was thumping so hard it hurt. Sully was brought up afterward, and he felt better.

Below, the goat clanged his hooves on the railing. There was a shout of "Goodness gracious, my stars and garters!" as he slipped. He clambered onto the balcony and was just tall enough to raise Sully and Koda through a hole in the wooden planks above them where the slide had torn sideways. The goat butted it, and with a sharp scraping sound, the slide tore the planks further. The top section fell apart along with part of the balcony. The goat and hare climbed the heap of debris to the third level.

In a huge puppet's head, they found a mirror and a hidden room. All the lights were on. It wasn't until they exited a labyrinth of sheets and into a hallway that darkness descended again.

"They crossed here. Their scents were all over the sheets," the hare said.

Koda stared down the hallway, trying to see if anything was hiding in it. After so much time spent in the carnival, the deadening of noise weighed on him like a bag full of bedding. He abruptly stood. He thought he had heard something.

Running footsteps. Racing toward them, the goblin-gnome's disembodied head floated in the darkness. The rest of its body below the neck faded from the green glow, which was so intense in the dark it lit the Trickster's face as if it were holding a flashlight under its chin.

"That's the one!" Hooves loud on the floor, the goat charged it into the drapery.

A blood-curdling scream brought Sully up on his feet. "Twiggy!"

The hare and Sully ran ahead of Koda into a soft, white light. The squirrel stood inside a room behind a tear in the wall. Looking at the hare, he screamed louder. Even in the low light his petrified expression was startling clear.

"What's happened? Are you hurt?" the hare pressed.

The squirrel's breath collapsed, and he wavered as if he were going to pass out. A dark shape teetered on the floor in front of him.

"Answer me, Twiggy!"

"What's the matter?" Sully cried.

At the sound of their voices, the squirrel seemed to focus. He glanced at Sully then back to the hare. "You're alive?"

The hare hopped into the room to look at the shape from the other side. Once in front of it, no matter how slight his startled expression, he visibly recoiled. Koda decided he and Sully weren't going into that room.

"What is it?" Sully asked, sounding shaken but also curious.

Koda heard fast incoming footsteps at the corner of the hallway. He scurried to the opposite wall, hitting it hard.

The goat trotted into the hallway. "Varmint disappeared on me!" He saw the squirrel and asked, "Was that you that screamed?"

Guiding the squirrel out of the room, the hare picked up something small off the floor and dropped it at Koda's feet. "Hide this quickly," he said.

Koda identified the object as a relic. A groove ran along it like the first one. Koda pouched the relic more greedily than he ever had any treat.

"Is that what did it?" The goat tromped over the wallpaper to the shape. He reacted similarly to the hare.

"What is it?" Sully repeated.

The goat said, mystified, "It's a trophy of Jack."

Sully asked what Koda was thinking. "Trophy? Like a gold statue?"

"Kinda like that." The goat looked up at the torn wall. He then considered the so-called trophy and stomped on it, caving it in like a squashed water bottle. White dust sprang up into a cloud.

"Some Trickster was a larkin' on you. It's paper mache."

The squirrel was leaning over, hugging himself. "Wh-what?"

"Human material. It's fake. Just like the other trophies on the wall."

"It spoke to me! In Jack's voice!"

Sully paled.

"Everyone tell me what happened," the hare said.

Each animal gave a brief account of their time in the carnival. Koda noted the hare's was the briefest, with such glazed-over details as the fox outwitting him and presenting him with cards that had no "reasonable meaning." Koda brooded with suspicion.

When they recounted leaving to find the hare, the goat turned to Sully and Koda. "I don't reckon I said 'thank you' to ya'll for getting me help. So, I thank ya'll." Koda felt oddly uncomfortable, he didn't know why, and wanted the conversation to move on.

The goat asked the squirrel, "How did you get the relic?"

"That *thing* chased me in here. It was hiding behind the furniture. When I came into the room and saw… *that*… it tripped over it and let go of the relic." The squirrel had his back to the room and the now destroyed "trophy." "I don't get it! If it's fake, how come it talked?"

The goat turned to the hare. "Jack?"

"I'm not sure." The hare's eyes lingered on the squirrel as if replaying how he had screamed in his mind.

Walking over, Sully nudged the squirrel with his head in a comforting gesture.

Koda said, "We found the relic. Why haven't we seen a Cracker Jack?"

"Maybe it's somewhere in the fun house," Sully said.

The group fell silent. Searching the fun house wouldn't be pleasant.

"If this is a human's idea of fun, they're even more demented than I thought," said the squirrel.

"Are you alright to move on?" the hare asked.

"I'm ready. Just embarrassed."

"Don't be. The Trickster's objective is to make us afraid. Let's recuperate outside, then we'll solve the matter of the missing Cracker Jack."

As they walked to the exit, the goat said, "It really is too bad. I would've liked to've given that Trickster a real reason to run for the— *What?*"

Koda, who had been half listening, frowned.

They rounded the corner…

… and met a dead end.

"If it ain't bedbugs, it's ants!" the goat exclaimed. "Where'd the sheets go?"

"Someone is messing with us," said the hare.

"Did *you* hear anythin'?"

"No, I did not."

"Then how did this wall get here, Jack?"

The squirrel whined, "It's the fun house! It's not going to let us out of here!"

Koda's panic festered.

"I've seen this in a movie," Sully said worriedly. "You have to be psychopathic to make it work."

"Psychokinetic," Koda corrected and stared fearfully at the dark.

"We'll go down the hallway. Nahiossi and Sully, I'd like you to stay close to Rowan. He sees very well in the dark," said the hare.

With no other choice remaining, they crept into the void. Koda stayed within about one foot of the goat, but that was as close as he was willing to get. He didn't want to get stepped on. Koda bumped Sully, making sure he was there, and counted his pawsteps, wanting, if anything, to know how far they were going. Once past one hundred, he felt himself leaning forward. He clenched his nails into the carpet to keep from slipping.

The goat's right. When it rains, it pours!

Sully grunted. "I'm going to fall!"

"Grab Nahiossi and Sully. The ground is steepening," the hare told the goat.

A sound of shifting movements hinted that the larger animals were leaning in to take them. Koda steeled himself, heard Sully gasp, and was bowled into. He snagged the carpet, tumbling.

Koda bumped his shoulder then head on a cold surface. Sully rolled to a stop beside him. Wherever they were, the air smelled old. He viewed the angled hallway in a concrete wall crookedly from his position on the floor which, because of lights flashing, made him feel as if the world were spinning.

He heard the rest of the group also lose their footing. The hare jumped out of the hallway and slid. After him came the goat, half running, half stumbling. The two spread out on the floor as if stranded on ice.

The squirrel leaped out of the hallway with ease.

"Well, how do you like that? Must be nice to be a squirrel," the goat said with a tired look.

"Says you," said the squirrel.

Koda saw them in strobe-like flashes. He wondered if his new vision was going haywire. As he examined the ceiling, he discovered that wasn't true. Square lights ran in either direction.

Like outside, this room was in ruins. In the center of a wide crumbling concrete floor, a large groove ran down a narrow tunnel that followed the lights, the end as dark as the hallway had been. Dilapidated support posts on the other side of the groove lined the space, and on a wall behind the posts, faded posters depicted retro lettering over a starburst background. They seemed to shout.

EXPERIENCE THE CIRCUS THEATER.
THE RINGLEADER AWAITS.

"We're not going there," said Sully.

"We're on the bottom level," the hare said.

That's right. Concrete, Koda thought. He shook his head at the lights. They were driving him crazy.

"Like a basement?" Sully asked.

"I know a few squirrels who lived in a basement." The squirrel's voice hardened as if remembering the flood again. "Trust me. This isn't a basement."

"It could be our way out," the goat said. Koda opened his eyes as he heard him walking over to the groove in the floor. The goat stepped on a large rectangular metal piece covered in plaster dust. A bit rubbed off in the upper right corner, uncovering a part of a word: TR.

The squirrel ran past Koda to join the goat. Koda scowled at him then wiped at the sign. He wasn't sure why, since he couldn't read, but this could be important.

"What are you doing, Koda?" Sully peered over his shoulder at what he had revealed.

TRACK 1

"What does that mean?" Sully asked.

"Let's go, Jack!" the squirrel called. "The Cracker Jack's got to be at the end of the tunnel!"

Koda looked up and saw the squirrel jump down into the groove. The goat stomped his hooves at the edge.

He went back to wiping and revealed more letters. CO. Then AS. *What could that be?*

He paused at a slight jerking motion in the concrete. The

132

vibration rapidly intensified, so much so that Koda felt it in his head. Metal rattled in the tunnel.

Sully flattened to the floor, trying to hold onto it. "There's not a T-Rex Trickster, is there?"

The hare stepped back in alarm. "Twiggy, get off the tracks!"

Koda worked quickly to uncover the remaining letters. He gave up wiping them off with just his paws. Walking on the sign, he used his belly as a duster. At last, the full sign flashed in the neon light.

TRACK 1
COASTER SUBWAY STATION

A booming metallic howl and screech muted the hare's shouts. The head of the roller coaster zoomed into the tunnel. Posters flapped and rubble trembled among shaken dust. At the last minute, the squirrel jumped out of the groove and the goat threw himself back onto the concrete. Carts skidded onto the tracks. As they came to a halt, the rollercoaster's passengers flopped in their seats.

Puppets turned their heads to the Critters, moving strangely between the gaps in light.

"Want to ride?" they said as one and sprung out of the carts.

II

THE SHOW MUST GO

I T WAS A RIOT of flinging wooden arms, marionette strings, and green auras as the puppets shambled across the concrete. Sully circled back toward the hallway and squeaked as one of the puppets grabbed him. He pressed his paws on its wooden hand and tried to push himself out of the top of its grip.

"Behave now. This will be fun," the puppet said, slack-jawed, clapping wood. Sully feared it would bite him.

Tapping shoes and exclamations buried a shout from Koda so perhaps he saw him. Sully, himself, had lost everyone. Traveling through the puppet mob, sliding between their theater and Mardi Gras costumes, they approached a black ghost-shaped figure seated at the rear of the roller coaster. But though it had the shape of a ghost, he couldn't see through it. The figure bent down as Sully was taken into the cart in front of it.

His puppet, dressed in pinstriped evening clothes, tossed a small belt over Sully's belly. Sully started to turn to watch the figure, but a tug made him face forward. Twiggy and Koda appeared over the side of the cart, clawing and biting two king-and-queen-fitted puppets.

"Rowan! Fight them!" Twiggy yelled as the puppets strapped them in.

"No fighting allowed on the roller coaster," said Sully's puppet. It secured his seat belt and flopped down next to Sully.

Blows clanged on the cart. Two more puppets held onto the side, looking down at some commotion. They dragged Jack upward by the ears into the cart. Sully flinched as his kicking legs swung down onto the opposite seat. The two puppets chuckled as Rowan jumped in on his own, pleased he had come without a fight. They wrapped a larger belt around him on the floor as he was too awkward to sit on the seats.

Twiggy yanked his tail. The queen puppet held onto it. "Do something!"

"I *can't*," Rowan stressed. "There's too dang many of 'em!"

The puppets crammed the cart, jumping in as if thrown in. Already they were becoming tangled with their strings. Koda clenched into himself. He was very green, and not only due to the Tricksters' increasing glow. Sully asked if he was alright but didn't receive an answer, or at least one he could hear. Meanwhile, Twiggy continued shouting and puppets kept jumping in, banging on the cart and hollering as if in competition with him.

Finally, swarmed together, the puppets tied their strings to the handles (their little wooden marionette controllers had been removed). "Make it go! Fast! FAST!" they shouted.

Under the clanking of metal, the carts jerked and slid.

"There's someone behind us," Sully said in a trembling voice, remembering the ghost-like figure. He was never really sure what Rowan and Jack were thinking—their eyes being the problem—but they were staring over his head.

"What is it?" Sully asked nervously.

"It's watching us," Jack said.

Sully gulped.

The strobe lights appeared to speed up as the roller coaster steadily gained speed. Its wheels clanged and shook on the tracks, filling the tunnel with frightening, blaring echoes. Sully jolted as one of the lights popped and shattered, glass raining onto the seats, and it sparked hanging low from the cracked ceiling. Then it zoomed backward as well as other things falling apart. Crooked signs and collapsed metal structures flashed by in purples, blues, and greens.

Sully writhed in his seat. Hamsters can't throw up like a giant, but he had to do something about the uncomfortable feeling in his stomach. The belt made it worse. He had to wriggle out of it.

The puppet wearing evening clothes—or as Sully was coming to think of him, Suit and Tie—held him in place. Sully fought to move, squeaking.

"Remain seated. Keep your arms and horns in the cart at all times," the puppet said. Between the seats, Rowan was shaking on his hooves.

With a jarring, rattling shudder, the roller coaster blasted from the tunnel. Posters flew up crazily from the tracks. The puppets screamed enthusiastically as they rounded the curve toward the fun house's side wall. Sully could see its roof peeking at an angle over the side of the cart, gone for a moment when they lifted above the building, then returning on their way back down to the ground.

Up they went again, going slower on an incredibly high climb. *cliink cliiiiink.* The cart tipped and hung vertically. All the blood went to Sully's head and he gripped the seat belt as he and Koda hung toward the back of the cart. Above him Rowan stood parallel to the floor on the backing below the seat, shaking more than ever. Above *him* Jack and Twiggy hung from their belts. The face constellations observed them with dread. At the highest point, when the carts ahead were a suspended trail above them, Sully thought their faces would touch his. *It's like we're in outer space!* The roller coaster gave a final lurch and rocketed.

Rowan slipped on the floor, now standing on the backing below Jack's and Twiggy's seats. Everyone hung the other way.

Weightlessness spread like wildfire in Sully's stomach. Wind blustered him—he could hardly breathe!—and stung his ears with cold. The cart shook fiercely, thumping him in the seat, the clinks insistent and running into itself.

Puppets flew upward by the strings. "It gooooes! FAST!" Their limbs knocked together, and their clothing flapped.

They went on like that, twice rolling backward as the world turned upside down, everyone bent at their middle, and Twiggy screaming, "You're gonna kill us!"

But the puppets just laughed and screamed, "It rides the air! The coaster! Like a slithering beast, it rides!"

They righted. The roller coaster rode the loop, punching the air, and propelled onward. The carnival's song faded.

Sully had to wonder if they were being taken to the end of the world. An expansive sight on a downward slope spread the indigo gloom, empty except for a pointed dot on the horizon. That red and white dot became a striped tent.

The roller coaster smoothed out. Sully slumped in his seat, his fur all frizzy. His nails had punctured the seat belt—so deeply, in fact, he had a hard time removing them. He tingled everywhere in body and heart. Beside him, Koda suffered the same bad fur day.

Rowan stood unsteadily between the seats. "There's gonna be big bruises everywhere, I can feel it," he said with a slight tremor in his voice.

Jack and Twiggy snapped to attention as the puppets began untying their strings and climbing out of the cart. The king and queen undid their seatbelts. Sully heard a small clang behind him as the black ghost jumped out onto the sand.

Suit and Tie grabbed Sully and hauled him out of the cart. He started to call for Koda and settled as the king jumped down with him. The greenness still about him, his brother remained almost obedient in its grip. A familiar dreadful, growing ache pressed on Sully's chest, and he asked Koda if he would be alright. Koda just nodded in reply.

The puppets towed Sully and his friends along the roller coaster. More jumped out of the carts ahead and formed a glowing mass like a crowd holding candles. Several already stood at the tent, whispering with their hands cupped to each other's ears. They made the tent appear even larger and more intimidating with only their small, flimsy bodies in front.

Twiggy tried pulling away from the queen, who was still holding his tail. He looked to Rowan. "You're not gonna let them take us into whatever that is…?"

"It's a circus tent," Sully said. Or more specifically, a building fashioned to appear as one. The "cloth" of the tent didn't move, which Sully noticed when he didn't hear any flapping sounds of fabric. The building was painted simply with red stripes and had a cone roof. Even so, Sully had heard most circuses weren't good places for Critters.

Rowan turned to monitor the silently following figure.

"What is that thing? A Trickster?" Twiggy growled and snapped at the queen. "Let go of it already!" If anything, she held his tail even tighter.

"It's wearin' a thick cloth. I can't tell if it has a glow." Rowan asked loud enough for it to hear, "What's the deal? Why'd you bring us all the way out here?"

The soft footsteps didn't falter, and the black ghost remained silent.

Sully had a bad feeling. "Jack, is it a totem?"

The puppets walked his friend by his ears. Head ducked, Jack said, "Tricksters wouldn't pack with a totem."

Why, then, did Sully feel there was something different about this one? It hadn't made a single annoying giggle or high-pitched laugh like the puppets. And it was hiding itself when

Tricksters weren't shy. Sully could only assume this was for an insidious reason.

Suit and Tie pet Sully's head. He cringed and didn't ask any more questions.

"Everyone try to relax," Jack said.

The whispering at the tent stopped, and the puppets faced them with their too-wide eyes. Sully dropped his gaze. Doll movies hadn't prepared him for this. The puppets opened the artificial tarp door, and in grand reveal, an eerie music box tune sprang into the night.

The Critters were taken into an enormous, softly lit room with a red carpet. Sully smelled lavender perfume. Presented in frame by two angular walls sloping to the floor, stadium seating hugged a curtained stage. To Sully's dismay, each seat was occupied and glowing. The puppets turned around in one simultaneous movement, causing Sully to jump at the sound of their wooden limbs knocking together.

They peered at him, their heads between the seats, and grinned their painted smiles as they sang, again in perfect unison.

"Come see. Come play.
You do not leave, you stay.
The ringleader dances, he sings.
To all of us... with strings."

The stillness afterwards nearly suffocated Sully. Wordlessly the Critters were led around the wall which supported the stairs parallel to the audience. Sully had time enough to see that the puppets seated in this section hadn't been glowing before they lit up like stove burners flowing up the rows. The same occurred to the puppets behind the other wall. Contrary to the song, not every puppet had strings. Most of them didn't except the roller coaster marionettes. Their captors forced them up the stairs and paused for the puppets in one of the rows to make room. Twiggy reclaimed his tail as he was seated next to the brothers, with Jack in his own individual seat. Rowan stood in the row.

The roller coaster marionettes lingered a bit to make sure they would behave, then threaded to the stairs where they could still monitor them. Shoving through, the black ghost appeared to walk backwards to center stage into the curtains. Since the next row was much lower than theirs, Sully was able to see the curtains remained open just a bit.

His attention snapped to a puppet sitting next to him in the end seat. It wore a steampunk tailcoat and a plague mask. Dark pupils settled in the corners. "Hello," it said in a smooth, creepy voice.

Sully and Koda cowered to the cushioned elbow.

Jack hopped onto the chair's arm. "What is your purpose for bringing us here?"

"You'll like our home. The show starts soon," said the plague puppet. Its eyes hadn't moved from Sully.

"What show?" Rowan asked.

The puppet didn't answer. Sully thought that a common bad habit of Tricksters.

Rowan gazed at the pointed, striped ceiling. There were no speakers up there that Sully could see. He had yet to find out where the music was coming from. Rowan said, somewhat marveled and ambiguous, "How are we gonna get out of here?"

"If we were seated at the bottom, we might've had a good chance of escaping," said Jack.

"What do you mean?"

Their row near the top of the seating provided an aerial view of the tent. Jack motioned at the puppets farther outward from the stage, so much so they were almost behind it. "Those miniature humans aren't glowing. They were when we entered."

"Can Tricksters extinguish their glows?" Rowan asked.

"I wasn't aware they could, but it all seems very suspicious," Jack said.

Twiggy scoffed. "Tricksters with human bodies. Two things I hate combined into one."

The seat jerked, pushing him and the brothers forward. Sully squeaked.

"Hey!" Twiggy exclaimed.

Sully felt what seemed to be little feet thumping on the back of the seat.

"I'm beginnin' to suspect we left the Cracker Jack at the carnival." Rowan kept his eyes on the plague puppet and lowered his voice. "Is it too farfetched to escape on that roller coaster?"

"We'd be clueless on how to get it started," said Jack. "Unless Sully or Nahiossi are familiar with how it functions."

"I'm sorry. I don't know," Sully said.

"Makes sense why the fun house was abandoned," Rowan said dismally.

Sully jumped as the plague puppet's hands slapped onto its lap. With this latest jolt to his heart, he wondered how many more frights he could take.

The puppet's eyes rolled forward. "*Shhh*. The show starts."

The music box tune faded to fast-paced drums. Sully could feel a sense of anticipation in the theater as well as his own increasing anxiety. Every puppet with a glow straightened in their seats.

"Ringleader! Ringleader!" they chanted, loudly slapping their legs with their wooden hands.

Little feet kicked the back of the seat again. Even so, Sully pressed against the cushion, wishing he could sink into it and disappear.

A theater spotlight lit the stage curtains. To an abrupt musical uproar, a Trickster leapt out, flinging itself around in a crazy, jumping dance. It was as if it was controlled like a marionette but by invisible wires, so chaotic were its movements. The puppets drove themselves more enthusiastically, if that was even possible. Sully's gasp went unheard as wild applause waved across the audience. The puppets cheered, bouncing, some high enough to poke above the seats, and the roller coaster marionettes became tangled in each other's strings again. Meanwhile, Sully noticed one startling detail that overwhelmed him with fright.

The Trickster wore clown clothes.

The clown skipped to a halt and raised his arms. "Did you miss me?" a playfully chilling voice shouted.

The puppets cheered harder. Sully and his friends watched in a dreamlike haze.

"Aww, well, I missed you, too. Now, I know you love a good opening, but you didn't come to tonight's show just to watch me dance, as entertaining as I am. Tonight is very special! We shall indeed dance and siiiing, and we won't do it alone…"

The clown beckoned with his hands. "Give the Critters a round of applause!"

All the puppets clapped. The plague puppet and everyone else in their row turned to stare at them. Sully squeezed himself farther into the cushion. He could hear the smirk in his voice as the clown said, "Bring them to me."

Sully started to run for the aisle but just as he jumped off the seat, the plague puppet caught him. It handed him, shrieking, to Suit and Tie.

Twiggy was faster and made it to the last seat when he exclaimed in protest as the queen puppet grabbed him. The marionettes from the roller coaster streamed into the row. Jack and Rowan surrendered as they must have known it was hopeless. But as they shouted at Sully's and Twiggy's handlers, not a word came from Koda who just struggled in the king puppet's hand.

The other puppets continued to applaud as their captors dragged them down the stairs, and the music thrived on it, speeding in rhythm. Sully fought Suit and Tie all the way to the foot of the stage. Scary clown images flashed through his mind. He wished he hadn't watched so many late-night horror movies when he was only a month old.

He froze. Large spotted shoes stood on the top step. Higher up were ruffled, white satin pants, a white satin shirt with purple pom poms, and—

Sully quickly closed his eyes.

"Why, this Critter is afraid of me," the chilling voice announced. Sully whimpered as he heard the clown speak close to his ear. "Open your eyes."

He kept them closed.

Loud, for everyone to hear: "The Critter needs some encouragement!"

"Open! Open! Open!" the audience chanted.

Hair that looked like cotton candy. That, somehow, was the first thing Sully saw. A burst of orange atop a colorless face that appeared bigger due to large, elephant-like ears made of bone. Within the shadow cast by the stage light, the eye sockets were black pits of terror. A heavily exaggerated jaw was raised into a permanent, deranged grin. Hornless with long nostrils and cracked teeth, the clown's head was a half-human, half-bull skull.

Sully screamed. He squirmed in Suit and Tie's hand.

"We'll have none of that! I'm the friendliest Trickster you'll ever meet." The clown's jaw clacked like the puppets' as he spoke.

Suit and Tie and the rest of the roller coaster marionettes walked onto the stage.

"Koda! Koodaa!" Sully cried.

Still silent, his brother wriggled in the king's grip, but it shook him until he stopped.

Jack threw his head back, and the marionettes holding onto his ears flew upward. He tossed them back down hard onto the floor, hard enough for them to let go.

"Easy there! Good quality puppets are difficult to replace!" The clown sounded genuinely alarmed.

The marionettes quickly stood and formed a line between Jack and escape. He barely looked at them. "Release my friends," he said firmly.

"No can do, rabbit. Small things tend to run fast."

Rowan started for the clown, but a few marionettes lassoed him with their strings while others wrestled Jack to the floor.

"You freak!" Twiggy lifted like a cork about to pop out of the queen's grip. "Quit terrorizing Sully and take us back to the carnival!"

"Rude, aren't you? F-Y-I: those are strong wire. They won't break." The clown clapped his hands together. "Let's have some more fun. First, I'd like to thank you for the new addition!"

"What addition?" Rowan yelled. He stomped against the strings' pull on his horns.

Facing the stage, the clown paused for dramatic effect, then pointed at several of the marionettes. "You there! Yes, pull back the curtains."

A skeleton hand slipped onto Suit and Tie's shoulder and brought them facing. Sully's limbs felt too heavy to move. The marionettes who weren't restraining the Critters walked floppily to the curtains and parted them. Seafoam green light poured out onto the stage. Already trapped in a circus theater by puppets and a clown, Sully had thought their situation couldn't get any worse. That is, until he saw the Cracker Jack imposing the wall.

"What a coincidence, right?" The clown laughed. "I assume

it has to do with you. At first, I was extremely angry, what with the damages and all. Then I thought: You can pay them off! I needed new performers."

So close!

Jack, Rowan, and Twiggy had ceased fighting. Koda, although motionless, showed an intense saddened anger.

The clown said brightly, "Say thank you, everyone."

"Thank you," said the puppets in unison. Oddly, their voices all sounded the same.

It had taken him some time, but as the clown turned to and away from the audience behind him, Sully saw that their glows winked on and off. When he faced them, they glowed, and when he was turned away, they seemed to lose control of their bodies. Their jaws dropping sounded as one loud *CLACK!* The clown never completely turned away from the marionettes on stage. Instead, he only turned his body sideways to them.

"I have no idea why it would trespass on my property," the clown said, looking inquiringly at the Cracker Jack.

That's why Koda isn't talking! He's protecting the relics inside his cheek pouches. Sully prayed the Cracker Jack wouldn't betray them.

"I've got an idea!"

Sully's hopes sank, but the Cracker Jack hadn't spoken. Its triangle eyes shifted to the theater's entrance.

The goblin-gnome thief was running down the red carpet. Twice tripping on the steps, it climbed the stairs onto the stage and, giving the Critters a vengeful sneer, raised the bloodied foot Koda had bit. Sully feared for his brother.

"Ah, another performer!" the clown said jovially.

The goblin-gnome pointed a bloodied finger at the Cracker Jack. "It wants my prize!"

"Your prize?"

"It's in cahoots with them! I saw them outside the carnival!

145

I won the relic fair and square, and that no-good Critter bit my foot!"

"Did you say '*relic*?'"

Sully's hope vanished.

"You fool. Now *he* will take it," the Cracker Jack scolded. It wasn't the one the Critters had found in the cave. Its eyes squinted angrily, looking as if it wanted to chomp on the goblin-gnome with its square teeth.

The marionettes seized the goblin-gnome. He grew very frightened, kicking and thrashing. "The clown is in on it!"

"At last, there's the connection," said the clown. "We had a play on this, actually. Long ago, humans carved fruits and vegetables to protect their houses from evil spirits. However, the Trickster world is upside down. You, my wall ornament, are their ticket out of here." The clown folded his hands. "So… which one of you is hiding it?"

Sully found it extremely difficult not to look at the bulge in Koda's cheek. His friends were indignant. Their only response was a grunt from Rowan as he resisted the marionettes' strings.

The clown walked slowly, each large spotted shoe set hard on the floor, over to Koda.

"Is it you?" the clown whispered. "There's blood on your fur."

Koda gripped the king's fingers.

"Yes, that's the one!" the goblin-gnome shouted.

Everyone resisted showing emotion. The clown lifted a hand—Sully's heart nearly dropped—and touched Koda's cheek with one bony finger. *Tap, tap.* Koda flinched.

The clown walked backward from him. The permanent grin was more evident than ever. "I ask you, what are you called? I'll invent stage names for you later."

"Listen, bozo! We're leavin' this place!" yelled Twiggy.

"Bozo?"

Sully winced. If the clown got angry, what kind of trick would he do? He fiddled with one of the pom poms on his costume. A crack ran across the ridge of his socket as the grin inched up the skull. "Hmm... I like that. Better than anything I've come up with."

The clown moved his hand to his chest. "You may call me Bozo. I'm glad we've bonded. Great timing, too! I was planning something big, and we're short of actors tonight. The show *must* go on... and I have lots of fun performances we can do." Bozo turned on his shoes. "Let's begin with a bang. Bring me the cannon."

Cannon?!

Half the marionettes hurried backstage. Rowan and Jack resumed fighting with their captors. Barking like mad, Twiggy shouted, "What are—*KUK!*—you going to do?"

"I have to take precautions," Bozo said apologetically. Sully felt a nauseating worry. "You know, in case you're tempted to leave. I'm not going to take the relic. It's useless to me, and I prefer not to poke around someone's mouth."

A loud thump and the heavy rolling of wheels sounded backstage. The marionettes wheeled in the cannon and spun the barrel to aim it at Koda.

Sully had never bit anyone in his life. He had never even thought to do so until now. Then Suit and Tie made a ring with his fingers around Sully's neck, pulling them up slightly at his chin, and he found he couldn't bite the marionette even if he wanted to. Sully desperately scratched him.

"You're a *horrible* Trickster!" he screamed. "Leave Koda ALONE!"

"This will look heinous to you. Really, it's just a slap on the wrist." Bozo shouted, "Fire!"

The shot muffled Sully's scream and his friends' struggles.

The cannon recoiled, knocking the marionettes to the floor, and exploded smoke like a dusted firework. Sully's ears rang. He couldn't breathe, and he couldn't bring himself to witness the aftermath. Sully drowned in his tears.

Jack shouted, "Sully! Sully, Koda is fine!"

How could that be?

The smoke dispelled, revealing the king puppet in one piece. Sully could breathe again once he saw Koda was still in its hands. Behind them a cannonball was lodged in the Cracker Jack's eye.

"What?" Bozo said, feigning innocence. "Did you think I'd harm the Critter? And my puppet, to boot? I take good care of my collection."

"He's gonna destroy it!" Rowan gave such a fierce yank on the strings the marionettes restraining him skidded across the stage floor.

Bozo spread his arms. As if beckoned by him, a screen of wire lowered to the stage. More of Bozo's helpers held the wire on a catwalk above. Everything became chaotic as the puppets onstage stringed the Critters and the goblin-gnome like marionettes. Sully tugged on his paw while Suit and Tie wrapped a wire around one of his wrists, before moving to his other wrist and his feet. After only a few minutes of Twiggy shouting insults and Rowan yelling angry southern exclamations, the marionettes left the Critters to dangle in a line.

Bozo folded his arms. "I'm very talented, so I have many professions. But a murderer isn't one of them. No, I'm going to make the Trickster *soft* to the point he won't be able to transport anyone. Then I'll push him out."

"Good luck!" the Cracker Jack said. "I want my relic first."

"It's MINE!" bellowed the goblin-gnome.

Bozo looked at Koda. "The *duende* is mad at you. You

shouldn't have cheated him and bloodied him so."

The music box tune faded, releasing to the harsh metallic whack of cannonballs. Out of nowhere, Bozo said conversationally, "Your 'giant'… she listens to oldies music."

The brothers ceased tugging at the wire. Sully couldn't resist asking, "How do you know that?"

Bozo snapped his jaw up and down, and the sound of his teeth clacking echoed throughout the theater.

"Let's change the tune," Bozo said and stomped his shoe.

A song began to play, a drum beat alive in the air. Horns blared, wires floated, and the Critters began to move.

"What is this?" Twiggy exclaimed.

Breathing hard through his nose, Rowan kicked and almost hit him. The wires rotated them in a circle, gaining speed very quickly. That same weightlessness blossomed in Sully again, clutching to him as if he were on a swing ride as it first starts to lift.

Bozo drummed the floor with his feet.

Have you heard 'bout a place
Somewhere up Broadway?

The wires twanged, and Sully bounced. The goblin-gnome squabbled irritably as all together the wires pumped their arms and made them dance. Inside the circle the marionettes took partners.

BOOM!

The cannon rolled back, churning smoke into the air. A cannonball drooped over the Cracker Jack's mouth. "'ot 'ooving!" it said defiantly. The marionettes fired again, breaking the stem on top. There was the tiniest flicker of the Cracker Jack's glow.

"STOP IT!" Koda shouted.

Rowan bucked. "Get out of the wall!"

Faster the wires forced them forward and back, forward

and back, in a twisting motion. The music picked up, and the marionettes swung their arms to the drums, flinging their partners for a twist.

Twistin', twistin'
Everyone's dancin' great.

Along the circle they twisted.

"Hey! Hey, stop! My body doesn't move this way!" Twiggy cried.

"Enjoy yourselves, Critters!" Bozo shouted joyously. "Not every show do I get to dance to rock 'n' roll!" He shook his arms in time to the clapping of the audience. The section behind remained aura-less.

Twistin' the night away!

During one of the flings throwing him sideways, Sully glimpsed Jack pull his paws together. He bit at the wire, but lost strength and his arms wrenched back into place. Sully tried to copy him as he kept track of the marionettes. Suit and Tie was dancing with a girl marionette in slacks. Like the others they seemed unaware of what the Critters were doing. Sully waited for the wires to turn them toward the audience. Bozo was looking down at his spotted shoes as he tapped with the rapid speed of a 1950s tap dancer. If he wore a hat, Sully imagined he would have held onto it as he moved his legs rapidly back and forth in front of each other.

Bozo popped his body upon another firing and looked upward at the Critters. Jack and Sully quickly released the wire from their teeth.

Bozo didn't seem to have noticed. "I changed my mind. You'll be tempted to escape so long as you have the relic," he said.

150

"I can always have a less pristine puppet open your very unhygienic mouth. I think I'll do it now."

Suit and Tie and the slacks marionette danced around Koda as the puppeteers on the catwalk floated him to Bozo. "A little dance before you give up the relic?" he taunted.

Koda's strings lurched and drove him hopping on the floor. Bozo mimicked him, snapping his fingers.

Let's twist!

The puppets in the audience, those that weren't behind Bozo, leaned over the seats. Their jaws clunked as they sang.

"Bend up! Bend back!
Bend up! Bend back!"

And Bozo and Koda danced.

As a saxophone drew out, Jack bit one last time at the wire on his wrist and it broke. He then hung by only his other paw. The wire snapped with a quick tug, and Jack fell onto the floor where he dragged by his hind legs.

Sully strained against his wires to look up at the catwalk. Two marionettes, one holding the two broken wires and the other holding the wires tied to Jack's legs, continued swaying their arms like conductors. Sully was certain the marionettes or the goblin-gnome would warn Bozo. He expected the goblin-gnome's squabbles to blare into a warning shriek, maybe pointing its finger at Jack. Once a tattletale, always a tattletale. But the Trickster was busy thrashing in the throes of a tantrum, and the marionettes went on conducting and dancing to the music made by leaping piano keys.

Jack was still dragging by his legs. He reached over his back with his teeth but fell short of the wire by more than six inches.

Rowan and Twiggy tried swinging toward his wires.

Jack, hurry! Sully wasn't strong enough to keep pulling the wires in front of his face. He was also getting dizzy from the whirl of bodies surrounding him. He could barely see around them as he heard Koda shout. His brother and Bozo had finished their dance, and Suit and Tie was removing the two relics from Koda's cheek.

Bozo clapped. "Not bad! Now… How about the rest of you?" he said, and his eye sockets focused on the Critters.

One more twist!

BOOM!

The song cut off in a rocket of smoke. All at once Bozo slammed to the floor and all the puppets in the theater stopped glowing. The Critters and the goblin-gnome dropped to the stage floor in the darkened theater. Something clanged above, and Sully shrieked as one of the puppets from the catwalk slammed onto the stage. Glass eyes rolled in the sockets, staring at him.

Stunned, Sully stood in the light cast by the Cracker Jack. Its glow was the only light in the theater except for Bozo's. The clown had nearly been thrown off the stage and lay limp on his back. The cannonball that had struck him bounced down the steps in loud thumps, then rolled onto the floor until it came to a stop at the bottom of the stadium stairs.

Sully and the others looked at the stage wall. The cannon had been turned away from the Cracker Jack, the marionettes around it spread in a loose circle as if they had been whacked to the floor. Jack stood beside the cannon, misted in smoke like a gunslinger in an old western. All that was missing was a tumbleweed rolling by.

"Yeah!" Twiggy shouted.

Jack hopped to them and began chewing their wires.

152

Twiggy's laugh rang much too loud in the dark. "How did you do that?" he asked.

"The puppets had already loaded the cannon. I just moved it around," Jack said, serious.

Rowan chuckled. "The Trickster misjudged your teeth."

"I chewed through quite a bit of wire when I was younger," said Jack. There was some pride in that.

"You're amazing!" Sully said.

Jack paused as if surprised by his compliment, before proceeding to free Twiggy, Rowan, and Koda.

Sully remembered the relics. He walked cautiously to Suit and Tie, carrying the strings with him.

"Sully, wait," Koda said. Jack finished cutting his wires and Koda hurried over to Sully.

"You needn't worry about them now," said Jack.

The relics had fallen from Suit and Tie's hand. Sully snatched them up and quickly moved away. When he looked back, the marionette remained still as if asleep, with an arm bent over his back and the rest of his limbs laying crookedly outward from his body.

Did he faint? Where's his glow? Sully wondered.

Koda took the relics and pouched them. He bared his teeth as the goblin-gnome ran toward them. But the Trickster ignored them as he ran down the steps to the entrance, mumbling fearfully with wires still attached to his limbs.

"Poor fella is traumatized," Rowan said.

"Good riddance," said Twiggy. "Good riddance to *all* of them."

Rowan shook the wires dangling from his horns. "What exactly happened? How did you get past 'em, Jack?" he asked.

"The clown Trickster positioned himself where he could see everything on the stage, including the puppets above. Even so, he became distracted. I was able to escape without him really seeing me."

"And the puppets?" Rowan asked.

"They were all the clown. If he wasn't facing them, they weren't glowing. They became lifeless," Jack said. "He couldn't control them outside his peripheral vision."

The explanation shocked Sully. He saw Bozo with new understanding. Though there was still fear, Sully couldn't help but feel compassion for him. He thought it must be very lonely having a theater all to yourself. Enough to pretend you were your own company.

"No wonder!" Twiggy said. "Who'd want to be friends with a lunatic?"

"Is he dead?" Sully asked.

"No, I don't think so," Jack said. "He's still glowing, and he won't be unconscious for long."

Sully very much wanted to leave. Free from their strings, the Critters gathered near the Cracker Jack. With the cannonballs stuck in its face, sinking it around the stem, it resembled a weirdly-shaped Bundt cake.

"I guess we'll find out if the Trickster softened him enough," Rowan said grimly.

12
LIZARD LEGS

FRANKLY, SYDNEY didn't care what had poked her nose. Her belly scales were cold, and the light was much too bright. "Go ahead and turn on the lamp. I'm not waking up!"

But Insect-Giver was persistent. She poked Sydney's nose again.

"You got worms? Otherwise I'm going back to—"

Sydney opened her eyes. She was on a pillow, not in her cage, and *those* weren't Insect-Giver. Two stunted figures, torsos glowing green, stood hunched at the end of the bed. Both were ghoulish to look at, eyes swollen shut, their heads shrunken. They were shrunken all over by the looks of it. Wet, raggedy clothes slumped on scrawny limbs completed their resin-mummy appearance.

"Halloween was two months ago, munchkins," Sydney said. Tasting the air, she compared their stink to crickets. While tasty, crickets smelled like armpits and feces.

Sydney tried to recall what she had eaten that day, and the day's events suddenly came to her. There had been weird trees and lots of animals. More importantly, she had been dragon-napped and thrown into some huge hole in the ground!

155

Annoyance gave way to anger. One of the munchkins hobbled forward, reaching out a gray, shriveled hand. Sydney dared it to come closer. She would imagine it was the owl as she chewed its fingers.

Munchkin One wiggled them. A braided ponytail on top of its head swayed. "Oo ooo li' soof?" said a powdery, vaguely feminine voice. Small, wooden pegs shifted within holes in her lips.

"What? You got something unsightly there in your mouth," Sydney said.

"We cooh som. Ooo cam 'elp." Munchkin One lunged and grabbed Sydney.

Biting down on two of her fingers, Sydney yanked as viciously as she could. The munchkin screamed, and it sounded like someone throwing up pebbles. Sand exploded out of her mouth. Munchkin Two climbed onto the bed to grab Sydney's tail, and she was pulled between the two munchkins like a rope.

Disgusted by the grimy taste on her tongue, Sydney released Munchkin One's fingers. It had tasted like she'd been biting two very hard sticks. Her jaws came away dry. *All that hard work and I didn't draw blood? Disappointing.*

After climbing off the bed, Munchkin Two lifted her up by the tail and dragged her across the carpet. Sydney raked her claws on the floor, shouting, "Forget me helping you with your 'soof!'"

"'uccome?" Munchkin Two's voice was male and sounded just as parched.

She stopped, surprised. No scaleless can understand a Hunter. *A scaleless doesn't glow, either.*

Sydney glared, not answering, and looked around the room. *How did I get here, anyway?*

The munchkins' passing glows drew furniture out of the dark: a black wardrobe and bed, gray club chairs, clothed books, and tabletop lamps. *Cheery*, Sydney thought. *And why is everything smeared?*

The furniture had a wavy, dreamlike quality as if they were images in smoke. Sydney realized she and the munchkins were the only things of color in the room.

Off center to a pitch-black window was an open chest on a table. Munchkin Two dropped Sydney inside it and shut the lid. Sydney scratched vehemently. "Open it up, you toxic waste!"

She watched the munchkins through a keyhole. Munchkin One kept her distance, sucking her injured finger near Munchkin Two's shoulder, whose purple-streaked ponytail swayed as he dug inside his rags and withdrew a canteen-sized cauldron. He set it on the table along with several rotten vegetables, mushrooms, garlic, and a wooden spoon. As each was taken from his clothes, he withered like a scarecrow who has been stolen of his straw.

"Soof a'mos' dom," Munchkin Two said.

Soup almost done. Sydney noticed their tongues, which were brown and shriveled like dried bell peppers, stuck out when they spoke. "No, it's not," she said contemptuously through the keyhole. "You don't even have a fire under it."

"Is col' soof."

"Of course," Sydney said sarcastically. She closed her mouth as she tasted a mold smell coming off two shriveled squashes.

Munchkin Two stripped the husk off an ear of brown corn. It made a *splash* and a *bloop* as he tossed it into the cauldron. Next came the whole mushrooms and garlic. Munchkin One fussed over the spoon for a bit, then they stirred together like voodoo twins.

A door stood ajar behind them. Sydney could already picture herself exiting through it. Once the chest opened, it was bye, bye, munchkins, and hello insects on the way home. *I've outwitted many creatures. What's two more?*

Finished stirring, the munchkins reached for the chest. Sydney smiled in anticipation. They grabbed the chest and rotated it so the keyhole pointed down at the cauldron filled with a greenish-brown soup.

"What are you doing?" Sydney barked.

"Mos' impor'an' imgrediem'," Munchkin Two said. The next two words were very clear. "Lizard legs."

The chest lid opened, and Sydney fell into the soup.

Sydney puffed her beard and splashed fitfully. Oh, the curses she could have unleashed on them if she had wanted to open her mouth. But oily lettuce pasted her scales, and brown carrots floated like an unpleasant surprise found in a toilet bowl. She wasn't tasting any of that. One of the moldy squashes plopped into the cauldron, and she struck it away, kicking faster, her tail stirring the soup.

"'as'y soofs 'afe flafor," said Munchkin One.

Oh, I'll give you flavor if I'm in here long enough. The insects she ate should be fully digested by now.

Sydney heard low voices not of scaleless speak outside the door, possibly on another floor. She wouldn't call for an animal's help. *The water isn't even boiling, and the munchkins obviously don't have the brainpower to chop food.* A shape moved past the doorway, but Munchkin One stepped closer and blocked it, humming and adding ingredients to the cauldron.

A while later, Munchkin Two poked his finger in the soup, sucked on it, and uttered a pleased *wheek.*

"I wan' a 'as'e," Munchkin One pouted. She held out her hand for the spoon. He shoved it away, leaning over the lip of the cauldron to sip.

Sydney splashed forward and grasped the spoon. Surprised, Munchkin Two lifted it out of the soup, giving her the chance to climb up the spoon and onto his arm.

"*Eeee!*" He swatted at her, shivering like a roach. Sydney kicked off his arm and landed on the floor.

Munchkin One threw back her misshapen head and made a dry heaving sound Sydney supposed was laughter.

"Idia!" Munchkin Two seethed. "'ome back! Ooo ruim soof!"

Sydney was already out the door. She stopped in a dark hallway. The stairs to her right seemed like they would be a chore, so she snuck into an unlit bathroom opposite. Hiding behind the door frame which was only slightly ajar, she saw the munchkins' blundering shadows on the hallway carpet. They receded with powdery shrieks as the ceiling thumped. One big *BANG!* straight out of a horror movie. Sydney could feel the vibration well enough.

What are they keeping up there? An elephant?

Something banged a wall twice before Sydney saw movement at the stairway's banister. A squirrel raced by the two munchkins still standing in the hallway and descended the stairs. Maniacal laughter rang out from the ceiling.

"RUN, RUN! LET'S HAVE A LITTLE FUN!"

"'e comes!" Munchkin Two said, his voice hissy and terrified. The munchkins quickly retreated into the bedroom and the door slammed.

Giving up so easily? Sydney ventured a peep around the bathroom door. That booming voice had come from the second bedroom.

There. In the slim wall between the second and third bedroom. The blond color caused her eyes to dilate. Sydney marveled at her luck. *Luck? Pssh! It's called "fine predatory instincts."*

Hiding inside a small hole were the two rodents.

Confident they hadn't seen her, Sydney started to crawl out. She paid no attention to the quake and fall of the ceiling in the other room, but a sudden voluminous shrieking made her pause. Flapping wings by the thousands flushed the upstairs like a whirlwind of leaves.

Bats.

Where did they *come from?* Irritated at the missed opportunity, Sydney hid. The crack under the door gave her a low-level view of the banister. The little bloodsuckers crashed into it as they swooped down and fell to the floor, stunned. Sydney jerked away as several slammed into the bathroom door. She heard an abrupt thud and a violent clattering noise—the sound of bolts coming free—before there was a slam as the other bedroom door crashed onto the floor.

More thuds. Sydney looked again and saw feet much too big to fully see through the crack under the door. They were definitely not scaleless feet. Scaleless feet weren't the size of bigfoot's, and they didn't have curved nails that looked as sharp as knives. But did Sydney care about them? Absolutely not.

Because now…

…she knew where the rodents were.

13

HAUNTED

T HE CRACKER JACK refused to let the Critters in. However, to their good luck and misfortune, it wasn't really in any shape to deter them. A cannonball rolled free as the goat lifted its drooping mouth and the Critters went in one after the other. The opening sealed.

The glow faded. That sense of nowhere within a crawl of time yielded to a ground crumbly and dry. Impatient and bursting with anxiety, Koda paced around Sully. He had a feeling they weren't just inside a dark place. Something was wrong. The texture of pumpkin skin remained like a burnt image on a screen. He didn't smell the sweet scent.

We're not in the Cracker Jack.

The goat shifted his weight. Koda heard something crunch.

"What was that?" the squirrel said, on edge. Hearing those words, Koda wanted to freeze and run all at once.

The Cracker Jack's texture disappeared, but it was still dark, only now it had brightened a shade and scents and sounds came into the air: moist grass, rustling leaves, crickets, and smells unique to giant life such as oil and rubber. The goat had set his hoof on gravel. Koda thought they were on the edge of a driveway, and he was proven correct by a two-story house he saw through gloomy

161

patches. It was strange yet also so normal. But it was terrible most of all, because the house didn't belong. He denied it was real, like it was a bad dream.

"Of all places…" the squirrel said, disgusted.

Sully pawed Koda's arm. "Koda… I can't see color anymore."

Koda did a double take at the scenery. Black trees. Gray grass and gray Sully. Koda stretched out an arm. His ivory fur was like sunshine in the ashen-colored world.

"Well, I mean, everything isn't in color except for us," said Sully.

Now *he tells me. Sully's gray because he* is *gray.* Feeling foolish but also relieved, Koda was surprised at how depressed he'd felt. He wouldn't say he had gotten *used to* the colors, but his new sight had certainly been helpful more than a few times. He had completely overlooked how vital it was to see potential predators so clearly. If you could get past the distracting colors, you could really focus on things, which kept you safer. Koda examined the area as well as he could despite how bleary everything was.

The squirrel rubbed his eyes. "You guys see this? It's blurred!" The goat and hare nodded.

"Is this the giant world, Koda?" Sully asked.

"No, there isn't a moon in the sky. And those faces are still there." Koda had overlooked their green color. He made a point to ignore the face constellations even though they were frowning slightly, staring at them as usual.

The goat said broodingly, "It took us longer to get here. Did you notice that just now?"

Sully, who had frequently watched Giant's mini TV, said, "It's like it was loading."

Koda assumed the animals' silence for confusion. He noticed the other Critters looked distinct and vivid apart from their forested surroundings. "What he means is the Cracker Jack got stuck trying to get us here." Still *is trying*, Koda thought. *Except for us, I'm seeing with my old vision.*

"That could be because of the beatin' it took," the goat said, and he looked to the hare for his opinion. The hare nodded, his voice low and wandering.

"Don't leave us in the dark, Jack," the goat prodded. "This world's done that enough to us already."

"I'm thinking of what the clown said to us concerning the Cracker Jack," said the hare. "He told us they were used to ward off evil spirits, but the Trickster world was upside down."

"He's crazy! He was talking gibberish," the squirrel said.

"Why's what he said important?" the goat asked.

"Because we have to stop to wonder why these relics are navigating us through the Cracker Jacks. Starting with what the clown really meant. The clue is in the words."

"Well, goin' off of that, the *meanin'* would be upside down. The opposite of 'wardin' off' being 'to welcome in.'"

"It's going to attract evil spirits?" Sully asked, horrified.

"Or wouldn't the opposite be good spirits?" the goat asked.

The squirrel switched from rubbing his eyes to rubbing his forehead.

"There may be no difference between them. Whatever comes through, comes through," the hare said.

"I don't know. I don't really see a totem usin' a Cracker Jack for transportation," said the goat.

"Perhaps you are correct. Either way, totems will not be stopped by a Trickster. They will find a way to the Haven, as bad luck would have it." The hare paused before his next sentence. He started slowly. "And to my knowledge, if I am to trust a Trickster, a totem *is* down here."

Sully looked as scared as he had been when meeting the

163

clown, and the squirrel jerked to his full height.

"Gather at the river! Jack, you sure about that?" the goat asked.

"If the totem wasn't in the Trickster world, though, it would be in the giant world or the Haven. The worst-case scenario depends on for what victims you are most worried."

Instantly, Koda's thoughts went to Giant. Shingles on the house's roof quivered, like they were mocking him. How very far away from home he felt. The national forest, and therefore the "portal" to this world, wasn't that far from Giant's nest. Maybe it was far to a hamster, but to a terrifying, mythological creature? Giant would be in danger. Koda would find some way to warn her if he were in the giant world, but…

He clung to the thought of the Cracker Jack. "The clown said the Cracker Jacks were used as protection. Couldn't that mean they're protecting the world outside of this one?" Koda asked.

The hare said, "That very well may be true, but listen carefully." The urgency in his voice held everyone still. "Rowan, you asked me if the relics were totem pieces. If they are, wouldn't it be likely that as each piece is leading to another, they are also leading us to the totem?"

The question hung in the leaf-cluttered wind like a noose. *Oooooo*, it sang. Sully made himself small beside the goat's hoof.

"I would like all of you to consider this while also considering I could be wrong," said the hare.

"You're not often wrong," the squirrel said with a troubled look.

The hare offered no response other than looking away at the house.

Dryly, the goat said, "That Addams Family house over there is your test. We arrived at its doorstep; it's as good a choice as any to search for the two remainin' relics."

The squirrel cut him off as he started for the house. "We've never been in a human's hovel!" he cried.

"You're afraid of *giants* being in there?" Koda retorted.

"Why not? Apparently, any monsters can pass through the opening now."

"Don't fight," Sully said.

"Listen to your fellow rodent, and let's get off the road. The next thing we should fear after roller coasters are speedin' cars," said the goat.

Koda and the squirrel glared at each other. Walking to the front porch, the house's bleary texture didn't refocus. The best Koda could see of the door was a shining circle like a miniature moon. He remembered the goat's difficulty with doorknobs.

The goat tripped on the steps. "Takes some gettin' used to, doesn't it?" He scuffed his hooves on the wood. "Stand back."

Koda was about to remind him that didn't work last time and to look for an open window when he heard a long eerie *creeaaak*.

The door had opened a crack.

"Who did that?" the squirrel cried.

Sully hugged the goat's leg, staring intently at the black void beyond the doorway. Sniffing, the hare hopped slowly up to the door. For a second, Koda saw a gray hand reaching for him as if it were about to grab the hare by the head. Then it was gone, and he guessed it must have been some trick of the light.

"No one," the hare said.

"No one? It had to be someone!" the squirrel argued.

"House is old. Old houses sometimes have doors that don't lock," said the goat. Releasing his leg from Sully's grip, he pushed the door. Everyone cringed as it hit the inside wall with a violent ring.

It's a house. You've been in one most of your life, Koda comforted himself. They left the porch and crept inside.

The downstairs was quiet and stuffy like a tomb, with crisp, white walls and razor-edged shadows. Curtained windows were a pitcher of black. An unlit Christmas tree stood in the dark. To the right deep set in the room a crackling fireplace smoldered lazily. Flickering light cast on the over-mantle, on faceless figures inside silver frames, on furniture, and on the carpet before reaching two flights of stairs. Koda got a bad feeling about them, and in a house like this, it was a haunted feeling.

He stiffened as a gust of air blew on his back as if someone had breathed very heavily on him. The door swung away from the wall. *BAM!* The door slammed shut.

"*KUK! Kuk kuk kuk!*" the squirrel barked while the goat stomped his hooves in place.

Sully squeaked rapidly from his chest. "Koda, this house is haunted!"

"Keep calm. We've had weirder things happen," the hare said, lifting a foot as if to thump the floor. He slowly relaxed it. Taking a minute to unbend his ears, the hare hopped cautiously into the living room.

"*Quuaaa…*"

"*Shhh,*" the goat hushed the squirrel. "It's been years since I've been in one of these," he said reminiscently as he made his way over to the stairs.

Koda had a choice to make. Out of the three, who was the lesser of the evils? The squirrel was obviously out of the question, and he still had his suspicions about the hare. The goat had been someone to rely on so far, he admitted. If any Critter could be somewhat decent, he supposed he could see goats being more trustworthy.

He motioned for Sully to follow the goat. While the hare and squirrel explored the living room, the three of them investigated the area behind the stairs, where the firelight didn't reach.

"It's a dinin' room," the goat told Sully and Koda. "A half wall divides it and the kitchen."

"Where they butcher Critters," the squirrel said from the living room. His comments were getting on Koda's nerves.

"Why does he talk like that?" Sully asked.

Entering the kitchen, the goat stubbed his hoof on a refrigerator door to open it. Stark light highlighted counter tops and a tile floor. "Not everyone has had great experiences with humans," he said, keeping his voice low.

Koda knew no matter what volume they spoke at, anyone with good ears would be able to hear them, so for the squirrel's benefit he said, "Any Critter who has stolen from them and *made* trouble."

Sully said to the goat, "*You* like giants, though."

"Yes, I do. Farm animals are popular with small kids."

The goat poked his head into the refrigerator. It was empty and Koda could feel the cold from where he stood. A surreal, frightening feeling came over him, the kind he had felt the morning the owl took him from Giant's nest—the morning he'd had the nightmare.

"Can you close that, please?" Koda asked, clenching his left paw.

The goat moved to close the door but paused as Sully asked, "How about Jack? Does *he* like giants?"

Koda noticed a shift in the goat's expression. "Jack. Well…" the goat said, evasive. "I've mentioned he learned a lot from his brother."

"Yes!" Sully said, remembering. "Did Jack's brother make it to the opening?"

The goat forgot about closing the door and turned away from the refrigerator. "I'm afraid he died a long time ago."

Sadness and extreme sympathy showed on Sully's face. He

was speechless for a moment. "How?"

"I ought to let him tell you." Likely because of Sully's voice and pained expression, the goat added, "It was a while back. I'm sure Jack is feelin' better about it now."

Sully mumbled sadly at this.

With a preliminary creak, the refrigerator door slammed shut. The kitchen exploded in noise as the goat hit the refrigerator trotting out of the kitchen. Sully squeaked as he and Koda raced out of the way.

"What was that?" the squirrel exclaimed from the living room.

The goat snorted like a frightened horse. "That's twice," he said.

Koda grabbed Sully's paw when he heard a small squeaking sound come from above the counter. A knob turned and a faucet blasted water. No one was on the other side of the sink.

The goat stepped back from the spray quickly, as if it were acid. "Let's search elsewhere, huh?" he offered. Sully was hugging the goat's leg again.

They discovered a storage room and bathroom adjoining the kitchen (both doors were open). A dim bulb in the ceiling gave them just enough light to see that the storage room contained an enormous stack of boxes. All of them appeared blurry unless the Critters drew close.

Koda inwardly groaned. "We're not going to find the relic in that."

"It's curious what they do with it all. Your giant keep this large a stock?" the goat asked. There still seemed to be an awkwardness to his voice after the conversation about the hare and his brother.

"Actually—"

Koda was inclined to believe the house was playing yet

another trick on them when a broom leaning against a box fell and hit a jar full of marbles onto the floor.

"Sorry," Sully said. A sudden interest overcame him as he saw some of the marbles roll between two columns of boxes and disappear into the wall. It was too dark over there, so Koda didn't like him getting so close by himself. Together they walked to the empty space behind the boxes with Sully in front. The path was narrow, and Koda had missed his chance to squeeze ahead.

Sully stopped... and gasped.

"You found it?" Koda could barely contain his excitement. Now that they had exited the boxes, he moved around Sully.

His excitement dispelled. There was no hidden relic. The hole the marbles had disappeared into wasn't special, just a jagged opening in the plaster as if it had been chewed by a—

Koda stumbled back and landed hard on his bottom.

Behind him, the goat stepped forward. "What is it? What did you find?"

Koda wondered why he hadn't figured it out sooner. After all, wasn't the layout of the house so familiar?

"We're at Giant's nest!" Sully cried.

The goat asked, "This is *your* house?"

"Sully made these holes."

"That's the one I made last month!" Sully exclaimed.

Koda demanded, "Why's it here?"

Softly the hare called the goat's name from the living room. The Critters left the storage room and passed the kitchen as quickly as they could.

The hare was sitting by an end table with its drawers pulled open. "Did you find anything?"

"Sully and Koda say this is their Giant's nest," said the goat.

The squirrel leapt off an opened ottoman with various clothes and slippers inside. The hare's ears bent forward.

Sully was both crazily excited and bewildered. "I've made holes all over! Except for the attic because Koda told me not to go up there. He said Giant was already scared I was a rat in the walls and—"

"Woah, slow down," said the squirrel. "Jack, this can't be their human hovel, right?"

"No, it's not."

"But…" Sully began.

The hare raised his head, gesturing at the house. "You normally see it like this, yes? Blurry, except when you get close enough? But houses aren't actually like this. They're clear."

For the longest time, Koda had assumed everything *was* blurry and colorless. At least until he noticed how Giant reacted to objects farther away, how she seemed able to tell what they were even when Koda couldn't.

"Then it's a copy? Who made a copy of Giant's nest? Why is it here?" Koda stressed.

"I may be giving too little credit to the Tricksters, but I don't think making a house on this level is within their capability," said the hare.

"What about the fun house?" the squirrel asked shakily.

"They're both peculiar," the hare agreed. "It confused me how the carnival existed down here."

No kidding, Koda thought.

"You can't construct wood and metal from blue sand," the hare continued. "Not even half of the carnival could be made without earth material. I'm not implying I know everything about the Trickster world. Maybe they were able to obtain said material from another location, who can know? But I've noticed this. And now Sully and Nahiossi's house…?"

"You're sayin' it was all created based on memory?" the goat asked.

The hare straightened, gazing at the goat before looking off into the dark. "Memory…"

"I mean, they're all rememberin' things from Earth," said the goat.

Ears perked, the hare faced him. "I think you're correct, Rowan. There's been something personal about everything so far. It would explain objects seemingly moving without explanation, but it *does* in fact have an explanation. The memories live on in the present."

"So… the house isn't haunted?" Sully asked. Koda thought he detected a little disappointment in his voice.

"No," said the hare. "I would go as far as saying what happened to Twiggy at the fun house was also related to memory. The faux head may be a coincidence—I resemble many jackrabbits. Though how did he hear my voice?"

The squirrel hugged himself.

"We are strange to this environment," said the hare. "Besides acting through us, it's acting *on* us, and perhaps in stranger ways than the Tricksters. For example, seeing in color. And it all likely comes down to the fact that we're foreign objects here."

"I'm not a UFO," Sully said as if he had been accused of some wrongdoing.

"I'm not sure what you mean," the hare said. "In short, my friends, these are the effects of us being where we shouldn't."

"Could we do anythin' that'll make things worse?" the goat asked.

"It's not so much what *we'll* do. If the Hunter Hototo dropped is still alive, there may be results even more severe than what we've experienced so far."

Koda held his paws together. *I was right. We're doomed to a world falling apart.* He reflected on how his world had been so composed. The everyday routine of Giant hugging him with her

171

hands. What was she doing now? How was she doing? Did she think he was dead? And here they were, a massacre and a world's impending destruction later.

The hare spoke soberly, "The relics are our security, and we thoroughly checked the furniture."

"Nothin'?" the goat asked.

The hare shook his head.

"Nothing except clothes," the squirrel said, frustrated. "What do they need it for anyway? It's unnatural not to go around naked."

"That leaves one place," said the goat.

Everyone looked to the stairway. Kindling crackled and fell through the fireplace grate.

Sully said, afraid, "The worst things are always upstairs."

"Since this is your house, I'd like you and Nahiossi to come with me," the hare said.

Koda refrained from showing his disapproval.

"You're just asking for trouble," said the squirrel.

"Rowan, if you don't mind, can you stay downstairs with Twiggy? It's better if we have all our bases covered."

"Yes, sir," the goat said respectively. "Reckon I'm searchin' the storage area again."

The hare hopped out of the firelight, Koda and Sully slowly following him.

A noise came from the kitchen as they reached the stairs. Koda thought it sounded like the chopping of a knife on a cutting board.

"Jack, wait!" Koda glanced behind them and saw the squirrel running after them. "Sorry, Rowan!"

The hare carried Koda and Sully. They hadn't been able to climb the tall steps. After a slow ascent, they stood in a dark hallway. There were four rooms with doors ajar: one facing the stairs (the bathroom) and three opposite each other. The room to Koda's left faintly glowed green. He heard splashing and dry voices, and he sniffed rotten garlic. None of the Critters peeked into that doorway, possibly fearing the door would loudly creak open and alert those inside.

Sully wandered to one of the two rooms to the right. Koda met him at the door. Squeezing past it, he identified the gloomy room as Giant's. Her scent was everywhere, though overlaid with smoke. Her bed stood between his and Sully's homes, just as it did in the real Giant's nest—Koda had to remind himself it was only a copy. He always thought he and Sully on the dressers were like guardians while she slept.

As they walked in, on their right, between the closet and the wall, was the dragon's lighted (empty) cage. Sully gave it a fearful, yet also sad, look. It wouldn't have surprised Koda if his brother *missed* the dragon. Maybe such a thing was possible when the world around you was even worse than the lizard. As the hare and squirrel proceeded to search, Koda and Sully went to the shaken Christmas tree to gaze at the shed bristles and shattered ornaments. The broken lamp lay a few feet away on a burnt rug.

I'd been hoping I wouldn't see it like this again, Koda thought.

"It's not here either," said the squirrel. He finished searching under Giant's pillows and jumped from the bed onto Koda's home. "They put you in these? Hototo did you a favor."

Koda glowered.

"You said there was an attic?" the hare asked.

Sully lifted uneasily in the direction of the closet.

"We don't have a drop-down staircase. It'll be a square in the ceiling." Feeling snappish, Koda said to the squirrel, "An attic is a wide room in the highest section of the house."

"I know what an attic is," the squirrel said, disgruntled. "I had friends who lived in human hovels during the winter."

"Good thing we never had any squirrels," Koda said.

The hare pulled the sliding closet doors. As the black strip of darkness widened, Koda's vision flickered as if someone's shadow had passed over him. His heart quickened. Whirling around, he saw no one, and the bedroom door, while still ajar, seemed untouched. *Impossible! We checked the whole room!*

A metallic screech returned Koda's attention to the opened closet. He waited for someone to comment on the shadow, though whatever it had been, it seemed they had had their backs to it.

The hare hopped back a bit to view the inside of the closet. A bare shelf was positioned a foot below the ceiling. Below that was a line of clothes Sully eyed suspiciously. "Be careful! Someone might be hiding behind them!" he warned.

The hare pushed a stack of boxes out of the closet, jumped on top, and grew slightly alarmed as the squirrel joined him. "I strongly recommend you stay down here," the hare said.

"What? No! *They* can, but we'll make the most of it going together." Hangers jangled as the squirrel jumped onto the clothes.

After a pause, the hare made the high jump to the shelf and, standing on his hind legs, pressed his head on the ceiling. A square section lifted into blackness.

Sully made a noise of dread as they climbed into the attic. "What do you see?" he asked.

"Many peculiar human things," the hare answered. He ducked his head into the closet. "Don't leave the room. I saw one of your holes by the door. If you hear the Tricksters coming, hide there."

Upon the hare's exit, Koda abruptly turned. Alone with Sully, the gloom beneath the bed and the shelves, inside the closet and shading the window, seemed deeper, infinite, and home to faces he shaped from the shadows. He couldn't be sure if his paranoia had conjured a figure crouching by one of the dressers. The ghostly space resonated with a Trickster's howl and Koda, huddled against Sully, felt it come alive somehow, as does a creak on the stairs or a soft shuffling at the door during the middle of the night. He swore he heard both, here, in the room, a few feet in front of them. A shadow passed over the wall toward the bed.

The hole was in the wall vertical to the door. Koda and Sully clambered in.

"Baaaabyyy…"

"I'm hearing things," Sully whispered quaveringly.

Koda darted glances at the furniture. "I heard it, too."

"Baby." The voice sounded worried. "Where'd you get to, Sully?"

"It knows my name!"

Koda quivered. He knew that voice. It was Giant's, except it couldn't be!

Soft footsteps. First, he looked to the door, then over by the bed, and as his eyes traveled, he saw them: impressions made in the carpet. They neared the hole, appearing like prints in the sand made by something invisible. There was a delighted gasp. Koda and Sully reeled as a shadow with eyes appeared in front of the hole. "I found you!"

They fled to another hole leading to the hallway. Sully was about to jump out when Koda blocked him. Two Tricksters stood, paused, in the doorway at the end of the hall, their shrunken heads tilted at the sound of thumps on the ceiling. There came a tumble as if something had fallen into the closet.

The squirrel raced out of the closet and down the stairs, chased by hysterical giant laughter. "RUN, RUN! LET'S HAVE A LITTLE FUN!"

Koda's fur stood on end.

"'e comes!" one of the Tricksters hissed. They retreated into the bedroom and slammed the door.

Koda jolted as, under a deafening crumble, a ceiling fan fell and clanged to the floor. Screeches traveled through the wall and bats flooded the hallway. He could hear something huge heaving itself around Giant's bedroom. Seconds later, the door smashed onto the carpet. Its hinges struck the doorframe close to the hole, and Koda jolted again. He stared at the huge clawed foot planted on top of the flattened door. Slowly he raised his eyes.

A haunting presence filled the entire doorway. It was a four-legged creature with matted fur, spindly wings, and a gargoyle face, and it didn't possess a green glow.

There was no mistaking it.

It was a totem.

14

CAMAZOTZ

YELLOW EYES, full of wickedness, scoured the hallway filled with swirling bats. The eyes were like the rounded glow of submarine lights that if blown out would likely reveal two hollow sockets. Slowly the totem turned its head. The crinkled ears and twirled horns were the only small features on its body. If it weren't covered in scraggly blue and purple fur—the fur of a wolf, as it was canine in build except the bat wings and monstrous face—Sully imagined he would have seen veins as thick as pipes pulsing throughout the muscular arms and legs. It breathed angrily with exhilaration and murderous intent. With each rancid exhale, the air wavered like desert heat. The terror Sully felt was small beside his amazement.

A bat trapped under the totem's foot beat its wings, appearing to vibrate as it screeched bloody murder. The totem squashed it across the flattened door. Its nails rotated toward the hole in the wall and Sully, oblivious, was in full view. A yank on his arm turned him to hide. Koda stared, petrified and paled to a lighter shade of ivory.

"Where are you?" the demonic beast said with a menacing playfulness. It spoke in human tongue.

Sully jumped and winced as he heard a series of high-

177

pitched chirps, strange to be uttered from the throat that gargled thunder. The totem gave a sigh that was like a gust of wind. "Two vermin are in the wall," it said. A clawed toe pointed into the hole. "There."

Sully's breath choked. Terror awakened, he and Koda bolted to Giant's bedroom.

"That's it. Flee!" said the totem raised in ecstasy. "I'm going to toy with you… Including the diseased filth downstairs and the hunted MEAT cowered in the attic."

Stopping at the other hole, the brothers sprang back. A bat thrust its head into the wall and twisted around, trying to wedge itself in. It made such awful noises, a kind of angry clicking that continued without pause even as Sully and Koda had to wheeze between their screams. Its fanged mouth bit rapidly, and the red eyes never once blinked.

"You're not leaving," the totem said, "but if you wish to prolong your deaths further, you'll get to choose who I kill next."

Sully trembled. He would never forget the sounds that followed. They were more horrible than the screams he had heard during the flood.

*****

Sydney listened to the commotion with a nag of intimi- dation. She might have to compete for the two rodents, and she didn't like the odds.

She scanned the bathroom for options. The sink was to her right (the lights above either turned off or burned out), and the sink's drawers were shut, of course! Beside the sink was the toilet, which was definitely out of the question, and tucked at the end was the bathtub. Sydney crawled to it but stopped as something slammed into the doorframe, nudging the door farther open. There was a pained shriek.

Stupid bats. Sydney quickly climbed the stack of towels beside the tub as they continued to open the door. She slipped and fell to the bottom with a loud, shrill noise as her nails scraped down the side of the bathtub.

Sydney tensed. Heavy footfalls thundered by the door. Why hadn't she closed it?! Looking through a gap in the shower curtain, she glimpsed the monster. Orbed eyes trailed shimmers in the sink mirror. Its grin was ghoulish and wide like a curved machete.

Sydney's tail wiggled in shock. *That is no Hunter.*

The monster passed by, gone in the mirror. She heard it bulldoze into the next bedroom and give a lively laugh—not an animal's but a *scaleless's* laugh—as the munchkins screamed. It should have been over quickly; she had gotten enough of an eyeful of the monster to know that. And the munchkins were frail, even if their fingers were as hard as tree branches.

One of them managed to run into the hallway. The bathroom door swung, throwing their shadow and hundreds more on the curtain. *Hey, no! Go somewhere else!* Sydney wanted to shout, but she didn't dare. The munchkin crumbled to the floor under the attacking bats. They were hell-bent on picking at it, tearing first at the rags—behind the curtain it was easy for Sydney to imagine they were stretching flesh—then at its body like bloodthirsty crows. The helpless creature flailed its arms, thrust out its hands to push them away, and they picked at those as well. It became some deranged shadow play. In the bedroom, the wails of pain died down, and she heard the thump of the monster.

The door swung into the wall, there was the sound of it all crumbling apart, and the room waved dark.

The tattered silhouette of the munchkin stumbled against the bathtub, pulling the curtain taut. "*'op it! AAAP IIIT!*"

An agonized scream. The silhouette jerked. The curtain

179

billowed upward for an instant, and Sydney was amazed at what Yellow Eyes could do. When the curtain began to yank and tear on the bar from the large teeth stuck in it, her blood, already cold, chilled to ice.

A final withered scream ended with a vicious croak and splatter. Sydney's nails squeaked on the tub.

Snorting loudly, the forbidding silhouette paused. Sydney's heart dropped in her chest—and it dropped even further as a rubber nose pressed into the curtain, pushing it closer to Sydney until the curtain swept into the tub. Blood dripped down it to pool under her claws.

The nose dragged. Yellow Eyes dunked his head, the curtain straightened, and he resumed eating loudly with grinding of teeth and bones cracking. The taste of pennies in the air, the coldness of her belly, it was all too well for Sydney to feel like she was in a meat freezer. The minutes crawled until the meat fell from Yellow Eyes's mouth. Thumps softening, the room brightened gray.

Sydney exhaled but was startled again, this time by the jangling of curtain rings. Tilting her head up, she saw a bat fly past the bar. Then another. And another. They crowded above her like a locust plague. A large low-flying pest set its red eyes on her and hovered, shrieking excitedly.

Shut up! Shut up! SHUT UP! Sydney silently yelled.

The thumps accelerated. Rings clattered into the tub as the curtain swiped off the bar, revealing Sydney to a hungry, yellow gaze.

***

Sully's teeth jabbed up and down. He was so incredibly terrified, they could have been stabbing the roof of his mouth and he wouldn't have known. His entire focus was on the bat that had wedged its thumbs into the hole and was pushing closer to him and Koda.

Just as Sully thought it was about to reach them, it was yanked out of the wall. Jack appeared, holding the infuriated bat between his large incisors. He discarded it and pulled Sully and Koda back into the bedroom. Sully looked around in disbelief, viewing the destruction of furniture among floating plaster dust and bats. A coffer had fallen on his home from a hole in the ceiling—a hole so large that he couldn't even hope to create one as big. That was all he had the chance to see.

Besieged by bats, Jack carried them into the hallway to the stairs. Sully heard the loud breath of the totem incredibly close, almost right next to them, and it sounded like its wings were scraping a doorway. He tried to lose the Tricksters' agony in the screeching.

Jack vaulted down the stairs a level at a time, Sully and Koda swinging hard against his chin. The brothers shrieked as a bat flew at them, and Jack raised his paws to knock it to the ground. It wasn't much later when another bat attacked them. Beyond the flapping wings in Sully's face, he glimpsed the downstairs completely overrun by red eyes. Jack must have been blinded for he almost ran into the storage wall several feet from the bottom of the stairs. He swerved at the last minute, ran into the kitchen, and up to the storage room door. It was closed.

He dropped Sully and Koda and stood pressed against the door. "ROWAN!"

Rowan can't open doors. Rowan can't open doors!

The door opened, and the bats swarmed into the storage room after the Critters ran in. Rowan raced toward them. "What in tarnation?!"

Koda was screaming. A bat clung to him, biting him. Jack bit its wing and flung it into the air where it flew to hang on a coat rack. "Where is Twiggy?" asked Jack. His chest inflated deeply as he breathed.

Sully went to Koda. He seemed like he was okay. "T-twiggy ran downstairs before us," Sully said.

"TWIGGY! Twiggy, run to the storage!" Jack beat the floor with his foot. He spoke in suppressed fear, "Ga bendiga. Dí t'olo ne yá ts'edi." Despite being unable to translate them, the words still frightened Sully.

The bat which had been fighting with Koda along with several others flew down at him. Koda and Sully ran inside the marble jar.

"For land's sake! You gonna tell me what happened?" Rowan was backed against the door. The bats caught in the frame behind his head flapped crazily.

Jack fought off the brothers' attackers, and they returned to the coat rack. "We found the totem," he said. Rowan gave a snorted sneeze, surprised. "Stay here and protect Nahiossi and Sully."

"Where you goin' that you'll leave 'em with me?" Rowan demanded.

"We have to leave!" Koda protested.

"It won't do us any good. We won't be able to outrun his wings outside, where he can fly freely." Jack gravely turned to update Rowan. "The totem is Camazotz."

"Then we have no hope of hidin', either," Rowan said, tromping around a little.

"It makes the chirps to find us!" Sully said. "They tell bats where things are like a map."

Sully had learned about bats and echolocation when he first started watching TV. That's why they had been the first thing he was afraid of. He knew bats weren't blind like the saying said; they were just like everyone else—except goats and animals like that— they can't see in the dark. And so, bats hunted by making echoes.

They frightened Sully because they could find you even if they couldn't see you. Camazotz was just a gigantic bat. An extremely evil gigantic bat.

Jack was regaining control of himself slowly, though there was still a slight shaking to his feet, as if he were fighting the urge to either thump or flee. "We have to stop him here somehow. Until then, I'll keep his attention—and don't follow me, Rowan."

"You're fast, Jack, you really are, but even *your* feet will tire!"

"I'm the only one who has a chance. I'll pray for a miracle." Jack hopped to the door.

"No! Stay!" Sully pleaded.

Rowan stood blocking Jack. Upstairs the screams wrenched short.

Jack said, "He'll come after us once he's finished with the Tricksters. Don't make it easy for him."

Rowan grunted and slipped as bats pounded on the other side of the door, pushing it open. A whole cloud of them slipped through in the second it took Rowan to push back against the door. He looked at Jack.

Finally, he gave in. "Make hell for him, then." He pushed his weight off the door, and the bats swarmed in like angry bees.

Crying out, Sully started forward out of the jar. "Stop!"

Koda wedged in next to him, pushing Sully to the glass. Jack was already gone. Lost in a violently moving screen of black, Rowan held the door.

A bat dived at the jar, forcing Sully to stay inside. "Why'd you let him go?" he asked, crying.

"We'd be surrenderin' everyone if I hadn't," Rowan said. The bats leeched on his ears, his face, his whole body. He reared to throw them off, but the door pushed farther open when he did. Rowan stomped back in place. "Damn it all!"

***

Sydney restrained herself from flinching as Yellow Eyes's claws slid out of the shower curtain. They held eye contact. Was he going to eat her in one bite? Or would it be many bites, to draw it out?

The monster's head entered the shower. Blood glossed its orange fangs and dribbled onto Sydney's back. The droplets felt very warm but weren't at all comforting. As he pointed his mouth down at her, more blood spilled into the tub. *drip drip drip*, very fast. She could see it flowing into the drain out of the corner of her eye. She didn't turn her head. Warmed by his meaty breath, she stared upward into the back of his mouth, as dark as the eyes of Death.

Yellow Eyes grinned, and as if telling her a secret, he rumbled in what was meant to be a whisper, "I don't kill what could benefit me."

He stood grinning at her for a bit more before backing away. The thumps made Sydney slide in the blood. Yellow Eyes growled and turned abruptly, destroying the rest of the doorway and part of the sink. A pipe burst, spewing water. Chips of the wall ricocheted off the mirror.

Stupid, idiot, crazy WEIRDO!

"ARE YOU PREPARED, CRITTERS? WHO IS THE SOUL YOU'VE SACRIFICED?" Yellow Eyes bellowed, and that arrogant non-Hunter stomped down the stairs.

Pay no attention to the bearded dragon behind the curtain, huh? Sydney thought and was relieved, if not a bit insulted.

She climbed the curtain onto the lip of the bathtub. The munchkin's head was laying on it, draped by the soaked curtain. She could see through the holes Yellow Eyes had made in the curtain, though it was too dark in the room to see any details. Its glow had disappeared. *Why didn't you go downstairs?*

Sydney jumped down onto the towels, which were also spotted in blood. They had fallen onto the floor sometime during the violence, and she saw that where they had touched the wall was a hole big enough for her to escape through.

Sydney had to control the urge to yell. *You have to be pulling my tail! It would've been great to know about that beforehand!*

A bat dived to bite at her neck. Sydney snapped angrily at it and crawled through the hole into a closet.

She had never been… *vigilant—yes, that's the word. I'm not afraid, if that's what anyone would think*—of the darkness, but right now it felt like the right thing, the intelligent thing, to do. When she touched a pair of boots that shuffled backward, she bloated herself and prepared to fight. Then she slowly looked inside and found them empty. The boots had simply moved because she had run into them. She licked the laces. They tasted like Insect-Giver. Sydney wondered if this could be her house (the hallway *had* looked familiar), but then the thought slipped her mind and turned to more important things.

Exiting the closet through an open door, Sydney found she was in the room beside the one Yellow Eyes had first entered. She ignored the bats flying around and saw a tree on the other side of the room, framed in an open window above a desk. She guessed leaving out the front door wasn't an option. Considering the ruckus she heard, it was probably a mess downstairs. She had a hunch it would be over in a few minutes.

***

Jack went swiftly to the living room. He stung from bat bites, everywhere they leeched onto him, but just then he was feeling so much inside he barely felt them. He knew what the totem wanted, though he wasn't as fluent in English as he was in the

Native American languages. Perhaps it was the totem's intention that none of them could understand. How very dishonorable. As Jack was about to call to the totem, someone else did it for him.

"Over here, you vampire mutant!"

Twiggy. Jack searched wildly for him. On the window sills. Under the furniture. Twiggy was nowhere to be found, but he had heard him somewhere close by.

The clang and boom of the totem descending the stairs forced Jack back over by the stairs. The attacking bats scattered high like dark butterflies. Either they didn't wish to be within striking-distance or the totem wanted them out of the way to get a good look at his next victim. Jack put some distance between him and the stairs and spread his arms, standing fully erect on his hind legs. His ears pointed up and backward.

Through the chaotic flapping mass, Camazotz, the Mayan totem, ducked his blood-splattered head around the ceiling. The yellow eyes were globes of fire set upon him.

Jack said a prayer.

The thumbs at the end of Camazotz's wings gripped the banister as he stalked the last flight toward the storage room's wall at the bottom. One of the steps cracked and splintered. Jack worried for his friends, hearing the fox Trickster's voice in his mind. *You're afraid for the others. Afraid you won't be able to help them like* before.

She doesn't know what she's talking about.

He stepped back as Camazotz reached the bottom and entered the living room. The totem took up a lot more space than Jack thought, and he was suddenly overwhelmed by his size. Camazotz snarled, making a gargling sound like deep purring. "Lovely choice. I'll feast on t'u'ul readily."

"You belong imprisoned in wood, devil," Jack said.

"Not anymore."

Both brave and afraid, Twiggy taunted unseen, "Are you as

blind as a bat as you are deaf? Come get me!"

"Don't interfere!" Jack yelled.

The totem turned as ponderously as an iron weight toward the front door. His feet fell like redwood stumps, and he carried his wings awkwardly in the confined space. "The one who called is hidden." He opened his mouth to chirp for the bats.

Jack leaned into his legs. He powered them to the totem's heel and bit as hard as he could before running beneath him and into the kitchen. Jack circled back under the stairs. A wing crashed the banister, and spindles struck bats out of the air and boomeranged off the walls with a loud metallic ping. The landing crunched from the blow, caving downward at him. He threw himself away hard.

Camazotz laughed and spat, "PATHETIC!"

Jack twisted up off the carpet and returned to the kitchen. It wasn't his intention to defeat the totem, but he would be dead on the floor before Twiggy or the others were killed—a very likely possibility as Camazotz dove through the flights of stairs. The landing obliterated around his head.

"You really mean to fight me, Critter? Now that I am free, there will be no way of containing me."

Jack darted to the end of the stairs by the storage wall. The stairs above groaned, jerked, and broke from the ceiling. He heard it all in an instant, the second-floor hallway and banister preparing to fall on him. The living room zoomed in as Jack increased his speed, and his shoulder struck a side table. He stumbled and fell.

He heard Twiggy shout again, though with much less muster and more fear. "Brainless wretch!"

"*HRAAAAA!*"

Camazotz rampaged the front door. First, it splintered down the middle, and the other half swung out over the porch, landing several feet out from the house in pieces. Then the rest of the frame and wall around the doorway blasted apart as if blown by a firework. What was left looked like the aftermath made by a shotgun blast into a piece of wood but on a much larger scale. Briefly, Jack saw a furry tail slip away into the remains of the wall. He could hear Twiggy running.

The veins in Camazotz's wings were like thunderbolts lit by the starlight shining on the porch. The muscles in his jaw spasmed. He looked like a wolf about to howl at the moon. Heaving around, Camazotz tore a wider chunk out of the house's front wall. The flights of stairs behind him were stacked on the floor in heaps of plaster and wood.

"Stop playing around! I toy with *you*, not you with me."

Seeing the opening in the house's façade, hearing it groan, it donned on Jack what he should be doing.

Level it out.

"I've made it easy for you," Jack baited him. "I'm right out in the open, and you still can't catch me."

The rusty grin was more of a sneer. "Enough play. All t'u'ul must suffer," Camazotz said and pounced like a lion.

Jack spun into the couch. He ran around it, hearing the vibrating *BONG!* of it overturning, and the dull blows following him to the end of the living room. He halted, looked back, and glimpsed the sudden up close view of the totem's jaws. Jack dove to the floor, causing Camazotz to race above him, his thick legs plowing past and demolishing the wall.

The totem did not stop. Chased by the increasing sound of stomping feet, Jack raced for the kitchen. He meant to drive Camazotz right through the opposite wall, but as he was about to make the leap over the rubble of the stairs, the bats returned. He missed the jump and crashed. His face and throat burned, and he thrashed around in the spindles as if caught in a snare.

Camazotz's laughter gradually rose in pitch even as his

movements were rapid and violent. Losing sense of direction, Jack darted toward the fireplace. A split-second touch of intense heat warned him, and he coursed sideways before racing into the flames.

The totem didn't follow him. Camazotz had made him panic, Jack realized, and he couldn't shake the bats. Blinded by so many surrounding him, he staggered into furniture before succumbing to both his fatigue and attackers, collapsing flat on his stomach.

"Should I let them eat you alive, poor, heroic, t'u'ul?" Camazotz jeered. "Or should you *burn?*"

Jack already felt like he was burning. The bats on his face flew back, and he could see Camazotz next to the fireplace, high-lighted in flickering light. He raised his wings. He flapped them, slow at first, then quicker, then fast. Embers floated out from the grate into the living room. They caught on the heap of spindles and steps, on the couch, and on the dressers. How rapidly the fire thrived. In a matter of minutes, it would block the Critters' path to escape.

Jack thumped his foot as hard as he could. "Twiggy! Rowan! Run!"

***

Rowan jerked away from the door. The bats pushed it open, and he grabbed Sully and Koda.

The upper section of stairs slanted to the wall. Fire crept along it and the wooden pile of debris. A strong wind blew the flames. Sparks crackled in Sully's face. He threw his paws in front of his eyes, feeling the heat, unable to breathe. At the last minute, Rowan backed against the half wall in the kitchen.

Camazotz roared his laugh. "What's the matter? DON'T LIKE FIRE?"

The totem loomed, his head arched high. Beyond him, the living room was ablaze. There were two huge openings where the front door and the house's side wall had been. Flames ringed the inside as if they were rings of fire that a lion would leap through. The false Giant's nest groaned and creaked, popped wood and burned brick, under the hum of the growing fire.

Jack kneeled on the floor, covered in bats. "RUN!"

The slanted flight of stairs was disappearing in smoke. Rowan charged under it. Sully thought his fur would catch fire. Then they were running to the porch. Camazotz swung at one of the dressers. It flew up toward Rowan's side, and it flew over as he ducked and smashed onto the pile. Sully felt himself slipping. He tumbled onto the ground as Rowan ran onto the porch without him.

A bat swooped at Sully. It grabbed him by his arm and flopped around as it struggled to carry his weight. Sully kicked his feet up at it, squealing. Wheeling himself around midair, he saw Camazotz advancing like a Cheshire cat. Backdropped by fire streaming up the walls and overtaking the fireplace, his wings flapping beside his legs, he looked more like a bat from Hell.

In the most heartbreaking cry for help, Koda screamed, "Rowan!"

Rowan steered back for Sully. It seemed like he was moving in slow motion as the bat got a stronger hold on Sully and quickly turned him around toward the totem. Sully's eyes were locked on Camazotz's yellow eyes when Jack and Twiggy appeared. Jack leaped, knocked the bat to the floor, and took Sully. Danger and peril pressed on him like a hot iron brand while chilling laughter rose louder and shriller, right on their tails.

They stumbled over the porch and onto the driveway. A few bats that had still managed to hold onto them flew up into the sky. Jack, Twiggy, and Rowan holding Koda spun on the gravel to face the house where Camazotz stuck his gargoyle head through its gaping doorway.

With a voluminous quake of wood falling upon wood and windows shattering, the weight of the upstairs and attic collapsed, crashing down on the totem. House and all. A brief enraged, twisted expression of shock disappeared under a flush of debris.

Like the forest, everyone was still. Even the crickets didn't make a sound.

Sully said very quietly, "There really *were* bats in the attic."

15
THE CRUELTY OF GIANTS

ROWAN SET KODA down on the driveway. They panted, gaping at the ruin of the false Giant's nest, a hill of crumbled brick and wood ablaze. Wind combed the flames. The engulfing smoke clogged Koda's lungs. He coughed.

"We're alright to leave now," the hare said. He hopped wearily onto the road toward the woods. Rowan and the squirrel followed him quickly.

Sully, looking as stunned as Koda felt, seemed unable to walk. Another look at the few bats that had fled the house and were now circling above pushed him to catch up. "Is it... gone?" he asked.

"You cannot kill a totem," the hare said.

Koda kicked up his speed to walk alongside the hare. "There's a whole burning house on top of the thing!"

"We've bested him for the moment."

Disturbed, Koda slowed in place with Sully, letting the Critters walk ahead. He realized they should be walking much faster, and they sped into line with Rowan.

The woods began off the side of the road. As the group entered under a low canopy, they were cast in broken shadows. Crickets began singing again, while farther in an unseen woodpecker jabbed its beak into a tree.

A piece of wall or frame snapped and fell on the burning pile. Koda jumped. Even Rowan and the hare stopped, stiff and with their ears up. Everyone listened longer than what was probably necessary, then they quickened their pace.

The squirrel glanced back at the house. "Are all totems that stupid?" he asked.

"He was blinded by cockiness and rage. Both are easily manipulated," said the hare, and Koda "be burrowed" if he didn't sound vengefully triumphant.

"When I said to give the totem hell," Rowan said with a fatigued, humorous air, "I assumed you wouldn't take it literally! You've got lucky feet. You alright?"

"I'm fine. And the rest of you?"

Koda's chest burned where the bat he fought had clawed him, and everywhere he stung from bites.

Sully combed his neck. "I'm not going to turn into a vampire, right?"

Smiling, Rowan said, "No. You're stuck bein' a hamster for now."

"I didn't get any bites." The squirrel sounded sour. "What I've got are splinters sticking out of my—"

"But I heard you in the livin' room," Rowan said.

"I was in the walls."

"Why didn't you hide with me?" Rowan asked, frustrated. "I'm missin' a lot of information here."

They pieced the story together from the beginning. It gave Koda's pulse time to slow. Starting with their discoveries in the hallway and attic, the hare recounted how he and the squirrel had been lost in the sheer number of rocking chairs, chests, and blank human forms wearing clothes. There had even been a piano wrapped in cobwebs like everything else.

"How did that get up there?" Koda asked, surprised.

Since neither him nor Sully had visited the attic at the real Giant's nest, the hare asked if they had ever given any thought to what was up there. Sully confessed, with some shyness, that he had, and the description of the attic matched his imaginings.

"We didn't see bats anywhere in the attic," the hare continued. "An ugly snap and ripping sound preceded their appearance, that's all." Hearing that, Sully tripped on a rock.

The bats appeared after the hare and squirrel heard the totem breathing behind a huge tapestry. They hid in vain. The totem, sensing they were there, made its chirping noises.

"Camazotz was said to see through walls. I hadn't known the reason for it until Sully revealed the purpose of his chirping," said the hare.

A look of pride came over Sully's tired expression.

"Of course, he found us. Twiggy was closest to him, and he ran." The hare asked the squirrel, "Why *didn't* you hide in the storage room?"

"Too many bats. I ran into the first hole I saw in the wall and hid there. At some point I realized, you know, we could bring the whole house down on the sucker."

"Bless you, Twiggy."

"It was a two-Critter job," the squirrel murmured.

At the mention of the storage room, Koda thought despairingly of its contents. "Where do we search for the relic next?" he asked.

The squirrel groaned.

"We'll rest somewhere secure, then decide," said the hare.

Koda looked at Sully. His eyes drooped, and he walked sluggishly. *I guess it's for the best.*

The group wandered far into the bowels of the woods until they found a grove mostly concealed from starlight. Rowan inspected the area as each Critter made themselves comfortable. Koda felt more secure once the squirrel scurried up a tree.

He bumped his nose on a tree trunk. Koda curled into a ball, shifted, and turned on his side. It wasn't the same without bedding and a hideaway. He waited for Sully to join him. When he didn't, Koda sat up and made out the shape of the hare lying under a grape bush. Sully was cuddled against him.

The hare lifted stiffly on his front legs. "Sully, wouldn't you rather sleep beside your brother?"

"I thought maybe you were lonely."

Koda was aware of Rowan and the squirrel paying close attention to them.

"I think it's best you keep him company," the hare said quietly.

"Okay," Sully said. Pawsteps found their way over to Koda.

"I'll take first watch," Rowan said, sounding slightly mindful.

The hare replied, "Wake me if you feel yourself tiring."

Snuggling beside Koda, Sully said goodnight. The image of his brother cuddled with the hare made Koda think. There was some sadness, but he found he felt more curious ever since Rowan told them about the hare's brother. But the thought of the hare was fading, sleepiness was taking over, and he said goodnight. Somewhere in the fog, the squirrel said something sarcastic. Koda drifted off.

Baabyyy...
Koda's nose twitched.
Wake up. It's time to wake up.
A cold breeze swept his fur. He had forgotten to stuff the hideaway window with bedding. Crickets sang especially loud, as if they were right in the room.

The hideaway lifted, and his burrow collapsed. *Hello, little baby.*

Soft, warm hands cupped Koda into the air. He kept his eyes closed. *Whatchu doing, huh?* Giant asked sweetly in his ear. She placed him in the crook of her arm against her stomach. Koda was at peace as she hummed.

He didn't question it when the scene changed, when his eyes were suddenly open, and he saw Giant from the bottom of a cardboard box. *He's like a little polar bear!* she exclaimed. After that, he was inside his home. Giant stood above him, clasping her bleeding hand. Koda shared in the sadness showing on her face with a metallic taste in his mouth. It lessened, was almost gone, as he was returned to her hands.

I love you.

Giant lifted him to her cheek, which rose as she smiled. Eyes closed, Koda pressed lightly on her nose—she always held him a little too close—then opened his eyes again.

It wasn't Giant who was holding him.

Ablaze, Camazotz leered at him. He threw back his head, laughing, and opened his mouth wide with a shocking snap and ripping sound. Teeth raced over Koda's head, and he was swallowed up.

His scream choked as he sucked water into his lungs. It bubbled—he was thrashing in the totem's stomach acid!—but he felt cold, and fish swam about him. He floated. Surfacing, gasping for air, Koda saw a glistening reflection of a blurred forest in the water.

He splashed ashore. Pawing himself, his fur was dry. The air was still; no wind blew in the trees or in the grass. The scent of decay wrapped around him as he heard something move in the brush behind him.

Running. Trying to run faster but slowing down instead.

Why was he slowing down?! Soon, he came to a complete stop. Something made him stay still. The scent of decay strengthened. Foreboding, becoming torment. It flowed onto him and to the dirt as a shadow as tall as a giant.

Panting hard through his nose, his lungs begged him to calm down. Koda tried to close his eyes, to move his head or any of his limbs, but couldn't. *I don't want to see!*

An arm extended from the figure. A finger pointed.

What do you want?!

The colorless forest that was now becoming green raced around them, giving the illusion they were moving with it. But they *weren't* moving. Koda could barely bend his fingers. He was a ghost among the grass, feeling just himself and the figure's presence. It rolled like night chasing the sun, crossed hills and swells of land through trees of bone-shaped branches, through wild flowers and high, flat stones.

Before long the motion eased them in front of a blank, imposing structure, house-like in that it leaned upward to a point. Though it was smaller, yet it seemed very large and heavy like a leaning gargoyle. The shadows parted as if from a break in the clouds and revealed it as stone with bold columns. A deep-set door opened to a space glowing green.

The shadow pointed on the ground, then it vanished.

Koda could move again. Standing to the sky, he saw it was ridged with purple gums and rifted with teeth. Beyond, Camazotz held in his massive claws a tiny, struggling figure. *Help me!*

Sully!

The totem swallowed him up, too.

Koda woke, nearly screaming. Thinking he had screamed, he checked on Sully who went on sleeping, dead to the world (and that was the only instance in which he should be). He saw a lump in the dark: Rowan slumbering. Up in a tree, the squirrel grumbled softly in his sleep.

Koda felt something in his paw, his left one, which somehow made it worse when he looked down and almost screamed all over again. The objects themselves weren't frightening; they had given him comfort many nights. But they couldn't possibly be here!

In his paw were several pieces of bedding.

He threw the pieces down and made a little too much noise scooting away from them. He hardly had any time to think before he heard whispers from somewhere farther in the trees. Koda identified the voice as the hare's. There were pauses as if he were talking to someone. Eager to leave the area, Koda still made sure not to wake Sully. He thought it would be alright to leave him with Rowan near. Later, he would realize how trusting that was, how completely unlike him.

Koda ventured toward the whispers, keeping his pawsteps soft. The crickets droned in and out like a heartbeat. His own thudded nervously. As he rounded a grassy rise of wispy trees lighted by a distant shine, he expected the path ahead to become green as it had in his nightmare. Instead, it remained blurry and black except for a brightness in the middle of a rocky grove. Koda waited for his eyes to adjust.

A pure white hare brighter than snow, so bright it appeared to glow, whispered to the brown hare. No shadows acted upon it. Somehow, it seemed the white hare wasn't there at all but was a ghost. And yet, Koda wasn't afraid. There was a kind of beauty about that light, as well as the soft whispering. The few words he was able to discern were in Native American.

As he took a step forward, the dirt grated beneath his paw, and the white hare darted to an open hill where it vanished.

"Try to get some sleep. It isn't a luxury we'll have often," the hare said.

Found out, Koda walked toward him. "Who were you talking to?"

"My brother."

Koda froze.

"Rowan told you," the hare said, sounding neither offended nor bitter. "It is another memory taking Muraco's form."

Koda thought back to the shadow with eyes and Giant's voice. Had it been a memory taking Giant's form?

He felt a twinge of awkwardness that the hare had overheard them talking in the kitchen. "He had white fur," Koda said.

"The name Muraco means 'White Moon,'" the hare said distantly. "As you and Sully are, Muraco and I were. Hares are solitary, if you didn't know, just as I understand most rodents are. So no, we weren't brothers biologically."

The hare spoke clearly, though with a kind of heaviness to him. His ears drooped low. His shoulders sagged.

Koda asked, "How did your brother die?"

"You wouldn't like the answer."

Koda stared at the hare's back. He realized what might have happened. "A giant killed your brother."

"No, but they had their role in it."

"You can't hold a grudge for an accident—"

"It was not an accident." The reply was quick and firm.

Koda was quiet for a moment, letting irritation boil inside him. He didn't hold back his anger. "Why do all of you except Rowan hate giants?"

"I never said I hated the humans."

"But you do, don't you?"

"I won't lie and say I don't hold any anger, but it's something… I try very hard not to think about."

Koda paid close attention when the hare lifted his head to

the trees while he paused. He was quick to move his face back away from Koda's view. As the hare had always been so diligent about analyzing *him*—*He has a good eye with small details,* Koda remembered Rowan saying—he noticed how strange it was for the hare to be hiding from him, like Koda might see something in his expression. But it was then, as he listened to the hare's voice, he thought there may be something else going on other than his suspicions.

The hare said, "I neither take credit for what they have taught me, nor what hand they had in healing you. If I hated all humans, how could I be so close to Native American culture?"

Gaining strength, the hare spoke solemnly. "Muraco showed me how strongly connected we are with the older tribes. They *listen* to us, Nahiossi. Not like how you and I are listening to each other right now, but they acknowledge there is something to learn from us. We are spiritual guidance for them. Many animals want to help."

"The squirrel doesn't," Koda grumbled.

"He has not experienced what Rowan and I have. It's important to *know* these things. That there is some good where you otherwise thought was bad. I don't want to hate someone who is good and to have that hate destroy everything I know.

"I knew they hunted. But because a being eats another doesn't make them evil. Even Critters eat insects. This is something Twiggy doesn't understand. What makes a being evil is the disrespect, the sinister pleasure it has when taking a life."

Strength and tiredness battled back and forth in the hare's manner. The ears and shoulders still sagged, and Koda could tell nothing from his eyes, but there was passion in everything he said.

The hare breathed deeply. "The world is different now. There are fewer tribes, and others have drifted from their culture. We are more separate than ever. My brother wished we would have the choice to decide which world we wanted to live in."

"Is he the one who told you the stories about the Tricksters?" Koda asked.

"Yes. Among many things, he told me of the Haven. It's a world without predators we're traveling to. There, a hare's life doesn't depend on how fast he can run."

The hare sounded like he was drifting. "I always looked forward to hearing about it. The first year of a hare's life is always the hardest; not many of us survive. Especially during winters, when slush is abundant, and leverets are drowning in cold, icy mud."

Koda felt a chill and discovered the woods had become cold. Small flurries fell around them. He thought it was snowing until he saw how they disappeared when they touched the ground. He began to see phantoms—memories—in the surroundings, strange images he couldn't identify racing by in the trees. It was as if past events were unfolding in the present.

Koda's pulse beat fast. He couldn't help but be curious. "What are you thinking about?"

The hare winced and stared at the snow, not moving his head. Every hair on his body was still. Almost as if fearful to continue, he said slowly and steadily, "It was a wet winter when Muraco found me as a leveret on my own. He was searching for the opening to the Haven, and he took me along." The hare's voice hardened. "It's a trying time for everyone, and there should not have been any humans in that desolate land."

There was a pause, then a swallow that sounded sore in the hare's throat. "He seemed pressured by some increasing worry that wasn't of the weather. With each day, he grew increasingly anxious. It took us a month, crossing human houses and forests. We feared we would never find what had become so important to us. Then we found the preserve.

"Every sound and detail are clear in my mind. The sun was breaking through the overcast. We were crossing snowy grassland when we heard barking—"

The hare drew in a rattled gasp as there sounded a sharp bark and prolonged growl not five feet from where they stood. Koda ran forward to his side, shaking. He searched the surrounding dark for something snarling and frothing at the mouth.

The growl tapered. The woods were silent.

"I shouldn't be thinking about this." The hare shook his head, closed his eyes tight, and raked his nails in the dirt.

"You said they were memories," Koda said, alarmed. "Memories can't hurt you."

"This memory has been wounding me for four years," said the hare. His voice began to strain. "I think of him now because I feel so close to him."

Koda waited, frozen in place. Even though he was touching the hare, he didn't feel the need to back away.

The hare blinked at the snowflakes as they fell and disappeared on his nose, then continued. "The barking was far behind us but getting louder. Somewhere in it I heard boots stomping and the jangling of loose metal. We fled, and it surprised me when a tussock to our left exploded and dirt sprayed on Muraco's coat. The very forest air seemed to shatter in one long, piercing echo. It became clear to me that humans didn't need to run as fast to kill us. To a Critter whose feet is his only real defense, I was paralyzed to think we would die at the hand of such a weapon.

"Muraco ran into me and got me running again. When we managed to make it past the preserve fence into the trees, he urged me to run ahead and not look back. I did only part of what he asked me. Some few yards away I hid behind the bark of a peeling tree. Down on the slope Muraco hid in a tussock. The snow wasn't terribly thick, it clung to the grass like dew drops, and there were no pawsteps to trace either of us.

"The barking turned from eager to anxious, but the dog had

stopped advancing. The forest went quiet. Then I heard a twig break. About ten yards directly across from Muraco was a human wearing brown fur so lengthy it curtained his legs. He was standing behind a large tree, weapon lowered, I assumed, as it wasn't in sight. A hood covered his head, and his hands were in his pockets. I wondered how he'd managed to cross the field without my hearing. To this day I've never been able to explain him being there."

Tensed, Koda expected to see the giant appear behind one of the trees.

"Muraco had seen him. With his speed he could easily make it over the slope. He saw me. We held eye contact, and I could see my brother thinking it. What we both didn't realize was that the human wearing fur wasn't the human carrying the gun."

The hare's voice strickened with grief. "My brother peered out of the tussock, and the human shot him. It and its dog had been hiding in the field. They hadn't even tried to cross it. But the shot didn't kill Muraco; it had grazed his shoulder. Though I could see it had dazed him, since he wasn't nearly as fast as he ran.

"The dog ran past the fence. Kicking up snow, it made such a terrible noise—"

The hare paused as if expecting to hear the dog again. Nothing happened, and he continued with a troubled breath. "After the human had let my brother suffer, it climbed the fence, grabbed him by his legs and stuffed him in a bag. I watched them leave. I just stayed there, like a coward. I didn't know what to do with him gone."

Koda stared out at the grove, feeling a way he had never felt before and repeating the hare's words over and over again in his mind.

"Eventually, Twiggy found me. It didn't take him long to figure out why I was staying, and he convinced me to travel the rest of the way to the mountain pass. Seeing the Haven doesn't mean as much to me as it did. But others have a right to see it, to live a life they deserve."

Jack said, bowing his head, "I wish that wasn't the last I'd seen of him. Muraco… he— It tore him apart!"

His voice raised with an anguish Koda hadn't ever heard. He lingered quietly for a moment more, then softly moved away and retrieved Rowan to trade shifts. He didn't say anything of their conversation or the state Jack was in. Rowan left, and Koda couldn't fall back to sleep until sometime later when Jack returned to the group.

16
AGAIN-WALKER

F LAMES SWISHED smoke and embers at Sydney's perch on a tree. As the bristles caught fire, she could feel the heat cooking the bark and scrambled under the low hanging branches for safety. Her perch tilted downward, dipping her over the grass roasting below.

Her nails slipped. Hanging by her fingers, Sydney clawed fitfully. Orange light flashed everywhere with a rushing roar and popping. She hooked her nails in the twigs, climbed over and maneuvered the end branches until she was near enough to the ground.

She jumped off and landed in the grass several feet from the fire. Pinecones continued to pop like roasting chestnuts. Within minutes the tree flared like a candle wick. Sydney's beard was as black as the ashy pile off to the side. Smoke drifted into the sky. An ugly shade of purple was made uglier by bizarre face constellations. They glared down at her. Sydney glared back.

"You don't see *that* every day." If this was indeed Insect-Giver's house, she wouldn't be happy when she returned.

Positive that Yellow Eyes was done in, Sydney benefited from the fire's warmth. She scratched her back with her leg. *Stupid soup bath. It's made me itchy.*

She turned in the direction of the woods. A short while ago she had seen the rodents and their three travel buddies enter. The odd thing was, the woods were blurry and bleak like the house. But she couldn't care to wonder why for longer than a few seconds.

Belly warm, Sydney scuttled through the grass. *Now to get those pests.* As she followed their scent trail into the woods, she heard a noise from the pile, like the wood had lifted. She dismissed it as the house settling.

***

Sully dreamed of the dragon peering out at him from her cage. Fright consumed him. The dragon's eyes flicked at something behind him, and her claw reached up to the glass. Reflected there, Sully saw Hototo stalking toward the bed. As the owl was about to run under it, someone pawed him awake. Sully jolted upright.

"Sully, Jack wants to move again," Koda said. In the background, Sully heard Rowan and Jack moving around.

Sully rubbed his eyes in a hurry to see his brother. The bad feeling lingered. It disturbed him to think he had left the dream before he could squeak, and a dream Koda was left on his own. Guilt ate at him again. It felt as if it had grown into a large lump in his heart. To tell Koda the truth, that he had been too scared to save him from Hototo that night, had slipped his mind. *I will. When we find the next relic, for sure. There's nothing bad about waiting a little bit, is there?* He thought he was being untruthful, and it troubled him more that he still couldn't confess.

"Did you have a nightmare?" Koda asked.

A little light had broken through the canopy, allowing them to see each other. Sully wished he hadn't looked so frightened. "I… think so." *Please don't ask what it was about.*

"What was it about?"

206

Sully sank inside. He wasn't going to lie. "It's... It's too scary t-to talk about."

Koda examined him. It might have been Sully's imagination, but he thought he looked hurt, sad. He most likely knew Sully was lying. "I had a nightmare, too," Koda said. "Could you move in yours? Was there a shadow?"

"Twiggy!" Rowan called, startling them.

Twiggy half fell, half scuttled down from a nearby tree. "What hornet's nest are we off to now?" he asked. Koda frowned at him as he and Rowan joined them.

"Huh?" Sully said. Twiggy had said a few peculiar phrases so far. They reminded Sully of giant phrases but translated to animal speak. Did Twiggy know that?

Rowan shook his head and winked at Sully. Apparently not. Rowan might have had something to do with the phrases.

Sully searched for Jack. He heard him walking over very softly, and he wondered if Jack had gotten a good sleep. "Are there any major locations nearby to your Giant's nest?" he asked.

Sully stated he didn't think so. "Giant said the nest was 'off-the-grid.' I think that means we're far away from where other giants live."

"We're done with human hovels," Twiggy said emphatically. "Didn't you guys ever go out and explore the woods?"

"Why would we do that?" Sully glanced nervously in the direction of Koda's irritated voice.

"We'll stumble upon somethin'," Rowan assured them a little half-heartedly, as if he predicted it would be unpleasant.

The land mimicked the roller coaster as they set out, sending the Critters on a ride of lumps and miniature hills. Wandering in the woods brought ugly memories to Sully of being alone in the national forest and overwhelmed by new scents. Here it was the complete opposite. The woods hardly smelled of anything. There

207

were no animal markings besides their own. The woodpecker they heard earlier was probably just a "sound memory," Sully thought, if there was such a thing. As the night darkened, he heard only his and the others' pawsteps (again the crickets had quieted), and he saw only vague, dark shapes.

"Where are we now?" Sully asked as they came to a stop. The path ahead formed an even lower canopy and was drawn in by curved trees. Since they were in shadow, Sully imagined them to be the ribs of an elephant.

Rowan answered, "The trees are gettin' dense. They're a bit odd. Maybe we should detour?"

"What do you mean by odd?" asked Jack.

"They remind me of bones."

Koda made a brief alarmed sound.

Sully stiffened. He heard Twiggy turn sharply. "What? What, did you see something?" Twiggy asked.

Koda urged, "We have to turn back."

"You recognize this area?" Rowan asked.

"Yes!"

"Well, is someone going to chase us?" Twiggy asked, impatient.

"Don't jinx it!" Koda snapped. "That part hasn't happened yet."

Twiggy complained to Sully, "Your brother isn't making any sense."

"Did you get scared of the trees, Koda?" Sully asked.

"The trees were in my nightmare."

"Oh, come on! Is that what this is? You're scaring us over a nightmare?" Twiggy said.

"How did I know these trees were here then, huh?"

"You live around here!"

"I told you we never went outside!"

"Quit that carryin' on," Rowan hushed them. "If we're seein' things outside of this dream, you need to tell us about it."

Reluctantly, Koda briefed them on his nightmare. He started at the pond, then how he hadn't been able to run away and someone foul smelling he couldn't see had taken him to a menacing structure. Sully shivered. *I really wish he had told us when it was bright out,* he thought.

"What do you reckon we ought to do, Jack?" Rowan asked.

"I think we should take a vote on this one."

"I'm inclined to go there," Rowan said. "As far as I'm concerned, we've got no other leads. Someone went out of their way to tip him off. I say let's check it out."

"They weren't friendly," Koda objected.

"It's stupid to take directions from an imaginary creature," said Twiggy.

"Then you and Koda are both against the idea," Rowan said. "Jack?"

"They could be setting us up, though we have no other leads. I agree with you."

Rowan said, "That leaves you to break the tie, Sully."

Sully shifted uncomfortably. He felt everyone's eyes on him, especially Koda's. *The shadow didn't sound very nice*, he thought. *What if it wasn't trying to help Koda?* However, in the end, he caved under the pressure.

"I… guess we don't know where to go… Maybe we should see if there's a Cracker Jack where the structure is," Sully said.

"Three to two. Let's go," Rowan said. He and Jack began walking again. Muttering, Twiggy followed.

Koda asked Sully, "Why didn't you say no?" Unhappy about the situation, Sully didn't answer.

Several times Rowan confirmed with Koda that their course was on track. The nightmare had been very vivid, Koda said, and he had no doubt which paths to take. He led them to a tree line. Dreary light from an overcast sky appeared, lightening the scene before them in muted color. Wild flowers, pale blue and clear, edged an open field of dead grass.

Sully gasped in fright.

Tombstones marked the land.

"Is this where you were taken?" Rowan asked Koda in a slightly disturbed voice.

"I hadn't been able to tell it was a cemetery," Koda said, aghast.

Sully asked softly, "Why's everything clear and not black-and-white all of a sudden?"

"You didn't mention a cemetery nearby. This may not have existed in the human world," Jack said.

Rowan stepped past a tombstone. The grass crunched like dead leaves. "Let's hurry through it and find the structure."

Do we have to? Sully thought with dread.

Twiggy asked Rowan, "Having second thoughts?"

"I admit it's not an ideal place…"

"It would be a clever spot for a relic. Look hard at the gifts," Jack said.

The gifts scattered among the tombstones ranged from dead flowers and clothes to small miscellaneous objects that at one time, Sully thought, probably belonged to the deceased Tricksters. On every tombstone (each unnamed and without an inscription) was a green candle. From afar they had made the acre appear as if it were ablaze from a green wildfire.

All of it made Sully think there were other Tricksters who cared about those that had died. He wasn't sure why he hadn't thought so before; maybe it just seemed Tricksters were too busy causing mischief. But looking at the tombstones and gifts, he realized at least some of them weren't all about mischief and nothing else. Despite their not-so-friendly experience with the Tricksters, he was saddened, and he thought it unfair to think of them as bad creatures.

Was there someone who would remember the two Tricksters who had been killed by Camazotz? Sully certainly would remember, and he plucked two wildflowers and set them beside a tombstone where he thought they looked nice.

Gradually the grass thickened and grew tall. Weeds and hedge leaves brushed Sully. He had the sensation he was traveling in a dying jungle. It all seemed very deserted and there were no signs of danger. Sully spread out a little from the group.

Koda didn't stray from his side. "What are you doing? That thing is somewhere out here," he whispered, agitated.

"I don't smell anything bad. I'm okay. I've been on my own before," Sully said.

"It's not smart going off on your own."

Sully felt a stab of frustration. "*You* went somewhere. I woke up when you came back to tell Rowan to switch places."

Koda's expression changed to one of having been caught.

"Where did you go? Did you talk to Jack?" Sully asked.

"Why would I be doing that? I told you. They're animals."

The grass in front of them rustled. Twiggy entered the patch. He gave Koda a dirty look, then ran off in another direction.

Sully said to Koda, "That wasn't nice."

"I hope you mean the squirrel."

Sully hadn't. To tell the truth, he wished they would just get along.

They passed a tombstone. It had been blocking the shape of a very large, very dark structure. Sully looked up to see if a cloud was casting an abnormally black shadow and saw a misty sky, that was all. So, it surprised him when a scrolling movement, very much like a cloud passing overhead, cleared the blackness away.

Close, high off the ground, was a mausoleum. The facing wall loomed like a gigantic slab. Rain water stained it from an overhanging stone roof that draped a heavy shadow over the door. Roman-like, weather-beaten columns stood solidly in front.

"That! Over here!" Koda exclaimed.

Twiggy, Rowan, and Jack hurried to them and slowed upon the sight. For once Sully went first. Followed quickly by the others, he climbed the marble steps to the open metal door. It slanted into the wall and was cut with vine work and crosses like a vintage iron fence. Sully sniffed dust and old, crumbling concrete.

Koda said to Twiggy, "Do you believe me now?"

Twiggy looked at him, then up at the mausoleum's cracked roof. "I hate human structures."

Rowan pushed the door open into a glowing room.

Twiggy warned, "I'm not really sure we should go in there."

He went quiet as Rowan walked in anyway. Sully, now a little hesitant, didn't mind walking in second.

Inside, the space was actually narrow with walls made up of coffins. Sully tried not to smell what was in them. He saw Koda panic for a second as he probably mistook the dry rotting scent for the one in his nightmare. Rowan and Jack coughed, and Twiggy covered his nose. The room ended about seven feet in, where they found the source of the light. A rectangular opening in the floor glowed mysteriously of the eerie seafoam green.

"We're gonna go down there?" Sully asked reluctantly.

Twiggy's tail bunched like a chameleon's tail curl. "There's probably a whole lot of those weirdos ready to ambush us! I'm not going through another Bozo fiasco."

A dull croak came from Sully's throat.

"There ain't nothin' more terrifyin' than our escape from that house." Rowan stared at the opening. "What could be down there?"

Sully scanned what small knowledge he had of mausoleums. Was there really supposed to be anything beneath it?

Rowan kicked a chunk of concrete into the opening. A small clattering sound echoed back at them.

"I hope it hit one of them in the face," Twiggy said gruffly.

"Doesn't sound that far." Rowan stepped forward and tumbled head first. The sound was like a bag of flour dropping.

"Rowan!" Sully and Twiggy exclaimed. Jack and Koda jumped forward.

Standing up, Rowan called stiffly, "I'm okay!"

In the echo, a faint unknown voice gave Sully a start.

"Who's that?" Twiggy asked, sounding on the verge of panic.

Someone replied, "Who's that?"

The Critters recoiled.

"They won't bother us," Rowan assured. "I'll stand below the hole."

"I'll stand below the hole," repeated another voice.

"How many are down there?" Twiggy whined.

Jack didn't wait for an answer. He jumped down onto Rowan's back before hopping to the floor, then looked around.

Twiggy leaned over the opening, his paws folded. "Jack?"

"Everything's fine." Jack called for Sully and Koda to jump, and he caught them as they slid off Rowan's back.

Tricksters covered the walls of a squared-off tunnel. Their heads stuck out like door knockers. Except for the green blush of their faces, they were uniform in color to blend in with the rock. They came in a variety: some with blunt noses and puckered lips, others without eyelids. They gawked at the Critters in static comical expressions of surprise.

Twiggy jumped onto Rowan's head. His eyes widened, but as he found out the Tricksters couldn't move, he said haughtily,

213

"These are Tricksters I can get used to. Immobile, so they can't harass anyone."

Rowan lowered Twiggy to the floor. The tunnel forked two ways in a Y shape like a snake's tongue. Within both paths, a seemingly endless line of Tricksters trailed out of sight.

"Which one do we take?" Rowan asked.

"Which one do we take?"

"Stop repeating what we're saying!" Twiggy ordered. "You're annoying!"

"You're annoying."

Twiggy chittered.

Three Tricksters, who seemed in mockery of the Three Wise Monkeys, were set in a frieze-like section above the fork. One peeled its eyes down, another cupped its hands around its mouth as if to yell, and the last cupped an ear as if to hear some gossip. See evil, speak evil, hear evil, as it were. They rhythmed in clownish sing-song voices:

> *"Choose wisely and you'll find a surprise…*
> *Pick another and meet your demise.*
> *Dear me! Wouldn't want to pick the wrong one!*
> *HA! Haha haaaaa!"*

The laughter constricted as the Tricksters tried to hold a long note.

"Oh, put a sock in it," Twiggy snapped. "No one likes you, Tricksters."

"Don't pay them any mind," Jack said. "Did you receive any directions beyond this point, Nahiossi?"

"No," Koda said.

Sully noticed his brother acting especially awkward around Jack, and Jack in a similar muted way. He wondered why.

"It's a fifty-fifty chance. Let's just go for it," Rowan said.

"Just go for it," one Trickster agreed.

Jack hopped to the fork. "I hear water dripping in the right tunnel, and there's almost nothing in the left."

Wary, Koda said, "Listen, we don't do well with water."

"Yes, little gremlins," said Rowan. "Out of courtesy for the youngins, better pick the latter."

Sully walked behind Jack and Rowan to the left tunnel, passing a chain of faces on the slim vertical wall between the tunnels.

The faces chimed, "Hehe. Goodbye, little Critters! You have something delightfully fun coming to yooou!"

Sully sped up a little.

Keeping conversation to a minimum, the Critters avoided the Tricksters echoing what they said. Twiggy glared at them, and in return, the Tricksters stuck their tongues out. It wasn't so bad compared to walking on the street with them, but still, Sully was uncomfortable. At least before he hadn't felt so trapped with the sky overhead. With graves above them and only the creepy tunnel ahead, he kept expecting something dead to pop up from around one of the corners. Though nothing had happened yet, Sully remembered bad things usually occur at the front and rear of a group, so he quickly chose to walk in the middle.

The tunnel curved multiple times before Jack abruptly stopped. Sully smelled something unpleasant.

He heard the start of Twiggy's strange purring. His friend whispered hoarsely, "Something's died down there!"

"It's the shadow thing. It smelled exactly like this," Koda said, distressed.

Rowan had been guarding the rear. "It gave you directions. It oughtn't be a hindrance to us."

"There aren't so many Tricksters on the wall, Rowan,"

Twiggy said. "Why do you think that is?"

The tunnel had grown dark as the Tricksters thinned out. The last of them scrunched their noses and clamped their mouths closed as if trying not to breathe in the stink. It came from farther down, where the darkness crept in. Koda and Twiggy warned them again. Sully thought about changing his vote. But the group traveled on, and the stink of decay thickened like mud.

The tunnel widened to a chamber of connecting rooms. Torches created crisp brightness against the dark. For a moment, it seemed like they were standing in a crude medieval underground. But if Sully were to close his eyes, he could almost imagine he was in an old, dusty library as his senses filled with limestone dust. That is, if it weren't for the decay.

Sully released a sudden cry.

Critter skulls filled the chamber floor to ceiling.

Twiggy lapsed into a barking fit, fueling Sully's shock. The intense shadows made the skulls even more gruesome, if that were possible, as each crooked jaw overlapped the next skull to appear as if they were eating each other. Rowan took an involuntary step back. Eventually, he and Jack were able to hush Twiggy.

Koda asked in a staggered voice, "Are they real?"

"They can't be!" Twiggy sounded sick.

Sully glanced at Jack. His ears were folded, and he muttered nervously to himself.

Rowan examined a porcupine skull on the floor by the entry. The teeth behind the large incisors clamped together in what looked to be a grimacing smile. "It's either a very realistic trick or..." He stomped on the remains. Unlike the trophy at the fun house, it didn't throw powder into the air.

"Rowan!" Twiggy scolded him.

"I'm sorry. I had to check—"

"DO NOT TOUCH THEM!"

The piercing voice full of rage startled Sully badly. A violent tremble shook the chamber as a wall collapsed from a huge impact. Within one of the rooms Sully glimpsed the presence, which seemed to be more than a shadow, with a swollen and blue fist held over the broken wall. The presence stood lanky and tall like a skeleton, with a thin layer of skin the color of pale wild flowers.

That was all Sully was able to see before his mind reeled. He crumpled onto the floor, uttering a garbled sound. His vision glazed red.

Chaos. Koda rushed to him. "What's wrong with Sully?!"

The words may as well have been in another language. Sully didn't understand anything. It was as if all thought, everything that had made him *him*, was going away, caused by some intense blow. Like he had been stunned onto near death.

"Close your eyes!" A rabbit pressed his face to him.

An animal with horns shouted. What kind of animal was that? It shoved something small that was yelling. Meanwhile, Sully's heart raced, and he lurched. "Uck… Uck…"

More shouting. Vision going dark red. *"Sully, stop! Stop it!"*

Sully's bones stiffened. He felt empty, like the skeleton in the chamber. For the first thirty seconds, he continued to rock on the floor like a rattling bone.

As the pain reached its peak, a kind of reverse blow stunned Sully out of whatever had just happened to him. He exhaled, suddenly and deeply, as if he had been holding his breath for a long time, and thoughts began to return to him. Slowly he unclenched his body, he breathed choppily, and his friends—he could recognize them now—materialized out of the red haze that was now fading to normal colors.

They all stood above him. Koda was hunched on his feet. Shaken, Sully didn't look anyone in the face.

As he moved to stand up, Jack pawed him lightly down.

"Don't," he said. Sully could now understand his words.

"That is your vorning," the presence said icily.

Sully thought there was something wrong with his hearing or that there were *two* presences; he heard *two* voices speaking in animal speak and in giant speak with what sounded like an Irish accent. But he smelled only one presence.

Twiggy struggled to speak past his barks. "*Kuk! Kuk!* Sully… hasn't… done anything! What did you do to him?!"

Jack stared at the ground. "Is he healed?" he asked the presence. His paws slightly trembled.

"Yes. Look no more, and do not anger me. I am the guardian of these skulls. I vill not permit you to damage them further!"

"What in the Sam Hill?" Rowan said in a shocked, distressed voice. "There's no green glow in here. It's not a Trickster."

Koda inspected Sully's face. He gasped uncontrollably from his tears, and his eyes were the widest they had ever been.

"I'm okay," Sully said. He tried not to move. His brain felt loose in his head, and he tried very hard not to cry.

Jack demanded in a firm, loud voice, "What other purpose do you have?"

"I am sent to you as a guide in your wravel through the catacombs."

"Who sent you?"

"That information is friwolous."

"Who sent you?" Jack repeated.

"Nameless," the presence answered irritably.

Sully guessed that meant it didn't know. He winced as he prepared for it to shout again and kept his eyes closed.

"If you were sent as a guide, where were you at the fork?" asked Jack.

"My reach is limited to the resting places of the dead and your dreams."

Sully said shakily, "I'll never sleep again."

"Why are these skulls here?" Jack demanded.

The presence answered, "It is not my place to question."

"Are these all of them?"

"There are more."

Twiggy's nails scraped the ground.

"How long have you guarded them?" asked Jack.

"For the entirety of my existence."

"That would be…?"

"Four years to this day."

Rowan turned his head sharply, and seeming to remember he wasn't supposed to look, he stopped at his shoulder to observe Jack. His friend stood as rigid as a mannequin. One touch, and he might fall over. Sully didn't even dare touch Twiggy. By the look in his eyes, Twiggy was likely to bite anything that got too close to him. Even Koda stiffened.

"What?" Sully asked.

No one answered him.

He listened for grinding teeth as the presence said viciously, "The skulls are meant to remain vhere they lie."

"My friend thought they were false. We will not interfere," Jack promised.

Rowan and Twiggy breathed hard through their noses. Sully waited fretfully.

"Wery vell. I vill take you."

Sully flinched uncontrollably at the sound of a lightweight stomp and drag. The presence limped farther into the chamber.

"Take us where?" Twiggy said in a high, strained voice.

"We'd be better off goin' back to the fork," Rowan stressed.

"You heard the Tricksters. There's doom and everything in that other tunnel," said Twiggy. "And for sure you're not making it back out through the ceiling."

Jack said, "It's best we go on."

"What are you saying?" Twiggy asked hoarsely.

"This is serious. We've stumbled onto quite possibly the worst thing we could find, and the only way we're going to find out why is from this creature."

"How are we gonna follow it if we can't look at it?" Rowan asked.

"We can on the odor alone. Keep your eyes closed. In case there happens to be light, it's too risky to keep them open."

Twiggy gently grabbed Sully under the arms and helped him stand. Sully waited for his brain to slide out of his ear, but he was stable, if not a little shaken up, and it already seemed as if he had simply fainted. He kept his eyes closed very tightly, however, as they left the chamber, distancing themselves from the presence by the volume of its footsteps. But because of their caution, the pace was painfully slow. Sully was sickened, not only by the smell, but to be venturing the catacombs blind. It was a place that could go on in darkness forever, because it was locked away from the world, from fresh air.

They had long since departed the room when Twiggy exclaimed, "I can't stand it!"

"My sense of smell is better than yours," Rowan said. He coughed.

"Jack, what are we doing trusting this thing?" Twiggy cried.

"Allow me to ask Nahiossi something," said Jack. "When you woke, was there an object you recognized from your night-mare?"

Koda took a moment to respond. When he did, he talked low and uneasily. "There was a piece of bedding. The stuff Giant fills our homes with," he said.

"How did it get there?" Sully asked, a little disconcerted himself.

"The object was given to validate Nahiossi's nightmare," Jack said, "so he would not dismiss it as being unreal. It intends to aid us."

Rowan kicked something like a lightweight rock. A small skull immediately came to Sully's mind.

"You're familiar with this creature," Rowan said.

"It's an aptrgangr."

"What's that?" Sully asked.

"Aptrgangrs, translated as 'again-walkers,' are Icelandic creatures," Jack said. Sully was pretty sure Icelandic and Irish weren't the same and rethought the accent. Jack continued, "They're often raised from the dead to protect their possessions or others'."

Sully caught himself as his eyes began to widen. "He's a *zombie?*"

"I'm not sure what you mean."

"I've got this one," said Rowan. "I reckon you could call him an old-world zombie. The original."

Sully had never heard of one you couldn't look at. "The zombies I heard about are bad."

"It depends on who they were when alive," Jack said.

"The possessions, the skulls. Did a Critter summon the aptrgangr somehow?" Rowan wondered.

"Other than Native Americans, I don't know of another living being that would value them. But it's peculiar the way they are displayed."

"I don't think a Critter would do that," Sully said. It seemed disrespectful to him.

"I agree," Jack said. "Perhaps it's an effect done by the world. Four years old… If that's true, they were killed long before the disaster."

"The skulls are fake," Twiggy insisted. "Those Tricksters put them there!"

"They're real, Twiggy," Jack said. "We can't deny it no matter how devastating."

"Then that thing murdered them!"

"I saw claw marks on those skulls. Whatever the aptrgangr is, it's likely both human and animal-like, considering its speech."

Sully admired Jack's attentiveness. He hadn't noticed the markings. "I saw an arm. It kind of looked like a giant's. I think it… walked like one, too."

"Even if the aptrgangr has anything like human hands, they don't have strong enough nails to make that deep a cut," Jack said.

"If it's anything like a human, I don't want to be following it anywhere!" Twiggy snapped.

There was a pause in the stomp and drag sound. Everyone came to a halt as they heard something crack like a joint popping out of place. The aptrgangr stood still ahead.

Sully swallowed. A scrape, then a drag, and the pattern continued.

Slowly, the Critters resumed walking.

"Is it your intention," Jack said. "to leave us stranded or worse?"

"I care about what happened to those Critters. 'We care for our own,' remember?" Twiggy sounded like he was glaring at Jack.

"Yes," Jack said evenly. "Which is precisely why we should be more careful of our actions."

Silence from Twiggy, as if he were thinking things. Sully felt very uncomfortable. "You wouldn't do anything, would you? Not even if you *knew* it was human," Twiggy said.

Rowan's head moved down above them. He scolded Twiggy, "Hey, remember who you're—"

Twiggy raised his voice. "Doesn't it make you angry, seeing them in there like that? Does *anything* make you angry at *all?*"

The outburst nearly caused Sully to open his eyes. He could feel the anger coming off Twiggy, and he shied away from him to feel for Jack's paw.

"You're supposed to be on our side! You—for sure!—if it was going to be anybody." Sully heard Rowan's hoof lift off the floor, a quick movement, as he tried to touch Twiggy in effort to quiet him. "No!" Twiggy cried defiantly. "Jack, you came to the mountain pass and started teaching everyone to *like* them. That's like telling baby ducks that foxes are their friends to the point they trust them enough to walk into their mouths."

Twiggy ran ahead, and Jack stopped as if he had cut across his path. Twiggy's watery and constricted voice rang harshly in the tunnel. "That's what happens to Critters who like humans. That's why it happened to Muraco, and if you go back to the human world, you're going to end up—"

"Don't you *ever,*" Jack raised his voice, lunging forward at Twiggy, "talk about my brother that way. He's not a *FOOL.*"

The word sliced the air. The others had stopped as well, and they stood in silence.

Sully listened for Twiggy. "I'm not going on," Twiggy said in a completely dead and hurt tone. He ran down the tunnel. Sully and Rowan called for him to stop, and a short time later, he did. Sully could hear him crying.

Rowan stepped up to Jack. "He isn't right to talk like that."

"What's wrong with Twiggy?" Sully asked in a small voice.

"He's been upset by the skulls," Jack said in an equally pained voice.

Sully worried about what Twiggy had said. What did he mean? He turned to Koda—maybe he would know—but his brother had been very quiet since the skull room. Sully hoped he

223

hadn't scared him too badly.

As he turned, the black behind his eyelids brightened. A dim light entered the tunnel, and the aptrgangr's footsteps stopped.

"A chamber is here," it said. "I am to show you vhat is inside."

***

Sydney was hot on the rodents' trail. Their scents had been changing frequently, and now it contained an assortment of things: blood (*had one been injured?*), pumpkin, cotton candy...? Also smoke (admittedly that may still be lingering in her own nose), and their rodent oils, which smelled like pooling grease. But she was sure they tasted a whole lot better.

Surprisingly, the trail was more potent than it usually was, what with the many forest scents missing in the air. The warmth in her belly kept her wide awake as the trees trapped the darkest shadows. *Like I need the light. I can practically see the stink cloud coming off those rodents.*

Sydney was pleased to find them asleep in a grove. She had gotten very close to the fat one, and for the first time, she wondered about the goat and rabbit lying nearby. The rodent would make a lot of noise.

Annoyed, she decided to wait for when, at some inopportune moment, they were to separate, and she couldn't be interfered with. She made sure to camp out a way, bored to death while they slept for an incredibly long while as if to inconvenience her. Then, when they woke up, Sydney stalked them at a distance as silently as she could, which was hard since the itching had only gotten worse.

She hid in the wild flowers until she saw the Critters enter a mausoleum. After a few minutes of anticipation, she crept slowly up the steps, found an opening to a tunnel, and jumped down.

The landing was a little hard on her belly. Sydney licked the floor. The trail had strangely gone, and there were two paths to choose from. More glowing creatures bearing deformed faces gawked at her stupidly on the walls. Three above the tunnels chimed:

"Choose wisely and you'll find a surprise…
Pick another and meet your—"

"More of you?" Sydney interrupted. "You see a whole farm go by here? There were two rodents. One's small, and the other has eaten too much cheese."

"The other has eaten too much cheese," the three repeated.

"That's what I said. Which way did they go?" Sydney demanded.

"Which way did they go?"

"I'm asking *you!*"

"The lizard, she seeks the Critters."

"*Bearded dragon.*" Sydney frowned and scratched her back. "Where's the exit? It's humid in here!"

"No cheating is allowed. No hint may you have."

Sydney's beard started to flare, then she sneered. "I take it the three of you can't move out of that wall," she said. "Captured prey is always the most fun."

Their jaws dropped.

"Always the most fun," a glowing face said on the wall next to Sydney.

"Yep. I'll use the faces below you as a step ladder."

The three gulped. "They went right."

Grinning, Sydney went into the right tunnel. "Suckers."

She expected to catch the rodents' scents almost immediately. Instead, there was only damp rock. She was sure of herself, though. They couldn't be that far.

Entering from a low passage, she was welcomed by the sight of a lake within an enormous, elongated cavern gleaming gold. Creamy stalactites dangled overhead, casting a reflection in the water which was like molten honey, and hung as a drapery behind the lake. A hole in the ceiling with the stalactites poking out from it shone brilliantly like a gigantic geode.

"I've seen better."

Sydney walked through the stalagmites on the stippled floor until she reached the lake; it stretched far down until the darkness turned the honey color into an aged amber. Before taking a drink from the lake, Sydney gazed at her attractive reflection.

She pulled away abruptly. A burning itch flared in her back, then outward to her limbs, to her face.

"These… stupid… itches!" Sydney scratched fiercely. "It's the humidity! It's making it worse!"

She squirmed and bent and scratched, feeling tremendously flaky as her shed skin peeled like tape from her body. None of it came off in patches. She simply wiggled out of it, pulling her arms and legs in as if from a sleeve. With a short, irritated puff, Sydney freed herself and, turning around, stared at the shed, amazed.

It was a replica of herself, body pattern perfectly duplicated, hollow and see-through like a snakeskin. All somebody had to do was fill it with cotton or beads, and they'd have a Sydney stuffed animal.

"I've peeled in patches but never a full body suit!" Sydney exclaimed. But though her clone was beautiful, nothing was prettier than the real her.

It was also creepy to look at. Sydney exited the cavern through another passage.

Once she left, the Sydney replica twitched.

***

Sully and his friends were about to enter the chamber when the tunnel jerked and shook. They stumbled and jittered on their feet.

"What now?" Twiggy cried.

A blast resounded above, followed by an earsplitting sound—through rock, dirt, and skeletons shaking in their graves, and through the sky above. Sully couldn't explain it, but it was like hearing a sound from space, a sound which could be entirely separate from the universe. Yet it plunged into the catacombs with the power and shock of a billion drills—or the shock of lighting striking a tree. He had felt such power during the flood, when he had smelled burnt wood. Rowan and Jack fell back as rock dove through the ground above, thundering on its way to the tunnel.

Sully screamed, "Cave-in!"

"Sully!"

Koda wasn't beside him. Sully had been walking ahead.

"Su—"

Koda's shout cut short as the tunnel caved.

17
SOMETHING IN THE WATER

"**H**E'S GONE!" Koda paced along the sloping mound of rock. It filled the chamber's entrance, teeming onto the floor and blowing dirt at him. He and Jack had run inside.

"Nahiossi," Jack said, not shouting, but with a distressed edge to his voice.

Koda dug at the smallest stones. They struck him as they fell from the wall of rock. "Sully!"

"We'll find him, Nahiossi. *You need to stop.*"

Koda spun around into Jack's face. "He could've been smashed in the cave-in!"

Jack pawed his head, and Koda flinched. He was a raw nerve. Dusty torchlight drifted through the air, as well as the stench of decay. The aptrgangr was in the chamber.

"We don't know that," Jack said.

Suppose Sully was alive? "Another totem has been destroyed," Koda said. "He needs me!"

Jack spoke with a measured calmness. "I know, and it's hard for you. Sully has been brave. Until we can get to him, he knows what to do on his own. You need to have confidence in him."

That's when this whole mess started. When they hadn't been together, and Sully had continuously gone off without him, doing these dangerous, stupid things. Koda had told him to stay together in the tunnel. And the one time he had allowed himself to lose track of him, wary to race ahead because of the aptrgangr, this had happened.

"He should have been walking with me. He's always wanted to get into trouble, but he doesn't listen to me at all anymore! You've done something to him. He's not the same!"

"You're used to him depending on you," Jack said, as if he were finally understanding. "Would you have him helpless without you?"

The anger was boiling, and yet Koda couldn't speak. He turned away.

"He is not. He has learned he can travel an entire forest, if he must, to save his brother." Jack paused, very quiet in front of him. "And we did give him strength while he cried over you. But we've not taken away your bond."

Koda's anger fell away so suddenly and with such heartache that he couldn't breathe. He sank onto his haunches. *I don't want to be here.* And more than because of Sully—because his eyes were flooding, and he couldn't wipe them without shame in Jack's presence.

Surprising him, Jack pressed his nose gently on his head. There was no feeling of dread or dislike. Koda only felt comfort.

Jack backed away. "He may have Rowan and Twiggy with him." There was worry in his voice, and Koda was ashamed he hadn't thought of the others sooner.

Jack said, "Aptrgangr, you have immense strength. You cannot take us through this rock, but I'm assuming the left wall of the chamber connects to the other half of the tunnel."

The aptrgangr answered defiantly, "You are correct. You are vrong in that I vould. The skulls vill remain untouched and undamaged."

"Are there tunnels that lead to our friends?" Jack pressed.

"You vould take your chances. My place is vith the dead's remains. I cannot wenture those vays."

"What good are you?" Koda snapped.

The creature seemed indifferent to the question and replied, "I am to show you vhat is in the chamber."

"Jack, we have to get to Sully," Koda pleaded.

A reply didn't come immediately, and he was frightened that Jack had given up hope. "Please hide yourself, aptrgangr." He added to Koda, "It's in our best interest to stay a little while."

The stench weakened slightly as the aptrgangr walked away from them. Koda panicked, then focused on Jack's tone of voice. He had sounded subtly cautious.

"Open your eyes, Nahiossi. Do it carefully."

Remembering the horrendous state Sully had been in when he saw the creature, Koda was reluctant.

"The aptrgangr is hidden. You are safe," Jack said.

Koda opened his eyes slowly. As he stood to peer over the rocks on the floor, an object raised into view on the chamber's right wall. It was wedged in a moose's eye and was the color of bone. He had almost missed it.

The third relic.

Jack nodded. The aptrgangr may or may not have something to say about removing it, regardless of it not being a Critter's remains. Jack chiseled his teeth around the relic to ease it from the wall. It popped out loudly.

He gave it to Koda, who hastily pouched it. He prepared himself for the rumbling that occurred before a Cracker Jack appeared. He listened. The chamber went undisturbed.

Fear jolted him as the aptrgangr spoke. "Center chamber," it said in some weird, calm anticipation.

Koda estimated the chamber was at least double the size of the previous one. No space was left uncovered. In fact, the skulls were packed tighter together, their jaws cracked and almost separated. As they walked to the center where a thick rectangular stone rested like a sacrificial table, they avoided stepping on fragments of jaws and teeth that had fallen from the skulls above. Low as the stone was, Koda couldn't see on top without climbing it. He hadn't any idea what it was they were meant to see.

Jack reached the stone. Koda guessed he was examining it. Then, taking an involuntary stumble backward, he released a strangled cry.

Koda asked, fitfully, on the verge of running, "Is it dangerous? What did you see?"

Jack bent his head to the side. His ears swayed. His whole body trembled. There was a grievous, wide shock to his eyes. As he hadn't fled, Koda was convinced enough to climb the stone.

A rabbit's—or hare's—skeleton lay in pieces. Deep grooves sliced the bones in crazed patterns. *Those are Hunter marks.*

A small groove smeared across the shoulder bone took Koda completely by surprise since he hadn't immediately understood.

These were Muraco's remains.

***

An aftershock jittered Sydney's nails on the floor. It vibrated as if it was a wave of water, and the flow of the current crashed from the cavern. The ceiling coughed dirt. With an abrupt, faltering rumble, the reverberations broke apart.

By the inner frame of the tunnel, Sydney stood frozen with her limbs stretched outward. After an unsure pause, she moved to straighten upright.

The cavern's golden sheen was now nearly extinguished under sheets of dirt. Brown light replaced the circle of gold above the lake and was downsized to less than half of what it was before. The light shone dimly on the water where the stalactites had stabbed into the lake. Dirt floated like algae. On the initial boom of the quake, Sydney had heard a heavy churn of water.

She turned her head at a small crinkling noise like a cracked eggshell rolling over. A flowing movement snagged her eyes to the lake's edge. *Water frothing mud?*

Then she saw it: her shed skin crawling like a worm.

The shell thickened as it expanded. Inside, a floating heart the size of a dime grew with each thumping beat. Other organs materialized: blood, muscles, and scales. Sydney's transparent leather pattern became opaque as something like black smoke flowed out from under the scales. Among the coral-shaped stalagmites, it may as well have been underwater like a strange squid-like parasite.

The black smoke faded. Tawny eyes brightened from it.

The Sydney replica was alive.

I've shed lots of times, and that's never happened!

A loud *CRACK!* jerked Sydney around to look at the tunnel wall. A large piece of rock split from it and fell to lie slanted against the bottom.

Sydney peered back at the corner.

Her twin wasn't there.

She had a sudden, frantic thought to hide. Sydney clamored behind the rock piece and pulled in her tail just as the sound of racing nails on the floor brought her twin into the tunnel.

The scratching halted. A pathetically optimistic picture of the rock piece looking flush to the wall held in Sydney's mind. In the dripping white noise of the cavern, she thought it more likely that her twin was staring directly at it.

A triangular shape of what could only be its nose pointed outward from the other side of Sydney's cover. Sydney stopped herself from clenching her claws, seeing it was a shadow. The *crick* they made on the floor was so small, it could have been her imagination. Her twin skulked forward to within a few inches of her, or so it appeared due to her nearsightedness.

It seemed to bask there, sitting and staring for so long, Sydney was becoming irritated. Suddenly, it took off into the tunnel.

Sydney crept into the open and tensed as she bumped the rock piece. It wobbled, but eventually stilled. Sydney glared.

"There's only one Sydney, and that's me."

Seeing as there was nowhere else to go, she tailed her evil twin. Down the tunnel she found, quite out of place, a single red card which had fallen out of nowhere.

Three skulls stacked on top of each other like a totem pole: one bare, a second with muscle. The third was a silhouette until it faded right before her eyes and, to Sydney's flattery, revealed her profile.

***

Sully shouted for his brother. "Koda! Kooooda! Rowan, did everyone make it?"

Rowan had fallen on his legs. He pulled himself up, sneezing and batting some dirt out of his eyelashes. He could feel the dirt settling on him as well, as he heard the last of the rocks rolling onto the floor.

"Yes, I saw 'em." Rowan coughed. "Koda's with Jack."

His words calmed the little Critter for he quieted a bit.

"What about Twiggy?"

"Trapped on the other side," Rowan said.

He had opened his eyes before the cave-in had shut out the light from the chamber. They had been going down a straight path, which opened on its right, then opened to its left, ahead of the chamber. He and Sully were now closed off, both in front and behind, in the long tunnel, with only the right tunnel still open to them. Twiggy was behind the rock mound in back.

"He doesn't have good night vision, so he'll probably wait for us," Rowan continued.

"Mm." A small worried noise was Sully's only reply.

Rowan looked around. He could see the tunnel as gray, though it would be virtually pitch-black to Sully. Down its black throat, the tunnel divided into three directions, forming a cross. The end straight ahead led to a spherical chamber. A deer's skull, left arm and leg sprang, frozen, from behind the wall out in front, barely seen under the awning roof.

"There's three tunnels. One of 'em might connect to the chamber they're in." Rowan thought he heard something dripping, though he couldn't be sure.

"I don't want to leave. We could get lost." Sully's tiny voice barely made an echo.

"Okay. The others have the aptrgangr with them. They'll find us quicker stayin' put."

"What if something else finds us?"

"Then we'll send 'em runnin'."

"That sound... Is another totem going to show up?" Sully asked.

"I wouldn't worry about that now. Besides, the tunnels are too narrow. There's no way one of those hulkin' devils could fit in here." Rowan tried to sound lighthearted. He sat on the floor. "We'll come out of this alright."

Sully found his flank. "Rowan?"

Rowan immediately picked up on the unsure, somewhat sorrowful tone. "Yes?"

"Koda says I saved him at Giant's nest."

Rowan did a mental double take. *This is a secret. There's guilt behind what actually happened.* "Well, you did, didn't you?" he said gently, feigning ignorance.

"No," Sully said miserably. "I was too scared. Giant's other pet scared me, and I squeaked, and that's what caused Koda to escape. On accident. Hototo got distracted."

"Sounds to me like you saved him."

Sully brushed Rowan's side with his head.

"The squeak came from you, didn't it?" Rowan smiled. The small humor didn't work on the little Critter, and Sully remained very still. "I myself don't have a brother, but I reckon Koda would understand."

"He's going to hate me."

The reply was pure and sorrowful. Rowan looked at Sully, a small, furry, innocent little Critter if there ever was one. "Don't you think that," he scolded lightly. "I've never known a Critter to hate anybody."

"What about Twiggy?"

"I *have* known Critters to lie."

Sully was still. Eventually, he spoke. "Do you think if I go to sleep and have a dream, the again-walker will show me if Koda is okay?"

"Worth a try," Rowan said encouragingly.

Sully shifted to make himself comfortable. While he slept, Rowan stayed awake, listening for any sign that they might not be alone.

***

Twiggy's tail was smashed under a boulder. It weighed on him like a stomp from Rowan's hooves. Pinned to the floor, he yelled for help. "Jaaack! Rooowan!"

The echo rang. *Jaaack! Rooowaaan!*

Whimpering, Twiggy pawed at the floor and wiggled his lower half. He wailed as a sharp pain twisted in his tail and clawed madly at the floor. He pushed forward, free.

Twiggy cowered against a wall he couldn't see.

"Are you there?" The echo mimicked the saddened, fearful cry and died in the distant tunnels. Darkness stared at him like a threat.

No light. No nothing!

Taking short breaths, Twiggy grabbed his tail, whimpering at another painful jab and hugging it.

Had there been the hollow sigh of underground, a faint whistling of drafts, he likely wouldn't have heard wobbly, tiny scratches coming in fast.

Someone's there! Terror firing, his mouth opened to *KUK.*

He clasped his paws to his lips, shutting them tight. He uttered an *ook*. From straight ahead, the scratches halted. Twiggy's fingers pressed very hard on his mouth.

The scratches went right. They screeched, swerving into another tunnel before fading. Twiggy smelled smoke.

It occurred to him, now it was gone, it could have been a surviving member of his family. He hadn't gotten that feeling, though. Conflicted, he questioned whether to hold out for everyone or retreat to a tunnel in case whatever that had been returned. He decided he couldn't stand the tension.

He used the wall as a lifeline. It turned right and went far until, at last, it echoed an inconsistent drop and splatter. Anxious to be rid of the tunnels, Twiggy scurried to the sound.

He entered a cavern with a lake cast in a brilliant glow. A

curtain of rock was like golden icicles in its shine. Never was he so joyful to see light. Not daylight, though; he didn't think it was considering it had been so bleak outside. But still! As quickly as the joy came, it became muted as Twiggy sniffed a strange scent. An animal scent he wasn't entirely sure was a Critter. Yes, he was positive it wasn't.

The Hunter from the flood!

He had a painful urge to alert the others, but how was he going to tell them now?

A shadow passed over the hole in the ceiling, causing the light to flicker in a haphazard way. A series of *KUK!*s that would have been as loud as a blaring horn almost made it out of Twiggy's mouth. His lips quivered as he tightened them together, and his shoulders jerked as if he were suffering from a bad bout of hiccups.

Twiggy bolted into a cluster of stalagmites. As a squirrel, he knew passes of darkness overhead were a sign of danger. What things did that usually? His petrified mind hadn't come up with the answer, but his instincts did—they remembered how large birds caused that kind of flicker when they flew across the sun.

Through the hanging stalactites, Hototo flew and landed powerfully on a leaning cliff wall. His talons—the same talons that had slaughtered Twiggy's family—caught the ledge with a sharp scrape.

Twiggy visualized the owl ablaze, gone up in smoke like Camazotz, but just a little bit slower. He wasn't even surprised that Hototo had made it into the opening during the flood. The owl was like a curse—a plague! Twiggy's whole family had been wiped out. They had all been lying there in the grass, never to play in the warmth of summer again, never another morning waking up to familiar faces belonging to those who would risk everything to bring them forage. They would never be given love again. Remembering them now, Twiggy knew his pup was gone.

In a watery blur, the totem leaned forward and back upon the cliff wall as it bobbed its head sideways and back like a rotating meridian ball. The eyes without a soul had focused on something.

Twiggy popped down. Had he been seen? As hard as he tried to be still, it was so tempting just to scream from the heartache, fear, and hate he felt.

He had failed to remember how silent the owl's wings were. About twelve feet to his left in the stalagmite maze, shrill scrapes lifted and dragged. *Scrit. Scrit.*

Owls could find Critters under multiple feet of snow. Their hearing, Twiggy knew, was more excellent than a goat's or a hare's. *He's not searching for Critters. Unless he's searching, he won't know there's one to listen for.* Was that plausible?

He tried not to think of that, or the fact he would never again hold his pup. Stifling his sobs, Twiggy inched toward the cavern's entrance. He kept his back low.

The scrapes loudened near an open pocket ahead. For a frozen moment, he surrendered himself. He waited for Hototo to step out and for his eyes to grow menacingly large before charging at him. Twiggy snuck right, away from the scratches, forced farther and farther from the entrance until he reached the cavern's end wall at the lake.

Hototo would soon catch his scent if he didn't hear him. A member of his family had said you could lose a dog by drenching yourself. Maybe that could work here, too.

You can't go back. Listen to those scrapes; they're right behind! And gaining! Plus, at this distance, he'll see you leaving anywhere else, so just get it over with.

Twiggy crept out of the stalagmites to the lake's edge. He was as far from the glow in the ceiling as could be, and the lake looked dark and alarming, like a pit of tar. Looking back, he saw just the tips of Hototo's ear tufts over the stalagmites. A gasp rose up

Twiggy's throat. He clutched it and practically choked on his own breath. With wide eyes, he watched the tufts lower and realized he was seeing them from farther away than he originally thought.

The lake stared at Twiggy coldly. He lowered himself in, forcing himself not to splash. Twiggy held his breath and dunked. Deep underwater, he clung to the rock wall and saw only endless black. A minute went by, but it seemed like three times that. A bubble streamed up from his nose. His lungs wouldn't have tightened this fast if his heart wasn't beating as fast as it was. Twiggy waited, waited for the muted *scrit scrit* drawing closer to reverse in the opposite direction.

The bubble floated up toward the top of the lake. Twiggy's lungs constricted just a little more as he thought of it bubbling on the surface. The *scrit scrit* had stopped.

In the end, it wasn't the bubble that had given him away. It was the clear patch he had made in the dirt on the lake's surface.

Twiggy opened his mouth to breathe when something jerked his leg. His view of the cavern above and Hototo standing over the lake shrank rapidly. He wheeled his arms and kicked, unable to scream without any air in his lungs. He didn't feel fingers on his ankles or anywhere else on his body, and when he looked down with the last of his strength, though there was nothing to see, he could sense something whirling around below. A kind of whirlpool but without pattern, like a snake trying to coil around its prey.

It was as if the water itself was trying to drown him.

His lungs flooded. His vision spotted and blackened, and that was when water streamed into his nose.

Yān. Yān sǐ bìng chéngwéi shuǐ de yībùfèn.

That wasn't his thought, but he heard it in his mind just the same. Pretty soon Twiggy heard nothing at all, and thoughts that weren't his own took over.

The *thing* inside Twiggy swam to the surface. His body climbed out of the lake, completely dry, and didn't gasp for air or run as his eyes saw the owl standing there. Instead, his body bowed to him in greeting.

"Bring me the relics," Hototo growled and scratched irritatingly at two small puncture wounds made by the goat's horns. "Kill the Critters."

***

"Aptrgangr," Jack said, raising his voice a little to try to seem normal. He was aware of how woeful and pitiful it sounded. He leaned away from the floor with his arms stiff out in front of him, head bowed so he wouldn't have to burn that awful display on the stone any further into his mind. "Aptrgangr, how did these bones get here?"

"That is not for I to know."

"You must!" Jack shouted.

To see him... in a lonely and dreadful place, Jack thought. *Is it better than where that human would have taken him? To be a trophy on its wall?*

He had seen the markings: nail marks belonging to a large dog.

"I saw it. It took him!"

Nahiossi appeared at his paw. He sat there, not saying a word. It donned on Jack that he was waiting, patiently, for him to recover and was willing to do so even as he was vexed for Sully.

Jack readied to leave the chamber. While he knew it would sink him further into despair, his emotions shaking him, he risked a last look to the stone.

Muraco's skull raised on his jaw, rocking on it as the bones rattled. "Why didn't you *tell* me there was a second human, Jack?"

240

Jack tasted blood gushing from his lip. He staggered, swayed, felt Muraco shaking him even though he was still on the stone. His brother breathed on him, a dry, earthy air, a breath of ground bone dust.

"I-it's the ch-chaaa-amber," Nahiossi said. The rocks in the entrance were spilling forward. The whole room quaked and cracked. That was all it was, an influx of compressed air. Muraco was still dead.

"Jack, l-let's go!"

They staggered to the tunnel beyond the stone. Nahiossi gripped at the floor. "I-is it the Craa-acker Jack?" he asked loudly.

"This feels more violent," Jack said, though most likely not loud enough for Nahiossi to hear. He shouldered the wall. As much as he was trying to keep his feet under him, he was trying extremely hard to focus on anything other than Muraco's bones, the way they hopped and buzzed upon that vibrating stone like stunned bees in cold weather.

"Is it th-the t-too-otems?"

"No." Jack tried to think. "No. It's just rumbling. There hasn't been another explosion since the cave-in. It's... It's the world, Nahiossi. It's collapsing."

"We st-stii-ill haven't found S-suully," Nahiossi yelled. "Or Rowan aa-and the squirrel."

The aptrgangr's odor became more potent at the entrance. Jack had the presence of mind to place a paw over Koda's eyes, and he was grateful for it.

"Can you find them?" asked Jack.

"I cannot guide you further. The next dream that one has, I vill be in it."

The walls of the tunnel fractured. Between the rumbles and cracks, Jack left the aptrgangr and felt his way along the wall with Nahiossi. He took them around a corner and was faced with complete darkness.

"Twiggy! Rowan!" he called.

"S-sully!" added Koda.

They kept right, repeating their calls. Ahead, Rowan called, "We're over here!"

"K-koda!" Sully's voice zoomed in. Jack felt them stumble over his paws as Sully met Koda head on.

Trotting up to them, Rowan slipped on his hooves. "Hototo's got what he wants. The whole darn place is fixin' to cave!"

"Where's Twiggy?" Jack conjured a terrible picture of him lying crushed under rock.

Beside him, Twiggy said, "I'm right here."

Jack reached out a paw to touch him and sensed Twiggy step back. "Are you okay?"

"I'm fine."

He didn't sound it. Somehow, he sounded distant. *He's still upset*, Jack thought. *I shouldn't have yelled at him.*

Rowan tromped his hooves. "Are we gonna high tail it out of here?" he yelled.

Jack put aside his concerns and let Rowan guide them through the dark.

18
SHUI GUI

S ULLY LISTENED, engrossed by Jack's tales. They were at the bottom of a sloping passage, which, as Rowan described, was as wide as a chamber in itself. He concluded that the landslide of rocks on which they sat, sinking down from the slope and then filling the bottom of the passage like a ball pit, had fallen from a gaping hole in the high ceiling. Rowan said it was like they were in a square tube slanted down at a forty-five-degree angle.

Though Sully couldn't see the ceiling himself, he stared nervously upward. Cave-ins had closed off everything but the chamber with a deer skeleton on the wall and the tunnel Twiggy had walked in from. Twiggy told them there was nothing in that direction, it had led to a dead end, leaving them the rock-filled passage.

In a deadpan tone, Jack told the story of the chamber the aptrgangr had showed him and Koda. However, when Muraco's bones were mentioned, he slipped, and a few words came out watery. Koda never interrupted. Since rejoining the group, he had glued himself to Sully.

"I'm sorry we weren't there to share that with you," Rowan said as Jack finished.

"It couldn't be helped." Jack sighed, sort of wandering in a depressed haze. "I'm sure you know what that explosion heralding the cave-in meant."

"Another totem," Rowan said dismally. "Too bad we don't have another house to burn down on it."

If at all possible, Sully would prefer the totem mind its own business and they do the same. "How many totems are we going to have to stop?" he asked, deflated by the idea of another Camazotz.

"We can't keep goin' on like this," Rowan said. "Somethin's gonna break."

"Maybe another Hunter crossed the barrier," Koda said.

"The trees were destroyed, so that's questionable. I'd assume another trigger took place," Jack said.

"Trigger?" Koda asked.

"Something like the Hunter from the flood. Or maybe the world is simply reaching its limit. It could be both. Think of the Hunter from the flood as a foreign object in a Critter's or human's body. It doesn't belong. Should it not be removed, it can cause a variety of issues. Including death."

"I see the parallel," Rowan said grimly.

Sully had been picturing the Hunter as a monster with eight legs, a mouth like a shark, cat eyes, and bat wings. Oh, and with clown hair. Incidentally, most of the things he was afraid of. "Could there be another Hunter that was already in the catacombs? Is that why there are Critter skulls?" Sully asked.

"That could very well be the reason, except in the scenario that there *is* another Hunter that killed the Critters in those chambers; it would've had to exist here four years ago," Jack said. "That would mean destruction was already happening to the Trickster world. I don't think that's the case. Look how quickly it's deteriorated since we've been here. There wouldn't have been a Trickster world by the time we arrived."

"That brings us to our current situation. We've got to get

out before the Trickster world quits on us." Rowan sighed. "The aptrgangr won't guide us further?"

"Not in person, and it would be impossible to backtrack now."

"We need an exit. Or a Cracker Jack. It's a bad stroke of luck ya'll didn't find a relic."

"Or did you?" Twiggy said.

He sounded kind of accusatory. They hadn't even asked Jack yet. Sully jumped a little, hearing him close to his ear, as he hadn't been able to tell where Twiggy was standing. He wasn't twitching or bouncing like he usually was, and he hadn't spoken since they found each other.

Twiggy continued, "There had to have been more than just what the aptrgangr showed you."

"Isn't finding remains enough?" Koda asked. Sully was sure this was just to give Twiggy a hard time.

"If Jack was going to waste our time talking, I would think it would be to tell us something useful." Twiggy asked Jack, "Why don't you just get over it? There are thousands of other dimwitted hares out there. Pick one. There'll still be some left after the humans get at them."

Sully was speechless, and it seemed Koda was, too, before his brother burst out, "What are you talking about?! Jack told me it was a human that—"

"Oh, shut up about the humans," Twiggy said sharply. "After all, what they're doing is protecting the environment. Keeping the waters clean. You should be thanking them."

Sully cried. He didn't understand. Why was there such spite in Twiggy's voice? How could he talk to Jack like that?

Jack said nothing. Intense anger radiated from him—Sully thought he heard him chitter—but he had to have been utterly shocked.

Rowan asked quietly, "Did you find a relic?"

"We will eventually," Koda said in a low, angry mutter.

"I, uh, I suggest we contact the aptrgangr."

"You said there's another passage," Jack said to Rowan. His voice trembled a little. "We'll pick a room for Nahiossi, so it's quiet. Of course, Sully can stay with him."

"I think just us should go. *He* can stay here," Koda said, obviously talking about Twiggy. "If anything happens, he can sneak away quietly."

The silence from Twiggy distressed Sully, but he was too afraid to move away. Koda helped him by nudging Sully's side.

The rocks were described to Jack and the brothers as having filled up to another smaller passage where the angular ceiling of the "tube" ended. After the four of them had went some ways inside, leaving Twiggy behind, Koda stopped. Sully got the feeling he was glancing over his shoulder.

"Jack, we need to talk about what happened. Something's not right!" Koda cried.

"I've upset him. He doesn't think I can protect him or any of you," Jack said with great strain as he tried to speak through his anger and mortification.

"Do you think he'd ever talk to you like that? He's not himself!"

Jack seemed to awaken somewhat from his depression. "What do you mean?"

"I don't know. But we should go back to that tunnel. The one he came in from. He wasn't like this before, and I think something happened to him. I think he was lying about there being a dead end. There might be something over there and we—"

Jack's scream pierced the tunnel. It coursed away raggedly and ended as a short, tearing squeak by a grinded thud. Sully had never heard a hare scream before then. It was an awful sound that sent bolts of horror and anguish into him, traveling up his arms from a shudder in the ground where a quick stab and clomp had just been.

It took Sully a moment to realize Rowan had hit Jack.

He had misjudged how fast Jack could move when scared. Heavy thumps, violent, panicked scratches; Sully fully expected to see sparks. Rowan's hooves jabbed and scraped, as if being pushed, while he struggled to keep Jack pinned against the wall. Jack continued to scream. Sully screamed, too. "ROWAN! RO—"

He felt a momentary, hot breath on his face. Suddenly, he was off balance as Koda cut in hard from the side. The one warning Sully received was a pent-up cry. There was a scuffle, and Sully could smell Twiggy. He had smelled different; it was a kind of wet smell, like damp clothes, and it only worsened, like sweat, as he fought Koda. Spitting, Twiggy hissed, joined in by Rowan's erratic snorts.

"What's wrong?!" Sully screamed.

Koda ran into him. "It's after the relics!"

Sully heard a sound, and he had enough fear of water to recognize it. A large wave—he was sure of it!—washed around, as if from a storm out at sea, somewhere in front. It drove him to run.

Sully ran off the ledge of the passage and nosedived into the rock pit. He grabbed blindly at rocks, crying, whimpering, trying to climb the slope and panicked that he was losing his grip. He tumbled to the bottom. Koda tried to push him upwards, but it was no good. Sully threw himself at the pile as the rocks slipped under him.

Someone was coming up behind them. Sully screamed and kicked weakly alongside Koda as they were pulled up by their scruffs. Then he recognized Jack's scent through puffs from his nose. He carried them, never stopping, as the rocks continuously shifted beneath his feet, until he stumbled at the top of the slope.

He let go of them. Sully heard Jack slipping, gripping the floor edge and scratching it with his nails as he thrust out an arm. At the bottom of the slope, Rowan's hooves crunched rock. The raging water crashed.

Koda yelled at Sully to run.

"No!" Sully cried. He refused to leave Jack behind.

"Listen to your brother, Sully. Go! Bring Shui Gui to the water!" Jack shouted.

Immediately afterward, Sully heard the water rising into the air. He felt it was alive, somehow, reaching up at Jack and then attacking him. Jack choked. Any words he tried to speak were drowned. That was exactly what it sounded like. Like Jack was *drowning*.

Sully's feet got the best of him and he started moving. He trained his ears on his brother's pawsteps and the hoofsteps stomping up the slope. He and Koda were probably exiting the chamber now, the one with the deer skeleton, and would soon be back in the tunnel—

Sully recoiled from a sudden hit. Adrenaline shut out the pain, helped him to turn the corner and keep going after he hit another wall. Light shone ahead. He chased it and Koda's darkened figure.

His brother ducked as Hototo appeared. Talons gleamed like metal in sunlight, wings flapped and swung them backward. If not for the low-arched ceiling—had it widened at the end like an upraised lip—Hototo might have flown right into the tunnel. He screeched and seemed about to chase them, when Sully and Koda lost each other in the stomping of hooves. Shrieking, Sully flung hard off the side of a wall with his head. It throbbed as if it had dented the wall; he saw white blotches. But a part of it had felt like there was a tapered hole. He found it, climbed in and yelled for Koda.

Sharp echoes blasted from Rowan's springing hooves like the blows of a hammer on an anvil. The sounds seemed to speed up upon Koda's shouts, wherever he went. Sully couldn't believe it.

He's trying to stomp on Koda!

Jack's scent came into the tunnel. In a faltering run, he sped up toward the fight, and Sully thought Koda was going to be saved. A second later, Koda cried out for Jack to stop. That smell hadn't completely been like Jack's. It smelled like water.

Koda escaped. He ran to the hole and jumped in. The passage channeled deep and inclined. They rolled downward while rumbling began. Sully didn't know of what he was more afraid: the sound of the walls crumbling within the hole or the rapid scratching of Twiggy's nails. He could feel him, close, and hear wet, excited breathing. It was like when Koda had been sick, when Sully had heard the clicking from his lungs. A claw sliced the air an inch away from Sully. He screamed as the walls fell apart and rock tumbled through.

He was flung out of the hole like a ball of snow leaping off a chute. Twiggy let out a scream of rage, and there was the sound of raging water again. It tried to blast through the rocks inside the hole, but the rocks held firm and the rapid scratching faded.

As the rumbling quieted, Sully trembled on his side, feeling tremors in his limbs, as if he had never left the passage.

Koda sneezed. He pressed on Sully's arm. "Are you sick? Are you hurt?"

He ached everywhere. His lungs, his ears, his throat. "Jack…" Sully croaked.

"He was running with them. The totem got him."

Sully had done it again. He had run away when someone he cared about needed his help.

"They're my friends!" Sully cried.

"They're not dead. Remember those movies? They're not

themselves," Koda said.

"You're— You're saying they're possessed?"

Sully twitched as some part of a wall crumbled. They were in another chamber with a bit of torchlight. It was empty; there were no skulls. Koda stood over him in shadow.

Sully scratched the ground to his feet and shrank away from him. "Are you... Koda?"

"Yes," Koda said cautiously as if realizing he didn't know if Sully was himself, either. "They'd be no reason for the totem not to attack with two of us left."

The brothers stared each other down.

Eventually, as nothing happened, Sully loosened his stance. "Koda... we're alone."

"They're going to find us." Koda glanced about the room as if to look for them. "They have just as good a sense of smell as us or better. And Rowan's night vision, there's that. But first they'll have to find a way to get to us," he said. "I *know* it's not them. They can't just change their scents like that. And I could just tell... something... something else was in the tunnel with us."

Sully's mind began to clear—there was a possibility his friends were going to be okay—but it was taking him longer to process, and Koda was talking kind of fast.

"How are you going to get the totem out of them?" He sniffed. "You need giant items to do an exorcism."

"I don't think that would work on a totem."

"Then how are we supposed to help them?" Sully pleaded.

"I-I don't know," Koda said. "We ended up going down the tunnel Twiggy said had a dead end. I was right. He lied. There's a whole cavern that way."

"Is that where the totem got him?" Sully asked.

"I think so."

"But what about Rowan?"

"After the cave-in, were you and Rowan separated from each other at any point? Sully?"

"N-no." Sully rethought. His eyes widened. "I went to sleep!"

"It possessed Rowan while you were asleep," Koda said gravely.

Sully swallowed. He could have been next.

"Jack was right," Koda said. "There's something important about those relics. Why else possess everyone instead of killing one and going onto the next? It'll be stronger in numbers."

Sully remembered what he had been meaning to say since the second relic. "I could hold one of the relics."

"Didn't you hear me, Sully? *Totems* are after them. Why? Why do you want one?"

"I want to help."

"Sully, no."

A low rumble. Sully listened for the beginnings of another quake, but it silenced. "Why not?"

"A relic makes you a target," Koda said. "What is this? Are you *trying* to get killed? Just like how you were almost taken over with Jack back there?"

Sully shrank, stunned by Koda's tone. "If something happens, at least we'd have a backup."

"This really isn't a game this time! We are on our own. And I can't protect you like Rowan or Jack."

"I don't *need* to be protected. I can do it myself."

"In other words, you don't need me."

"Yes, I do." Sully didn't understand where such a thought had come from. "But everyone rescued us all those times. Rowan and Twiggy protected me when you were asleep. Jack, too, during the flood, and at the carnival and with the clown. And Camazotz! I want to help someone!"

"You've done that already," Koda said. "You went to get help when I was sick."

"And you yelled at me. You've been upset with me ever since."

"Because I'm afraid you're going to get yourself killed! It's hard for me to let go, even if you can do all these things on your own."

"I don't want to do them on my own," Sully said sincerely. "I'm with you no matter how scary things get."

For the first time since they left Giant's nest, Sully thought, *really thought*, about what his brother must be feeling. He understood why Koda had acted the way he did when he woke up in the burrows, and why he had gotten angry every time Sully got a little too adventurous. Sully felt selfish, for he had let his excitement distract him from Koda's feelings.

"You don't have to give me the relic, Koda."

In the silence, Koda paused. He touched Sully's arm. "You're still trembling. Are you sure you're okay?"

"I feel a little better."

Koda seemed to consider. He began to unpouch one of the three relics. "I'm doing this because the totem thinks I have all of them. It seems to know everything the others do, so it will think that." He gave Sully the relic. "Pouch it. Right now."

"No one's going to find out I have one. I promise," said Sully.

Koda was quiet. "It's the one Jack and I found."

"You found another one? But you said—"

"I knew something wasn't right. I didn't think the squirrel was possessed so much as I'd thought he'd gone crazy. And with all the craziness, it just seemed like I should expect anything could go wrong. And it did," Koda said. "I guess it pays to be cautious in the right doses."

Sully exclaimed, "There's gotta be a Cracker Jack somewhere! Ask the zombie—"

"After we return everyone to normal. There has to be a way." Koda seemed to think. "Jack said 'Bring Shui Gui to the water.' What water? And there was that comment Twiggy—the totem—made about giants 'keeping the water clean.' Sully," Koda stepped forward, "what if this thing came from the water?"

Sully remembered the crashing wave as Rowan and Twiggy chased them. Was that… was that the totem?

"You want to bring Shui Gui to the water? Was there water in the cavern?" Sully asked.

"I think I might've seen a lake, but Hototo was in the way."

"Hototo will get us if we go back there again."

"You found a passage here. There could be one leading into the cavern," Koda said.

"How are you going to get everyone there?" Sully asked. "If the passage is too small, Rowan and Jack won't fit, and we'll have to go the front way anyway and—"

"I know, Sully. I know all of that," Koda said, exasperated. "Maybe we'll have to let the owl see us, and he'll screech or something, and the others will come running in. I know 'maybe' isn't good enough…"

It *could* happen. However, if they made it to the lake—should there be a wide enough passage—and Hototo didn't kill them and take the relics beforehand, the water totem would see their intentions. It would probably already know once it got to the front entrance.

"I'm scared to go back, Koda."

"Me, too," Koda said. "But I want to see home again. The *real* nest. Giant is there waiting for us."

Sully wanted to watch movies with her again. She would scrunch the blanket a little on her lap, so he could hide during the

253

scary parts. He would try to sneak some of her popcorn. Sometimes she caught him and would smile and pet his head. He had never really felt scared with her around, not the kind of scared he was now in this dark and miserable chamber.

At the mountain pass, and even while on the painful journey there, he hadn't been homesick. During the flood, Sully had wanted to leave for the Haven. *There are no threats where they're going!* he had said.

Why had he ever wanted to give up those nights with Giant?

"We'll think of a better plan on the way," Koda said. "It's alright to whisper; it can't be louder than our pawsteps. Anything more and the echoes will carry our voices."

Sully walked with Koda to the chamber's exit. Some of the firelight spilled out into the tunnel. "Do you know where we're going, Koda? It all looks the same."

"I'll keep going right. That should get us back to the cavern," Koda said, but he still sounded unsure.

All the way through the catacombs, Sully listened, paranoid, for the others. Every crack and crumble in the wall sounded like them entering the tunnel. He constantly fought the urge to run. Run to where? The catacombs were like a maze. Unlike the ones Sully had been in during playtime, there was no scent of cheese to lead him to the end. He trusted in Koda completely.

Finally, light fanned around a corner. After so long in the darkness and because of how bright it was, Sully blinked many times before he was able to see a mountain of rubble blocking another tunnel. The light shone over the top from the other side.

"Koda, sunlight!"

The outside was just a climb away.

"We've gone the wrong way then. At least for now. When we get the others—"

Sully recoiled as the light flashed brighter. It filled the tunnel like a subway train's headlights. He had never seen such a bright light. He wondered if that was all it was, as where it touched the walls and rubble, the textures smoothed and faded from dark brown to beige to white. The walls and rubble became part of the light, disappearing inside it.

Koda stepped backward. "That isn't sunlight."

"Huh?" Sully said, afraid.

"It's a gap in the world."

The tunnel lurched, throwing them, and the ground vibrated. Sully held on for dear life.

"We've got to hurry!" Koda exclaimed.

The brothers turned another corner, still with enough light to see by.

"This tunnel goes right," Koda said.

He hurried them down it. He was going so fast, Sully was afraid he would trip and be left behind before Koda realized he had vanished.

Soon the light faded, and the quakes began to calm. Koda allowed them to slow just enough so they wouldn't hit any walls. The farther they went, the more cracks and beveled plates in the tunnels. Sully expected they would run out of tunnels going right.

"What was that, Koda?" Sully huffed. "What was happening?"

"Jack was right. The Trickster world isn't going to last."

"We need to warn Twiggy, Rowan, and Jack! We need to find the Cracker Jack! Before it disappears and—"

"It's going to be okay, Sully. Don't think about it now."

Koda was scared, too, Sully knew it, just as he knew if he let himself get any more frightened, he would freeze. And then who would there be to help their friends?

Sully forced himself to focus on the golden light entering

the cross in the tunnel ahead.

Koda braked. "Stop! We're here."

The cavern was at the top of the cross. The arms were made up of two tunnels, left or right, and Koda planned to go down one of them. He hoped, he told Sully, at least one of the tunnels would go along the outside of the cavern wall and go to the passage they needed to get inside. They would figure out the rest of the plan once they found it.

Koda whispered, "Owls have excellent hearing, right?"

"Oh, no," Sully groaned. Hototo was apt to hear them going by.

Koda panted. "I'll go and walk back a little to make it seem like I went the whole way. Then you go. We'll make Hototo think we're one Critter. The squirrel."

Would that fool Hototo? Wouldn't the path of pawsteps make him suspicious?

To turn the right corner at the cross's arm, Koda had to walk toward the cavern. Sully clenched his paws. His brother's pawsteps were very light and quick. They paused before returning. Afraid he would cop out if he thought too much, Sully jumped on his cue. He rounded the corner too quickly. Standing beside Koda, Sully squished his eyes shut and prayed he hadn't doomed them both.

Talonsteps. Beating wings.

Sully's imagination. He was hearing water dripping and irregular splashes. Did owls like to play in water? No, that was too innocent a picture.

Then he thought of another one. Of something alive in the water, wanting to get out. Wanting to claim another victim.

They went a long way to another corner and went straight a longer way, just as Koda had hoped. They had to be walking outside of the cavern wall now. Sully said a prayer of thanks.

He smelled something foul, like a combination of rotted wood that had been left in the sun, oil, sand, and something like the last dying breath of fire.

Scrunching his nose, Sully opened his mouth and could taste the stink. *"What is that?"*

As he heard Koda pacing, he remembered why they were there. Sully felt along the wall with unsteady paws. An edge rose off the ground at about his height and continued for an undetermined length. Sully climbed into the recess and very cautiously pawed his way farther in.

His nails snagged on cloth. It was draped on something long and bony, like a tree branch. At the end lay five ridges. As Sully walked over them, he found they weren't fixed to the floor. He touched one, feeling a jagged finger nail.

Sully slipped on the edge and fell. "There's a body in there!"

Koda sniffed, frightened. That smell couldn't belong to just one body. Sully expected the wall contained rows upon rows of burial niches packed with corpses.

Sully pleaded, "Let's look at the other tunnel."

"And chance the owl again?" Koda said.

Sully chewed his lip.

"Try not to cough or sneeze." There was a small scrape as Koda climbed the edge of the niche, or loculus, as Sully had learned they were called in the Catacombs of Paris. Again, he had sabotaged himself into fear by watching documentaries.

Sully couldn't get anywhere near the loculus the first two tries. *Why is it always something I'm afraid of?*

He crawled over many more bony limbs. The skeletons had skin like scrunched paper. He heard them constantly scrape against the rock as he and Koda made their way to the back wall. It only added to Sully's illusion that the corpses were stirring in their sleep, as if from night terrors, and at any second, they would sit up to look at them through the dark. There was also the sound of sand being pressed, the kind one made when walking along the beach. By the width of their sunken torsos, so sunken Sully could feel the granules inside and the ground beneath, he realized very quickly that these were not the bones of Critters.

"Koda," Sully whispered, shaken. "Are these giants?"

"I think they're Tricksters," Koda answered, also sounding disturbed.

Sully touched something tacky and bulbous, about the size of a knee. He grasped a slightly raised, triangular patch of skin. There were two pits above it. Shivering, he pawed upward over various grooves to a strip of hair.

Sully squeaked and jumped to wipe his paws on the floor. He was positive he had just climbed over someone's very shriveled, very small face.

Koda pawed Sully.

Flustered, Sully apologized, "I'm sorry. I made too much noise."

"No. That's not it."

Sully tensed at the fear in Koda's voice. "Do you hear them coming?"

"I remembered something."

"What?" Sully couldn't stand it.

"The aptrgangr said he couldn't guide us farther," Koda said shakily. "He could only guide us where there were remains, and they ended tunnels back."

The shocking realization hit Sully hard in the stomach. He gasped in horror, feeling like he was going to be sick.

The corpses aren't dead?!

Something shifted and snapped like a dead flower stem. Sully backed up into Koda.

The head had turned.

The body murmured as if waking from a deep sleep. An arm brushed back a flap of cloth, revealing a green glow. More murmurs. Across the recess, glows lit shrunken faces. They glowed like a light held to an egg. One by one, Tricksters lifted on their arms and seemed to look around with eyes that were sewn shut.

The rumbling had been dormant for a while. Now it erupted again. Tricksters leapt about as if in the throes of convulsion, shouting, pushing their hands up to the ceiling like dead weeds and throwing dust. Their images shook as Sully bounced. From behind him, someone thrust out their hand and shoved him and Koda into the crook of the Trickster's thigh in front.

Shriveled fingers batted at them. "Rats! Rats are 'rawling on me!"

In a pause of the quake, Sully sprang into the path of another Trickster dragging toward the end of the loculus. He caught his paw in a stitch in its mouth and was swept under to its chest. He dragged along with it toward the other Tricksters scrambling over each other to the tunnel, like newly risen zombies from the grave. They began to gather in the tunnel, but another quake sprawled them onto the floor.

Twiggy and Jack appeared at the opening of the loculus. The totem had *drowned* them, Sully was sure of that despite they were dry. That is, except for their noses which glistened as if Twiggy and Jack had a cold. The look in their eyes upon seeing him chilled Sully. It was a look only a totem could have, a cold, deadly look. Glaring at him, their fur sticking up in the green glow of the tunnel, Sully wondered if they were completely different animals.

The Tricksters on the floor split away from them. "TOTEMS! TOTUUMMSSS!" But Sully knew there was only one.

Sully's Trickster swerved away from the opening. Sully scurried beneath its raised chest as he saw Jack rushing at them and about to jump. The Trickster flattened on top of Sully. The weight was as light as a stack of foam. He could feel Jack's claws through the paper skin. Jack lifted the Trickster, who was screaming terribly, by its head. He stood over it with his legs in view. Sully raced out, glimpsing Jack's claws stuck in the Trickster's scalp. He would always remember how its head looked: like a small, deflated soccer ball. As Jack removed his claws, the sound was like a knife pulling out of hardened burlap.

Sully dodged the Tricksters, terrified he was going to stumble from the vibrating ground. Above him, the ceiling of the loculus jerked downward, the CRACK! as a fissure opened in the rock like a whip to his spine. Sully drove himself harder, and the ceiling fell with a heavy slam.

He could barely move after he fell to the tunnel floor. He lay there in shock, his heartbeat practically lifting his chest off the ground, as all around shriveled hands and feet scraped over the floor in a green haze. Tricksters fumbled on their knees, grappled each other while trying to stand, tearing cloth and tangling their fingers in stitches. Past shredded clothes and limbs, Sully saw a few of them sandwiched between the fallen ceiling and bottom of the loculi. Still more Tricksters dropped from the higher rows. As they landed, they shrank away from Jack, who, having just made the jump out of the loculus, raised himself very slowly.

Sully heaved against the floor. He thought his whole body might fill with air, and he strained against his breath as he began to panic, watching Jack go very still. For some reason, it made Sully even more terrified.

The force of water bursting out of Jack's chest threw his head back, his ears flopped, and he remained as limp as a doll as the water struck a Trickster. The Trickster twisted at the waist, cracking like a twig, and fell on its knees. The water, moving as a tendril suspended in the air, streamed into its nose. It struggled, its head rocking back from the torrent like a balloon tied in front of a fan, and Sully thought how horrible it would be if its head rolled off its shoulders. The Trickster threw its hands into the spray until, at last, the tendril collapsed. It crawled away, whimpering, as again and again, the tendril connected to Jack's chest slung at the Tricksters, throwing them every which way.

Apparently Shui Gui couldn't possess them and was resorting to the next best thing: getting them out of the way and clearing the path to search for Sully and Koda.

Where is Koda?! The thought of his brother pushed Sully back into action. Searching for him, his frightened gaze fell upon Rowan emerging from the end of the tunnel. Behind him, the erasing light glided around the corner, shadowing him in its brilliance. Rowan forcefully bowed his head and stabbed two fleeing Tricksters with his horns. Then he threw them, screaming, directly into the light. Another fell on its knees at his side. As it hurried to stand, Rowan bucked, and it fell right back onto its knees and onto the floor, unmoving, where a lock of its hair dangled on Rowan's horn just above its head.

Someone kicked Sully. As he rolled, he glimpsed a stitched mouth that reminded him of a growling dog.

"'Aavv-*fuh* the Critter!'" it shouted.

The Trickster smacked him. Sully rolled and struck some-one's leg. He lifted on shaky arms to see, past the panicked crowd, Rowan staring at him in the glaring light. His eyes had changed, too, to a baleful look, one reflecting a grinning evil.

Rowan ceased throwing Tricksters and rammed straight through them. Sully, beginning to hyperventilate, ran. The rumbles drastically rose in volume. The light closed in on both sides of the tunnel. Tricksters were disappearing, and Jack was still in the same spot at the wall, frozen, while the tendril moved sporadically. It dove in a zigzag current, throwing Tricksters up by their feet. The path was clear, with Sully completely out in the open, except for a single shrieking Trickster.

The Trickster batted his chest as if something were in his shirt. Twiggy sprang out of his sleeve and hissed across at Koda, who was clinging onto another Trickster. The Trickster rose abruptly, and Koda jumped from its head onto a higher level in the loculi that was still intact.

There was light up there, shining out of the back wall.

A passage to the cavern. With all the quaking, it must have opened.

"I have to get up there!" Sully cried.

Fingers wrapped around him. Sully was afraid he was going to get hit again. Then the Trickster threw him onto the edge of the loculus. Sully swung by his claws and pulled himself up. With no time to catch his breath, he ran to the back wall where Koda was positioned in front of the passage.

Sully didn't stop; he meant to push them both out the other side.

Seeing his intention, Koda's face lit up in horror. "Sully, we can't!" He ran right into Sully, stopping him.

"Why not?!" Moving around Koda, Sully looked through the passage at a destroyed cavern bombed with rocks. The lake splashed many feet below.

He saw a rippling face in the water: Twiggy. Twiggy's spirit, that's what it had to be, as he was see-through. He paddled beneath the surface with hungry eyes, just as the water totem might have looked when it had waited for Twiggy to come along. Had Twiggy taken its place? Sully thought so, and the process would keep repeating if anyone else were to step too close to the lake.

Koda shoved Sully. "Run! Get out of here!"

The erasing light shone into the loculus. The quaking finally etched cracks into the rock. Twiggy was paused on the wall outside the opening, encompassed in light, looking in with a water tendril shooting out of his chest.

They hadn't figured out the rest of the plan. But Sully knew what to do. He had the idea to dart out of the way as the tendril struck, so it would go through the passage. Sully darted, and the rock under him teetered down, sliding him right back in front of the opening.

The tendril struck him.

Water streamed into Sully's nose and down his throat. He choked as his lungs filled like pitchers. He expected to feel cold but instead was warm. It was the feeling of someone else possessing his body.

Sully had the sense he had blacked out sometime between being hit and floating up out of the lake. He paddled, gasping, feeling as if he had swallowed an entire forest's wind, and looked frantically about him at rocks plummeting into the water. A wave soared high and threw him against a boulder. Sully coughed, sputtering as more waves flowed over his face.

They must have won. The feeling of someone else within him had gone. *Bring it to the water*, and that was what he had done, so everyone else must be themselves again. Sully called desperately for Koda and the others. Looking up at the cavern wall, he discovered the passage wasn't there. The gold light of the cavern was being replaced by the erasing light, and it had swept over the wall. Rocks had stopped falling since there was no longer a ceiling to fall from. The light overtook everything; the lake faded like a trail of water-color. The world was becoming white.

"*Koooda!*"

Sobbing, Sully paddled helplessly. He stopped paddling altogether when he saw something he could only describe as *invisible* trailing a current moving toward him. It gurgled as if in a rage, then the light reached it, and it was gone.

In a beam of light, the Trickster world was no more.

PART III
PURGATORY

19
STRANGERS

ONE DAY Giant placed Sully in the wrong home. Walking into the bedroom, she was distracted while talking to a visitor in the next room.

Sully left her hand, and she started to walk away.

"Wait, this isn't mine," he said.

Giant closed the door.

As he waited for her to realize her mistake, Sully took a look around. The home was like a gnome garden—if there had been any gnomes—with the sunlight shining in and all the quaint ceramic houses. There were dried forage hideaways (Giant was trying out all sorts of houses to see what the newcomer liked), though all were empty and smelled only of coconut. As always, Sully wondered what color they were. Curvy shadows (tubes and seesaws) and chews without chew marks broke up the "lawn." There were no burrowing trails, and the bedding was perfectly flat. *It's all so organized!* Sully thought, who had the bad habit of digging under his furniture, sometimes burying it. Giant had to right his wheel practically every day, and the dried carrots on *Sully's* hideaway (its roof bald in places) were scattered everywhere.

From the back corner of the home, he heard chittering beneath a small plank. Sully was bemused. *He sleeps all the time.*

He knew the hamster was a boy. He had waited all day the first night for Giant to reveal their name.

Sully walked along the plank as he looked avidly for eyes or a nose. "Hi!"

Bedding stirred. A young voice barked, "Leave me alone or I'll bite!"

The warning stung Sully a little, but he quickly recovered. *He's been very shy. Giant did say I was a large hamster. But it's all fur!*

He tried to sound his friendliest. "My name is Sully. That used to be my plank. It's really good for passing out on after you've run on your wheel. But you can use it as a tent if you want to."

Sounds of frantic burrowing. The log jumped.

"I won't come in!" Sully inched forward, hoping the bedding would collapse so he could see him. "Giant gave you lots of cool stuff. Huccome you haven't used your wheel?"

"Because I want to *hide*," the hamster answered brusquely with a sort of shake in his voice. "Go away!"

He's really scared. Why? Nothing bad ever happens at Giant's nest.

Sully walked away. *That bite he gave Giant was scary. I don't want to be taken to the vet because he bit me.*

He abruptly turned, hoping to catch the hamster peeking at him. No such luck.

"I'm happy you're here," Sully said. "I've always wanted a brother."

"Brother?"

Sully hadn't expected a response. He brightened. "Yep. It would be nice to have someone to look out for."

The bedroom door opened, and Giant rushed in. She scooped up Sully.

"Good morning, Koda. I'll see you in the night," Sully said cheerfully.

Giant turned him on his back to rub his belly. Sully giggled, but it seemed she was looking for something under his fur. She didn't find whatever it was, and for some reason, that made her exhale in relief.

"That scared me," Giant said, flustered. "You're fine."

She plopped him in his home, and Sully immediately went to the glass to look out at Koda's. He thought he could see a face underneath the plank in the white blur of the sun. It could have been wishful thinking, though Sully chose to have confidence in the first.

Sunlight lazed on the hideaway's snowy, coconut roof, making it very bright. He considered maybe he should have pouched some coconut. But that would have been rude. Then he was thinking of the sunlight on top of it, how extremely white it was.

Had he ever seen something so white?

The erasing light.

As the bedroom door slammed shut, Sully bolted up straight. He remembered.

The Trickster world was destroyed!

Sully looked around the room, frightened that he had lost himself somehow—like someone had used him to reenact a play and had rewired his mind into the past to do so. The room was still blurry and black and white.

"Koda…? When did we get back to the house?!"

SCREECH!

Sully squeaked, but it was just a tree scraping the window.

"Koda!"

The sunlight softened on the hideaway and the plank, making it disappear to Sully's eyes. No other light came from a Christmas tree. He realized there wasn't one anywhere in the room, the carpet wasn't burned, and everything looked as it was before the fire.

"Is everybody okay?!"

Clouds obscured the sun, and the room darkened. The memory was gone.

"Where did you go?" Sully said quietly, though his heartbeat couldn't be any louder.

He drifted into his memories. He remembered it had been a long while until he saw Koda again. Eventually, Sully saw him burrow out from the plank like a cautious turtle.

Giant coaxed him out of his shell. First, she set her hand in the home, letting Koda know she was there. Later she would place a chair next to his home and sit in it, sometimes reading, to get Koda used to her being around. Then there was the first handling test, and that didn't go so well. But so many more things to get Koda comfortable did work. After two months, Koda could sit in her hands without biting.

It took him longer to trust Sully. What pushed it, Sully thought, was the time Sully had become lost in the walls; he hadn't made many holes yet. He could hear Giant crying loudly one night. Koda had searched for Sully, and he found him. That's what started Koda thinking he wasn't so bad. Everyday Sully called something friendly to him, and it took a really long time, but after many adventures, Koda finally called back to him.

How happy Sully had been during the months that followed. Telling Koda about movies, music, and forage—all kinds of forage! He hadn't even known about cheese! There was the day Sully told him about fireworks, that they were a good thing even though they were loud, because Giant spoiled them with treats to keep them calm. At night, they would snicker across to each other, making fun of the dragon (*Come see the bearded lady!* Sully would joke).

He became his friend, then his brother. Still, Sully was worried when he finally asked Koda about the nub on his left paw. He hadn't ever answered him. Koda always found some way to distract him from the subject. That was a little hurtful since Sully thought they were so close, but he knew Koda must have a very good reason not to tell him.

Now alone, Sully pawed the glass, wishing the sun would shine through the window again so he could see Koda's home.

"Koda! Are you in trouble? I'm going to jump out!"

I really wish you would stop escaping.

The memory of Koda's words stopped Sully for a second. *Just one more time*, he thought. Determined, he climbed onto his wheel.

Twistin' the night away!

Sully nearly had a stroke. Giant's radio had turned on full blast. That must have been it.

He jumped over the glass wall onto the carpet. Darkness blotched the light. How could he have ever seen this way?! As he focused his eyes, he could just make out Giant's bed directly across from him, and at the ends, the homes. That itself wasn't strange. But somehow, Sully had dropped from his home to end up in an entirely different part of the room!

He paid closer attention to the light. There hadn't been any light in the room before. Sully's heart fluttered. The song was beginning to frighten him. Stepping backward, he felt a dangerous warmth on his side. The Christmas tree burned in a terrible display of shattering ornaments and withering branches. The comforting smells of Giant and Koda were overpowered by heat, burnt carpet, and an animal scent that smelled dangerous.

He heard a clack like the snap of a beak. "THERE YOU ARE."

Under the bed, behind the overhanging blanket, was the nightmare Sully kept returning to in his mind.

Hototo was about to kill Koda.

Sully stepped back against the dragon's cage. Turning around, he prepared himself to see her.

But the dragon wasn't staring at him…

… because the dragon wasn't there.

Sully screamed at the owl, "I'm here! I can do it now!"

The chase never came. Hototo, a standing figure of black, exited the blanket. Koda squealed in his talon. The talon rose to the owl's horrendous face, and Koda's little body flopped like a ragdoll in Hototo's beak.

And then he swallowed him.

***

Koda gasped sharply. Just a split second ago, he had seen the water tendril strike Sully through the passage and the erasing light enter the loculus. Splashes like ocean waves throwing a ship had become louder than the quakes. Now he was here, wherever that could be, staring at a cool gray wall.

Did Sully do it?

Even if he did, there has to be nothing left.

I'm somewhere. I think I'm alive.

Where is everyone?

Sully isn't safe. He's got to get warm.

The wall wasn't completely gray or solid. Through a plastic film smudged in grime, he saw dark, squirming shapes like hissing cockroaches. The movement made Koda ill to his stomach. He could smell them. A moist, rancid smell violated his nose and burned his eyes. They were out there in another bin, and he could see they were small with little to no fur. There were things much larger behind them. One of them looked directly up at Koda, the black-pebbled eyes dulled by the plastic between them.

Déjà vu hit Koda hard. He staggered away from the wall, stepping in oily liquid. Every movement brought him closer to becoming conscious of himself, and he was finally aware that his cheeks were lighter.

The relics were gone.

His paws thrust upward into the hollow of his cheek. He shouted, "No, NO! Who took them?!"

Turning around, his fear was almost too great. Koda uttered a small, indistinct sound. He realized that though his sight had reverted to black and white, it wasn't the reason why his vision was blurring. He was about to faint.

He had meant to run until his paws were swollen. Now, he swiped his arm over his ear, reaching across his face to the other. His paws came away dark gray and wet. He groomed himself repeatedly without any real thought to the fact that he was covered in waste.

His siblings crowded the bin. They hobbled around, most covered in filth. One hamster spun in circles, stopped, and repeated the cycle. Another batch of small, wriggling shapes bunched in a corner.

Koda thought, *The humans. The humans haven't taken them out yet. They're too busy filling the cages. Cramped. They just keep getting more cramped.*

Sound came into the space. Outside the bin, metal clanged and rattled. *The animals almost never come out of their cages. There are so many rows out there. Row after row after row.* Dogs whined. One of them was strong enough to bark. Another howled mournfully, and others answered with their own woeful call. Koda wished they would stop. He remembered hearing them in and out of his sleep, going on nonstop, just as he always smelled them. Ammonia, sickness, and death clouded the air.

I can't stand it! Why don't they ever take them out?!

Cold air seeped through the plastic as something outside the bin kicked on and started vibrating. Possibly an air conditioner. Or a freezer. Right next to the bins for easy access.

They put the mice and rats in plastic bags. I bite when I see a human hand. I don't want to be frozen!

Koda shivered to his core. He lost his voice but dug deep for it. "LET ME OUT!"

It seemed impossible to be this frightened. Maybe if he hadn't experienced this scene so many times in his nightmares, hadn't been reminded of what had happened so long ago every day since, he might have been confused. But he wasn't. Koda understood all of what was inside the building as much as he understood what was going to happen when he took a moment to actually feel his fingers.

He looked at his left paw.

And saw there were four.

Koda gaped, so shocked he couldn't process the large hamster approaching in the corner of his eye. He stared at both paws, seeing they were the same size as when he was only a few weeks old.

What caused the hamster to attack him? Did he appear too small or weak? Or had he simply been in the way? The hamster bit Koda on the hip, and in reaction to him crying out, jumped on him. Koda flipped onto his back. Nails raked his stomach. Without thinking, he pushed his paw into the hamster's chest. Its head ducked down. Vicious pain flared in Koda's finger. He screamed until he couldn't breathe. And the hamster rolled them into their other siblings, agitating them.

They began to join in.

20

THE SMOKING BEAST

SEVEN MONTHS Koda had gone without biting anyone, and still he kept his teeth sharp to the point he was afraid he would chop off his fingers when eating or asleep—all for the chance he might need them in another fight.

Summoning a burst of desperate strength, Koda kicked the hamster off him and raised his paws, screaming angrily like a hornet. His sibling stumbled in the misted shade of hemlock trees. Koda didn't give the scenery change a second thought, though he became incensed at the hamster gaping with wide eyes as if his finger hadn't been between its teeth.

His fury shattered as he stared at Sully. Gone was the larger hamster. Sully stared back, shocked and unsure. All at once the forest in all its strange light, complete clearness, and colors came to Koda, and he was confused. His heart thumped. Why had everything changed?!

"You're alive," Sully said, overcome with relief. He walked forward. "Koda, I have something to tell you. At Giant's nest—"

Koda rapidly backed away.

"What's wrong?"

Ears back, Koda narrowed his eyes. "How did you get here?"

"I don't know. It's scary."

"Shui Gui got you in the tunnel."

"Yes, but—"

"How do I know you're not the totem?" Koda asked, his voice rising in fear.

The hamster watched him as if uncomfortable. "It *is* me. I fell into the lake, and I wasn't possessed anymore. I think it worked for everyone else, too."

Why isn't he wet? a voice inside Koda asked.

The hamster's face brightened. "I'm so happy you're okay!" It leaped at Koda to attack.

Koda ripped into the soft flesh beneath its arm. It squeaked and tried to flee, but Koda would not let it. In a quick and furious outburst, Koda squeaked, too, and struggled with it before the hamster kicked away from him.

It gaped, blood streaking its side. The eyes were innocent and afraid. They didn't look like Shui Gui's eyes at all. And just like that, Koda's mind woke up. The image was too much. The realization that he had done something beyond terrible suffocated him.

Bushes rustled. Koda started as Rowan, Jack, and the squirrel walked into the clearing.

Koda lunged for Sully, and his brother shrank away. "Sully, be careful! They—"

"It's us," Rowan said. He stood precariously as if he would fall over by any wind. Jack and the squirrel had a haggard look to them.

Koda turned back to Sully. His brother recoiled. It was his eyes that hurt Koda's heart the most. The others saw the blood, and they shared in a moment of undecidedness.

Koda examined his left paw. The unbloodied stub was seamless to the skin again.

276

Am I going crazy?!

Gently, thinking there would be pain if he moved it, he set his paw down on the ground. "I didn't know you were you. It was a nightmare," Koda said, pleading. "I was in the mill."

If Sully understood, it didn't show in his eyes.

"He knows what he's talking about," the squirrel managed to say. "I had a nightmare. Hototo was murdering everyone in the rain." The squirrel gripped his stomach. "He got me."

"I was at the carnival," Rowan put in. "Koda and Sully hadn't shown up in time, and the crystals covered my face. I couldn't breathe," he finished with a kind of stupefied amazement. "What about you, Jack? Any nightmares?"

Jack shook his head. Even afterwards it quivered a little. "None that I can remember."

"Was it real?" the squirrel asked. "It felt real enough, so how could it be a nightmare?"

"Probably because it's not a nightmare," Rowan said. "You know, my owner, he sometimes hosted Bible studies at his house. I heard the word 'purgatory' mentioned once or twice. If my English is right, I'd say it was described as 'the place you went after you died.' The 'place of sufferin'' before you moved on. What we've experienced is kind of like that, don't you reckon?"

"We're dead?"

Sully glanced worriedly at the squirrel.

"Not exactly. But we're movin' on, alright. The Trickster world was destroyed, so perhaps we're waitin' for the next."

"Is this it?" The squirrel gestured at a dreary sky empty of face constellations. "Is this the Haven?"

Koda tried to put aside his emotions to focus on their surroundings. A light breeze swayed leaves and devil's club shoots circling the foggy trees. Daybreak in a forest.

"No," said Jack. "If this were the Haven, I'm sure we would

have already seen other Critters."

Koda didn't smell them or any other creature, either.

Rowan scanned the trees. "I don't recognize this forest."

"The relics," Jack said. "Do we still have them?"

Koda was startled to feel the weight had returned to his cheeks. "Yes." *I'm not going to say I gave Sully a relic*, he thought. He hadn't entirely let go of his suspicions.

"Hototo wanted the relics," the squirrel said, remembering. "After the water totem possessed me in the lake, Hototo told it to steal them and kill you. It was going to use me to do it!"

"And failed. You have no blood on your paws, Twiggy," said Jack.

Rowan stared hard at Jack's hind leg. A weeping red line capped the knee. "I'm madder than a boiled owl. I really am, and that's exactly what I ought to do to Hototo." He looked at Jack. "I'm sorry."

"Don't blame yourself. The wound will heal," Jack said in a hidden tone Koda had come to understand meant he was uncomfortable. Soon he would change the subject.

Sully winced at Jack's injury. *He doesn't know how similar his own injury is.* Koda felt an overwhelming need to stand by him but forced himself to wait.

"We should be moving on." Jack stood. His leg trembled.

"I can carry you," Rowan offered quickly.

"I'm fine." Jack eased his leg down and hopped with a limp to the farthest trees. Rowan and the squirrel followed, an unsure gate in their steps. Not without weariness, Sully took his place next to Koda, who kept his movements passive.

The forest opened onto a deep, grassy incline. As the wind blew stronger, its breeze swayed the hemlocks which sloped into a valley thick with them. Out of the wooded hills and high, green, rocky walls, fog rose and clumped into the sky. Among all its grayness Koda spotted a blob of color, what he assumed was a balloon. More drifted up from the valley, crinkling.

They weren't what had initially caught their eye. After a glance of offer and a dismissal from Jack, Rowan grabbed Koda and Sully and trotted down the incline. Jack had a difficult time of it. He lost his balance halfway and tumbled to a stop directly on his injured leg. He winced, huffing quietly with a tightening of his chest as if he were trying desperately not to cry out in pain. Koda and Sully asked if he was okay. Their answer was a distinct nod.

The squirrel kept close to Jack as they lowered deeper into the valley. A nearby stream burbled softly. There was the occasional branch snap, which sent the squirrel into twitching fits. His twitches turned to barks while through the trees a group of rowdy Tricksters chased phantom carousel horses.

It was occasional at least to Koda as he heard the noises mostly on the edge of his hearing. He had a lot to think about. Sully hardly looked at him, and he hadn't even tried to clean the drying blood on his fur. Noticing that the others' noses were no longer wet, same as Sully's fur, Koda realized they must be dry because Shui Gui's power had been released from them.

What have I done?

It wasn't until Koda walked into Rowan's hoof that he saw how much the scenery had changed. In the shadows beneath a thick canopy, it was like an entirely different world. Arcade machines and food carts sat out of the shoots like unearthed treasures. The target sign from a dunk tank sat in the arm of a tree, and on a popcorn cart, a small glowing bird wearing steampunk goggles picked at the buttered kernels spilling out from the broken glass.

Rowan kicked a large yellow ball, the kind that filled a ball pit. It bounced lightly to rest beside the cart, and the bird flew away.

"A junkyard. The whole carnival's here," he said.

"As well as items from the house and cemetery," said Jack.

In the grove to their right, blurry armchairs sat next to clear tombstones. The sight disturbed Koda. They gave him the feeling of someone invisible seated in them.

Far ahead, light glimmered off something silver and tall. It brought them to the bottom of a mountain. The shoulder was steep. Two metal supports leaned inside its cleft. Koda gazed upward at a Ferris wheel. The fog softened it like a castle in the clouds. Carts hung in the spokes, and many sat in the crowns of trees. The canopy had broken up here, cluttering the ground with broken branches and leaves.

Koda stood defensively, causing Sully to flinch, as something clanged in the spokes of the Ferris wheel. A non-glowing marionette caught on a tree branch where it dangled above them.

"I thought everything was destroyed," Koda said, unnerved.

"If that were true, we'd be dead," said the squirrel.

Remnants of the carnival, the false Giant's nest, the cemetery, and the catacombs littered their path. There were also items apparently from other locations they hadn't seen, such as disturbing paintings Koda guessed were from a gallery. A bald Trickster held his hands to his head and screamed silently from a charcoal prison. The scenes had all the character of a demented dream. String lights adorned the trees, and what miscellaneous objects there were on the ground were sunk in dunes of indigo sand. The smaller Critters at the rear of their group pulled back to avoid getting dusted.

Koda felt numb to it all. In all the clutter, he hadn't seen one Cracker Jack.

"What a mess," the squirrel remarked. He jerked to his full height as Jack tripped on a bump in the grass. Jack's leg shook as he stood.

"Let me give you a ride. You're gonna beat yourself up," Rowan said with firm care.

"Nonsense." Jack grunted and made a visible effort to hop steadily.

Sully asked, "Are you okay?"

"Don't worry yourself," Jack said patiently.

Rowan and the squirrel flanked him as they walked. Jack quickly caught on.

"You don't need to slow for me," he said.

They reluctantly gave him his space.

Surmounting a knoll, they dove steeply to a dense grove. A circus tarp hung in the crown of one of the largest trees, slumping to the ground like a curtain. Monochromatic objects Koda had seen in the red tent spotted the grass. The squirrel scurried to Jack's flank, leaning away with his paws curled in.

Koda didn't like it here. It was especially startling to see so much red after a while of little to no color, though his eyes didn't hurt anymore. He was getting tired of looking at the trees, especially here, in this dark lighting. He hated how behind every one, he expected something to peek out.

Light bounced off a small, falling object. It wasn't strange considering there were many shiny things flying in the wind, but Jack paused at this one. It fell right at his feet as if the wind had dealt it to him.

"What is it?" Rowan asked.

Jack stepped back. His face tightened, whether from pain, surprise, or both. "It's one of the fox Trickster's cards."

The red card had landed face down. No one moved to flip it over.

Rowan asked, "You said you saw two of the three?"

Jack nodded.

"You hadn't really gone into detail."

Jack sat in the grass next to a toy gypsy caravan. Sully and the squirrel glanced around nervously as they realized they wouldn't be leaving soon. *I can see Jack wants to, but he's hurting. What really happened in that tent?* When Koda had first wondered that, he hadn't been ashamed to think Jack was up to something. Now he felt only sympathy and guilt.

"The first card, Deception, was of three Hunter skulls." Jack described them. "That somehow indicated that one or a few of my friends was hiding the truth. The second was a devil, which supposedly symbolized totems. From there, the fox went on to pry into my past." He said this slightly bitterly. "All the cards were to point to one outcome."

"I reckon it's important we see that last card," Rowan said.

"Why?" the squirrel asked grouchily.

"'Cause Jack never said the Trickster was incorrect. She told his past perfectly, I'd bet."

"You're saying we're lying to Jack?"

"Don't get tore up. I'm just sayin', if we can get ahead of the game…"

Jack frowned. "It was a mistake not to give the fox more credit. Now that I think of it, it's possible the skull card was depicting the Hunter from the flood."

"Wha—? None of us knows anything about that! So, we can't have been lying," said the squirrel.

"Those cards are comin' true," Rowan said broodingly, his haunting words causing a sense of foreboding. A breeze Koda hadn't felt threw the card into the air, startling everyone. It rode on the wind, somehow never revealing the reverse side to them, and landed in the far grass.

"I'll get it," Sully said. Guilt or no guilt, Koda went with him without slowing his pace.

They found the card face-down against a rock on the other side of a tree. The fir leaned dramatically from its roots, which seemed to stretch painfully out of the ground. Sully crawled underneath the tree but froze at an approaching sound.

Koda perked his ears, sniffing. Jack and Rowan had paused walking toward them and were a distance away still. The squirrel was hidden to him, probably in the grass. Koda made eye contact with Jack. He was watching attentively.

The ground rumbled. *Not again*, Koda thought. Then he listened more. The sound evolved into rapid tearing of grass and shifting noises—a glassy sound like small mouths grinding crystals.

Koda shoved Sully, stopping him from running farther out from the tree and grabbing the card.

"Stay put," Koda said.

To their ears, the sounds roared with the power of a horse stampede. Koda and Sully tucked in their bottoms as the first wave struck. Geode Tricksters raced by them through the grass, tearing into the blades, their crystal feet sounding like the slight crack of glass.

Koda jolted as a geode sliced a blade close to his face. He feared the Tricksters would try to kidnap him and Sully, but they seemed to be unaware of them. Or maybe they didn't care to take notice. Tricksters. Not caring to take notice of Critters.

What's going on?

The card fluttered at each gust of earthy air. Sully watched it nervously. "Why are they running?"

The geodes tore up the land into the thick fog beyond the grove. The last of the pattering diminished as quickly as it had arrived. A few stragglers hurried to keep up with the rest, looking back apprehensively with their shifty eyes.

There was a rustle toward the knoll as if Rowan, Jack, and the squirrel were flailing in the grass. Warnings were shouted. Jack thumped. Koda questioned at last why they hadn't come to the tree. The answer came with a thud and a loud scrape.

SCREECH!

Koda heard the wind passing through the owl's feathers. His dangerous scent swept underneath the tree. As it trespassed into Koda's lungs, a part of him felt that it would poison him. The owl had smelled like this, too, when Koda had hid from him under the bed. His blood went cold just the same as before, and his little rodent heart beat very fast and very loud.

Tap… tap. The tapping of his talons.

Was he toying with them?

Koda and Sully stared upward. Wood dust flaked off the trunk. The owl's talons wobbled on the bark, digging into it like a saw.

What's it doing?

The owl's wings beat frantically without flying. The talons dug harder at the bark, shaking the tree. An increasing feeling of warmth made them cower flat to the ground and away from black smoke pouring out like dry ice.

***

Jack, Twiggy, and Rowan ducked at the foot of the hill. Jack tried to resist thumping. Even lifting his leg sent a searing pain into his thigh.

The owl's scent trailed overhead before dropping with the threat of a guillotine blade. Most any Critter can distinguish a Hunter from their own scent, and while that thing certainly smelled ominous, it didn't smell like any bird on Earth.

They had forgotten it was daybreak. Sunrays showered the owl, and he didn't flee. Jack finally noticed—after his mind had cleared a little from fright—that the owl wasn't anywhere near the size of the great totem who could lift Rowan off the ground or attack cougars. In fact, the owl was about the size of a normal horned owl.

It's not Hototo.

For the moment, at least, Jack didn't expect it would be able to move. The beast shuddered as though about to burst. Wings batted. Feathers splayed like broken fingers and began to rip apart on its body. Smoke seeped through the tears.

There was a shift of light and movement in the grass, and Jack fought the instinct to flee. A sound like millions of cicadas rolled across the grove as the grass waved at a great speed. Prints that were not his own, nor his friends', stamped the soil, a spring's worth, as well as scattered leaves crisped from autumn. Twiggy bounced hard at the *CRACK!* of settling trees.

Rowan snorted in confusion. "It's loadin' again! Like Sully said!"

Cold penetrated Jack's coat. Where mist had wandered thickly beyond the trees was now clear grassland. Frost rapidly overtook shrubs, freezing stems and branches of stranded trees into icicles. The entire feathery landscape tinkled from building ice. A frozen fence bordered it.

The sun was breaking through the overcast.

Jack jolted at a creak and saw of branches. The circus tarp tugged in the wind and cascaded free to the ground—right at the roots of a tree with peeled bark in front.

"Muraco died here."

Showing surprise in his expression, Rowan said with a mix of sympathy and disconcertment, "You said you didn't have a nightmare. That's because it hadn't started."

Jack forced himself to stand on his leg and winced.

"This is fake," Rowan said, growing more excited.

"That *beast* isn't," Jack stressed.

I should have recognized this place, Jack thought angrily. *But without the snow... Would it have been in my mind if that fox Trickster hadn't planted it? Made me remember what I didn't want to remember?*

285

"What's happening to it?" Twiggy's disturbed, constricted voice gripped Jack like a cold fist. He did a double take at the thing spoiling the owl's feathers and skin. The sun's rays had fallen. Shadowed in the bruise-colored gloom, a scarecrow creature stood at five feet tall and was still growing. It wore the beginnings of clothes that steamed with heat. Smoke and long hairs streamed out of its ballooning head. The beast buckled, using a still forming human hand to hold itself up.

The spectacle held Jack still before urgency propelled him on his feet. He ignored the splitting pain in his leg. *Fight through it! If I never run another day, let me flee this world first.*

Rowan moved to shelter him. Jack snapped, "Precious time is already lost!"

The scolding was like a fired gun, a comparison that came to Jack from the pole shape hidden by the camouflage jacket. Rowan obeyed him. At his hooves, Twiggy twitched frightfully.

"Now run!"

***

Sully darted forward and snatched the tarot card. Running with it, he and Koda turned back for the knoll. They swirled up smoke upon the bitter ground. The chill latched onto Koda's fur.

At the top of the knoll, the erasing light cut away the last of the horizon's golden strip. It had arrived as a silent threat without any rumbling and increased in brightness as it flashed forward. The snow looked dark gray against its brilliance.

Sully and Koda halted with the others. Jack said, "We've entered the light! It will take us to the Haven!"

Unlike before, when the light had swept over the tunnels, everything it touched now burst, like a star had exploded in every blade of grass.

Rowan paced like a frightened horse. "Forget it." He charged in the direction of the leaning tree and the creature.

After less than a minute, the smoking creature was nearly completely formed. Sunlight cut under a brimmed hat, revealing a cruel face. The body still shook from a puffing movement under the jacket.

The squirrel and Jack were quick to follow Rowan. "Rowan, stop!" they cried.

Rowan sped up to the trunk… and passed it. "I'm not stupid!" he shouted.

Koda and Sully ran. The grass frustratingly slowed them and blocked their view. In his mind's eye, Koda saw the hunter jump down from the tree and grab the gun with its one free arm, dragging the barrel in the dirt. He could *hear* it happening.

Ahead, Rowan's beating hooves slowed a little, probably for Jack. Jack, a swift blur of brown fur above the grass, passed Rowan and Koda both. He had lucky feet, Rowan had admiringly said, and apparently so even when injured.

But Jack was staggering along. His pawsteps weren't as sure sounding as Rowan's. Approaching the fence, Koda heard him stumble and running to him, he saw fresh blood soaking Jack's knee. He could no longer hide the obvious pain on his face. His eyes darkened in the dimmer snowy light. Koda heard excited Trickster voices out on the grassland. They were running, too.

"Stop! It'll have a clear shot!" Jack warned as Rowan trotted up and veered.

"There's nowhere else to go!" Rowan cried.

Koda, Sully, and the squirrel stood like prairie dogs. The erasing light broke up the leaves in the grove.

The squirrel said to Jack in a high, strained voice, "Let Rowan carry you—"

"I will slow him," Jack replied impatiently.

"Now's not the time to be proud!"

Koda turned to see how close the light had gotten to them. He hadn't expected to find someone standing hidden by a nearby tree.

A human wearing brown fur. Those had been Jack's exact words. Slanted branches obscured the figure's head. *How high is that? It's got to be at least twelve feet!* Its hands were shoved inside its coat pockets. It was watching them, Koda was sure, waiting to see how everything would play out.

A sharp echo pierced the grove. Bark exploded, and grass flew like fireworks. The squirrel lapsed into a fit of barking.

A tussock to our left exploded.

Light cut into a tree where a bullet had shot at an angle to the grass.

Rowan moved to grab Jack, and Jack kicked his feet at him. "Damn it, Jack!"

The hunter's boots rapidly crunched leaves and dirt. Jack bolted to the fence and gasped as his injured leg caught on a board. Rowan charged the fence. The frame creaked and bowed. He charged again, and it snapped. Everyone else scurried under.

Geode Tricksters, carnival creatures, and other miscellaneous Tricksters were breezes of color in the tussocks. Koda slowed as much as he dared for fear of cutting himself on the icicles. It was not a natural snow. He knew the world had gone crazy. Beside him, though falling behind, Sully refused to let go of the card. It bent upward at his face and fought him.

"Let it go!" Koda shouted.

The gunshot fired louder on the grassland. Rowan collapsed out of view. Sully screamed, the others shouted, and Koda felt terror. He was relieved as he heard Rowan heaving his weight off the ground and his hooves trotting clumsily to catch up to them. The tip of one of his horns was missing.

The erasing light rounded the landscape and shone thinly throughout the tussocks. The land rolled upward onto a hill, and Koda was awestruck once more.

It was like another planet was sitting on the edge of the grassland. The edge wavered like blazing heat, yet the colors inside were cool. He saw another world inside, somehow looking down at its landscape from a starry purplish-gray sky. There was no moon. Windows to other purgatories and the face constellations appeared in the sky. Tricksters plummeted to the ground like tiny green fireballs. Because it was night, Koda was fooled into seeing mountains where the wind had shaped the desert sand. A river divided the desert and real mountains in a long, wavy line.

Animals, hundreds of animals, herded in its pass. They sounded strange calls, more spectacular than the trumpeting of elephants. Sully had watched enough dinosaur movies for Koda to recognize the brontosauruses and stegosauruses. The calls became so strong, there had to be millions more. Somehow, Koda knew no matter how strikingly earthlike the land formations, there were no giants inhabiting this world.

"The Haven!" the squirrel yelled. "We're gonna lead it right into it!"

Koda kept Sully in sight as he ran up the hill. The erasing light encompassed all sides of Jack's purgatory and was drawing in. The one thing that remained untouched was the window into the Haven. Some of the Tricksters had made it to where the grassland ended and were launching themselves inside. Koda's perception of them changed. Like the rest of the world, he viewed them from above.

The squirrel barked. "We'll be killed!"

Jack shouted, "No, they're floating!"

Once level with the mountain peaks, the Tricksters hovered abruptly as if pulled by invisible parachutes.

Koda heard a sound—*Jangling of loose metal*, as Jack had described when telling his story. As Koda dodged the tussocks, he glimpsed something white like a ghost running up one of the hills. It *was* a ghost, in a way, for Koda saw it was Muraco drawing in close alongside them. His shoulder bled on his white fur like wine spilled across a white cloth, and somewhere below—if what Koda was seeing wasn't simply a memory—there would be a groove within the bone. The blood and his limp seemed so real, but in just one second, he changed from Jack's brother to the hunter's dog, a mean, gray-haired, chomping brute.

Jack's legs threw him instead of propelling him forward. Seeing Muraco, his head ducked and almost hit the ground. The gun fired, and it was Muraco, not the dog, who lay dead. Jack uttered a strangled sound that was meant to be a scream.

"It's not real!" Koda shouted.

Another echoing roar ended in an explosive shatter. Ahead, a geode Trickster's crystals stabbed into the ground. As Koda and Sully ran around it, the tarot card struck a shard and jerked out of Sully's mouth.

"The card!" Sully cried.

"Don't!" Koda shouted.

Someone collided with Koda, and he rolled. He curled into a ball as the stampede hurdled over him. The Tricksters kept coming, and Koda was frozen. He had been ignoring the cold. Now that he wasn't moving, it rushed into him.

In a break in the stampede, Sully and the squirrel helped him onto his feet. The three of them shortened the distance they had lost and ran in line beside Rowan and Jack.

Sully hadn't returned for the card. But now it made its way back to them, flying above their heads without ever flipping over, on a wind that didn't exist. It was like it was trying to tell them something.

Jack's final card unexpectedly dove, the movement somehow so precise and aggressive that Koda stumbled before he kept on running. The card kept with them, turned itself over, and hung in the air in front of Sully just long enough for him to gasp at what was on the reverse side. Koda, managing to run close by him, at first could not process what was pictured there, it was so terrible.

Jack's final card portrayed a robed skeleton clutching a scythe.

"What is it? What did you see?" the squirrel cried.

"It's Jack!" Sully screamed. "The card is his death!"

The card flew behind them. Twenty feet from the Haven, Jack stumbled on a mound and fell, landing on his injured leg. He squealed. The knee was as bright as a red pinball.

Everyone skidded to a stop.

"Keep going!" Jack ordered.

He urged me to run...

"We're not leaving you!" the squirrel screamed and tried to pull Jack's arm.

Jack pushed him. "Protect them, Rowan!"

Rowan had run the farthest of them. He swerved back and looked at Jack, tormented.

We held eye contact...

"Jack, get up!" Sully cried.

Koda realized he no longer heard the hunter's footsteps. He spun when he heard a precise *click* from a nearby hill. He never did see the hunter or his gun. There was just the sound it made, a strident blast.

And the human shot him.

Jack's body fell. The squirrel leaped away, then turned back to him, his face tightened in horror. "Jack!"

Rowan grabbed him and raced for the Haven. As when fighting his sibling, witnessing Sully convulse at the sight of the aptrgangr, and at everything else terrifying that had ever made Koda feel helpless, a sensitive part of him froze. The rest took flight, only thought of taking flight, and steered him among Sully and the others to the edge of the grassland. The erasing light closed in.

A surging sensation blossomed in Koda, like he was in the seat of the roller coaster. The Haven spun and steadied as he felt a strong pull in his stomach. They landed softly among the Tricksters in the desert. While the Tricksters ran for their lives, Koda and the others stayed still in the sand. They were in another world. Free from purgatory.

At last Koda could understand Jack, how something so important to you, that you had sought after, could become so meaningless. He and Sully may be one step closer to home, had found something he thought impossible from the beginning, but he found he couldn't take any of it in. His mind froze upon that last image of Jack, his body jerking from that bullet and hitting the ground with a final thud. Had anything ever hurt this much? Knowing they had come this far, knowing who had helped them and kept them safe, and knowing he'd been shot close enough for Koda to see his blood staining the grass.

He cried, remembering.

The others cried, too. It seemed they would stay still for a while until the squirrel, Twiggy, scattered the sand in chase of something. Koda looked up at the sky at a burlap bag floating down. They all rushed to it.

Jack was tucked into the bag, only his upper body laying out of it. His ears lay limp over his face, fur swaying in the light breeze.

Sully sobbed. "Jack."

All the twitching movements had gone out of Twiggy. He brushed the ears apart and exclaimed, "He's alive!"

Blood trickled at the corner of Jack's mouth. His teeth, smeared with it, jabbed up and down.

Rowan sat heavily from shock.

"We can help him! He's breathing!" Twiggy cried.

Sully held up a paw to Jack and recoiled with a wretched cry as Jack suddenly kicked uncontrollably. Sully backed away to sob beside Koda, still with horror at Jack's squeaks. He gasped, fell still. His paws folded like the dead hands of someone laid to rest, but he breathed in short bursts.

Twiggy shook as he held his head in his paws.

Jack said weakly, "Worse things will happen now. Look out for each other."

Sully said in a voice muffled by tears, "Don't go, Jack."

Walking gently past Twiggy, Koda recalled the sound of rocks settling, the shouts he had made to Sully, and the comfort he had felt from Jack. Koda pressed his nose on Jack's ear. He hoped it would mean something to him. An apology for all his suspicions.

Jack focused on him. His expression changed as if Koda were someone else. Dying, would he have appeared to him, with his ivory fur, like a white jackrabbit?

"Muraco, I'm sorry... I wanted to forget." Jack's eyes seemed to stare at nothing. His breathing stopped.

PART IV
THE HAVEN

21

THE COLLAPSE

THE SOUND was spectacular. Louder than the harshest thunder, explosions pounded in Sully's chest and took over the beat of his heart. They ripped the world. It was as if the sky was breaking.

"Stay close to me!" Koda shouted, wincing.

Sully hardly reacted. *It's too horrible. Jack can't be dead!*

Rowan cried. The sight of his tears, so painfully sad, made Sully feel faint with grief. Rowan stood unsteadily, looking at the sky, and said with wretched realization, "The totems! They've all been released!"

Jack's death had been the last straw. The Haven just couldn't take it.

An enormous tremor hit the desert. Almost immediately a deep crashing echo dove toward them. Sully toppled into Koda.

Twiggy clung to Jack. "They're not going to get away with it! They can't kill you, too!"

Rowan grabbed Twiggy as an overpowering burst of air like the opening of a shaft pushed Sully across the sand. He cowered from the sheer volume of cascading sand as he struggled to stay afloat, squinting in the cutting wind. A hole appeared and collapsed right in front of him. A kangaroo rat jumped out, spun and darted into the fumbling crowd. There were more than Tricksters. Camels, ostriches, and other desert Critters ran for their lives. The ground cracked behind them in an arc of separating sand. It completely split apart and a chasm formed, cutting across the desert like a lightning strike, forking in all directions where the desert dunes poured in.

And the Haven's crust separated. Jack's lifeless body drifted on a piece of tectonic plate. Sully, Koda, Rowan, Twiggy, and all the other Critters, trapped upon their own platform of the Haven's crust, drifted as well.

Rowan kicked his front hooves, his lower body submerged in sand like a horse swept by a wave. He released Twiggy to grab Sully and Koda just as they were about to be buried.

For a second, it seemed Twiggy was going to go after Jack. Then he stopped in his tracks. Restraining the part of his voice that wanted to choke, he yelled, "Here! Come on! Over here!" and scurried onto Rowan to grasp his horn.

Many more kangaroo rats had fled their burrows. They hurried to Sully's group with what appeared to be a hundred more rattled Critters.

The ground ceased shaking, and they stopped sinking. Rowan pulled himself out of the sand and brought Sully and Koda beneath the cover of his belly. The other rodents crowded them. Feeling all their fright as well as his own, Sully could feel himself bordering on a whole new kind of terror. He couldn't tell what squeaks were his and what were someone else's. He just knew he had to get away from here or very soon he would lay down in the sand, weakened by a failing heart.

He was too afraid to run, but what brought him back, if just a little, was Koda's comforting grip on his paw. His brother stood up and looked over the crowd. On the other platform, someone was screaming. Soon the urge to scream was like a wave passing onto the others. The explosions ceased, and Sully heard a tremulous shout next to his ear. "Totem!"

Jack was no longer on the edge of the platform across from them. The thought of him falling into the chasm sucked the air out of Sully. He struggled to breathe. Tricksters and Critters tried climbing over the edge of the platforms, lost their footing, and fell to where a huge cascading rumble absorbed the splash. Great waves rolled into the chasm from the ocean.

Frenzied, running from something. The Critters on the other platform fell over in a panic. A gap of about fifty feet separated Sully from something large and white chasing them to the edge. A jerboa hopped in front of Sully, and he lost it.

He didn't try to look again. He was distressed to hear the scene continue. The screaming! They were Critters just like him and Koda. Brothers. Sisters. Whole families like Jack, Rowan, and Twiggy had. It was all the same throughout the Haven. Monstrous calls turned ravenous upon hearing the agonized screams.

"I can't take it!" Twiggy bawled.

"That's too big of a jump. It can't come over here," Rowan said, bewildered and confused with a growing sense of horror. It magnified in his voice as he shifted toward the south. "Somethin's there! Behind the mountains!"

Sully stepped to the side, anxious to see past the crowd.

"What do you see?" Koda shouted.

Rowan ducked into Sully's view and put them onto his back. With the dunes gone, the desert spanned as a flat and broken landscape made up of many chasms. The platforms glowed like florescent mushrooms. The windows to other worlds were gone. In their place, the face constellations glared malevolently at the mountain peaks. Sully scrutinized them. Between silent flashes of light, he thought he had seen five peaks instead of the four he now saw.

He waited for another lightning flash.

***

Hunting her doppelgänger had ended in failure. Sydney lost it soon after it left the cavern. She blamed the rumbling and the Critters yelling at each other. *You think they could be any louder? They'll wake the dead.* The tunnel had caved, and she had become trapped with a strange light. Next thing she knew, the scenery changed.

I didn't faint, Sydney thought bitterly, as if someone had accused her. She'd had a nightmare, a very vivid one where she was again carried by the owl in the pouring rain. The flood washed over the roots of a large tree where they landed. Sydney stared at the beak in her face. Her scales had protected her a little, but the owl flipped her to expose her soft underbelly. The pain had been incredible! But she felt perfectly fine now.

The scene around her changed again. There was no need to panic as she fell from the sky. *For all I know, I'm still dreaming.* Sydney landed safe in the desert—at least for a couple of seconds, until someone nearly trampled her. Prey animals and glowing creatures (many quite different from the two at the house) stumbled while they ran. In one direction, a wolf as big as a house whined like a frightened dog with its tail between its legs. In another, a centaur-like creature with a satyr for a torso raced into a group of ghosts. They floated outward from it with drawn, tortured faces. Sydney thought they would only have to wildly wave their arms to complete the chaos.

Thunderous explosions sent the crowd into even more of a frenzy. They covered their ears and shrieked.

Wimps.

Sydney jolted, gaping as another explosion detonated directly behind her, like a grenade going off. But instead of gun powder, a pungent BO smell dispersed into the air.

She heard a growl and a sound of falling sand. Under a

growing shadow, Sydney turned to face coal-gray fists quadruple the size of scaleless hands. Her gaze drew upward. Sand streamed off hulking shoulders and over a barrel chest. The creature grunted and huffed aggressively through its nose. White fur surrounded a dark silver, apish face.

"Abominable snowman? Aren't you, like, extinct?!" Sydney exclaimed.

Lips pulled in a snarl while the Yeti's cold eyes darted at a running camel. It snatched the Critter by the neck, and the camel let out a long, horn-like cry, kicking helplessly as the Yeti dragged it in the sand and pulled it high to a pair of long canine teeth.

Sydney fled. *Dream or not, I'm getting out of here.*

The ground rumbled. A brutal shatter sounded all around. Sydney froze, listening, as something like a dam broke somewhere in the desert, letting in huge waves of water. Sand rapidly sank beneath her.

She was stunned only for a moment. Running like a desert lizard, she took advantage of everyone fallen on their knees or bottoms to shove her way to the edge of a platform. Glowing creatures drowning in sand hung on to the side of a cliff. Sydney had to continuously step back as the sand pulled her toward a bottomless chasm.

"I'd have to be Godzilla to make that jump!"

The glowing creatures went over. A lucky few hung onto the cliff wall farther down and were unharmed when they splashed into the water. Sydney intended to do the same and was infuriated when she realized she was building up the courage to do so.

Someone kicked her as they ran up to the edge. Sydney dug in her claws. "Watch where you're going, you stupid—!"

With impending dismay, she watched the darkness of the chasm draw closer. Sydney fell three hundred feet in a shower of sand to crashing waves.

***

Sully tried not to blink. Lightning blinked for him and again he missed somewhere between the flashes the fifth peak appear.

It was not a peak, after all. A talon gripped the mountain. Following the next flashes, another talon appeared on the opposite side.

A joined whimper raised on the platforms. Now a gargantuan monster, Hototo raised over the peak. His cruel eyes hung like two evening suns eclipsed underneath the deep shadow of feathers. They fluttered in the wind and made his face disheveled and gruesome. Higher and higher his head went as he climbed on the back of the mountain.

Camazotz's scalded head rose behind the lower peaks. The bat demon glared, his scars angry and pink. What little fur he had spotting his flame-eaten skin shed into the wind in tufts. Red pupils in the center of his yellow gaze scanned the landscape—possibly for the Critters who had burned him.

As though suddenly breathing in after a near drowning, Sully awakened fully to the horror about to occur. The sandy plains in front of the mountains cut downward into the chasm as one long rock wall. Critters and Tricksters on the plains simultaneously realized where they were, and they fled to the cliff.

Hototo pushed off the summit and swooped onto the plains. Camazotz descended the mountain, unable to fly because of his fire-eaten wings. The totems were nearly the size of a mountain themselves. Blinking in and out of the dark amongst the rumbling of thunder, they stood pressed together with their wings thrashing... and fused. Their inner legs joined before disappearing altogether as Hototo's feathers transferred onto Camazotz's body. His face jutted forward at his beak as if someone were poking it from the inside, and it slanted until he was more like an eagle on the head.

A wave rose high over the Tricksters climbing down the rock wall before it crashed against the cliff, dragging them into the sea. When the waves calmed, the Tricksters disappeared, a water tendril shot over the plains. It dove between the two totems' heads and connected as their tail.

Now one, the totems flew like a tornado with one owl wing and one feather-bat wing. Crowds on every platform erupted in panic.

Sully jerked forward. The crowd shoved Rowan, forcing him to walk. Yells of surprise were followed by immediate splashes as they neared the platform's edge. It was the flood all over again.

Twiggy barked so loudly Sully feared for his lungs. "Rowan, pick them up! You're killing each other!"

Shaking, Sully looked to the other platform. Critters and Tricksters willingly threw themselves into the chasm. The Yeti stopped at the gap, had discarded a camel, and was observing their platform murderously.

The Yeti jumped and sunk behind the crowd. Sully desperately waited to hear the splash. It never came. A hand as large as a boulder raised over the crowd and smashed down on them with a violent shake.

Koda squeezed Rowan's neck. "There's no way off here!"

"For me there isn't!" Rowan corrected him.

Twiggy tightened his grip on Rowan's horn. Lit by the flashes in the sky, he looked like a pirate clinging to a mast. "For *all* of us!"

"Twiggy, I've seen you climb trees taller than—"

"*No!*"

Mountain goats can climb really well. Rowan's a goat. There can't be that big of a difference! Sully thought desperately.

The Yeti raised itself onto the platform. Each dramatic step shook the ground.

Rowan took off into the crowd with Sully and Koda gripping his shoulders. He trotted right up to a Trickster. "Please, can you take—" he started to ask, but the Trickster sped away from him. Rowan tried another. "Can you take these Critters?!" he shouted, but it, too, ran away screaming as the Yeti advanced.

Rowan spun in place. "I need your help!" he yelled and flinched at someone touching him.

A lanky, yellow Trickster had come running by while pulling up his vermillion shorts. He grabbed three jerboas who had at some time climbed onto Rowan's back and tucked them into his pockets.

"What are you—?!" Twiggy began to protest.

Initially alarmed, Rowan spoke quickly. "You can climb down this thing, can't you?" he asked.

The yellow Trickster watched him with glazed eyes (they reminded Sully of misty fish bowls). Drool coated his lips and two beetle-like fangs. He took Sully and Koda and put them into his other pocket. Twiggy clutched Rowan's horn even harder as the Trickster reached for him.

Rowan shook his head to loosen his grip. "Twiggy! Let go! You gonna leave Sully and Koda alone with a Trickster?"

The drooling Trickster snatched Twiggy from behind— hastily, as he was apparently afraid of getting bit. The twisted shape of his body further contorted as he hunched down at the sound of the Yeti roaring. It had spotted Rowan. Seeming to sense an escape, the Yeti tossed a Trickster over its shoulder like a gorilla throwing shrubbery in a display of dominance. The totem pounded on its chest and charged.

Sully and Koda jostled in the pocket as the drooling Trickster ran. Restrained in his hand, Twiggy screamed, "ROWAN!"

Grief chipped at Sully's soul again. *I don't want to lose another friend!* As he looked back, he saw Rowan standing his ground, horns thrust forward. Never at any other time had they appeared so small and so dull.

By now less Tricksters and Critters remained on the platform, and the path to the end of the platform was mostly clear. The drooling Trickster bent his legs against the pull of the sand. There were but a few Tricksters on the edge, hesitant as below the chasm sea crashed and swallowed more victims.

"We can't get wet," Koda said shakily.

The drooling Trickster seemed unsure what to do. Then with slight hesitation he removed them from his pockets and took off his shorts. He wrapped them in the bundle.

"I'll keep you dry." A bead of saliva wet Sully's face. The bundle closed, and Sully felt their new companion lower over the edge. Meanwhile, the Yeti roared. The ground shook fiercer.

***

Had the fall not been from so high, Sydney wouldn't have had the time to see limp bodies floating in the water. The scene was like a premonition of her death.

On the way down, Sydney struck the overgrown werewolf who was scaling down the rock wall. She slid down its back, using its tail as a slide into the sea. She felt an instant cool upon her back sliding up to her head. Then Sydney breached out of the sandy sea, all scales in place. She bobbed lightly on solid ground.

Sydney spit out the salty taste. "The water's not even that deep!"

Glowing creatures appeared to walk on water as they scattered into a labyrinth of platforms. Those deceased no longer glowed, Sydney noticed, and none who had made it were prey animals. Ostrich, camels, and rhinos sat out of the water like dead fish. There were quite a lot of those, too.

A kind of light, high-pitched barking turned Sydney around to find a zebra flailing in the water. It appeared to be stuck as if something had pinned its legs beneath. The front legs kicked, and the head nodded in rapid jerks. Sydney could see the whites of its petrified eyes. She jumped a little inside as the zebra fell violently back into the water from a sharp yank. A wave had risen on it. Something like two blow holes puffed sprays high into the air.

"What the heck?"

It had been difficult to tell in the unruly whitecaps that there were things like shark fins between where the zebra had been and Sydney's spot in the water. Now the waves washed softly over them, making her sway. What she thought was the ground started to lift toward the surface, pushing bodies and fish out of the water. The surface under her shined like a dolphin's skin, and it pulsed as if breathing. Lightning flashed before abandoning the chasm in momentary blackness, and the ground could be seen snaking about during each flash.

The light fractured and displayed a shape rising out of the water as a silhouette. With a small stubby head like a periscope, the monster looked exactly like its infamous photo.

"You've got to be kidding me! The Lock Ness Monster?"

Sydney glided on her stomach to turn at an enormous splash and downpour. A reptilian tail trailing as high as Nessie's head whipped around crazily, flinging bloody sand water, then slammed into the platform. It snapped and began to lean.

***

The drooling Trickster made a small splash. He managed to keep the bundle mostly dry by keeping it lifted above the water. Sully peeked through a fold in the shorts. Their platform, blocked in by tall silhouettes, stood high like a wooden stake nailed into the sea. The leaning platform across cracked and groaned.

"Watch out!" Sully yelled as both crashed.

The Yeti dug its fists into the ground as it leaned sideways and hung there on the platform like King Kong on the side of a tower. Rowan slid by him. As the Yeti tried to grab him, Rowan jumped onto the next leaning platform. The first to break turned forward off the side as if on a crooked neck and fell opposite to the other in an X shape. The remainder of the crowd plunged into the sea.

"Get us out of the water!" Koda forced Sully away from the fold and it closed. Outside the drooling Trickster whimpered, splashed frantically and climbed onto what Sully assumed was another platform. The Trickster tucked them between his body and the wall.

The sea splashed with a strength that chilled Sully. It was the world's largest flood, all churning with rock, as if all the water in the clouds had poured into the chasm. Sully imagined that if a tidal wave had swept away three very tall buildings, this is what it would sound like.

He couldn't stand the suspense and peeked out into the rain. Critters and Tricksters rode the wave, some slamming into rock and being thrown under. Splashed furiously by the sea, the platform Rowan and the Yeti had stood on was stacked on the other two in pieces. Neither one of them was in sight.

***

Sydney shambled on the monster's body away from the falling rubble. With a fierce slap and crash the tail swatted down. Water flowed, enough to float her for a few seconds.

As she slid off the Loch Ness monster's fin which was like a thick rubber pad, a glowing creature—some pig-faced guy—cut in at her left. A flailing hand sent her back onto the fin. Cursing, Sydney hurried and as she did, felt the fin rising like a lifted bridge. She slipped through wet granules of sand until her claw caught in one of Nessie's scales. Sydney climbed to the top and dropped several feet. The water slapped her underbelly like a paddle.

Puffing, choking on water and sand, she paddled fiercely to catch up to pig-face. They were out on open water. "Come back here, you idiot! I'm gonna make you pay for that!"

A sweeping shadow draped her as the tail struck another platform. A groan, a cracking, and the shadow shrank rapidly with a whistle in the breeze.

Uh oh.

The tail cut into the sea, sending up two colossal waves. Sydney lost all sense of direction as she tumbled underwater in the current. The intense pressure of wave after wave weighted down her head and neck, so much so that it might have been choking her. Ribbons of starlight sheened green over many, many dead bodies. They floated in the surf as the sea finally calmed and Sydney whipped her tail kicking to the surface. Catching her breath, she swam around. Behind her, pulled back by the raging sea, the glowing creature was coughing and soaked to the bone.

"Hah! I'm ahead!" Sydney yelled.

Beyond the rubble, the creature and Nessie's forbidding dark shape, was a long split in the chasm labyrinth. The path glowed that off-kilter green like a pool of radiation. The glowing creatures swam farther into the chasm, hurrying away from Nessie who lowered her head into the water. She didn't seem to be interested in them. Meaning, the glowing creatures should be sufficient cover for Sydney. Though if there were any Critters still alive, she expected Nessie's attitude would change real quick.

Sydney huffed. *Is going after these rodents really worth all this trouble?*

22

IN THE CHASM

KODA AND SULLY peeked through a fold in the bundle. Rowan swam around the collapsed platforms, panting and soaked to the skin. He glanced behind him as if in awe of what had happened there.

"Rowan!" Sully cried with relief.

Twiggy shoved between them and jumped out onto the platform wall. He waited for Rowan to swim below (had the water not been polluted by dead bodies, he might have gone beforehand) and let go of the wall to land on his head. He hugged Rowan around the ear.

"Let's get movin'. The totems aren't done," Rowan cautioned. They could still be heard everywhere as brutal echoes in the chasm.

The drooling Trickster lowered himself from the platform and Koda, Sully, and the jerboas walked onto Rowan's back. Blushing, he then put on his shorts.

Rowan turned back toward the collapsed platforms.

"Where are you going?" Koda asked, deciding that was the absolute worst direction for them to go.

"The desert spans widely to the north, east, and west, so I'll go south. Right now, I just want out of here," Rowan said.

South. To the mountains, and out of the water. Koda supposed so but not before summoning the image of that disturbing conjoined thing. How ironic that the one mythical beast he had known before this whole adventure started was the chimera. Typically, the chimera had three heads—a lion's, a dragon's, and a goat's—and a snake for a tail. *What version, the Greek or the totem's, is worse?* Koda wondered. *And how did they get so big?* The totem-chimera had landed somewhere in the chasm. It had to be far away now, for he couldn't see any of their heads. But he could still hear them. Laughing.

Bodies drifted in the water as Rowan swam through them. Anyone who was still alive fled, and the few who were Critters cried out upon seeing their own who hadn't survived. Koda watched, distressed, as an antelope with a badly injured leg tried to pull a much smaller, unresponsive antelope out of the rubble. As the antelope began to cry mournfully, Koda thought he should look away, and he did.

Twiggy called to them. "Come with us," he said, but nobody paid attention to him.

The collapsed platforms formed a crumbled island. "How did you make it out of that?" Koda asked.

"By pure luck and right timin'," Rowan said. He also seemed to be avoiding looking at the antelopes. "I jumped one platform to the other as they were fallin', and then I landed in the water."

"What about the totem?"

"He was crushed by the platforms. But like Jack said, you can't—"

Rowan stopped and made a small, miserable sound. Twiggy loosened his hold on his ear in reaction. He then tightened his arms around him again, collapsing into a fit of tears.

Nahiossi, I hold true to my promise.

Jack had promised to take them home. If it were still possible to return to Giant's nest, it would never be the same. Just when Koda had finally found someone he had a connection with— someone who had felt as alone as he himself had before he found Sully, and Jack had found and lost Muraco—Koda had lost Jack. And it seemed so cruel that even though he knew Rowan would protect them in his place, that even as he'd come to understand Twiggy, there was still an emptiness in him that could never be replaced.

Rowan swam on, and they honored Jack mostly in silence. Sully cried softly. Once Koda asked if he was alright. Sully mumbled no, so Koda pawed him. Physically Sully was fine; his fur wasn't cold. Even a few minutes in snow could make a hamster very ill, so this much was a miracle for them both. Emotionally, however, Koda worried for Sully.

The Haven had been broken up into many chasms. Koda imagined if an ant, or something even smaller—microscopic, even—were crawling on a chess board, it might have been like the Critters swimming below the gigantic, towering platforms of the Haven's crust. Koda eyed them nervously as Rowan used the platforms for cover. There were a few close calls when an intense cracking warned them, and they had to find a path around before the platform tipped over and fell into the sea.

Wherever Koda looked, he saw death in the water. Twiggy clutched Rowan's horn, motionless in a seemingly fearful, sad rage. His fur bristled. He ground his teeth. Koda thought he might chip a tooth, until at last, he burst out in complete devastation.

"They killed everyone!" Twiggy exclaimed. The three jerboas, who were huddling together, flinched.

"They can't have," Koda said. He searched for a smell or a noise. Both screams and the call of totems had eventually died down. "Where are they?"

"It's a big world," Rowan said. Koda watched him, waiting for him to speak. About a minute passed until he spoke again. His voice had deadened and become hollowed and quiet. "The totems will be occupied wipin' out the Haven of Critters where there are still many left. If all goes their way, they will be the only ones left."

Koda frowned, struggling with the anger inside him. He wasn't sure what to say at first. Then he said, "It doesn't make sense. Any Hunter that has ever killed a Critter would want to eat it. They'd think it was a waste to leave them all here like this. Why do they want to kill everyone?"

Rowan said, full of resentment, "Why do humans like to kill for sport?"

That stopped Koda. If Jack hadn't died, he would have wondered from where that had come.

"Are you sure you want a Trickster following you?" one of the jerboas, a female, asked.

Behind them, in a narrow pass between a large, curving platform and a tall island, the drooling Trickster swam in shadows, whimpering. He had removed his shorts again and wrapped them around his chest to conceal his glow.

Koda couldn't help being suspicious. He thought he would always be that way. But at least he had learned to give creatures the benefit of the doubt, and he would for this creature. He had saved their lives, after all. Just as Jack had done.

Out of nowhere, Koda winced hard at a sharp pain in his eyes. He nearly cried out. Blinking, he saw the drooling Trickster's glow and the landscape in only black and white. Koda gasped. When he blinked again, the color returned.

Sully asked if he was alright. Confused, Koda nodded.

The female jerboa's companions gawked at the drooling Trickster while chattering. "Tricksters are liars!" one exclaimed. "Never trust a Trickster!" said the other.

Twiggy flinched hard. "Shh! I agree but keep it down."

Rowan froze. Thick, sandy water swished about his legs. By then the dreadful aromas of fish, blood, and damp earth were thick in the air. Swimming quickly into a dark, low-ceilinged cleft in a nearby platform wall, Rowan sank as low in the water as he could without getting them wet.

Twiggy laid flat on Rowan's forehead. He whispered quaveringly, "What did you hear?"

Rowan didn't answer. In the narrow pass, the drooling Trickster rested its chin on the water like a waiting alligator. Koda didn't see any ears in the swirly cartilage which made up his scalp, but in the next instant, as he heard faint flapping noises, the Trickster dropped under the surface like a startled crab.

Koda walked backward into the jerboas, who were trembling except for the female one. Sully stared at the sky bordered by platforms. Even with the starlight creating two small specks of light on his eyes, they were dull and dry from having leaked so many tears. Up there in the sky, the face constellations glared, their stares more intense as a flapping noise grew louder.

A colony of bats flew overhead. Several ducked into the chasm, their little red eyes shifting, and created chaotic shadows over the chasm sea. Like vampires, they cast no reflection; the sand darkening and thickening the water wouldn't allow it. Koda remembered their heightened hearing ability. One shriek and he and his group were done for. But the bats were abnormally silent, and apparently uninjured by the house fire. Koda wondered if the totems' transformation had anything to do with that. As the bats went north, and the last flapped away behind the platforms, Koda and the others could finally breathe again.

"Camazotz," Rowan said quietly.

Twiggy tugged on Rowan's horn to ease him out of the water. "He's got a grudge against us."

"He's sent them on a hunt for Critters," Rowan said.

"And the relics," said Koda.

"They've probably been told to only shriek when they find someone," Rowan said.

The jerboas whimpered loudly. Koda wished they would be quiet. Except for the female, they were hopping about. "We want to go back to the burrows!"

"There are no more burrows," the female jerboa said impatiently.

"We'll make new ones!"

"It makes sense to go to the mountains," Rowan said. "It was shaken up hardly nothin' when the totems showed up. We'll find hidin' places there."

"What does it matter? Do you want to live in a world overrun by totems?" Twiggy said.

Rowan paused. He swam out from the protection of the platform. "They're gone now."

The female jerboa hushed her companions. They almost never took their eyes from the sky. Somewhere to the northeast the bats screeched. Roars and screams ensued. Even when it stopped, Koda couldn't get the sounds out of his head.

It was during one of these times that the drooling Trickster swam ahead, his eyes glued to the top of the chasm. He backed into an extremely wide platform, wide enough to fit an entire house, and felt his way to the other side. Then he reappeared again with an odd expression on his face. He paddled quickly into the shadow of another platform.

"What's with Drooler?" the female jerboa whispered.

Koda's heart fluttered madly with trepidation as Rowan swam them toward the platform. When they did, the Trickster grew agitated. He threw his hands up into his mouth as if he wanted to chew on his fingernails (he had none) and drooled profusely over

314

his fingers. But they hadn't heard anything—there shouldn't be a totem—so Rowan turned them around the platform.

Koda saw that he had been mostly correct. An immense, open room was set into the crust. It was empty but for an unlit fireplace piled with coal that reached some forty feet to the roof, and a few pine garlands adorning the walls and holiday remanence scattered on the floor. The floor spanned as far as thirty feet where it ended at two massive doors standing like the gate to Heaven (or Hell, depending on the contents behind it). How could such a thing exist in a world without humans? And it was so clear and had color, that no one could have imagined it here.

Dumbfounded, Koda said, "How did that get here?"

"It's like a very big dollhouse," Sully said.

Rowan regarded a slanted pile of rubble at the side of the platform. "Looks like the platform split in half and destroyed part of it." He gestured at the doors. "We'll probably be safe in there for a while."

Koda thought of Giant's nest burning. "What if it collapses?"

"Other than the missin' chunks in the walls, it appears otherwise sound," Rowan said.

Drooler, as he had been named, said shrilly, "Different way. Diiiferent waaay!"

"I agree," said Twiggy. "What's this even *doing* here?"

"There won't be any humans inside, Twiggy," Rowan said.

"I'm not worried about that. Remember we found a totem in a human place the last time."

"There could be Critters in there."

Twiggy paused.

"If I may," the female jerboa cut in. "I'd like to see if there are Critters."

"Burrows!" her companions chorused.

"There aren't any burrows."

"It's a long way to the mountains. We have a whole desert between us, don't forget that." Twiggy gazed forlornly at the room. Koda remembered his comment from earlier. What did it matter? The totems would find them eventually, but the thought of others being alive appeared to have brought hope into him.

Rowan looked down at a floating, dead armadillo curled on his back. "We need to get out of this water," Rowan said.

None of the Critters protested as Rowan swam over to the ladder of rubble. The smaller Critters jumped onto the rock and climbed.

Light splashing drew Koda's attention to Drooler. "I don't like it!" said the Trickster.

"Thank you for helping us," Sully said. It was said so weakly that Koda paused to look at him.

Drooler wrung his hands. He dunked into the water, mumbling frightened words, and peered at them once more before swimming away.

Physically and emotionally exhausted, Koda found it a long climb to the room. There was no Jack to carry him, and Rowan had gone quiet again and didn't offer. By the time Koda's paws touched solid ground, he wished that everything would be over. He longed for a warm, comforting space, and unfortunately, the room only mirrored his loneliness. The pine garlands' bristles had shed onto the floor, covered in white dust like fallen trees in a snow drift, left to be buried. A few baubles and wicker baskets lay beside the fireplace. Koda wondered who had lived here and where they were.

Twiggy sniffed. "There were Critters here before but not now."

Rowan clomped up behind them. "They could have entered through a niche in the back." He dripped wet sand and reddish-brown water as he walked to the two massive doors. One stood ajar.

He shoved the door, opening it wider with a heavy groan.

The smaller Critters were the first inside. There was a chill, Koda swore that there was, even if he could no longer feel any bit of cold afterward. Already he knew something terrible had occurred here, sometime long ago. Though, at first, there wasn't anything but that chill that could give it away. In the center of the room, large chestnut blocks displayed empty snow globes. Over them loomed a tall, triangular shape veiled in silver drapery which glowed from some light beneath it. And on shelves curving around the circular walls were many, many nutcrackers.

Being a house rodent, it didn't hit Koda immediately. Giant owned at least four nutcrackers—with fur, but synthetic, of course. He assumed these were the same until he sniffed a scent like old parchment. It was the same scent he had smelled in the catacombs, in the loculus. The scent of dead skin.

The hides of animals had been used to dress the nutcrackers.

"There *have* been humans here!" Twiggy exclaimed.

Koda heard a noise behind them, something like Rowan's hooves scraping on the floor. He spun around.

What happened next shattered their world. After everything horrible they had seen, after everything heart-wrenching they had experienced, nothing could be as impossible as what occurred in front of them.

Rowan changed. Standing there on his hind hooves, he tripled upon tripled in size until he was as high as the doors, and his shadow stretched over the floor. His horns twisted, and his face grew long and dark behind an appearing leather mask. A long, red tongue, hot and giving off steam, slithered at them. Worst of all, his hands—yes, they were hands as he had grown arms—were tucked into the pockets of a familiar fur coat.

"Willkommen," the totem said, grinning, "to my castle."

23
ON DISPLAY

SIEZED TO THE INFAMOUS fur coat, Koda sniffed pine trees, sausage, and a muskier scent of goat. He savagely bit a black finger that was long like a charcoal stick and tasted ashes. He could smell them, as if they had just been taken from the fireplace. Beside him, in the totem's other hand, Twiggy overpowered Sully's cries with rapid teakettle shrieks.

Humming *Carol of the Bells*, the totem stomped to the center of the room. As it set Koda on a chestnut block, an arctic chill raced upward through his limbs like a cramp. Koda tugged on his arms and feet and found them fastened in a layer of ice. The totem winked a large, brownish gold eye, one that reminded Koda of someone he knew, and down the line it went, freezing Sully, Twiggy, and the squeaking jerboas to the blocks.

"First things first," the totem rumbled in a German-accented voice. Its hands cupped Koda and pressed into Koda's cheeks with its thumbs. Koda wriggled with outrage as the two relics fell onto the block.

Twiggy bellowed, "WHERE'S ROWAN? TELL ME WHERE HE IS!"

Deep chuckling. *If a mountain were to laugh, that's what it would sound like,* Koda thought, and he felt utterly small.

The totem placed the relics in its coat pocket and the charcoal hand moved over to Sully.

"Leave him alone!" Koda shrieked.

The hand passed slowly over Sully's head to the snow globe behind him and removed the glass. Koda watched, hardly able to stand it, as a long, black fingernail trailed the ice around Sully's ankles. It melted. The totem placed Sully on the vintage stand and imprisoned him under the dome with a screeching twist. The others followed until Koda was looking at them inside his own snow globe.

Twiggy leapt at the glass. "WHERE'S ROWAN, YOU DEVIL!" The two smaller jerboas gawked at him as if he were the sole reason for their distress.

Sully fell against the back of his snow globe, staring, petrified, at the totem. He asked in a low, shaken voice, "Did you kill him?"

Taking its time, the totem swung one of the blocks away from the group and sat on it with a piercing *CRAACK!* The demon goat leaned forward, elbows on its knees, as if leading up to a delicious secret. "I *am* Rowan."

"*Liar!*" Twiggy screeched.

"Rowan is my friend. He wouldn't hurt us," Sully said.

"He would, and he has," said the monster gleefully.

"You're the Smoking Beast!" Koda exclaimed. "You killed Jack!"

Twiggy released a pained, fitful scream and vehemently scratched the glass.

"Scratch and jump!" the totem goaded him. "It used to be baskets instead of snow globes, but the rodents were chewing their way out of them. Now, what is it you said? The Smoking Beast? No, I am not. But I owe it many thanks for finishing the job for me. If you'll remember, it's very messy when it changes." The red tongue curled, hanging like a ribbon. "No, I've been fooling you since the

319

beginning, and a while before that for everyone else.

"Twiggy hit it on the mark. A little too late…" The totem reached inside a pocket in its coat and, to Koda's disbelief, held up one of the fox Trickster's cards. The horned devil Jack had described sat on its throne.

Koda stared, feeling an ache in his chest as he tried to calm his breathing.

The totem grinned. "She was correct, you know, the fox Trickster. This card, if you don't mind me reminding you, represented Jack's past—of which I was very much a part."

Twiggy's claws raked off the glass. "What did you do?"

"I'm getting to that." The totem slid the card on the block in front of Koda as if *he* were the fortune teller.

"Funny how things work out. For every difficulty and inconvenience, I was there to see it through. At the carnival, I hadn't planned on getting injured. Lucky for me, because of it, Jack didn't get to see his last card."

Sully had a look of shock on his face. Koda thought, *All the things it's saying… Wouldn't only Rowan know them? Maybe if he's like the fox, then—*

Stop denying it.

Memories from the past few days came to him. Rowan laying on the ground covered in crystals. Rowan fending off Camazotz's bats. The tears in Rowan's eyes after Jack passed away.

Those same eyes as he had seen them in the lit tunnel bore into him now. Sneering. They flicked to Twiggy and gained a terrible glow. "I must admit, I enjoyed myself immensely when I slammed Jack into the wall."

"YOU TRAITOR!" Twiggy screamed on the verge of breaking into sobs.

"You think me a traitor, but despite the tales the humans have created, I am the companion of no one."

The totem emanated darkness. The charcoal hands became strips of night, the holes in the mask pitted the eyes and mouth in blackness, and the tongue turned the color of wine. "I am Krampus, the totem of winter. As such, your kind fears me more than any other. Winter is the destruction of life, is it not?"

Somewhere outside, another totem hunted a Critter. Twiggy struggled to keep in his sobs. Koda stared at the embellished rim of the snow globe, positive this was it for them. They had finally run out their luck.

Then Krampus inclined on his block and the darkness reverted. "I'll answer your question now, but really, this all began centuries before Jack's 'brother' was shot. Not every mythological creature mankind has ever known existed, though we were many and popping up all the time. Thirteen great totems… and one disappointing failure." Venom crept into Krampus's voice.

Fourteen totems? Weren't there twelve at the mountain pass? Koda thought.

"In those years, we killed humans almost exclusively. Alone, of course. We like to hog the glory. The very thing that got us all in trouble," Krampus said. "However, there was one occasion when our unequal trapped us in those wretched poles."

"And there you should have stayed," Koda said contempt-uously. Sully glanced anxiously at him as if he couldn't believe his courage.

"Careful," Krampus said. "If you speak out of turn again, I'll be forced to kill someone—and it will almost certainly be Sully."

The jerboas whimpered. Sully himself was silent. Not saying a word, Koda glowered.

Krampus continued, "As I was saying, it was an unfor-tunate occurrence. Our traitor didn't go free; that is one consolation. He was trapped like the rest of us. For decades my essence was contained, and, in that time, mankind was altered. Mythology was a dying culture. The only creatures that still believed in us were the Critters.

"They conspired with the traitor. He told them everything they needed to know. About how he planned to enchant us evil totems—Yes! They knew all about it in advance!—and how afterward the poles would appear and would protect them from Hunters as long as they stayed within the protective barrier."

Krampus said mockingly, "They couldn't have guessed there was a weakness in the enchantment. Turns out this 'unique Hunter,' as Jack coined, the one Hototo carried in during the flood, isn't so unique. There are more of them out there, and it happened upon chance that one day one of these unique Hunters crossed the barrier between two totems. Totem heads break from the top as you've seen. Of the two, one was going to be released that day."

The block snapped as Krampus leaned forward and the jerboas shrank from him. "Let me pause there. This is a small detail, but I'm inclined to tell you as it brings me so much enjoyment. When we first met, *Nahiossi*," his use of Jack's name for him jabbed at Koda, "you asked what totem head was missing on the pole. I replied, 'You've met him.' You misunderstood me, thinking it was Hototo. But what I really meant… was me."

"Hototo is a totem, and there were no other totem heads missing," Koda replied hotly, forgetting to mind his temper.

"Ah, and the answer to that will come soon but here's where I'll resume. On the day the Hunter crossed the barrier, I was given my escape. In a way, I was *still* trapped as I arrived secretly in a corner of the Haven. I caught on shortly that I hadn't arrived on Earth. The air was putrid with the stench of Critter.

"Against my wintry nature, I traveled to the desert—discreetly, of course. I didn't travel like this." Krampus gestured to himself. "Oh, no! I transformed myself to hide among the neighboring Critters. I won't bother you with details of how I built my cozy underground home, though I'll say it wasn't difficult at all with my power.

"It wasn't my intention to stay forever. As I've mentioned, we totems were obsessed with scaring humans out of their wits. And so, while I waited for the flood, I made do," Krampus gave a smiling glance at the nutcrackers, "making merry with my *nussknacker*." The word was pronounced "noose cracker."

Krampus grabbed an unfinished nutcracker without fur, clothes, or paint off a shelf. He gazed at it reminiscently, then waved it at them. "Wood crafting is tedious—I had an extremely long time to wait—but there are easier ways to enjoy the art of crafting Critters."

He stood and walked to the tall shape hidden by the drapery. Everyone turned to see him. Grinning, slithering his tongue, Krampus paused in front of it. Immediately, Koda felt a terrible unease and almost shouted as Krampus yanked the drapery to the floor. Frosted light made the ceiling aglow and the nut-crackers appear double in number as their shadows were cast long behind them. A Christmas tree rivaling the totem's height shim-mered with clumps of snow. Its bristles shook, sending flakes onto the floor in a flowery white skirt.

There was a crisp chiming sound. Amid sparkling frost were hundreds upon hundreds of ice ornaments in the shape of Critters.

"Jerboas, do you recognize a few?" Krampus taunted loudly.

Sully stood against the back of his snow globe as if the light were pushing him there. "Those are real Critters?" he uttered.

"I assure you."

Twiggy curled into a fetal position and covered his ears. In their snow globe next to him, the jerboas hopped in dizzying panic.

The female said with a faraway look, "We heard the

explosion above, not *below*, so we didn't think that when Critters began to go missing…" She glared at Krampus, sorrow on her face. "They were lost in a demon's burrow."

Krampus flicked lint off his coat. "Yeeess," he said, as if trying to hold interest. Koda turned from the light as the totem stormed to his block and sat. He produced an oversized carving knife from his coat. Wood shavings from the nutcracker's face glided onto the floor like dead flower petals.

"The fireplace was where most of these unlucky souls fell into my castle. It's positioned under a system of burrows—sorry, *was* positioned. There aren't any burrows now. Four feet from the surface, most dig that far, and they end up here," Krampus said.

"Spare us the details," the female jerboa snapped. "Haven't you done enough?"

Koda mistook the length of the totem's arm. It blurred over the jerboas' snow globe before the knife stuck into the top, the glass cracking around it. The light from the Christmas tree shone along its edge. As Krampus pulled the knife out of the glass, Koda saw the globe was fractured like a thick spider web. Squeaking loudly, the jerboas shrunk to the stand, unharmed.

Another blur and the knife sliced at Twiggy's snow globe. He cried out in surprise and the paws over his ears trembled, shaking his head.

"Remove them," Krampus demanded. "You'll want to hear this."

Twiggy was as Koda had seen him after the flood. Removing his paws, he moved fraily to sit. Most of his strength had collected in his eyes. They burned with animosity and repressed panic.

Krampus chuckled. "It's been too long since anyone's seen me as I truly am. When the other totems were freed, and you showed terror, I was beginning to feel jealous."

He resumed carving. "You can sense when a flood is coming. The sky begins to fog like the flood is seeping through. Four years ago, I said goodbye to my home. As a bird, I flew out through the opening and greeted the mountain pass.

"The poles were new. I say new, but they had been standing there for generations. The trees were sealed, and the descendants of those who conspired with the traitor were running. *Screaming.* Some entered the Haven—there were too many to grab at once—but I had what I needed," Krampus growled.

"I tortured them until they revealed what I am now telling you. The traitor's totem head was shattered, and I knew the Critters had risked freeing him by attracting a unique Hunter. I'm positive that if he had arrived in the Haven, it would only be fate that we meet each other, so he had to be on Earth. It's all about chance, you see, whether we end up here or there, at least back in the day. Rules change all the time when the world starts to go downhill." Krampus said mockingly, "Obviously, the traitor hadn't made it to the mountain pass before the flood."

Again, he lapsed into blackness, and his tongue darkened like wet leather. "I had my revenge that day. I may not have killed those who conspired to contain me, but I killed their descendants. I made sure it was slow and painful, then threw them into the opening. I, uh, reckon," a smirk, "you'll recognize them as the skulls and bones in the catacombs."

Koda gazed once again with mad fright at Krampus's charcoal fingers. The long, thick fingernails. They ended at a ridiculously sharp point, and Koda thought those claw marks Jack had seen could have, without a doubt, been made by Krampus's hand.

The totem placed the knife on his lap and brought out the relics to play with them in his hand. He lined them up, pressed them together, and Koda saw that they fit perfectly like two puzzle pieces.

Krampus said, "Jack was correct. The relics *were* leading us to a totem. To the traitor. These are the salvageable pieces of the traitor's totem head."

Sully still has one, Koda thought. He tried to disguise his hope. *Krampus doesn't know I gave it to him, and he doesn't know Jack and I found it in the chamber, because I lied when Twiggy wasn't himself.*

"I threw the relics into the opening as well. I'd say I should have destroyed them if they weren't our key to the Haven and the human world," Krampus said.

Abruptly, Koda stood. The human world…

"Too bad. You were almost there," Krampus mocked. "I'll have to tell your giant you didn't make it."

"*Leave her alone!*" Koda screamed. "And leave the giant world alone!"

"Weeell, that would be very unfair, wouldn't it?"

Koda turned away, trying to suppress his fear. *He's not going to hurt her. Maybe I didn't want to believe the bad about giants, but I do believe there are good giants like mine.*

Krampus slipped the relics back in his pocket and took up the knife. Etching it deep into the nutcracker's face, he continued, "The traitor and Hototo were on the same two-totem pole. Of course, with the traitor freed, there was only the owl on the bottom. I was so clever to think of what I should do next. I gambled by walking next to the pole out of the circle, and wouldn't you know it, another win for me: Hototo's totem head exploded. There was no more fifth pole. I had to get rid of it, so I could cover my tracks. With my totem head gone, it would be quite suspicious to any Critters in the future if I were to go into hiding and no totem showed up. They might begin to expect exactly that, that I was hiding amongst them, if I am to give credit to simpleminded creatures. But I, myself, am a careful totem. So, I took the chance in destroying the fifth pole—no one would ever know there had been five instead of four—making it seem it was Hototo's head missing atop the pole and not my own. Ingenious, wasn't it?

"Anyway, Hototo appeared flying past the trees. I suspended a thick sheet of ice into the Haven opening—it's quite strong with my power—to keep it open, and I went to him. He's always been a terrible conversationalist, but as he couldn't kill me, we tolerated each other's existence. Having me around, I was a secret killer. On scavenging trips with Critters, sometimes I came back alone. Played it off as the owl attacking from the shadows."

A mischievous glint shone in Krampus's eyes. "Hototo liked that. To him I was a pawn—just as Shui Gui was—to retrieve the relics. Shui Gui didn't overtake me, by the way. I was in full control."

There was a point in which Koda had stopped paying attention to details in the loculus tunnels, but he had noticed Jack's and Twiggy's wet noses, Shui Gui's signature. The fact that Rowan hadn't had a wet nose didn't occur to him or mean anything to him until now.

Krampus viciously pointed the knife at the Critters. "I'm in charge. I've *always* been in charge. You've wasted your time competing against the lesser monsters. I'm the one you need to worry about."

The knife slacking in his hand, Krampus smiled at Koda. "It's ironic, isn't it? To think you thought Jack untrustworthy, and yet, you trusted *me*."

Koda stared. He wouldn't give him the satisfaction of any other reaction.

Krampus waved the knife in a *tsk tsk* motion. "Never trust a goat."

The knife straightened in his grip. He gripped the nutcracker tighter and carved savagely. "I have something special to tell you, Nahiossi. Something Jack didn't tell you about his story."

He was there that night. In the blurry forest. He overheard.

Sully looked, battered and confused, at Koda.

"Here's the part you and Twiggy especially will find interesting." A sharp flick of the knife. The nutcracker's face had become gaunt. "I left the mountain pass to find the traitor. To my surprise, he wasn't traveling alone."

Krampus ensured he had their attention and accentuated his next words. "*He was crouched in a tussock* just ahead of the forest preserve fence."

It took Koda moment but, as Jack's story again came to him, he realized with a jolt Krampus's meaning.

Jack's brother? A totem?!

"You're a lying RAT!" Twiggy shouted.

Krampus laughed. "I could have done the evil deed myself, but I decided it would be more satisfying to see Jack witness his brother's death by the hand of a human."

Sully fell back on his haunches, completely stunned, by the look of it.

"He's a hare on the surface," Krampus said. "Inside, it's a different matter. But perhaps that is why he's so fond of Critters."

If it's true, that's why, besides him trapping you, you hate him, Koda thought. *You and all the other totems gang up on him. Gang up on him like my siblings did to me.*

Krampus continued, "So, I crept into the shadows of a tree. I *purposely* confused the traitor by cracking a twig as if the hunter was walking at a distance. What a surprise it was that even with my help, the gentleman hadn't made a killing shot. Even more so that the dog should be the one to see it through."

"He couldn't have died if he was a totem," Koda said, glaring.

"Aha! Then that would mean Jack's brother is alive, wouldn't it?"

All at once Koda felt a smoldering fury he couldn't remember ever feeling before.

He could see in the totem's face Krampus was enjoying his anger. "The hunter, his dog, and I an inconspicuous bird, left Jack to his despair. I didn't take Muraco until we were concealed from his sight and no sound could reach him. I'd have murdered the hunter and dog, just for kicks, but he and his mutt were quick on their feet!"

Thundering laughter boomed out of him. Koda bent his head; he wasn't sure his ears could take it. As the laughter lowered, he could hear the jerboas whimpering again.

Stifling another chuckle, Krampus said, "I returned to the mountain pass with the traitor. When I arrived, I transformed accordingly, unfroze the ice, tossed him and the totem head pieces into the opening, and then I was done with him. Jack and Twiggy eventually made it to the mountain pass, and that was when I became Rowan."

The knife jerked upward to the nutcracker's jawline. Krampus gripped it vertically, as though he were going to stab it, and carved notches between its teeth. "As much as I love Germany, I couldn't have my full revenge without waiting for the next flood." His voice raised until it was deafening. "Without waiting to *kill every last Critter* THAT TRAITOR IS IN LEAGUE WITH!"

Rising shrieks came from the jerboas, and Twiggy couldn't restrain himself. "You can kill us, but you can't kill all of them!"

Krampus smirked. "I hardly think we'll need to try very hard. You've seen how quickly and efficiently the totems cleaned the desert. We were made to kill. We'll be rid of your kind by morning."

Faint shrieks sounded outside the room, stealing everyone's attention. Through the open door, Camazotz's bats hovered in the doorway but didn't enter the room, as if even *they* knew there was a superior evil inside.

"What took them so long?" Krampus said. The nutcracker was finished. He set it and the knife in front of Koda. "I better move fast…"

The jerboas' whimpers raised to squeals as the totem reached for their snow globe and uncapped them into his grip. They bit at him wildly.

"PUT THEM DOWN!" Twiggy screeched.

"*Shhhh*. Watch. This is fun."

Frost flowed from Krampus's hand and onto the jerboas as they struggled and screamed. Koda remembered the cramp he'd felt when Krampus had frozen him to the block, and as he heard a crisp hardening sound, he wondered with dread if the ice had invaded the jerboa's skin, turning their bones into icicles. Sully and Twiggy banged on their glass, shouting for Krampus to stop. The jerboas could no longer move. They froze, sparkling with expressions of terror. Krampus pinched them by their tails, and they dangled, chiming like crystals.

Sully gasped. He must have had the same thought as Koda, that Krampus would drop them. The totem continued to dangle them precariously, admiring their frozen form as one would admire a bracelet. He walked to the Christmas tree, took a thread from his coat, tied it around the jerboas' tails, and hung them on a branch. "There," he said jovially.

Returning to them, Krampus placed his hand on Sully's snow globe. Koda's heartbeat nearly stopped.

"Now for the rest of you. Which way do you prefer to die? By snow…?"

Snowflakes began to fall inside the snow globe. Frost built up rapidly on the glass. Whimpering, Sully scurried around inside.

"STOP!" Koda screamed.

Krampus removed his hand and the flakes continued to fall.

"By becoming a part of my ornament collection? Or by donating your fur to my new *nussknacker*?"

Twiggy released a stream of curses at Krampus.

"*You* don't get to choose. I'll eat *you*," Krampus said.

Koda forced his weight against the glass. *Are you going to let him die? Think! How do you get him out of this?*

Suddenly, inspiration hit. Without a trace of hesitation, Koda shouted, "Sully has a relic!"

Sully gaped at him. Krampus's eyes flicked to Koda. "He does, does he? And when did you find another?"

"The catacombs. When Jack found Muraco's bones. Open the globe and take it."

Krampus let the snowfall thicken. Koda's heart thumped.

The totem smiled. "I could take it now, but there's no reason. Once he's dead, I'll pry the relic out of his mouth."

"*Take it!*"

"You'll pay for this," Twiggy seethed.

Krampus ignored him. "Look how desperate you are," he told Koda, fascinated. "Willing to do anything for him. Here's another funny thing: Sully's incapable of doing *anything* for *you*."

Sully pressed his paws against the glass.

Krampus continued with an air of smug teasing. "He confessed to me. That incident you had at your giant's nest? You have your owner's pet to thank, for if it hadn't frightened him, you would not have been given the chance to escape."

Koda looked at Sully, and his brother avoided his gaze.

"Where was I? Oh. Yes. The squirrel." Krampus turned Twiggy's snow globe upside down and slammed it on the block. It shattered. Dazed and cut in several places, Twiggy barely lifted his head before Krampus grabbed him by the neck.

"*Twiggy!*" Sully wailed.

Krampus forced him flat. Twiggy kicked, making short,

irregular gasps. "I can't let your fur go to waste. You'll make for an excellent *nussknacker*."

Koda yelled, "Put him down!"

Krampus slowly raised the knife above Twiggy's back. Outside, a platform tipped over. Bats shrieked.

"Please don't hurt him!" Sully pleaded.

"You've won! You have the relics!" Koda shouted. "There's nothing else you can take! If you kill him, what do you gain?"

"Power." Krampus gazed insanely at Twiggy, gasping with anticipation. "This might take a few tries."

He brought down the knife.

A huge sweeping wind outside shook the room, and it jarred forward from the sudden blast of shattering rock. In a burst of overhead light, Koda's snow globe slid toward Krampus's coat. Koda hit the glass. The Christmas tree must have fallen, for the top was canopied by pine bristles and ice ornaments. Another silver gleam caused him to look to the side, where he saw the knife buried in Twiggy's tail.

Growling, Krampus lifted the tree with his fist as he wrenched the knife upward. Twiggy emitted a croaking scream. Sully's scream joined his from somewhere past the line of snow globes. The ice ornaments created splashes of reflected frost before Krampus tossed the tree aside; it was like Koda was looking through the window of a dark Christmas store display.

Krampus gripped Twiggy tighter around the neck, choking his screams and yanking him off the block. The coat slipped off Koda's snow globe. He tumbled, recoiling as glass splintered in his face. Through the cracks he saw Sully in a blizzard in his snow globe. They rolled back and forth on the floor before they stopped with a huge groaning thud as the platform settled back in place.

The room had tipped at an angle before righting again and was cast in green starlight. The ceiling and back wall were shattered around the chimera, floating in a fog of dust. Camazotz fought for room on the side of Hototo's outstretched neck. His red pupils shrunk to tiny dots of hatred upon the Critters.

"I'VE FOUND YOU," Hototo bellowed.

Krampus stumbled on the nutcrackers which had fallen off the shelves. They snapped under his hooves. "*Backpfeifengesicht!* Couldn't you have come through the front door?!" Krampus shouted.

Hototo saw the knife in his hand. Twiggy was still screaming. "Drop the knife! I want the vermin for my own."

"I've done more than my fair share. This one is mine."

"THE VERMIN ARE MINE, AND I AM TO HAVE IT! *Give it to me or I will have your* HEAD HUNG UP WITH YOUR COAT!"

"A stupid thing to say to a being you cannot kill," said Krampus.

"Camazotz!" Koda yelled.

The chimera, Krampus, and Sully all focused on him.

"It was my idea to burn you!" Koda shouted. "Come get me!"

An insane smile flickered on the edges of Camazotz's mouth. His growl vibrated in the air. Ignoring Hototo's command to stop, the bat totem shoved his head into the opening, rupturing the walls and floor as he dragged the rest of the chimera in with him.

24
FAMILIAR FOES

HOTOTO'S FURY rolled like the inside of a volcano. "*IMBECIIIILLE!*"

Sully's lungs filled with an icy gasp as behind greenlit snowfall, the owl reined his head, stabbing his beak forward. Camazotz hovered in the enlarged opening. The walls and ceiling of Krampus's lair crumbled, and Sully's view changed from the nut-cracker room to a speeding drop of the platform.

Hailing rock *tink!*ed on the snow globe. Sully spun out of control with all the falling snow whirling about, screaming as he expected the glass to implode and cut him to ribbons. Like a violent heartbeat, vertigo surged through his body as he halted in the air, punching the inside of the globe for the dozenth time within seconds.

The swirling blizzard glided down, and the glass didn't break. What had happened? Sully looked through frosted glass into another floating face blobbed by drool.

Drooler.

Holding onto the wall with one hand, the Trickster swept Sully into a pack hanging on his neck. It was white and knitted like a yarn sweater, so Sully was able to see through it. Drooler lunged forward and narrowly caught another falling snow globe. He placed it in the pack. In the dark green light, Sully saw Koda stumble on the vintage stand.

Drooler jerked as if a large rock falling from the platform had struck him. Sully had the terrible thought he was going to fall into the water, unconscious or dead, but then Drooler clung back to the wall. Sully was unsure how safe their position was going to be in the next few moments. The chasm's sea sloshed with waves of rock and nutcrackers. He could hear the totems slipping, throwing more rock and flapping frantically, on top of what remained of the platform. *It's gonna fall on us!* Then Sully was relieved as he heard the booming shatter of the totems landing on another platform.

Krampus was fuming. "YOU DESTROYED MY CREATION! AND YOU ALLOWED THE CRITTERS TO ESCAPE!"

"They've been *crushed*, you fool! When they should have been mine to crush!" Hototo berated. "You are both FOOLS!"

Camazotz growled, whether he was really paying attention or was merely upset he had misplaced the Critters.

Drooler let go of the wall with one hand and swayed them before snapping back to the wall. Through the knitting Sully saw Twiggy held to the pack. He was unmoving and silent.

Rubble rolled on top of the platform. Krampus yelled, "They may have a totem piece!"

The relic weighed heavier in Sully's cheek. He lowered to the snow globe's stand as if the totems could see him.

"You had them long enough to take it!" Hototo accused. "How many are you keeping hidden?"

A slick, watery voice belonging to Shui Gui said, "I was in the mind of one of the rodents. The furrier one had a totem piece."

Sully opened his mouth to gasp but for some reason couldn't find the energy to do so. His eyelids drooped slightly. Koda stood at the glass facing him.

"I won't waste time looking for it," Hototo said. "Look at the sky, you idiots. If the Haven is slower to open, it will be your fault. Krampus! Give me the relics."

Drooler placed Twiggy in the pack. Blood streaked Sully's snow globe where Twiggy's tail had wiped the glass. He couldn't see Twiggy's face since he was turned away from him. Sully wished desperately for him to move.

"NOW!" Hototo yelled.

Above them, the platform cracked as if Krampus had stomped forward. There was a huge clacking sound on the other platform, followed by a gulp. Sully realized Krampus had thrown over the relics, and Hototo had just swallowed them.

"Have them, then. Your success is my success," said Krampus.

"You don't deserve it, but you will take your place. Stop wasting my time and hurry up!" Hototo demanded.

Rocks spilled down from a heavy landing on the totems' platform. Sully could only describe the strange noise that followed as being like palm trees thrashing in a hurricane. This was the sound of Hototo's feathers shifting... shifting wildly. It was like when the totems first joined, and they became—they became...

"Drooler, open Sully's snow globe! He's falling asleep!"

Koda's panicked voice startled Sully awake. Falling asleep? At a time like this? He realized he had been ignoring a feeling like ice cubes in his stomach.

Drooler climbed swiftly and quietly into the water and uncapped their snow globes. Immediately Koda pawed Sully, trying to warm him.

Sully felt like an ice cooler. He tried his hardest not to stutter. "I'll... be... okay. I'm mostly... fur."

Drooler tied a rope around the top of the pack and swam away, closer to the other platforms. Hototo's and Camazotz's hearing, Sully assumed, were being blocked by the irritated sea, the bats flapping above, and the movement of Krampus joining the totems. His sneering voice, deeper and darker like approaching thunder clouds, cracked in the air. "IF YOU'RE ALIVE, CRITTERS, I HAVE A PRESENT FOR YOU!"

Sully tensed as Krampus took a huge, swooping breath and then exhaled. He looked through the pack's threads. Drooler was already rounding the platform, so he couldn't see the totems, but from where they stood, frost showered down like shaved ice. The water instantly chilled to ice where it hit the sea, and the frost smothered the columns and froze the sea toward them in a wave of peppermint fragrance. Drooler raised onto an island before it could reach him; if he hadn't, he probably would have been caught floating in the water inside a block of ice. Frost thickened on the pack, making it harder for Sully to see. But he still could, and what he saw through the icy film was a snowy wonderland. The same crisp hardening sound as when the jerboas had turned into ice ornaments amplified to a fantastic grinding crunch as the sea became one long ice bed in a realm of glaciers.

Sully and Koda buried themselves in a wool blanket in the pack, listening to Krampus boom with laughter. The wind kicked up, strong as a hurricane's wind, and sent Drooler sprawling backward as the totems flew away.

The Trickster picked himself up, removed the pack and gently took Twiggy out. Peeking from under the flap, Sully saw it was snowing, and they were on a kind of bank made from the Haven's crust. Twiggy lay on a stone, breathing but unconscious. His bleeding tail bent horribly at a large cut.

Koda peeked beside Sully. He told Drooler with purpose, "Tear off a piece of your clothes. A long one."

"What are you going to do to Twiggy?" Sully asked, concerned.

"We're going to stop the bleeding like the giants do," Koda said.

Drooler was wearing a hoodie. It was thoroughly layered in white frost, not a speck of cloth or glow showing through. He wiped the frost off his face, pinched his teeth on the ends of his hoodie, and tore it into a rag.

"You—you need to wash the wound," Koda stammered as if trying to remember the next steps.

Drooler jumped as somewhere far away, the totems crashed into the sea. All four let out a call.

"Quickly!" Koda rushed.

Drooler shrieked in surprise as he thrust his hand into the ice. He scooped out the water with his palm and splashed water on Twiggy's tail. Koda instructed him, and Drooler tied the rag around the wound. Sully grimaced but didn't look away.

Twiggy woke suddenly. He gasped and was about to scream. Drooler quickly held his hand over his mouth.

Sully lunged forward. His heart beat nervously with concern. "Koda, he's tying it too tight!"

Koda pawed him back. "It needs to be tight to work."

Slobbering profusely over frozen drool, Drooler finished tying off the knot and flinched as Twiggy pulled his hand away. Twiggy panted, trembling as he tried not to move. He gaped at his tail and the red droplets stark on the white rocks. The rag had already become soaked with blood.

Sully paced around Twiggy, giving him room while at the same time hardly able to stand not giving him comfort. "Twiggy, are you going to be okay?"

"No." Twiggy swallowed the tears in his throat and said with a frustrated rage, "They've won! Those *evil savages* murdered Jack, and they stole the relics!"

"Keep your voice down," Koda said firmly. "This isn't over

yet, unless you attract them to us. And we have one relic."

"Yeah, I remember, and you told them who has it," Twiggy said bitterly.

This appeared to hit home to Koda. Sully wanted to defend him. But Twiggy's attitude and the whole terrible situation had shocked him into silence.

Koda said, "They think we're dead."

"Krampus doesn't think so!" Twiggy snapped, breaking off with a tremble. He had flexed his tail. "Or whoever that thing is now," he croaked.

Frowning, Koda scrutinized Twiggy. "We can do this without Rowan."

Sully drifted further into sadness at the name. *Why is he doing this to us? We never did anything to him. Why would he do it?*

"We'll go with Drooler like we should have," Koda said. "Wherever we end up, we'll think of a plan."

Twiggy looked up at Koda, sullen and angry. "We had our chance. We tried to keep all the relics safe, and we failed every step of the way. You want me to parade around with my nearly-sliced-off tail—it's bleeding everywhere!—and to do what? We. *LOST.*"

"And you, what, want to hide? The Haven could end up like the Trickster world. Either way, you think you could hide from them forever?"

"I don't know! But trying anything now would be pathetic."

Koda let the quiet stretch out. There were no screams, no totems. The chasm was silent as if intent on their conversation.

Resentment shadowed Koda's voice. "Everyone dragged me into this. And now that I'm finally on your side, you want to quit."

"Well, what's changed your mind?" Twiggy said begrudgingly. "Or do you just want to get home to your giant's nest?"

"That isn't fair," Sully said.

Koda's frown deepened. "I remember who promised to get me there," he said.

"Well, I *do* know who's going to get to the giant world. The totems. Like Hototo said, look at the sky!" Twiggy exclaimed.

Sully did, and he quailed. It was like looking at the most frightening cloud shape, so strange and so large, up there like a harbinger of death. In the sky above the southern mountains was a Cracker Jack constellation larger than the moon and the sun. The face constellations glared at it. The Cracker Jack seemed to be pushing them away as it grew. Growing and growing. Slowly, but Sully expected its mouth (closed, for now) would be big enough to fit even the four totems in a few hours. It had been meant for the Critters; maybe it had even been there when Koda had found the relic in the catacombs with Jack.

So far away. Sully shrank inside.

"It's the Cracker Jack we'll never pass through," said Twiggy. "Jack is dead. So is everyone at the mountain pass. And Rowan is a traitor. Everything has been taken away, so there's no use in fighting."

Twiggy looked at his tail, head bent as he might have been aware of Koda staring at him with accusatory anger.

Koda said, "Did every Critter left here have to live at the mountain pass to be your family?"

"*Jack* was my family! And up until an hour ago, Rowan was, too."

"*We're* still here with you," Sully said. He locked eyes with Twiggy. It had been hard for him to do so in the cave after the flood, but somehow Sully now found it easier to do. Not that his heart didn't ache doing it.

"How do I know you're not totems?" Twiggy broke eye contact with him. Moaning, he fell back on the rocks.

Koda looked at Twiggy until it seemed the anger was too

much for him. He asked Drooler, "You want to help us, right? Did you leave to go somewhere safe?"

Drooler looked uncomfortable again. "There are more Tricksters…" he said timidly.

"Have they grouped together somewhere?" Koda urged.

"You let him take us there and we're going to be ambushed," Twiggy complained but not at all with his usual energy.

"We're ready to leave. Take us," Koda said.

Drooler observed them as if unsure he wanted to go against Twiggy and make him angry. But then he picked him up carefully with both hands. Anxious, Sully watched Twiggy whine as his friend tried to hold back from crying out. Drooler slipped him into the pack. The brothers followed him in.

Drooler kneeled, and Sully heard him pick up the two snow globes. Leaning hard into his arm, Drooler threw them, and they shattered on a platform. Afterwards, he seemed to think better of making so much noise and ran on the snow-covered ice.

Soon Twiggy fell asleep. Sully focused on his breathing, paranoid he would hear it stop. He became very frightened when Twiggy began to make soft squeaking noises, almost like gasps, until Sully figured out he was snoring. As he thought Twiggy would be alright, other worries clouded his mind. The soreness lingered in his side where Koda had bit him. *I can't blame Koda for that. It wasn't his fault.* Besides, there were worse things Sully had done which were recently revealed about him.

"You did a good job with Twiggy," Sully said carefully. "How did you know to do that?"

"Sometimes I saw the giants doing that. When they were around," Koda said quietly.

Since he couldn't see him very well in the darkness, Sully listened for anger in his voice but found he couldn't sense at all what Koda was thinking. He only sensed his own fear like black ink spreading throughout his body.

"Was this when you were at the pet store?" Sully asked.

"Before the pet store."

"But I thought you said you were born there?"

"Earlier I mentioned a mill. It's the place where most Critters are born before they are brought to the store. I don't know if every place is like that, but you were lucky to be born in the store. I'm so grateful for that."

Sully wasn't sure he wanted to know. "What happened there?"

"The giants kept us together even though we were old enough to be separated," Koda said and quieted before speaking in a soft voice. "One of my siblings attacked me. And that's why I only have three fingers."

Sully didn't know what to do with all the emotions racing inside of him. The hiding under the plank, the attitude toward Critters; it all made sense. He'd been holding in his tears since finding out who Rowan really was and seeing Twiggy injured. It was, in a way, a relief to cry. Sully had an urge so strong to hug Koda tight, but he was afraid Koda didn't *want* a hug from him. Not after what he had done.

Sully sniffled. "That's a very ugly thing. I'm sorry, Koda."

"I should have told you, but it's always been very difficult to talk about."

The silence was loud to Sully's ears.

"Koda… I wanted to save you."

"I know, Sully."

"I always thought I'd be very brave if you ever got into trouble. An older brother is supposed to be. And I haven't been helping you a lot."

Sully paused for Koda to tell him he was a coward, that he was as much a traitor as Rowan. "But I can save you now! I did it in purgatory. I yelled for Hototo to let you go."

"I'm not angry, Sully. If something like that ever happens again, I want you to hide and be safe."

"No! I don't want to let you down ever again."

"Sully, you—"

"Not even if you tell me to." Suddenly, Sully needed to get everything out. "I know I haven't been listening to you very much. And you've always known what to do. You're always right. I shouldn't have taken you around everyone in the mountain pass and trusted Rowan. You told me to be careful of other Critters. And all these terrible things have happened. But I have to be there for you. I'll listen to everything else you say, but I'll save you when you need me. I promise!"

"Sully," Koda said, trying to calm him. He had been trying to cut in while Sully talked. "I'm not right about everything. I was wrong about Jack."

Koda took a deep breath. "And about Twiggy, too. I've told you too many of the wrong things and made you afraid of Critters you shouldn't have been afraid of. And *we* are Critters! Twiggy was right. Why did I have to hate my own kind, but I never even remembered about the giants who treated them so badly in that awful place. It's so stupid now to think that because of my own fears, I worsened yours.

"I'm so sorry. Don't let the totem ruin it all. Rowan was never a Critter to begin with."

Sully stayed quiet, holding his own paws. Koda had never spoken so sincerely.

"And you don't need to be upset about what happened at Giant's nest," Koda said. "The dragon didn't save me. *You* did."

"It's my fault we're here. I brought you to the mountain pass," Sully said.

"If you hadn't, I'd be dead. And so would everyone left in

the Haven. There's still others out there, and we're the only ones who can fix this."

"We can fix it?"

"Yes, and this depression we're in isn't going to get us anywhere. I miss Jack. He's the other reason we're still alive, but it's for him and everyone else we care about that I'm not going to let the chimera win. I need you and Twiggy to help me."

Sully couldn't believe it. "I can help?"

"Yes," Koda said. "After traveling a forest, protecting the relics, and freeing Jack and Twiggy from Shui Gui, I believe you can. I'm proud of everything you've done, Sully."

Fear gone, Sully hugged Koda, and Koda hugged him back. It was the best feeling in all the worlds.

Completely out of nowhere, Sully cringed hard from a piercing pain in his eyes. He felt Koda flinch as he released their hug to rub at his face. Sully opened his eyes, and what he could see of Koda was blurry and black and white.

"Are you alright?" Koda asked, frightened.

Sully blinked. After less than a minute had gone by, clarity and color returned to his vision, and the pain subsided. "I don't know what that was."

"If it's something to do with your sight, I had that happen, too."

"Huccome?"

"The Trickster world gave us our new sight," Koda said. "Now the world is gone. I think our new sight will go, too."

Outside, the snow crunching from Drooler's footsteps stopped. "Critters," he whispered. "This is where more Tricksters."

Sully could hear more footsteps somewhere ahead. They sounded sneaky and rushed, as if the Tricksters were darting around trying to hide. The frost had thickened on the pack, preventing Sully from seeing through it.

Koda said, "What is——?"

"It's not good to talk," Drooler interrupted with his usual nervousness. "Tricksters are afraid of what happened. When the *totems*," he whispered the word, "showed up. They blame Critters. *They don't want them around.*"

Sully thought back to the Yeti, and how the totem had mostly been after Critters. The Tricksters were just in the way.

A moan startled them. Twiggy was waking up.

"Stay quiet. We're in Trickster territory," Koda whispered.

Twiggy lifted into a sitting position, or at least what he could manage with his injured tail. Everyone remained quiet.

There was a shifting sound as Drooler adjusted his pants. He walked toward the low, playful shrieks of Tricksters. Someone fell in the snow, and Sully could hear wood knocking. The Tricksters hooted softly—obviously trying to keep quiet should there be a totem nearby—like they were taunting someone, huddled around and bullying. Sully wished he could say something so they would leave the Trickster alone. As Drooler approached, the Tricksters giggled some more, and the someone who had fallen made the wood knocking sound again as he or she abruptly moved in the snow as if to lunge at one of the Tricksters. Their footsteps hurried away.

"Numbskull! Numbskull!" they jeered.

"Dreaded oafs! These are expensive collectibles!"

Sully sat up straight and felt Koda and Twiggy tense. He recognized that boastful, chilling voice.

Bozo!

Drooler began walking toward him. Sully, Koda, and Twiggy whispered, "No! No! Don't go over there!" But Drooler must not have heard them, and when he stepped in close to Bozo, they were forced not to say a word.

Drooler leaned down as if to help Bozo up.

345

"Mind your own business!" Bozo snapped.

Drooler recoiled and started to leave. A tug yanked him back. As the pack bounced, Twiggy whimpered but the sound muffled as he covered his mouth. His tail must still be sensitive.

"On second thought, make yourself useful, and hold this puppet here while I try to untangle the strings," Bozo ordered.

The sound of wood knocking resumed—the sound of Bozo's puppets dangling against each other.

"You're tangling them all up again!"

Drooler mumbled self-consciously.

"Never mind," Bozo said impatiently. The puppets knocked harshly as he yanked the puppet from Drooler.

Drooler stumbled, and the pack bounced harder. Twiggy couldn't quiet himself this time and whimpered loudly. Sully's eyes widened.

Drooler uttered a small surprised sound. He and Bozo seemed to pause.

"What was that?" Bozo asked suspiciously.

"Uh…"

"Are you… hiding something in there?"

Sully sensed Bozo's eye sockets focused on the pack.

Drooler made a run for it but was abruptly yanked back around.

"What are you hiding?" Bozo demanded.

Drooler uttered a startled cry as Bozo violently pulled the pack off him. Twiggy shouted.

The pack opened around Bozo's skeletal fingers. The fallen snow dimmed the bold orange color of his hair. In the darkened shadow created by the face constellations' light, his permanent grin was accentuated by a new crack wavering out of his mouth. It resembled a laugh line. Even so, Sully sensed the clown was inwardly glaring at them.

"So, it's *you*." Bozo chomped his teeth over his lower jaw. "You remember me, don't you? Of course. I'd remember someone I shot a cannon ball at."

Sully shrank.

"You know how many fractures I got from that?" Bozo said angrily.

Drooler's head leaned away from Bozo's skull. "You— You know each other?"

"Yeah, we know this split-personality *clown*," Twiggy snarled.

"I see you've paid for ruining my play," Bozo said, noticing Twiggy's tail. "Well, I think I'll take care of the rest!"

He reached in. Koda stood with his paws raised, mouth open and ready to bite. Twiggy, a blur of motion, cut in from the side. He shoved Sully farther into the blanket. Dangling in the air, his foot scratched Sully's nose. There was the unmistakable sound of rodent teeth chewing on bone. Then Twiggy yelled out, falling on them as the pack wrenched backward.

In the fray, the blanket had shifted. Sully wriggled out of it to find the pack was bunched in. Drooler clutched the pack to himself. Through a clear spot where the frost had been rubbed away, Sully saw they were in a more closed-in section of the chasm. The platforms appeared so much taller and darker because of it, like the Critters were surrounded by huge blocks made of volcanic rock.

Drooler backed away from Bozo, who stood by a huge shard-shaped platform. He looked a complete mess with the entangled marionettes (not glowing) under his arm and half the pom-poms missing from his satin costume. Because it was torn in several places, Sully could see he was a skeleton underneath as well.

Sully called to him, "Leave Twiggy alone!"

"Oh, not so frightened anymore?" Bozo jeered.

"There's scarier things than you," said Sully.

Bozo stepped forward, hunching his shoulders. "Well, you should be scared now, Critter."

"Critter?"

Sully squinted to see a Trickster hiding at the edge of the frost. She had the body of a squirrel with green fur and the head of a baby panther. Scurrying out from the cover of a fallen platform, she was followed by at least a dozen more Tricksters. Most were missing fur or were scarred. A duck-billed alien creature with two rows of eyes lining its forehead was bruised purple all over its body.

"Yes, there are Critters here," Bozo said smilingly. "In that pack."

"They're not supposed to be here!" the alien Trickster said.

"Get rid of them!" said another.

"I'm working on it," Bozo said. He advanced, and the Tricksters joined in, tightening a circle around Drooler, who took a step back.

Twiggy trembled. "Are you crazy? You're seriously gonna do this out in the open with totems on the loose?"

"They're not here for *us*," Bozo said with a sneer.

Koda was looking out with Sully. "We'll scream. Then you'll be right in the middle of it," Koda said.

The Tricksters behind Bozo hesitated.

One of the Mardi Gras puppets under Bozo's arm became aglow and lifted a star-crowned head. Piercing eyes shone out of gold and purple paint. "They're bluffing!"

"That's right. And not very well-acted out," said Bozo.

The Tricksters murmured agreement.

"You dunces! He's controlling the puppet!" Twiggy barked.

"You're released of your acting roles," Bozo said. "What would I need actors for when I don't have a theater for them to act in!"

"That's not our fault!" Sully protested.

"I'd say it is." Bozo glanced at the glowing puppet under his arm. "What do you say we tie them up with string, gag them, and leave them somewhere far from here for a totem to find?"

The puppet looked up at Bozo then back to the Critters. Its painted mouth seemed to genuinely smile. "Yeah..."

Someone grabbed Drooler by the shoulder. Sully and Koda yelped as various hands snatched at the pack and tried yanking it out of Drooler's hands. Twiggy, in pain, shouted.

"What is this commotion?" a voice called out good-naturedly.

The hands on the pack stopped moving. There was one last shout from a Trickster. Sully's chest heaved. They had tossed them around pretty good, and he pulled himself up to look out through the threads again. The crowd turned toward a figure moving to the front of the crowd.

The fox Trickster from the carnival stepped a little way behind Bozo, her werewolf feet crunching the snow. Like Bozo's costume, her red dress and cloak were in tatters (since seeing her the first time, Sully wondered if it had been stolen from a little girl carrying a picnic basket), and there were coins missing from her headdress. Her large face sagged around an empty eye socket. Staring was rude, but Sully couldn't help it.

She grinned. "Ah, here you are, Critters! What are you doing with Bozo?"

"We're acting out a play," Bozo said. He was the only one who hadn't turned to look at her.

"You'll have to do it another time. Come with me, Critters. I've been waiting for you." The fox winked her one eye and walked back into the crowd. The Tricksters loosened to let her by, fidgeting as they calmed down from their frenzy.

Bozo was clenching his fists. On impulse, Sully stuck out his tongue.

The blanket shifted over their view outside. Koda kept it in place and shook his head disapprovingly at Sully.

Drooler slipped away from the Tricksters holding him as their hands let go of the pack. Eagerly, Drooler walked up behind the fox, close enough for Sully to see the snow gathering on her tail. Before they were too deep into the crowd, racing footsteps brought a Trickster up to the pack. Both Drooler and Sully squeaked as a loud, growling bark halted the Trickster in its tracks. It whined and continued to whine as the sharp, startling breath beneath the fox's bark quieted.

Just like a werewolf, Sully thought.

The Trickster hurried away like a frightened pup. The fox resumed walking again as if nothing had happened and hummed a tune Sully recognized from their visit to the red tent. Drooler was more tentative to follow.

Twiggy panted. "Who is that?" Careful of his tail, he moved between Sully and Koda.

"Don't—"

He didn't listen to Koda and removed the blanket. His expression became one of intense anger.

"That's her, isn't it?" Twiggy said sharply. "*She's* the one who started all of this!"

"Are you really going to blame Krampus's evil on her?" Koda said. "Jack was going to find out about his death until we interrupted because of Rowan."

Sully felt a stab at that. He told himself it wasn't their fault.

Twiggy chittered. "Who knows if she made it all happen."

"Twiggy, what are we going to do?" Koda asked, frustrated. "You can hardly move, and Sully and I can't survive in the snow." He paused. "She might be able to help us—"

"Help us?!"

"Can you just hear me out? Listen, I've been thinking about

the relics, and we might still have a chance. The first Cracker Jack said there were four relics. There's one more left," Koda said.

"That's *if* the relic wasn't destroyed in the Trickster world," Twiggy said.

That stopped Koda. Suddenly, Sully felt sick. They reflected on the possibility in silence. Even though Twiggy had brought it up, he uttered small, worried chirping noises.

"It *has* to be here," Koda said with determination. "Let's try not to get caught up in 'what ifs,' okay?"

"Okay," said Sully. He would try.

"Remember what Hototo said about the sky?" Koda asked.

"He said if the sky was slower to open, it would be Krampus's fault," Sully said.

"Yes. He said that because Krampus didn't get the relic I gave you. And there's another one out there. If what Hototo says is true, and they get their hands on it, the sky is going to open faster. The fox could give us a fortune that leads us to the last one."

"Oh, sure! Give her the opportunity to hex us as well," said Twiggy.

Sully tried to think this through. There were so many things to worry about! "What if the fox Trickster only gives bad fortunes? She could be a witch of some kind!"

"I don't know from who else we can get help. At least at this stage," Koda said.

"What do you mean?" Sully asked. "And won't the Cracker Jack open eventually even if we have two relics?"

"Yes, it probably will. But we'll have more time to get rid of the totems."

"How are we going to get rid of them?"

"By getting help from Muraco."

Twiggy jerked upright and cried out at his hurt tail. "Muraco?!" he exclaimed.

"He trapped them before. It's the only way," Koda stressed. "I'm not ready to give up yet. Not after all we've been through and lost."

Overwhelmed but also a little excited—this was the first bit of hope they'd had since the really bad stuff!—Sully considered Koda's plan. No one could ever replace Jack. If he had to trust someone, though, Jack's brother should be dependable. "I think it's a good idea," said Sully.

"Look," Twiggy said. "I know you're trying to help but think about this for a minute! It's insane! If I can believe any of what that devil said, Muraco is a totem. And the fox is a Trickster. She's more likely to jinx anything you're planning, I'm telling you!"

"Give her a chance, Twiggy," Sully pleaded. "Drooler's a Trickster, and he saved us! They're not all bad like we thought they were."

"You guys are so sure, aren't you? If you *are* Sully and Koda..."

"If we were totems, we would have gotten you while you were asleep."

Twiggy looked at Sully in the dark as if surprised at what he had said. He leaned against the pack. "I don't like this."

Sully gently moved around him to peer out as Koda continued to press Twiggy about the plan. By the sound of it, they would be going on for a while, and Sully wanted to see where the fox Trickster was taking them.

She stood before an icy platform smaller than the one the totems, or as Koda called them, the "chimera," had sat on but not by much, which meant it spanned close to two mountains in width. The top rose higher than Sully's view. Near the bottom, it had been cracked like a cleft in a glacier. The fox gripped the edge, cracking it more, and it broke away as a large piece of ice about her height. She moved it to the side from where there was now a dark opening.

She insisted Drooler walk ahead, and he did, though very slowly. To Sully it felt like they *were* entering the inside of a mountain. He imagined they would soon be attacked by an army of orcs and a fire demon with a whip. They faced a split in the crust, a vertical strip of black between two high walls fifty—no, one hundred feet high! Or at least as Sully guessed. How big was the Empire State Building? The walls might have been that big, he couldn't tell, because by one hundred feet high (give or take), the walls faded to darkness. He wondered why it was this dark. If the platform had cracked, it should have done so all the way to the top, where the starlight would shine in. Behind them, the fox hauled the ice door back into place, and the walls darkened.

Koda and Twiggy stopped arguing. There was a moment in which Sully was sure they were all remembering the massive doors closing in the nutcracker room. The moment Rowan had transformed into Krampus.

"Let's go," the fox said cheerfully. She moved into the black strip past Drooler and nothing happened.

Because the platform was so large, the miles and miles of crust between them and the outside seemed to be insulating the inside of the platform. Drooler had been shaking fiercely from the cold, but now the temperature warmed. As far as Sully could tell, little pieces of ice glistened on the walls, and it thinned the farther they went in. They coursed such a long way, going left, right, left, right, in a zigzag. Sully heard low voices ahead, a loud shout, then giggling.

Twiggy sniffed nervously. "There's more of them. *Lots* more," he said.

Sully found he could smell more than Drooler; the Trickster's scent was strangely a nutty smell—like Twiggy's, though Sully wouldn't mention this to him for he might be offended. Blowing in over top of the scent was another not much unlike what

353

he had smelled at the mountain pass: a blend of various animals. An animal den.

A bit of green light highlighted the corner of a wall to their left. The group turned it to another corner where the split opened dramatically. So too did the voices rise in volume.

Gone were the sleet, snow, and ice, and in their place, thick spiderwebs covered every wall. In a silly way, they swayed in the peppermint air like toilet paper hung in the trees on Halloween night. *What spider made that?* Sully hoped he wouldn't have to find out. He knew whatever spider it was, besides the spectacular size of the cobwebs, it must be very talented for there were countless cobweb gypsy caravans parked along the zigzagging walls and cluttered in the center of the split. With their white knitted texture and Trickster glows lighting their curtained windows, the caravans reminded Sully of the lit Christmas decorations Giant set outside the nest. Each one of them glowed, and a few jerked about as some Trickster inside jumped and made noise. Other Tricksters ran around the caravans—*joyously*—as if oblivious of the danger outside. Their glows lit up the huge zigzagging walls.

Twiggy asked impatiently, "What's going on out there?"

"It's a trailer park," Sully said.

"Caravan site," the fox corrected.

As their group trailed through the caravans, around more and more corners, Sully heard less giggling and mischief and more sounds of pain. They passed numerous Tricksters bandaged in cobwebs. One of them slumped against the wall, crying. The fox touched their shoulder as she walked on.

"Are they going to be alright?" Sully asked.

"He'll be fine," said the fox. "The more sensitive of the Tricksters are more shocked than anything."

Koda asked, "Are there any Critters here?"

"There were. They ran like mice. Some were actually mice.

The rest were chased away by the Tricksters."

"And offered to the totems?" Twiggy asked harshly.

"No, just chased away," the fox answered casually. "I highly doubt the clown would have actually sacrificed you. He's already put in a request to the spider that she build him a new theater."

"It built all these?" Sully was impressed and very creeped out.

"And the cobweb laying over the top of the split in the platform. It acts as a ceiling. With the snow on it, it doesn't look like there is a split at all. Keeps us safe. Keeps us away from suspicion." The fox sounded pleased. "So long as we keep everyone quiet, of course."

"We're talking about Tricksters," Twiggy scoffed.

They rounded another imposing wall and were met with a low hanging, daunting cobweb mass. A humongous egg sac weighted it down, as well as an even larger tarantula. Sully jumped away from the front of the pack. He recognized the building-sized tarantula from the carnival. Its rider, the scarecrow, was kicking back in a cobweb hammock higher up.

"This way…" the fox said happily. "The spider is too busy caring for her eggs to bother you. I've chosen this spot since she's deemed it the safest place for them."

Sully was really going to be uncomfortable if millions of tiny spiders started crawling all over the place.

The tarantula twiddled its fangs as the fox and Drooler ducked beneath the web. Sully shivered. On the other side, they stood in what might have been a quarry before the water froze and was topped with snow. There was still the effect of water as orange light shined on the sparkling frost from the windows of a single cobweb caravan, much more elegant than the caravans in the other site. The flower-patterned webs in the windows created a kind of stained-glass effect, and little cobweb charms and fancy pots decorated the steps.

"My new 'tent,'" the fox said proudly and turned to Drooler. "You can take them out of the pack now."

The Critters looked at each other. "She's up to something," Twiggy said. "I'm warning you. Last chance."

Drooler had already opened the pack, letting in the slightly chilly air. He took Sully and Koda out and was starting to remove Twiggy when the fox shook her head.

"No, just them two. The squirrel should rest," she said jovially and beckoned Drooler closer to the caravan, toward the Tricksters bunched on the steps. They hobbled back and forth, giggling and hooting as if taunting something in front of the door. Sully paced a little in Drooler's hand, trying to see past them.

"Hey! Not by the tail, you dim-witted mutant!" an angry voice yelled.

The brothers twitched in alarm. Sully looked at the fox Trickster, who smiled at him.

"Critters, I'd like to present to you 'the Hunter from the flood'..."

The Tricksters parted, smirking over their shoulders. A gap appeared in the strange dance. An animal wriggled by its tail in a Trickster's hand. She had scales and intimidating rusty-gold eyes that fiercened at the sight of Sully and Koda.

The dragon.

25

SHEBARI

IN SHOCK, KODA barely processed seeing Twiggy climbing out of the pack. Huffing through the pain in his tail, Twiggy rushed to the caravan—to the dragon.

Sully shouted, "Twiggy, stop!"

The Tricksters broke out in a hollering wave, leaving the steps as Twiggy darted around their legs. The Trickster holding the dragon by the tail dropped her. She inflated herself and opened her wide triangular mouth full of teeth, preparing to bite.

If not for a Trickster stepping on Twiggy's tail, he would have run straight into her. He screamed.

Drooler stepped forward as if to help Twiggy, but the fox Trickster, calm and collected, held him by the arm. He cringed. "Seize that Critter for me, would you, please?" she said.

The Trickster who had stepped on Twiggy's tail, a humanoid wolf about teenager size with blue eyes and antlers, didn't lift its foot until it had Twiggy firmly in its claws. Twiggy bit its fingers. The Trickster yelped and almost let him go. It looked helplessly at the fox, obviously more afraid of disobeying her than suffering another bite.

She grinned. "That was certainly exciting."

"IT'S YOUR FAULT!" Twiggy bellowed. "IT'S ALL

THAT STUPID HUNTER'S FAULT!"

"Crazy rodent!" the dragon spat. "It's not even you I'm hunting." She sneered at Sully and Koda. "It's those two rodents!"

The Tricksters grouped at the bottom of the steps. They began giggling again, as if preparing to cause more mischief.

"Enough," the fox silenced them. Though her manner was calm, the giggling quickly diminished.

"What is *she* doing here?" Sully asked.

Koda felt completely out of himself, and it took him a bit to process the expression of dread on Sully's face.

"Sydney, here, followed the Tricksters after the Haven's collapse. She tells me she has come a long way to meet with you," said the fox.

"She's the devil in disguise!" Sully exclaimed. "Like Elvis says!"

"We don't want anything to do with it," Koda said loudly.

Twiggy shouted at the fox, "You planned this! You brought it here to kill us! Sully! Koda! Run! It's a trap!"

And there it was, like a worm wriggling inside him. The old fear. Koda stressed about what to do.

"It's not a trap. I have good reason for bringing you to her," the fox assured.

"What good reason could there be?" Koda demanded. His gaze never left the dragon.

"There's so much you don't understand about her. I'll explain if you enter my caravan."

Twiggy breathed in harsh bursts. His chest rose up and down in quick succession. "Are you going to listen to her?" he shrieked.

"I want to," Sully said. "We didn't do it before."

Twiggy calmed his breath, and the two looked at each other. It was a simple statement but with it brought hurt into

Twiggy's expression. He pushed at the Trickster's paw.

"Can you release him?" Koda asked.

The fox nodded to the antlered wolf. "Go ahead but keep him off the floor."

The Trickster placed Twiggy on its shoulder and stood there nervously as Twiggy ground his teeth.

"Alright now. Shoo, Tricksters. If you want any more of a show, you'll have to ask Bozo and his puppets. I'm sure he'd be flattered," said the fox.

The Tricksters dispersed reluctantly to the tarantula's web. Drooler followed the fox to the caravan. As they walked up the steps, Koda and Sully gawked at the dragon from Drooler's hand. She sat there insolently, refusing to move out of their way. The fox took Twiggy onto her shoulder, dismissed the antlered wolf, and swung the caravan door open.

As Drooler stepped over the dragon and took them through the beaded curtain, Koda viewed objects mostly woven from cobwebs and a few he recognized from the red tent. To their left, close to the wall, a cobweb tea kettle whistled on a cobweb stove that couldn't possibly work. Across was a couch, similarly made, and behind the open door stood a large cabinet woven with curly vintage designs. A modest collection of red leather-bound books stacked its shelf, as well as an orange-glowing lamp and a gramophone with a dent in its horn. Gypsy music played softly.

The fox Trickster gestured to the far end of the caravan where a bed lay high to the ceiling. Below it, inside a frame with a curtained opening, was another bed. "Seat them there, please."

Drooler snuck timidly past her. He placed Sully, Koda, and the pack on the bed. Sully noticed the sheet was the ruby fitted cloth he had seen on the table in the red tent.

The fox Trickster held the door open for the dragon. The bane of Koda's and Sully's existence crawled in and climbed a small cushioned stool onto the bed. The brothers stepped back. She sneered at them, prolonging their uncertainty.

"You can relax for now, rodents," said the dragon. "The fox scaleless said you'd be up to something, and I'm interested in hearing what she thinks two pellet-munchers can do."

Drooler took Twiggy from the fox and flinched as Twiggy lightly bit him on the hand. Drooler settled on placing him on the floor.

"I refuse to sit next to a Hunter," Twiggy said brusquely.

Instead of being offended, the dragon elevated herself proudly on her arms.

"Can't we all get along?" the fox said. She was enjoying this. Koda could see it in her one remaining eye.

"It *killed* Jack," Koda said, frowning at her.

"The *Smoking Beast* is what killed Jack."

The beast's whereabouts had slipped Koda's mind. There had been too many things occupying it since Jack's death. The beast hadn't appeared when they landed in the Haven. He assumed the erasing light had destroyed it.

The fox Trickster shut the door and knelt behind a Japanese style table in front of the bed. Drooler moved away. He had seemed paranoid ever since she snapped at the Trickster outside.

"Jack was very intelligent, I could tell," said the fox. "He probably already figured this out, but I don't think he had the time to tell you. His second card, Deception, foretold the Smoking Beast. In the Trickster world, Sydney's shed created a new species of monster."

"The dragon made the Smoking Beast?" Sully asked, shocked.

Twiggy suddenly looked at the dragon, infuriated and distressed. His voice choked, and he jumped onto the table on his way over to the bed before the fox set a claw between them. The fury in Twiggy's eyes intensified, but there was fear in them as well. Koda didn't blame him, not with those razor-sharp werewolf claws.

"Refrain from getting too worked up. As I understand it, you have little time, and I have a good deal of information to tell you."

Twiggy glowered at the fox—Koda could see the struggle on his face—and he jerked away, turning his back on her. He quivered from rage. The dragon sat there, looking smug.

The fox removed her claw. "Shedding is a normal, uncontrollable process for a reptile. It was hardly her fault."

"But Jack told us you said the Deception card meant his friends were lying to him," Sully said.

"I told Jack that tarot cards have many meanings, and this is true. The Smoking Beast is a deceptive creature, in that it shapeshifts *and* you knew who Sydney was, but you didn't tell Jack she was the Hunter from the flood. You were keeping the truth from him in an unintentional way."

"We didn't know she was the Hunter!" Sully cried.

"I understand," said the fox. "But you see how it's not always that simple. And neither is your situation. I'm afraid, since the Haven's destruction has allowed such things to happen, even though it's not a totem, this Smoking Beast can be very unpredictable and, therefore, extremely dangerous."

"What do you mean by 'unpredictable?'" Koda asked, unsettled.

"The beast isn't capable of thought or emotions. Like an instinct, it only reacts," the fox said. "Sydney told me that immediately after it formed, it turned into her duplicate. There are likely no rules to how it reacts. It could be based on the environment or someone's thoughts. The latter is true for Sydney, I think. She had been the only thing around at the time, besides the cave itself, and what was she doing? Gazing at her reflection. So, we're left to assume the beast picked up on the overwhelming infatuation she has with herself and became another her."

"Well, hey, you would be infatuated with yourself, too, if you had my looks," said the dragon.

Sully asked, "What about in Jack's purgatory? It was this kind of memory that—"

"Yes, I know," the fox said. "In Jack's purgatory, as you call it, the beast was likely fitting in. Purgatory had already created Jack's brother, the dog, the cloaked figure. What was missing?"

"The hunter," Koda realized with dismay.

"Yes, the human with his gun. You see, the beast is unpredictable by reacting to *anything* in whichever way it happens to. In Jack's purgatory, the Smoking Beast was likely still acting off Sydney. Its version of Hototo was smaller."

"Probably because the owl's not all that impressive," the dragon loftily remarked.

Twiggy turned around, his eyes narrowed at the fox. "How do you know all this?"

"Sydney told me."

"No, the reptile wasn't there when that thing killed Jack." Twiggy continued to glare at the dragon off and on. "Your card said he was going to die, but you didn't know how. I don't think you did."

Drooler and Sully stared worriedly at Twiggy. His voice had lowered and become threatening.

Seeming indifferent to his tone, the fox explained, "The Tricksters who ran with you to the Haven's opening in Jack's purgatory gave me that information. I've made sense of what I can from it. And some things I'm gifted to know on my own."

Twiggy's face darkened, shadowed by resentment and ill-contained grief. "Did you know he was a totem?"

"I did not."

"You know who I'm talking about!" Twiggy snapped.

"You've not caught me in a lie. I learned of the goat totem after, when I held my own reading. Your adventure was, and still is, very intriguing to me, and I sought to investigate further," said the fox. "I assumed, while giving Jack his fortune, that there was only one totem, the owl, in the image in my crystal eye. However, there were two—the goat was there as well—and that was my mistake." She bowed her head. "I apologize. Sometimes fortunes are late coming."

"What good are your cards if they show up when something bad is already happening?"

Koda wished Twiggy would stop arguing with her. *You don't act rude and then ask for favors.*

"I can't make sense of anything you guys are saying," the dragon said loudly.

"How did it get through?" Koda asked. The dragon turned her head at him, frowning. "What makes it so special?"

"Well, that's the juiciest part of it." The fox paused for effect. "Sydney... is a Critter."

Twiggy cussed in disbelief.

"I'm not some frightened weakling!" said the dragon.

"Oh, but by their standards, you are! Lizards eat insects—"

"*Bearded dragon!*"

"—and so do your roommates, here."

"Not me!" Sully quickly interjected.

"After all," said the fox, "a Critter is an animal who is mostly an herbivore, pardoning the eating of insects. Sydney tells me her diet is mainly greens and vegetables."

"Yeah, and it *shouldn't* be," said the dragon.

I don't believe one word of it, Koda thought. "If it's really a Critter, why did it destroy the opening to the Haven?"

"*Her. HER*, you cretin," the dragon hissed.

"Because even Critters can become Hunters of their own kind," the fox said slyly.

Twiggy started. He frowned at her.

"Is that true, Twiggy?" Sully asked fearfully. "It's not true, is it?"

Wincing, Twiggy turned in the direction of the door. "It's a disgusting thing we never did at the mountain pass. But… But Critters who are starving or new mothers under stress… they're capable."

He kept talking as if in fear of their silence. "To keep us safe, the barrier allowed Critters to enter but not Hunters. If a Critter were to eat a—another Critter—and walked into the mountain pass, I don't think the barrier would know what to do," he said.

And that's why the barrier and the trees were destroyed.

Sully was aghast. "Giant never fed the dragon any Critters!"

"What about before her?" Koda said.

"Huh?" Sully faced him, his expression twisted with worry.

"The dragon was a rescue. Previously owned by someone else," Koda said.

The fox asked, "Does our guest care to explain?"

"I don't need rescuing, and I've never been 'owned' by anyone." The dragon scowled at Koda. "Yeah, before meeting Insect-Giver, I did eat a small mouse or two."

Sully recoiled.

Koda stepped in beside Sully as the dragon smirked, putting a claw forward. "I found out it's not good for my stomach. Too much indigestion. But it'll be fun to catch you anyway. And then just spit. You. Out."

Twiggy jumped onto the bed between the brothers and the dragon, surprising them. His shoulders arched like a cat about to fight. "You'll be losing all the scales on your face before you even get the chance," he threatened.

"Just try it, rodent," the dragon snarled. "I've been harassed by an owl, a bat-eared freak, and severely deformed creatures who made me skinny dip in a stinking soup! I'm *looking* for a reason to attack you."

She and Twiggy glared at each other. Drooler wrung his hands by the stove.

Koda heard a clap. "Well, now that you're all friends, why don't you tell me what it is that's on your mind?" the fox said brightly.

"We need your help," Koda said.

"And what is it you need my help with?"

"Can't you tell us?" Koda was irritated with her. *She doesn't seem too concerned. Not that her world's been destroyed or that the next is just about to.*

The fox said, "Of course not! I'm not a mind reader."

"But you're a fortune teller," Sully protested, suddenly worried.

She smiled. "I am Shebari."

"How could you possibly help us?" said Twiggy. "You steered Jack into trusting Krampus more than anything, and now the totems have the relics."

"Forgive me, but that is no fault of mine."

"Three of the relics were stolen. There's one still out there. We need you to tell us where it is," Koda said.

The fox Trickster, Shebari, leaned forward, her claws sliding on her legs. She was so close, Koda could see how very irritated the empty eye socket was. The raw, pink flesh glimmered wetly, and the fur around it was soaked as if she were somehow weeping from it. In the corner of Koda's eye, he saw Sully watching her intently.

Shebari said, "*Three* relics were stolen?"

"Yes," Koda said. *Too much bad has happened today to let her know we have one.*

She examined him. A tense moment passed.

"Alright," Shebari said, leaning back. Koda felt relief. "It'll be fun. Though I will be using my cards, and your friend isn't confident in a reading."

"Whatever you need in order to help us," said Koda.

Shebari nodded, pleased.

The door to the caravan opened. The antlered wolf walked in carrying red plastic trays piled with food.

"Bring it here, please," Shebari said. "I'd like to get started."

"You have forage?" said Twiggy, who seemed unable to help gazing hungrily at it.

"You'd think we wouldn't have much, but some Tricksters had the foresight to bring what they could from the Trickster world," Shebari said.

Drooler snatched a baked treat, shrinking as the antlered wolf growled at him. Before leaving the caravan, it placed the trays on the bed. French fries spilled out of striped boxes and drizzled pretzels larger than Koda or Sully were bunched around candied apples. Buttered corn on the cobs with reddish seasoning were stacked against a wedge-shaped bowl holding a banana split.

Sully's eyes lit up. "Carnival food."

"I'm sure you haven't had a nibble since eating black-berries," said Shebari.

"How did you know we ate blackberries?" Sully asked, intrigued.

"I can smell it."

"Oh."

Before Sully could bite into anything on the tray, Shebari grabbed his paws. The movement was so quick it startled Koda—to think she could move like that. However, her intent wasn't vicious.

She brought Sully to face her and trailed his paw with a light touch of her finger. Sully made small noises through his nose; it obviously tickled him.

When she released him, he immediately returned to the tray. "Thank you," Sully said, his mouth already jammed with fries. Ordinarily, Koda would have advised against eating giant food. But the fries weren't anything really harmful, so he said nothing. He thought it silly to worry about things like that now.

The dragon stepped up to the banana split. "No meat, I see," she said disapprovingly.

Shebari grabbed Koda's paws next. Koda, who has never particularly liked having his paws held, shifted uncomfortably. As he looked up at her, he saw she was eyeing his left paw and the nub there. She smiled at him, like she knew. He looked down quickly, and as he waited, he noticed there were two holes in the ruby cloth.

"An old trick," Shebari said, a tease in her voice.

Koda was glad when she let go. She pulled a deck of red cards from a fold in her dress and shuffled them. Koda hated seeing the cards. He wondered why Twiggy's paws hadn't been examined. He handed Koda a pretzel crumb. It tasted as sweet as a yogurt drop.

Shebari spread the cards in a fan on the table. "We're without a crystal ball, unfortunately." She sighed. "I lost my eye in the collapse. *Bunked!* right out of my head. Someone has probably squashed it by now."

"Is it important?" Sully asked.

"It would be useful in clarifying the meaning of the tarots. Also, it is preferable to keep one's eye, whether one can see out of it or not."

Sully said, embarrassed, "I'm sorry."

"But you are lucky. We'll try something different. If it's a specific question you want answered..." Shebari moved the throw pillows off the couch and to the floor. "Then I think I have the right bird for the job."

Bird?

The couch seat opened upward like a chest lid. Shebari reached in and, to the sound of wings flapping, removed a black iron birdcage. A raven Trickster, feathers so black they were tinged with blue, squawked as she set it on the bed. The cage clattered.

Koda wasn't as frightened as he thought he should be. More... mindful, than anything. He had seen far too many totems.

Sully's expression was more like one he would have seeing a strange new toy Giant had given him. "What's it going to do?" he asked.

Shebari patted the cage, and the raven bit at the bars. She didn't seem to notice. "The process is called 'Parrot Astrology.' Though a raven will do just fine. Unless you prefer haruspicy."

"What is that?" Sully was quick to ask.

"It's the practice of telling fortunes by the livers of animals."

Sully froze in the middle of chewing through the candy apple. Twiggy opened his mouth to say something argumentative.

"Not a method I use," Shebari said, raising a claw.

She removed an iron key from the couch and gave it a twist in the cage's padlock. The door swung open, and the raven, green eyes wide, flapped out of it. The Critters, and even the dragon, stepped back.

Shebari folded her claws in her lap. "State your questions. You may find an answer or two in the cards once they've been selected."

As Koda began to speak, Twiggy interrupted him. "Wait, what are we—?"

"No, don't!" Sully stopped him. "You're gonna give away our question." He cautioned Koda, "Remember the story 'The

Monkey's Paw.' Be careful how you say it."

Koda heeded him long enough to feel even more nervous than he had before. He asked the raven, "Where is the living totem, Muraco? And where is his totem piece, the one we haven't found?"

The raven picked at its feathers and, cocking its head, approached the cards. Seeming to think carefully, it plucked one and flipped it over. The red foil twinkled in the orange lighting.

The card revealed one of Bozo's puppets glowing and wearing a three-point hat with bells and baggy, ruffled clothing. Its arms and legs were frozen mid dance, bending at different angles throughout the picture. Old buildings partially buried by desert sand bordered the night sky behind the puppet. Koda's gaze fell to the print at the bottom.

"What does it say?" Sully asked curiously.

"'The Fool,'" said Shebari. "This is Koda's card."

"Ha." The dragon smiled.

"Its meaning is new beginnings, taking risks. Trust." Shebari held eye contact with Koda. He didn't like her questing eye.

"Which aren't necessarily foolish," Shebari said.

The raven plucked another card. In contrast to the first card, this new one was painted during the day. A sun sent rays down on a boy wrangling a kind of hybrid serpent.

"Strength. Inner, to be more specific. It's a card of courage." Shebari eyed Sully. Looking wary, he held a corn kernel in his paws and didn't move to eat it until the raven chose their final card.

Shebari placed her claw on it. The raven squawked.

"What are you doing?" Twiggy asked, raising on his haunches.

"Jack's last card was the outcome of the first two. A spoiler now wouldn't be any fun."

Twiggy dropped his pretzel. "This is what happened last

time! If we—"

"When the time is right, you will receive this one card. It's not the outcome you asked for; it's the location of the relics. Go on and tell them, raven."

Twiggy started to protest, but Koda hushed him as the raven began to speak. Its grating, shrill voice randomly rose in pitch. "Te' lu'umo' ku fluye, wook suaves ku pisas."

Twiggy groaned.

"But we can't—" Sully began.

Shebari pressed a finger to her lips.

"Tu cheeeemo' Ameeeh—" The words constricted in the raven's gullet, causing it to screech several times before being stifled altogether. The raven lurched and spat out a golden coin.

"Hmm, I was looking for that." Shebari reattached the coin to her headdress. "Thank you, raven. You may go in your cage now."

"That's it? Seriously?" Twiggy said. "You give us an answer in another language, and we can't even hear it to the end?"

"Hmm... I suppose it could be difficult."

"Can you tell us what it said?" Sully asked hopefully.

"I'm not nearly as old as this raven to be able to understand the language," Shebari said.

Koda had stopped eating. He asked Twiggy, "You can translate it, can't you?"

Fear crossed Twiggy's face. "I can't!"

"You had to've learned from Jack. You'd know more than any of us!"

Twiggy tried clutching his tail and winced at the pain. "Jack is the one who could translate stuff. Not *me!*"

"You're going to be able to do it. You had to've picked something up from him. Just focus," Koda pleaded.

"'Pisas' means feet," said Sully.

Koda and Twiggy perked up in surprise. "You can translate Native American?" Koda asked.

"No, I wish I could. Pisas is Spanish. It's kind of silly, but sometimes I try to learn giant words. If I hear them a lot, sometimes I remember them. Well... I learned a few Spanish words when Giant was taking classes. She practiced with flash cards on the floor, and I remember she said 'pisas' when there was a picture of a foot. Jack told me some Native American languages have a little bit of Spanish in them." Sully shifted a little under their gaze. "'Suaves' means smooth, I think. I don't know what 'wook' means, but part of the sentence probably, I don't know, says 'soft feet'...?"

"That's fantastic, Sully. That's how you two can do it. You don't need to know every word. Just piece it together," Koda said. He gave into the excitement, the hope.

Twiggy inhaled deeply. "It's Mayan. I know that much."

For the next half hour, Shebari and Koda remained patient, and Drooler snacked quietly on his treat, as Twiggy murmured to himself. He only broke away from his concentration when Sully filled in a few words or when the dragon made some remark on how bored she was.

Finally, Twiggy said, "I think I got it."

"Tell us!" Sully urged.

Twiggy recited the translation slowly:

"On wavering land, soft footsteps you tread.
By boat Amet–Inet, to... bed.
In the... of someone dead."

Twiggy said, "I imagine it's something like that. But there are still parts I don't know."

Sully frowned worriedly. "That doesn't sound good," he said. "And what does it mean?"

You may find an answer or two in the cards once they've been selected, Shebari had said.

Koda forced himself to examine the cards. His focus centered on The Fool. Buildings that looked like ruins in quicksand.

Sand.

"'On wavering land, soft footsteps you tread.' What if the riddle is referring to the desert?" Koda said.

"Good luck finding a tiny piece of wood in that wasteland," the dragon remarked. Pieces of mushed banana from the banana split smudged her nose. Koda and Twiggy glared at her.

"I think the desert is it, Koda. We still have the rest of the riddle," Sully reminded.

Koda concentrated. "What about those two words? Amet? Inet? You didn't translate them?" he asked Twiggy.

"The raven said only one word. I don't know if it's Amet or Inet or something else." Twiggy tossed up his paws. "I couldn't hear. I'll tell you this: Both aren't Native American words."

"How about a totem?" Koda asked with sudden hopefulness. "Is there a totem named Amet or Inet?"

"No," said Twiggy. "But I didn't know there was a totem named—" He frowned. "Named Krampus, either."

He bowed his head with force. "Jack was good at this stuff!"

"Don't get frustrated. Think," Koda said. "Let's put Amet or Inet aside for now."

Koda tossed the words around in his head. "'To something bed.' Why would there be a bed in the desert?"

"It could be left from the Trickster world or made by the huge spider," Sully offered. "It could be here!"

"Shebari said there are more Tricksters in other places. So, this bed—if it is a bed—could be somewhere else," Koda sad. "And is there someone dead lying in it?"

"I really hope not," said Sully.

Koda returned to the cards for help and noted the sun on Strength and the buildings on The Fool, which appeared stranger than at first glance. Something about the two were *cultural* to him.

"What are these objects?" he asked.

"What do you mean? I see a sun and a human place," said Twiggy.

"A normal sun doesn't have hands at the end of its rays. Also, it's got a weird shape on it." Koda pointed to a squiggle on the top. He didn't care to touch the cards. "And I've never seen a giant's nest with a round roof."

"I have," Sully said.

"Where?" Koda asked quickly.

"I think it's a 'mosque.'" Sully carefully pronounced the word. "They're usually in older places, like the one in Aladdin, or in places they show on National Geographic. They remind me of Egypt." He wasn't afraid to touch the card, and he set his paw on the sun. "Maybe this is an Egyptian symbol."

"Both these objects are from Egypt," Koda said. *It has to be!* "Twiggy, could Amet or Inet be Egyptian words?"

"I have no idea. I have difficulty translating Native American, let alone Egyptian!" Twiggy picked up his pretzel and gnawed on it aggressively.

"Sully, do you remember? Was there a documentary or something that had this word in it?" Koda asked.

Sully thought and said dejectedly, "I forget."

"Try thinking of the various stories they had," Koda urged, wishing he had paid more attention to Sully's programs.

"There's a whole bunch. I'm not sure if I understood everything, but there was this half-giant, half-bird they really looked up to. Whenever the show put up their picture, I saw this sun symbol."

Sully paused. "Um… And they had a really gross process of removing all the brains from a mummy through the nose. I'm not sure why they did that, but they put them and a lot of other… stuff in jars. By the pictures they showed on the program, I think the dead person was supposed to go somewhere and take the jars with them. Some more strange half-giant, half-animal creatures would weigh the stuff in the jars and decide whether they were good or bad. Then they could travel to somewhere by crossing the Nile river on a boat—"

Sully straightened on his feet. "Boat!"

"'By boat Amet or Inet,'" Koda said.

"It's not Amet or Inet. It's Amentet!" Sully exclaimed.

"What's that?" Twiggy asked.

"The place they were going to travel to. It means 'west!'"

Shebari's grin was as wide as Sully's.

"I saw a river when I skydived here," said the dragon. Her beard had enlarged like a frog's throat from the banana she had eaten. "I watch Insect-Giver's television, too, sometimes. They showed a diagram comparing the size of this Nile to a bunch of other rivers. Isn't the Nile, like, the longest river in the world?"

Sully slumped.

The dragon swallowed her food and tilted her head all-knowingly. "The *human* world?" she said.

Startled, Koda questioned if it would be possible for the relic to not even be in the Haven. *No, as much as I hate what he's done, I believe Krampus tossed the relics down here,* he thought. Then, there was another worry: *What if the relic was in the Trickster world? Most everything that was there was destroyed!*

Sully must have seen the alarm on Koda's face. "What's wrong?" he asked.

Koda did his best to force the worries aside. *One thing at a time. Don't get worked up. Trust in the cards, and everything will be alright.*

"Nothing," Koda answered him. He steered himself back on track. "I don't think it matters. The riddle is making a parallel. In a way, the Haven is a copy of the giant world."

The dragon rolled her eyes. "Whatever, rodent."

"The desert is the chasm now, and there's all sorts of rivers running through it," Twiggy said. He had finished his pretzel. "How are you going to know which one?"

"Erosion," said Sully.

"What?"

"Erosion. It's what happens when water keeps running over land and shapes it in this weird way. So, we should look for where the rock is shaped weirdly at the top of the chasm," Sully said. He was on a roll now, and his embarrassment was giving into pride. "I'm afraid of water, so I thought I should learn a lot about it."

Shebari swept the cards back into their stack. At the beginning of the session, Koda had dreaded starting. Now that it was finished, he felt a pit in his stomach.

"Wonderful! Finish eating and have a restful sleep. I'll have everything ready for you by the time you wake," Shebari said.

"We should go. Every minute matters—" Koda started.

"Oh, yes, but better work is done when your body and mind are in shape for it."

Koda took a moment to actually see Sully and Twiggy, the state they were in. Sand stuck in their fur, bat bites irritated their skin, and Sully's injury, which still made Koda ache from sadness, had crusted over. They all smelled like sea water and other creatures' scents.

Everyone needed their rest.

"You, Sydney, should get some sleep, too," Shebari said.

Twiggy shot her a look. "Why?"

"Because she's going with you."

The Critters gaped.

"No way!" Twiggy exclaimed.

"She'll eat us!" Sully cried.

"We don't need any more traitors!"

The dragon demanded, "Why should I go with *them?*"

"It would be wise for all of you," Shebari said.

The dragon scoffed. "Sure."

Koda barely heard the arguing. He couldn't force himself to concentrate on any of them, not with the worried thoughts swirling around his head. There were prices to be paid when you didn't listen to Shebari. Yet it was hard to consider a danger he couldn't see versus the claw-baring serpent in front of him.

He turned to Shebari. "Tell us why."

"I thought you trusted me," she said.

Koda said in frustration, "She'll hold us back. She doesn't care about any of this."

Shebari smiled. "I'll not warn you again."

She started to stand, then reached across the bed to turn on an overhead light in the wood frame. "I forget. You need heat to digest," she told the dragon. "In addition, there is one other thing I would like to do for you."

Shebari grabbed a string necklace under her cloak, snapped it free, and set a small glass bottle with a cork in front of Twiggy. "This is my last healing potion. You may have it."

"Why didn't you give it to me when we first got here?" Twiggy hesitated, eyeing Shebari suspiciously.

"Go ahead, Twiggy," Sully said. "You need to get better."

Koda remembered Twiggy hadn't been there when he and Sully gave a similar-looking potion to Rowan. He could understand him being reluctant. Eventually, though, Twiggy took the bottle—by the expression on his face, his tail still must have felt very painful. He removed the cork with his teeth, then, with a last-minute hesitation, he gulped the potion.

He shut his eyes tight as if expecting a terrible pain. But, for whatever reason, unlike in Rowan's case, almost a minute went by and nothing dramatic happened. He opened his eyes and slowly, cautiously, untied his rag. Beneath the dried blood, there was no cut in his tail.

"All better," Shebari said cheerfully.

"You can't resist playing games, can you?" Twiggy said.

"You forget, I'm a Trickster." Shebari walked to the door.

Drooler leaned over to touch Twiggy's tail and retreated as he jerked it away from him.

"I'm not sleeping on the bed," Twiggy said, glancing angrily at the dragon, who had moved to lay under the heat lamp. She grinned at him.

"We'll sleep in the cabinet," Koda told Drooler.

The Trickster took the Critters over to the cabinet, Sully quickly pouching what he could of the food. After a bit of confusion, Drooler found the gramophone's volume knob and lowered the sound of violins. The orange lamp on the shelf would act as a nightlight.

"Sleep deeply," Shebari said. "Sometimes there are answers in nightmares."

Koda froze.

Shebari winked and stepped out onto the porch. Both the caravan and cabinet door closed as Drooler shut the Critters in.

It occurred to Koda he had forgotten someone.

26
AMENTET

THE APTRGANGR'S footprints guided Koda on the wide-open land of the chasm, lonelier and more snow-heavy than he had left it. One foot seemed to have dragged, creating long, slushy smears. Koda avoided them. Where he felt the heat rising into the air, snowfall evaporated above. The other print made it clearer for him to see that the again-walker wasn't at all human. Two long marks, which could have been made by a hand instead of a foot, raked the snow. The shape wedged out to the side as if it may have had other toes at one time.

Koda walked while staring at the ground. He heard the aptrgangr's voice, angry like a hiss of a fire, and realized he would soon have walked straight into it. The smell of spoiling of bodies underneath the ice flowed upward into the air as thick as vapor, masking the aptrgangr's own stench of decay.

"The thief has come to wisit me," the aptrgangr said.

Koda stopped and closed his eyes, shivering. The winter chill numbed his bones, or at least he imagined so as vividly as a nightmare could allow. "W-we thought we n-needed it to..." he gritted his teeth, "to get to the H-haven."

"You put it at *RISK!*"

Koda bunched tight around his stomach. Usually his paws

were warmest there. Somehow, they felt even colder, like he was freezing from the inside.

The aptrgangr seethed, "Like you vill the next." The snow crunched. "Do not seek after me."

Koda paused before pressing his paws back on the ground. He suppressed the cold ache in his teeth that would make him stutter. "You know where it is," he called after it.

"Aye. I still have yet more miles to go in secret. The totems are familiar vith my purpose to protect my master's possessions. They vill look for me, though I von't let them find me."

My master's possessions. The relics. "Muraco? Muraco is your master?" Koda asked, speaking over the *whooo*s and whistles of an arriving snow drift. Farther and farther away, the snow crunched and slid around the aptrgangr's lame foot.

"Vhatever his name may be."

Koda scurried after the sounds, blinking at snowflakes on his eyelids, struggling against the wind swirling at him like an avalanche. The footprints swept into it like dust.

"I sensed you and the hare take the totem piece from the chamber. The master vished you vould, so I did not interfere. And now I see the totems have ate them," the aptrgangr said bitterly. "I can travel now vith the dead in the vater under me. There are dead inside the totems, but I cannot get close. They grow from the Haven's destruction and there is much meat in the vay."

Koda remembered the chimera matched an entire mountain in size. The strong winds blowing against Koda were like gusts from its wings. He tumbled backward onto the snow.

"I am not your ally. Do not seek after me."

The snow fell with a speed only a downpour of rain should be capable of. It buried Koda under its weight like dirt in a grave. The numbness in his bones spread closer into his chest then to his head. Heartbeat and thoughts slowed.

"Wake up, rodent!"

Koda started and opened his eyes. The dragon was frowning down at him. "You're getting your rodent stink on me!"

Koda stumbled into Sully. His brother blinked sleepily and abruptly grew alert. Twiggy was already on all fours.

"You were acting all crazy in your sleep," the dragon said.

"How did you open the cabinet?" Koda tried to calm his heart.

"It's made from cobwebs. How hard can it be?"

The door to the caravan opened. In the corner of Koda's eye (Twiggy's as well since they wouldn't take their eyes off the dragon, even for a minute), Shebari stood in the open doorway carrying a cobweb pack.

"Up already, I see," she said cheerfully. "Good. Come outside. I have everything ready for you."

Drooler was laying on the couch. Eyelids drooping, he groggily moved over to where the pack had been left on the bunk beds.

"Oh, don't bother with that. I have gifts." Shebari produced two small cobweb sweaters from the pack, which Koda noticed were hooded as Drooler gave them to the brothers. The bit of cold that had slipped in from the door was shut out as Drooler helped them into the clothes.

"Nice ugly Christmas sweaters," the dragon mocked.

"Don't speak so soon. You get one, too," Shebari said and handed Drooler a lizard-shaped sweater with a sleeve for the tail.

Drooler moved to put it on the dragon and backed away as she snapped her teeth at him. Shebari took the sweater and didn't have nearly as difficult a time putting it on. Her werewolf teeth were especially shiny just then.

The sweater fit the dragon snuggly. "No one say *anything*," she threatened, glaring from under her tiny hood.

"Those *sweaters*," Twiggy began skeptically, "They're going to keep them warm?"

"They are tightly sewn," said Shebari, "and are as warm as the spider's egg sac. They'll keep you from becoming snowballs."

Koda glanced at her from beneath his hood as he instantly thought of the jerboas frozen by Krampus. The sweater rubbed too tightly on his fur. *How does Giant wear these things?* Beside him, Sully chewed on his sleeves.

Shebari brought her arm around Drooler, bringing him onto the porch. The Critters remained in the doorway, and Koda looked up at the top of the quarry beyond the caravan's awning roof. As Shebari had said, a vast cobweb blanket roofed them in. He could see it shuddering slightly from the high winds outside and crinkling from ice shattering on top. Koda grunted. *Your ice storm didn't work, Krampus. And if these sweaters work, it's not going to work when we're outside, either.*

Drooler walked down the steps. As his foot moved to lower onto the ground, the snow caved around a dark shape. He cried out and fell back on the steps.

A crocodile's head floated in the slush. Its glow in the water lit the underside of its flabby, scaled jaw. The jaws opened and snapped shut.

Drooler shambled up the stairs on his back. The dragon snarled in annoyance and moved awkwardly out of the way in her sweater. "Oh, big deal. It's an alligator," she said.

"Crocodile," Sully corrected. "Their faces are more pointed."

"It's an alligator," the dragon insisted grumpily.

Shebari rested her arm on the railing. "He's your ride."

"What do you mean, 'ride?'" Twiggy asked, backing into the caravan.

"How else do you expect to retrieve the totem pieces?"

Grinning, the dragon gazed at the crocodile. "You rodents are dead meat."

"It wasn't an easy task convincing him to accompany you. Tricksters aren't interested in risking their own necks. I assured him, however, that he'd be safe below the ice, and he agreed. That *is* the way you should travel. Underwater. It's the safest, and I assure you, you can do so for a while. Crocodiles can stay submerged for up to two hours."

"What would keep it from eating us?" Twiggy asked shrilly.

"Oh, don't worry about that." Glass knocked around inside the pack. Shebari removed a clear jar about a Critter's size with a decorative crocodile head on the top. She twisted off the lid. "They're modern canopic jars. I themed your equipment for the occasion."

"That's the jar they put a mummy's body parts in!" Sully exclaimed.

"I'm glad you like them. The crocodiles will hold them for you with you inside. The air will last a while," Shebari said.

Twiggy looked beaten, which reflected what Koda felt. *Why's it always water?*

Shebari gave the jar to Drooler and took out several others like it with different heads. More crocodiles popped out of the ice. Koda wished she hadn't brought so many.

Koda said to Sully and Twiggy, "There's no reason why all of us have to go."

Sully turned to him, alarmed. "Koda, I'm going with you. You can't forget everything Shebari said. The fortunes were for *me* and *you*."

"Yeah, and we're not going to let you go alone," Twiggy said, frowning. It was the kind of frown that showed caring. He might have *always* cared. *For Sully I* know *it's true.* But Koda thought of a memory of just Twiggy and himself. He remembered how

Twiggy had grabbed his arms in the lantern cave when it had been so painful to see in color and Koda had pushed him away. *What was I thinking back then?*

Twiggy had always cared.

Koda said, "I thought you wanted to give up."

"The more I think about it, the more I'd hate to let anyone else take revenge on those totems," said Twiggy. "Especially Krampus. For Jack and everyone else he's killed."

Koda looked from him to Sully to the crocodiles, wondering just what he had gotten them into.

"Don't get too worked up over us. All it gets you is running around with your tail cut off," Twiggy said. He grabbed his tail.

"Yes, go calmly," said Shebari. "But you might afford some fear. It warms you up when it's so very cold outside."

She and Drooler placed all the jars on the porch. Besides the crocodile, there were two with cobra heads and one dog-shaped with an unusually long nose and straight, pointed ears. Drooler uncapped them, put Twiggy and Sully in their own individual jar and with extreme uncertainty set them into two of the crocodiles' jaws.

As it came to Koda's turn and Drooler put him into his own jar, he wondered if he might be just a little bit crazy. He looked at the crocodile's teeth clasped around the front and sides of the jar and had frightening flashbacks of Camazotz in his nightmare. For the first time, he felt claustrophobic. Water sloshed about inside the crocodile's mouth, cooling his feet.

"Wait," Koda said.

Through the cobra's head (a lovely, absolutely *fantastic* choice that had also been made for Sully), a glassy version of Shebari leaned forward on the last step.

Koda thought back to The Fool card. The dancing puppet. Ever since seeing it, an idea had been forming in his head. But he wasn't sure he liked it. Hesitating, he asked Shebari, "Can you ask

383

one more to come?"

"Already have, dear."

Twiggy looked back and forth between Koda and Shebari. "Who?"

"Bozo," Shebari said.

"*Bozo?*" Sully and Twiggy exclaimed.

"You mean the Trickster off his nut from the theater we almost didn't make it out of?" Twiggy asked incredulously.

Shebari examined her claws. "It doesn't have to be four against thirteen if you have hundreds of puppets…"

"*Five hundred* puppets."

The voice echoed from the entrance to the quarry. Bozo entered from behind the wall, puppets now untangled under his arm. The Critters took a step back as he walked up to the caravan. The crocodiles snapped at him, and he flinched his leg and his arms to his chest like a—well, like a frightened hamster. Bozo quickly stumbled past them, straightening his arms and leg with an effort to appear as if nothing had happened. The dragon stared at him judgingly.

"Spying?" Shebari asked playfully.

"You invited me." Bozo crossed his arms. "Is this the reason why? It shouldn't come as a surprise, fortune teller, that I'd use my talents elsewhere."

"What do we even need him for?" Twiggy said loudly. "I thought we were going to be discreet about this."

Shebari listened to them both, her eye shifting mischievously at Bozo. "It's my understanding you have put in a request to the tarantula for a new theater. It's my worry, though, that she's a very busy mother, and your theater may not be built for a very, *very* long time."

Bozo's skull practically spun on his neck.

"Oh, I like how she works," said the dragon.

"Heinous!" Bozo stormed, slamming his fist on the railing. "Preposterous! Vicious skullduggery!"

Shebari looked at him with a sly expression.

"You don't have that kind of control around here!" he continued. "This fortune stuff is a lot of hooey! *Hooey!* I perform *real* magic, and if those Tricksters out there weren't superstitious—!"

Bozo stomped around in place, grinning his permanent grin but with a glare that was unable to appear on his skull. Shebari said nothing and continued to smile at him.

"Fine!" Bozo spat. "But I'm not taking my puppets. I don't have five hundred anymore, and I'm not about to have the rest destroyed."

"Then what good are you?" Twiggy said.

Bozo ground his teeth. "I have other play things."

"Where are they?"

Suddenly, the permanent grin on Bozo's face seemed genuine. "They are here already."

Twiggy frowned. "What's that supposed to mean?"

The clown Trickster grinned at everyone in turn.

"No," Twiggy said firmly. "I'm definitely not gonna have him around if he's not going to—"

"Better get a move on, Tricksters and Critters," Shebari said, "before the constellation in the sky opens. You're in luck. If the Haven were in a better state, perhaps it would have opened quicker."

Drooler grabbed the last jar, the crocodile-shaped one, and moved cautiously to take the dragon. She jerked away from him.

"No way. All this sounds like a lot of work. I can stay in the caravan," the dragon said.

Bozo snatched the jar and grabbed the dragon by her lower back. As she wriggled like a frog, he shoved her inside.

"What the heck!" the dragon shouted.

"If *I* have to go, *you* have to go." Bozo roughly handed the jar to Drooler, who cupped it in his hands in his usual discomfort. He placed the dragon in the last crocodile's jaws.

"Hey!" the dragon yelled at Bozo. "No wonder they don't like you! I've been chasing these rodents all over the place! Come on!"

"Are you afraid?" Koda said, not caring if she was.

"You wish, you rat! I don't care what any of you say. I. Am not. A *Critter!*"

The crocodiles began to submerge. Sully called over the dragon's yelling to Shebari and Drooler. "Thank you for helping us," he said.

Bozo gently handed over his puppets to Shebari in exchange for a cobweb hoodie. She hung the marionettes in the beaded curtain and set her gaze on the Critters. "You'll do well."

"Is that a fortune?" Sully asked hopefully.

"It's an honest opinion."

The water encased the whole jar. Hearing a dull underwater thrum, Koda took a deep breath.

"If you succeed, Critters," Shebari said from above, "I ask that you take the two relics—oh, I'm sorry, one—to Muraco in the southern mountains. Word gets around. He will be in the pass under the largest mountain."

So, she knew about our relic, Koda thought. Thinking of the southern mountains, Koda sank. *That means a longer journey.* He had been assuming they would find Muraco near the river where the relic should be. After all, weren't the answers shown in the cards? But they never did get to see the last one. Maybe he should have been more aggressive about seeing it. Maybe… Maybe it was best he didn't see.

He could just see the others and their crocodiles swimming close together in a blaze of Trickster glow. Swimming through the sandy waters wasn't so easy. The light didn't reach the chasm floor. As they passed under the caravan site, Koda heard the alarming sound of ice cracking as caravan wheels jolted in the snow. He guessed Tricksters were still jumping around inside.

The wind above the water blew fiercer. They were outside, and the water didn't brighten at all. Koda expected there was too much snow piling up for any of the starlight to make it below. When he looked above, he saw what looked like an artificial sky puffy and full from rain clouds spotted green, but what was really frost and snow coating the ice. Somewhere past it crunched two pair of feet: Bozo and Drooler. The two Tricksters stayed with them only until they moved past the entrance. It was probably best they didn't stay. They might give away their group.

Koda stared into the dark green vastness that was the chasm's sea. He sat at the back of the jar and tried to block out the thought of drowning or of any sharks or totems like them, so not every misshapen shadow he saw would be something to fear. He wondered if Sully was feeling well. Sometimes he heard him and Twiggy scratching in their jars as if they, too, were afraid of the shapes. More than once the shapes happened to be fish. The dragon mocked them, calling them "scaredy rats," but mostly she was quiet. For this reason, Koda thought she must be spooked as well.

Too often the crocodiles had to break through the ice—a sound dulled underwater but still too loud to Koda—to look for landmarks he had seen in his recent nightmare. They listened intently for bats. If they heard them, they hovered still in the water until they passed. At other times, there were sounds of the chimera, rumbles and angry shouts, some too close for comfort.

And the winter wind wore on, becoming thick with shards of ice; Koda heard them hailing down on the platforms.

An hour and a half later, the crocodiles slowed to a stop. Koda strained his ears, thinking he had missed some small flapping of wings, and heard instead a new pair of footsteps. One that dragged a foot.

The intense stench of decay permeated underwater.

To the side of him, the dragon's voice echoed inside her jar. "What is it?"

"Shh!" Koda hushed.

The footsteps stopped, and suddenly the Tricksters' glows seemed all too bright. Koda stared at the sea's frozen top, hoping desperately it was thick enough to hide them. But he could see the shadow of someone standing, just standing there, wobbling back and forth from the high winds blowing into it.

Some few yards opposite from where the aptrgangr stood, snow crunched as if from a heavy animal. Koda waited for the inevitable, the garbled sound from when Sully had seen the zombie still stuck in his memory. The heavy animal may have been behind a platform, as there was simply a snort and then their footsteps stomping away.

The aptrgangr stepped forward against the wind and the shadow quivered. Koda and his group waited for him to turn in another direction. They must have realized, like Koda, they would be going on the same path if they were correct about the relic's location. The crocodiles swam as quietly as they could as they coursed ahead, and the dragon hardly waited until the aptrgangr was behind them.

"Who was that? And don't *shh* me," she said angrily.

"The aptrgangr," Koda said.

"Who?"

Koda told Sully and Twiggy, "I had another nightmare with the aptrgangr earlier."

"Did he tell you where the relic was?" Sully asked.

"He's upset we even took the other one. He made the nightmare worse, so I couldn't find out where the relic was."

"You're really ticking everyone off today, aren't you?" the dragon said. Twiggy gave her another angry glance.

"Did the aptrgangr try to hurt you?" Sully asked.

"No, but I think he might if we get in the way," Koda said. "He's going after the relic, too. But he can't be the one to keep it. Shui Gui possessed you. That means it knows about the aptrgangr, and he's probably looking for the relic. The totems are going to find him and take it if we don't get the relic first."

"He's rotted all the way to his brain," Twiggy said. "He's practically delivering it to them!"

Koda wasn't sure if the effect the aptrgangr had on Critters would be the same for totems or if he would have any effect on them at all. Koda didn't know about the Tricksters, either. Just in case, he warned the crocodiles not to breach when smelling the decay. He smelled enough death as it was—even more terrible than what he had imagined in his dream, from all the bodies beneath the ice—but the aptrgangr's stench... its pungency was unlike anything deceased in the giant world, Trickster or else.

The dragon scoffed when Koda warned the crocodiles. "Why? What's something dead gonna do?"

"You see it, and it'll fry your brain," Twiggy said, perhaps in the hopes he would strike some fear into her.

It was still dark out when the crocodiles took their final look above the ice. Koda was beginning to wonder whether the Haven had always been constant night or if the totems had damaged the world from ever again having daylight. It had stopped hailing ice, though it was still snowing, and the winds howled. Glazed by the green starlight like a scene through night vision goggles, Koda spotted more platforms behind a broken-up wall of crust. Their ridged tops slanted down in strange sloping curves that, if the platforms and broken wall were to be pushed together, would form a groove in the crust. A river line.

"Sully, is that what you were talking about? The erosion?" Koda whispered.

"I think so."

"Finally!" the dragon exclaimed.

"Shhh!" Twiggy quieted her.

"I told you no *shh*ing me! If this is the place, start searching. I want to get back to that cobweb trailer thingy."

Koda tuned out their arguing and thought over the riddle.

On wavering land, soft footsteps you tread.
By boat Amentet, to... bed.
In the... of someone dead.

Bed still doesn't make sense. Could "someone dead" be the aptrgangr?

"One of us needs to go up there and look around," said Twiggy. "That fox Trickster didn't think of who was going to open these jars!"

"Where did Drooler and Bozo go?" Sully asked.

"Who knows. That clown is up to something."

Was it right to invite him? He might be more interested in sabotage, Koda thought.

He dared to look up and see the chasm floor awash in Trickster glow. It had gradually risen enough for him to see plants. They weren't rooted into the ground but floated through the muck, like eels. Like seaweed. Koda guessed the plants had been brought into the chasm from the ocean.

And what did the giants call the underwater ground covered in seaweed?

Seaweed bed. Koda remembered from one of the few times he had paid attention while the National Geographic channel was on. Like Sully, he had a kind of frightened fascination with water. "Bed" seemed to be what the humans called what covered the ground. And what covered it now?

Rocks.

Rock bed.

"It's not above ground we're supposed to search. It's the rock bed! It's got to be. Quick, go past those platforms and search the ground."

Surprised, Sully and Twiggy watched the crocodiles move forward and lower to the chasm floor. There was a low shifting and crumbling sound as they sped through the plants and sifted up sand on Koda's jar.

"I don't even know why I'm here anyway," the dragon complained. "Hurry up and find the stupid relic so we can go back to the trailer."

"Then get out of your jar and find it for us in the dark," Twiggy snapped. "The fox Trickster thinks you're so useful. That'll prove it to me."

"This is your dumb rodent world, not mine."

"It's your fault it's destroyed!"

"Quiet," Koda said.

"Some of us don't have a death wish," said the dragon. "When I get to Insect-Giver's house, I'm rewarding myself with a bowl of hornworms."

Rewarding herself for what?

"Is Giant looking for us?" Koda's focus strayed at hearing the innocence in Sully's voice. He would make sure the dragon got more than a nip on her tail if she said something cruel.

"She'll be looking for *me*, that's for sure," the dragon said. "I found you, and I can say I tried when you don't come back with me."

"*We're* her favorite," Sully mumbled.

"What's that?" the dragon asked sharply.

Even in the low light, Koda clearly saw Sully smile.

"I hear you rodents at night! Calling me 'the bearded lady.' You're so confident when you think I can't hear you, but I do, and if I hear you say it *one more time* at the house, I'm gonna—"

One moment Koda had been listening to the dragon's threats, and the next he forgot her completely as he clunked to the back of the jar, hitting his spine hard. The view of the sea moved violently upward. Koda's crocodile flipped head over tail, bouncing him around in the jar, and Koda *thunk*ed to a stop as the Trickster righted itself. The large shape that had hit them from below swiped back down. Dirt and rocks floated up through the water from where the shape had been laying like a strip of dead seaweed. The first thing that came to Koda's mind was an octopus tentacle. But it looked too dried and shriveled to be that. And it had hairs, like a long, mostly bald caterpillar, whacking up and down.

"What the— What is *that*?" Twiggy exclaimed.

An angry cry carried like a live current in the water. Trembling on his feet, Koda looked outside. He saw he and his crocodile had drifted far from the others. A split in the ice, which had been made by the large shape, brought in the starlight, creating a shining light as if from the heavens. The shape thumped up and down on the chasm floor before swinging away into the depths, striking one of the crocodiles into a platform. Koda heard a splitting crack of glass. Someone's jar had been broken, and he couldn't tell whose due to all the dirt clouding up. Thumps, which were so loud and powerful they could have easily been made by the chimera, brought in two gigantic paws, and Koda realized what had hit them was a tail.

All four crocodiles crashed out of the water and onto the snow, surfacing inside the straight formed by the two broken lines of platforms. In a tremendous crackling wave, the sea pulled apart and shoved them back into the ice. Koda could hear it parting around the Tricksters' scales like they were cutting glass. Wave after wave splashed onto his jar. Once they rode them more calmly, like a boat easing from the rapids, he could see a totem as large as a breaching blue whale rising out of the water.

Mummified, cloth wrapped its body and parchment skin hardened by resin stretched over the skeleton-thin face. As the totem growled, hissed, and spat with its ears lying flat to its head, a tight snarl revealed sharp canines. Like the fangs of a centuries-old vampire.

It was the worst possible thing a hamster or any rodent could ever face.

27
BASTET

SULLY SHOUTED, "Cat!"

The cat totem arched its back and pounced. The sea surged forward and rammed Koda and his crocodile back so hard his teeth felt loose. It was the greatest force he had ever experienced. He wondered if the shock alone was powerful enough to kill him.

Twiggy screamed, "Swim! Get out of here!"

Koda tried yelling out about leaving the relic behind but lost his voice when the sound of the cat pounding on the chasm floor caused the crocodiles to violently dive and swim back in the direction they had come. Sully's and Twiggy's crocodiles swam ahead of Koda's, their tails swishing madly in the debris.

"I thought cats were afraid of water!" Sully cried.

"It's an Egyptian totem! Bastet!" Twiggy yelled, "Where is that clown? Bozo! Bozo, you—!"

A green glow zoomed by Koda's jar. He spun back to see what it was, and it disappeared in the gurgling water. Then another glow zoomed by. Soon a whole trail raced the opposite way, lit up like sparks from a firework in the night sky. Koda's group had been thrown deep underwater, far from the starlight streaking through bits of shattered iced, and were quite a distance from the rapids. The water leveled out. Something hit Koda's jar, and the crocodiles paused in the slowing surf—long enough for Koda to register a face.

A hare not much older than Jack appeared to be staring at him. But outside Koda's fears, the eyes weren't focused on anything; they were lifeless. At least until a green glow brightened from its stomach. The body twitched, and the eyes, a translucent green by the light of the glow, moved just slightly. All around the body, farther in the water, more floating bodies became aglow. Koda had compared the movement once before to lighting stove burners. At the time, he had been sitting amongst a puppet audience.

It had never occurred to Koda that Bozo could do such a thing. To bring life to the dead.

The thing winked at him and swam to the surface in a swift conjoined movement with the other newly risen Critters. A group of them stayed to gather around the crocodiles. With sudden weight and no longer floating, they herded the Tricksters to the chasm floor.

Twiggy gasped. "This is wrong!"

"Look for the relic!" Koda shouted.

The crocodiles regained their composure and shoveled into the rubble. Much of it had been shaken up by the waves. Koda could hardly see, even worse than before. Bastet let out an angry feline scream as the undead Critters attacked out of his view. How long could they possibly stall her?

"Koda, it's not here!" Sully shouted.

"We have to keep looking!"

Bastet pounced. The water pulsed with energy from the undercurrent, pushing the crocodiles deeper into the rubble. A large rock knocked against Koda's jar. Panicked, he searched for a crack in the glass.

"It's the wrong place!" Sully cried.

Koda watched the swirling chasm floor with panicked dismay. If there was a relic here, it was useless trying to find it now. *Forget it! Was it really here anyway? Did we miss something?*

By boat Amentet, to rock bed.

Something was there. Something was forming, if he paid attention to how it was worded. Should it say "By boat west," it was simply a direction to go in!

"What if we passed it?" Koda shouted.

"What?" cried Sully.

"The riddle never said the relic was in the river or to cross to it. It could just be around the area!" Koda shouted at the crocodiles, "Take us back! Go! GO!"

The crocodiles jerked out of the rubble and swam them ahead of the growling cat.

***

Water flooded the jar from a gaping hole. Sydney huffed, keeping her nose at the top for barely a few seconds before it, too, was flooded. She held her breath as the jar filled and it sank lower and lower until it settled in the rocks. It was all craziness outside, like looking at a tornado with everything swirling about. Sydney couldn't take it anymore and opened her mouth. Bubbles streamed in front of her face.

The jar lifted. Suddenly, what would have been her watery grave was pouring out into the sea. Sydney greedily sucked in air and tried to slow the panic in her body upon seeing Drooler.

"What took you—?!"

Drooler clung to the bottom of a platform. He shoved her and the crocodile jar into his pocket, tugging on his pants as they went up the wall into a high cleft. More than once, he nearly flashed his bottom.

Standing as far inside the cleft as he could, the skull-clown overlooked the raging waters below. The scene there was a real rodent apocalypse: a gigantic cat in a catfight with glowing zombie Critters. More appeared out of the water in a fine snow mist. Hissing, the cat sent up a huge wave under her striking paw. Pronghorn and bighorn sheep kicked their front legs like charging water horses in a fantasy movie.

As it was utterly impossible for a Critter to fight like a Hunter, Sydney naturally concluded that Bozo was responsible; he never looked away from the fight, and he kept pointing to everything, calling out "You! And you! And you!" like he was picking out candy or something.

Bozo laughed.

"What's the big deal?" Sydney said. "Why don't you control the cat?"

"Because the Critters are dead. There's no life in them," Bozo answered irritably.

"The cat's a mummy. It's dead, too."

"*No*. It's a totem. And the totem is *alive*."

"Testy, testy!" Sydney mocked.

"Let me do my work." Bozo scrunched his shoulders. "Set your lizard eyes on *this*."

Sydney saw there was some organization to the fight, more than she had given Bozo credit for. The larger Critters (hippos, a few rhinos, and one—was she seeing that right?—triceratops?) snuck under the cat as she was busy batting away the smaller ones. Those with tusks stabbed her in the legs, wrenching them upward like a group of enraged elephants. There was no blood, but the feline screamed, backing up, and took hold of them, shaking them like a dog with a rabbit in its mouth. Then she tossed them. They slammed into the platforms and fell into the water wherein they swam with increased speed toward the cat, no worse for wear except a slight wiggle in their spines. Such was the advantage of being dead.

Bozo laughed. "How was that?"

"So-so. Make one of them bite the cat's tail," Sydney said. She grinned as the cat yowled.

Taking advantage of the distraction, the three rodents rode the waves away from the straight carried by their crocodiles. Sydney's crocodile was swimming away from the fight. She hoped the cat would think it was a large fish and eat it as payback for deserting her. But the cat ignored it. She charged after the rodents, her head bobbing above the platforms.

Bozo yelled, "Hey! Get back here!"

"Like it's going to listen," said Sydney.

She expected Bozo to send his minions. Instead, they became faint and floated on the water. The glows winked out.

Sydney turned her head up at Bozo. "Get those dead Critters to fight!"

"I can't see the water over there! They'd just drop dead again once out of my view."

"Well, get over there!" Sydney barked. Her voice echoed in the jar.

"You're crazy! I'm a distraction. If the totem really means to go, it'll go," Bozo stressed. "I can't control a one-thousand-foot cat!"

"Wow, your cockiness really flew out the window there, didn't it? I'm personally gonna pay that fox scaleless a visit and tell her how brave you're being. Expect your theater revoked."

"Alright!" Bozo snapped. "Let's get the devil over there."

***

Speeding along the sea, more propelled by the raging water than anything, Koda spread his arms and legs on the glass, trying to grip it with the pads of his paws. The crocodile's breath fogged the jar. It was tiring and yet beat the water faster, all the while constantly tossed out of the sea chaotic with slush, blood, and bodies. It stuck on the glass like bile. A hardened clump, with something that might have been hair, struck the jar. Then a hail of rocks. Koda pushed back—everything was moving so fast and so close.

It was by chance they had avoided crashing into a wall so far, the water wild and waving in hills. A huge withered paw batted down in Koda's window between the crook of the crocodile's jaw. The wave pushed them up, tipped them sideways, and threw Sully and his crocodile ahead of them. Koda lifted off his feet, hitting his head and spine on the glass. Struggling to keep his paws under him and breathing fast, he watched as more debris shook onto the jar. As it cleared, he strained to see the rock bed. The bodies whirling around in the water became aglow and, just speeding out of his view, swam back toward the totem. Bastet released another fur-raising yowl as the crashing steps came to an almost complete stop.

Koda and his crocodile shot up out of the water. A wave crashed into them, throwing them sideways, and Koda glimpsed the glowing Critters once again attacking the totem. They hung on using their teeth, sinking them into its skin to climb farther up its legs. Koda looked to the top of the platforms where Bozo and Drooler ran like chimney sweeps.

"Hurry! Curve around a platform!" Koda yelled.

The crocodiles swerved, their eyes blinking from the wind. The waves calmed, and they slowed to their own pace, though still moving swiftly. In line with each other, they dove into the muddled mist. Their glows lit the corner of a platform as they rounded it.

Twiggy slid around in his jar. "Koda, what do you got?"

Koda strained to think and felt his thoughts slipping to the battle somewhere not too far away. How long would Bozo be able to hold off the totem? Were they winning? Were they losing? Was the totem about to return? There was a possibility that the relic *had* been in the false Nile and had been crushed by Bastet.

"Koda!"

His attention snapped back to the waters and the floating bodies slowing from the waves, some upside down like dead fish. He found himself staring at them, thinking they would soon be among them, until, by some miracle, he shut out the thought and remembered the riddle's last line.

In the… of someone dead.

Koda knew he must be grasping at straws, but it was all he could think of. "What if the relic is in one of these Critters?" he exclaimed.

"Which one?" Twiggy cried. "Bozo might've taken them!"

Bastet screamed, full of rage. A platform collapsed, and the ground quaked from several blows as if she were spinning around in a circle chasing her tail.

"Start looking!" Koda shouted.

The blows raced toward them, then stopped again. Bozo was having trouble keeping Bastet at bay. More bodies became aglow and headed for her.

"Bozo, stop!" Sully shouted.

"You're gonna hand the relic right to it!" yelled Twiggy.

"He can't hear us." Koda pointed at what remained of the bodies drifting farther out in the water. "Go to that batch there!"

By the teeth grinding on his jar and the jerking movements as they swam, Koda sensed the crocodiles hanging onto the last of their nerves. They wouldn't last much longer before they decided to bolt. The crocodiles hissed, as if in agitation at the crack and boom of the rock bed, and attacked the rubble. Digging with their snouts, they uprooted the rocks, and bodies floated upward.

"Hurry! Before Bozo takes them!" Koda hurried them.

Another great thud sent the crocodiles backing out of the rubble. This was it. They were going to flee.

Bastet's claw slashed downward at Twiggy's crocodile, catching it in the tail. Blood inked into the water. The Trickster flung itself, snapping wildly, and its jaw clamped on a manatee that had been laying in the rubble on his back. As the crocodile thrashed, tearing its teeth back and forth in the flesh, the stomach opened. There could have been something that floated out then, there was so much rock swirling. During the collapse, perhaps the manatee had been thrown into the chasm from the ocean. With all the rock falling from the splitting ground, the manatee could have been pinned by it and, possibly drowning, may have sucked in the relic as the waves spun it out from wherever it had been hiding. Now, as Twiggy shouted, his crocodile swung around, hitting the relic in Koda's direction.

Koda's Trickster had its wits about it and opened its jaws. It may or may not have caught the relic; Koda couldn't be sure as the view from his jar filled with rocks—as he fell from the crocodile's mouth. What had happened? What had gone wrong? Koda assumed the crocodile had been hit. He heard it make a kind of hissing scream. And when Koda stood up shakily inside his glass prison, without any hope of someone picking him out of the rubble, he placed his paws on the glass, looking outside, terrified of the look in the crocodile's glazed eyes. Thrashing, convulsing, it made a new sound, an *uck uck*, so much like the sound Sully had made while collapsing in the room with skull-covered walls as the ancient scent of decay intensified.

Here it was again, that awful odor. The aptrgangr was somewhere there in the water with them.

"Close your eyes!" Koda screamed. He swung himself to the bottom of the jar, scrunching his eyes closed, and screamed again as his jar lifted. The scent flared, as dangerous as smoke before the fire starts, and he could hear the bony fingers wrap around the glass, tightening on it with rage, and he could picture the again-walker holding him up to its decayed face.

"I varned you."

Koda shrank from the glass and slid down the jar. Somewhere close (he couldn't tell exactly anymore), the water surged with bubbles, the rock bed crunched, and Bastet growled. One of the crocodiles might have returned then as, amongst reptilian hisses, there was a meaty thud and a brittle crack—the sound of the aptrgangr's bones as the Trickster rammed into him. Koda opened his eyes to see himself falling back into the crocodile's jaws, facing its throat. The crocodile gave a violent jerk and swerved about, stuck in place. Koda couldn't understand why they weren't moving. But all thought escaped him as he looked up at the Trickster's teeth clamped on the jar. The glass shattered piercingly around a tooth. Koda flattened to the bottom, watching the tooth wiggle a few inches from his head. He screamed, feeling himself sliding farther into the crocodile's mouth, and, without thinking, moved around to look outside.

At a high, steep, upward angle, Koda beheld the inside of Bastet's jaws. There was no uvula or tongue, just a cavernous opening going farther and farther away as Koda and his crocodile sunk into the throat. Koda screamed. He screamed until his little body shook.

***

The cat mummy had left a trail of destruction in her wake and was now paused in the middle of the attacking undead Critters. Sydney, Drooler, and Bozo viewed it all from the top of a platform where they lay on their stomachs like scouting soldiers. The skull-clown was having a bit of fun now. Laughing hysterically, though trying to keep it low, he sounded like an old man having a coughing fit. Spitting a violent growl, the cat whirled in a circle, throwing the Critters leached onto her tail.

"Dance, cat totem! Dance!" Bozo taunted.

The cat stumbled forward into the crocodiles, tearing up snow and ice and swishing it everywhere in the fray. A moment later, it brought up a crocodile smashed between its teeth. One of the rodents, still in the jar in the crocodile's mouth, screamed bloody murder.

Sydney frowned. "Hey, Bozo, pay attention over there."

"Stop ruining my fun. I'm doing the best I can," Bozo said.

"Well, it's not enough," Sydney said harshly. "Look, he's gonna be eaten—"

Immediately after she said it, the crocodile fell into the cat's jaws. When they opened again, the crocodile was gone.

"You let that happen!" Sydney accused.

"No, I didn't! Look at them down there! I've got the totem surrounded, and she's still not going down, I tell you!"

"Not good!" Drooler cried, drooling more than ever, and started to chant it.

"Tell me about it," said Sydney.

"No! Y-yes! Th-that, too, but—"

"Spit it out! And I don't mean that figuratively."

Drooler pointed. "Look at the sky!"

Sydney didn't know what she expected to see, but certainly something that didn't come with such bad news. The Halloween pumpkin in the sky had grown and become more than a constellation. It was now a solid object, like a moon lassoed close to Earth. Or a UFO. The mouth puckered then widened into a grimacing, partially open grin, as if something were forcing it to smile. Moonlight from another world spilled through. It was *exactly*

403

like an unidentified flying object. At any time, Sydney expected it to beam someone up in its light.

"Something's making that happen," said Bozo.

Another scream brought Sydney back to the scene below. The undead Critters were un-glowing in the water, and Bastet had cornered a crocodile against two platforms. Bozo wasn't looking at them. He gazed at the sky.

"Keep your eye sockets on the cat!" Sydney commanded.

Bozo looked back. The undead glowed again and stormed the totem. With a short, high-pitched scream, the cat thundered her body sideways to the platform, batting them up into the air. The crocodile dove underwater.

Bozo said, "If any other totems come over here because of that pumpkin, I'm out of here."

"Get the Critter out of that cat!" Sydney barked. Drooler whimpered. "I'm not gonna explain a dead rodent to Insect-Giver." Sydney didn't want them to get the wrong idea.

"How am I supposed to do that? None of the dead Critters can climb!"

"Figure it out!"

Bozo grumbled. In the end he obeyed her, and he was smart to do so. Otherwise, he would have been a very sad, very beaten, clown.

***

Koda's jar popped out of the crocodile's mouth and onto something soft. He let his scream leave him in a ragged gasp that rushed in his skull. Quivering, breathing fast, he turned around on his stomach to face his panicked reflection. Beyond it, the Trickster's glow illuminated a layer of what looked like stomach lining out of the darkness.

Oh, God, please help me. Help me. Please.

Tears burned Koda's eyes. Saltwater had wet his face, and pain returned to his eyes. His vision went black and white and lasted that way for longer than it had before. The sweater chaffed him as his chest heaved and made him feel like he was suffocating.

He stumbled to the hole in the jar and felt a tug as his sweater caught on the glass. Crying harder, he yanked himself forward. The sweater ripped, and he fell. Though the ground was moist, it didn't wet him too badly. He registered this only a little as he crawled farther into the glow ahead. One of the crocodiles, most likely either Sully's or Twiggy's, lay a few feet in front of him without a jar.

"Suuully? Twiiiggy?" Koda wailed and slipped onto his stomach. The outside boomed constantly with waves and rock, and he could hardly keep his feet under him.

Stumbling around, Koda faced his crocodile, who was brokenly sucking in air. A large tooth stuck out of its back. The crocodile lay there in a slowly fading glow that winked out entirely as the Trickster breathed its last breath.

Shebari promised them they would be safe.

Overwhelming sadness shocked Koda to his senses. His lungs settled. He wiped his eyes and forced himself to look around.

Now with one less crocodile glow, Bastet's insides were further darkened. But Koda could see just a little, and that was enough to make him thoroughly sick. The "stomach lining" was actually pounds and pounds of torn fish parts. Some fish, for the most part whole, flapped among deceased Critters. The mass churned far underneath, making a wet, unpleasant noise. Should the totem tip onto her side, Koda would certainly be crushed. His fear swarmed heavily in him again. Before it could drag him into full blown panic, he forced himself to focus on the walls. An oily brown slime coated the totem's skin and ribs. Higher up in the chest, a shrunken heart crinkled like a blown-up paper bag with each beat. There were no other organs. Strangely, despite being in what should have been a dead body, a lavender fragrance clashed with the fishy odor.

Koda rocked forward as Bastet jumped. He shouted again, "Sully! Twiggy!"

A squelch came from the darkness to his left. Koda spun. He listened and realized the next squelch that came was made by something a lot larger than either Sully or Twiggy. The sound was like grease squeezed out of hamburger meat and was followed by another noise, a slick sliding across the fish.

He heard a slip and an upheaval of weight. It had risen out of the fish parts, a zombie dragging itself out of its grave.

The aptrgangr.

Koda's heart raced. He shut his eyes tight and scurried away, his paws patting wetly. He squeaked as a flapping fish swatted him.

"BOTHERSOME CRITTER!"

Outside, it sounded as if a platform had split. Koda thumped hard into the fish, feeling their stickiness on his fur. The stretching of Bastet's skin was like scrunching sandpaper all around him. Her mouth opened, bringing in the starlight and rushing water. Closing his eyes, Koda ran from it in the direction he thought had to be the back of the stomach.

The aptrgangr huffed angrily. "Are you voried I vill kill you?"

Koda slid, his nose whistling from the seawater. He struggled to keep down his breath. His lungs strained. Behind him, the glass jar clanked, and the crocodile hissed and swerved as if to hit the aptrgangr. Koda didn't hear an impact—the crocodile must have missed—and the again-walker went on crawling.

"I von't kill you unless you interfere."

Koda thought about giving in. Why not let the aptrgangr take the relic? It would be so much easier. He could guarantee his life if he did. But no, he really couldn't. Bastet, Bozo, and his puppets were attracting so much attention. Could he really bet everyone's lives on guessing the totems wouldn't find the aptrgangr and the relic?

The answer was no.

Koda tried to shut out all the other sounds and focus on where he had heard the voice. The aptrgangr crawled with purpose, like he knew exactly where he was going, and it wasn't toward Koda. Why would that be?

In the chaos, had Bastet swallowed the relic?

Koda thought so. It was both good news and bad news. He couldn't avoid the aptrgangr if he wanted the relic.

Koda forced himself to move into the crocodile's light, trying to keep quiet even as Bastet's movements jerked him into the pile of fish. The squelches and dragging loudened. The aptrgangr was crawling toward Bastet's ribs in a line that crossed where the jar was. If Koda had only stayed there and turned left toward the ribs, he would have had the relic. His irritation with himself was replaced with intense fear. He may not be able to see the aptrgangr, but the aptrgangr could see *him* if he bothered to. Koda prayed his attention was elsewhere.

He stopped. If he coursed correctly, he should be directly across from where the aptrgangr would meet him. The squelches were about thirty feet away.

Koda felt around. The more he searched, the more he realized he was searching for a needle in a haystack. *It has to be here somewhere!* That is, assuming the relic was *on top* of the pile.

There were bodies in the water when the totem swallowed us. The relic could be buried under all this! How am I going to dig it out?!

The footsteps loudened: about fifteen feet now.

Koda headbutted the nearest flapping fish out of the way and spun around in a crazed circle where it had been. He found nothing. He butted another fish, searched, tried again. The decayed stench swarmed him.

Not caring how much noise he was making, Koda huffed loudly and shoved his last fish. He searched around the spot and a hard object poked his nose. A ball of panicked energy, he dug it out and pouched it along with a chunk of flesh. A squelch made by the aptrgangr's hand was heard clearly at Koda's side.

He bolted.

The aptrgangr released a rage-filled scream. Koda opened his eyes to see a green glow sweeping over Bastet's ribs. Hissing, the crocodile lunged, and there was yet another snap of the again-walker's bones without a scream of pain from the creature at all.

Koda halted as the totem's skin lit up as if from a flare. A draft flushing in the scent of seawater through tears in the skin cooled the marinated fish guts on his cheek. Through tears in the skin, he could see silhouetted platforms from high up.

There was another snap, and the squelches returned. Koda visualized the aptrgangr as nothing but a torso dragging closer to him while the crocodile discarded the other half. The body hefted upward with a brittle snap. Bones rattled.

"RECKLESS CRITTER! YOU ARE CURSED! YOU ARE *CURSED!*"

There was a slick slide in the flesh pile, and somewhere above, the aptrgangr's shadow reached out a hand. The crocodile leaped up behind it, snapped, and suddenly the shadow was missing a head.

Koda jumped out of a tear.

***

408

Bozo conducted the undead Critters to stick their tongues out (for those that still had them) and managed to goad the cat into running too fast. The feline slipped down and, turning in a fit of erratic high-pitched screams, Sydney saw some tears in her side. A small shape jumped out of one, like a flea jumping ship. It would have gone into the water had Bozo not taken advantage of the many ground squirrels found atop the platforms. Sydney had seen the glow inside the cat, made Bozo aware of it, and because of her superior intelligence, there were a dozen squirrels ready to catch the rodent. A moment later, a crocodile slipped out of the same tear after him and splashed into the sea.

Sydney said, "I'd say that's something you don't see every day but…"

Mouth raised in a grimacing snarl, the cat paused to bite at her ribs. She gave a sudden whirl as she saw the squirrels escaping with Koda. The platform they ran on jarred precariously from the hit and began to fall, but the Critters kept running until the platform ended.

Sydney could see the cat was rearing to lunge at them. "Keep that cat occupied," she told Bozo and slapped her claw impatiently toward Drooler. "Come on, let's go!"

Drooler grabbed her jar. Sydney bobbed in his pocket as he ran for the Critters. They would have been able to run straight across to them, but the cat had destroyed most of the platforms around her. There now stood a kind of circle of platforms like Stonehenge with the cat in the middle, a fifteen-foot gap between each platform. They would have to jump five of them by going around in a half circle to reach the rodent. As the first gap approached rapidly, Sydney steeled herself in her jar. "You know what? No. Let's just climb down and swim—!"

Drooler slowed abruptly and skidded right to the edge of the platform. He took the leap, springing in the air, and struck the ledge of the next platform with a jarring thump. Sydney's jar bounced and pulled the pocket down.

"Pick up your pants!"

Drooler let go of the ledge with one hand and tugged on them. Sydney's stomach surged as she felt them jerk downward and begin to slip. Drooler's feet kicked frantically one thousand feet above empty air, where bits of crust fell into the waves crashing over sharp rocks below. His grip on the ledge loosened. Sydney glanced upward to see the crust was crumbling where his hand clutched the ledge. Drooler placed both hands on the ledge and stabbed his clawed feet into the wall. Yet again the jar pulled on his pants and dipped farther and farther out over the sea. Sydney yelled at Drooler.

He climbed the platform wall and raised himself over the top. Drool gushed out of his mouth, and he drenched his shirt in it as he dragged himself over the puddle and away from the ledge.

Sydney shouted angrily, "Invest in a belt!"

From there it was a long stretch until they had to jump again. Sydney looked up at the sky. The Halloween pumpkin's mouth had stopped opening, so it was now frozen in a stupid, half-open grin. At this point, a plane might have been able to fly through but certainly not a mountainous creature. Sydney didn't stop to wonder why the pumpkin had stopped opening as her attention snapped to a crazed voice that rumbled from afar. Speak of the devil. She recognized the voice as the owl's, that fiendish bird who had dragon-napped her.

"WHAAAT?"

"Here comes trouble," Sydney said.

The ground boomed far in the chasm. The wind gusted in bursts. A humongous shadow raced over them and the platform tops ahead, shading the entire Stonehenge landscape. The platforms behind fell in a cascading crash. Sydney turned in the jar to see the two-headed creature—now three-headed—half flying, half storming through the platforms. She, who was rarely impressed by anything, couldn't help but recoil at the colossal form looming dangerously toward them.

The goat head laughed. "CRITTERS! YOU *ARE* ALIVE!"

"I don't like that guy," Sydney said, her tail twitching like mad in her fear.

Drooler jumped again and had barely lifted himself onto the ledge when, with a bruising slam and *BOOM*, the three-headed creature landed. Not even if a mansion had been thrown by a tornado into another mansion would the sound have even compared to the force that blasted its way into Sydney's heart. The shadow loomed, coming in above the owl's head as large as a skyscraper. The beak cut down into the platform like an obsidian wall within a few feet of Drooler. A gigantic fissure opened in the crust. In a hail of rock, Drooler jumped it.

It was there, in the fissure splitting the platform into the water, that the pocket sagged again. Sydney's jar tipped dangerously over the side. "Pick up—!"

As the jar fell, Sydney forgot to hold her breath. She choked on the water rushing in, even in her panic trying to give Drooler a good tongue-lashing. She watched him through an ever-darkening veil of water, completely oblivious as he jumped onto the last platform and joined the rodent, all while the waves threw Sydney out to sea.

Not again!

She sunk. She thought she had hit the bottom of the chasm, but it was an awfully soft landing. Sydney tried squeezing through the hole in the jar and mistook the slight rocking movement as her own doing. The whole jar lifted into the water then floated back down into the rocks by something that had moved underneath her. A large, forbidding shape closed in. Maybe it was Nessie or some

411

whale. Either way, it just floated there and cast their shadow over the jar. Salt in the wound. It really was, drowning and then being eaten on top of it. Or maybe it would be the other way around. Meanwhile, Drooler, Bozo, and the Critters were free.

Sydney gurgled water.

Rotten creatures.

***

The undead squirrels hurried Koda off the platform to join Bozo, Drooler, and the three crocodiles in the water. The ice had been too broken up to stand on the snow. One of the crocodiles carried both Sully and Twiggy.

Sully's eyes were wet with tears. "You're alive!"

Drooler took Koda from the squirrels. They lost their glows and fell into the water.

"Yes." Koda panted. He struggled to speak loudly over the quakes of the totems. "And I got the relic."

"When Bastet swallowed it, the Cracker Jack opened its mouth. It's stopped again for now thanks to you," Twiggy said.

"And thanks to me. I'm getting out of here," Bozo said. Without waiting for a reply, he splashed away from the quakes.

The undead Critters would no longer fight without him being able to see them. And so, as they heard Bastet halt behind the platforms, the crocodiles and Drooler chased after Bozo.

Sully asked Drooler, "Did you find the dragon?" Koda noticed the third crocodile wasn't carrying a jar.

"I have her in my—" Drooler patted his pocket and stiffened. In his other hand, Koda looked up at him to see his face frozen in shock.

"Did you find the dragon?" Sully repeated, his tone one of worry.

"I-I'm sorry!" Drooler wailed.

Sully gasped.

It seemed Drooler was struck dumb with guilt as he didn't move for a moment, just stilled in the water until a wave pushed him. He stumbled and nearly dunked Koda into the water. He shielded him, cupping him in his hands, as water sprayed into the sky. Gaps in the broken wall of platforms to their right showed them passing the chimera, who had crashed directly in front of Bastet. She raised her back threateningly and had to crane her neck to hiss up at the totems. Their heads raised high over the top of the chasm, looming over her. If not for the waves crashing around and helping the Critters and Tricksters along, Koda was sure they would have been heard. The darkness shielded them and feeling relief, the scene raced behind.

"We have to go back for her!" Sully cried.

"We-we can't. A hole in the jar. Th-there was a hole in the jar!" Drooler said pitifully.

Bozo and Twiggy snapped at him to be quiet, but their voices were completely muted by Hototo's roaring behind them.

"THE SKY OPENED. YOU HAD THE RELIC. NOW WHERE IS IT?"

A razor-sharp voice, Bastet's, responded angrily, "It is here, in my stomach."

"IF IT WERE, WE'D BE FLYING INTO THE HUMAN WORLD!"

"IT IS *HERE!*"

Koda shivered and not from the falling snow. Krampus's malevolent voice rang like a Notre Dame bell. He imagined the goat totem grinning as Krampus paused to look mischievously at the other totem heads. "She insists, fellow totems," he said.

The group of Critters and Tricksters headed south as the chimera leaped into the air. An earth-shattering slam bruised the chasm floor. And while they rode the waves, Koda having been stuffed quickly into Sully's jar, they had yet to pass the chimera's thousand-mile-long body now pinning a screaming Bastet. Tons of body weight lurched while cloth and papery skin shredded.

28
IN GOOD COMPANY

T HE JOURNEY to the southern mountains was long and strenuous. Fatigued from battle, the group traveled in silence. Bastet's screams finally ceased, and the chimera's calls went further west.

They caught Bozo trying to sneak off soon after they first headed out. "I've done my good deeds for today," Bozo had said in an agitated whisper. "You've got your relic. Now it's back to the grand reopening of my theater."

After arguing back and forth, Koda snapped, "There's not going to *be* a new theater, let alone an audience, if the world ends!"

Grumbling, Bozo gave in and Twiggy whispered to Sully, "No one bothered showing up even before."

Sully hadn't felt like laughing. He didn't feel right since leaving the battle. Days ago, he would have said there was nothing scarier than the devious dragon. Despite finding out he was wrong, she had still seemed invincible to him. Sully worried for Giant.

Twiggy said that maybe the point in her coming along was that she would die and not be able to betray them. His expression was stunned when Sully told him in a raised voice that it was ugly to say such things.

Barely alive and cut up in places, they arrived at the million-mile-long trench (or so it seemed to Sully) leading down from the plains. With its dark crevices and grooves, and a strange sheen created from the Cracker Jack's starlight, it looked threatening somehow. Like it was a creature all its own. Shrieking calls and strange sniffing noises reached them from above.

From the jar next to Sully's in the crocodile's jaws, Twiggy whispered, "They're up there."

Drooler had placed Koda in Sully's jar. He had fallen asleep. Sully pawed him gently awake and the two of them gazed outside through frosted glass. The snow storm worsened, though being deep inside the jaws kept the jar mostly ice free so far. The same couldn't be said of the crocodile's teeth. They had turned into icicles. Luckily, the ice and snow had formed back over the sea. Otherwise, they might have frozen in the water.

"It's a wide-open stretch from here to those mountains," Twiggy said apprehensively.

"I'm small. I won't be seen," said Koda.

"So are we." Twiggy glanced at Sully, nodding as if to urge him to show his agreement.

"For sure," Sully said.

"No sense in trying to go alone," said Twiggy.

Koda was quiet for a moment. "Then Drooler will take us up. But once you do, Drooler, stay here with Bozo. We might need you if something happens."

The thought of going without them bothered Sully. Drooler was like a friend now. And Bozo and the crocodiles were protection.

Bozo leaned against the wall of rock and folded his arms.

"Don't even think about running back," Twiggy threatened.

Bozo bent forward, again with that sense of inwardly glaring. "Get going. You're as bossy as that lizard."

Drooler took the jars from the crocodiles. He found a chunk in the wall to grip onto and raised out of the water. His cloak flapped loudly in the wind. From under his arm, Sully apprehensively stared at Bozo's hair becoming smaller and smaller below. Once they reached the top some minutes later, Drooler removed them from the jars and set them on the ledge. He departed quickly.

Sully turned to meet a gradually rising wall of snow. It reached about ten feet at its highest point. The snowfall *poured* like sugar spilling out of a bag. Already the winter chill nipped at him through the hoodie. Krampus's winter was strengthening.

They didn't speak but hurried into a rocky landscape. Mountains no taller than two giants (though they had to be taller underneath the snow) provided cover for Sully, Koda, and Twiggy. They tensed as a totem chewed somewhere nearby, hidden by one of the mountains. Though maybe "chewed" wasn't the right word. It sounded more like the totem was *sucking*.

There weren't many Critters still aboveground—Sully assumed the deceased had been buried by the snow, though the recently deceased, those who couldn't have been dead for more than half an hour, painted the snowdrifts red. Those bodies looked to be without blood. Various puncture marks grouped in a circular bite pattern imprinted their necks.

Twiggy looked forlornly at the neck of an adult brachiosaurus stretching twenty-five feet from behind one of the mountains. Its stomach formed an even higher mound. Sully wondered what it must have sounded like when it breathed. But now it was still, and he could see the cause: two deep puncture wounds in the dinosaur's throat. A trickle of blood leaked from them and had turned white from the frost.

"These marks are different from those other ones," Twiggy whispered.

"Did Camazotz do this?" Sully asked. Perhaps the totem was a vampire bat after all.

"Somehow, I don't think so," Koda said.

417

Sully often wished the friendly dinosaurs could return from extinction. The brachiosaur wasn't the only one they had come across. There were also hadrosaurs, stegosaurs, and triceratops. *The opening to the Haven must have been around for a very long time*, Sully thought and shed a tear.

His eyes hurt again. They had been acting up a lot more since they arrived at the plains, the usual blurring and vision going black and white. Sully rubbed his eyes, then batted his ear at a ringing sound ghostly playing over the wind.

Twiggy stood at alert. "What's that?" He jumped at a sudden loud boom.

A long, white arm stretched over the brachiosaurs, and a gigantic skull eclipsed in starlight peeked out from behind the mountain. It wasn't entirely human, for there were animalistic features, like a werewolf in mid form. Two fangs dripped blood onto the snow. As he stared into its eye sockets, Sully thought he must be staring into the hollow eyes of a demon.

The Critters were in direct view. Eyes or no eyes, the totem had to have seen them. Sully readied to run; he could see Twiggy was, too, but Koda gripped his arm. By some miracle, none of them had screamed yet. Sully realized it *was* a miracle, because the skeleton looked away from them—it had never been looking at them in the first place. It couldn't see!

The totem dunked its skull down toward its ribs, and as it did, the spine bent up behind the skull. It moaned, a mournful humming sound, and stuck its hand between its ribs—they rivaled even the largest elephant's bones—to clench at empty air where the stomach would have been. Removing it and trailing knuckles on the ribs, they chimed as deeply as church bells. Trailing off, they left the air ringing softly.

Sully flinched as the totem's skull jerked up at the sky. A vulture-looking totem with a female giant-like face flapped to the ground nearby. It reminded Sully of the dog with a giant face in the *Invasion of the Body Snatchers*, the movie he had nightmares about days after watching it.

The skeleton turned abruptly, striking the brachiosaurus with its arm. The ground boomed and trembled. The other totem shrieked and flew up into the sky again. She must have been over two dozen yards away, yet in three gallops, the skeleton had almost reached her.

A groan. Chiming ribs. The booming continued away from them.

"What totem was *that?*" Sully whispered.

"Gashadokuro," Twiggy whispered. "'Starving Skeleton.' He'll go on killing even though he'll never be satisfied. What a cruel waste of Critter life."

Sully couldn't imagine life on an empty stomach. Thinking about it made him feel ill.

Sometime later (what seemed longer than it really was), the Critters left the buried mountains to enter the larger ones. Sully remembered with horrific detail Hototo's head peeking above the peaks.

He will be in the pass under the largest mountain, Shebari had said. The group gazed upward in the blue shadow of a mountain that was so large, it may as well be Mount Everest's twin. Thick mist climbed it a way until just the snowcapped peak was visible like a fanged tooth. Above it, the Cracker Jack was an enormous orange moon.

They were currently sheltered a little by frosted boulders. Twiggy groomed himself, breaking the snow on his head. It clumped onto his shoulders. "You sure the fox Trickster isn't leading us on a wild goose chase?"

"I don't think so," Sully said innocently. "She knows we were looking for a totem, not a goose."

"How are you feeling?" Koda asked.

Sully had been trying to keep his mouth closed, which was difficult because of his long rodent teeth. He was afraid his tongue would turn into an icicle. His nose already felt quite frosted. "Do I look like Rudolph?" he asked.

Koda tugged on Sully's hood to better cover his face. "You're fine. Let's go in quickly."

The land between the sloping mountain shoulders resembled a deserted road at night and seemed to breathe ice. Sully would have said it was beautiful if he hadn't known who was responsible. He breathed everything in and realized how much clearer the air was compared to the giant world. Granted, he had smelled most of it while in a dying forest, but not even the woods where Giant lived was this fresh.

There were no trees here. There was no cover, and since the face constellations weren't very bright in the southern mountains, the pass darkened. A hamster can't be afraid of the dark, they're nocturnal, but he had grown used to Giant's night-light and very recently discovered there really could be monsters in the dark.

One moment they were alone, then someone ahead of them said, "I will not harm you."

After so long with only the snowstorm for sound, Sully squeaked, setting into motion several *kuk*s and squeaks from Koda and Twiggy.

No sound came from the unknown creature.

"Who are you?" Twiggy asked loudly.

"My name is Muraco."

When Koda first mentioned he wanted to find Muraco, Sully had only been thinking of him as Jack's brother. Now he remembered he was a totem. Muraco could be an enemy to the other totems while still being an enemy to them. Sully sensed Koda and Twiggy hesitate.

The voice was gentle, though also somewhat playful.

"Handi ko ngeki Ante ir colillas ar congelen."

Twiggy said with a slight tremble, "We understand animal speak better."

"I said 'Come with me before your bottoms freeze.'"

The Critters shifted, bemused.

"It's warmer where we're going," Muraco said, and they heard the figure turn to leave.

Twiggy made small stuttering noises of protest as Koda was the first to follow Muraco. Was he *really* Muraco? Sully had learned to be more suspicious. Part of him thought he could be Krampus in animal form. He was not very large; Sully knew that by the sound of his pawsteps. He squinted into the darkness. The face constellations stubbornly remained dim.

"There was some excitement over the plains several hours ago. Was that you?" Muraco asked.

"Yeah," said Twiggy.

"They must be furious." There was a smile in Muraco's voice.

The Critters did a double take.

"We... We know you're a totem," Twiggy said.

Why does he have to be so blunt about it? Sully thought worriedly.

Muraco asked, "Oh? From whom?"

"Heard it from a Trickster." Twiggy seemed to be *daring* Muraco to reveal his true nature.

"So, you had help. I assumed so. That commotion in the chasm had to have been done by more than just Critters. Not that I'm doubting you."

"The Tricksters are waiting at the end of the plains for us," Twiggy said boldly, then seemed to rethink his statement. "I mean... they're *close*."

"I believe you," Muraco said nonchalantly.

The Critters halted as the pawsteps stopped. As if on cue,

the face constellations glowed brighter and revealed Muraco to them. Sully could hardly tell him apart from the snow. He was a shimmering white, every hair appeared to sparkle, and as he turned to look back at the Critters, Sully saw soft blue eyes as clear as crystals. No matter the color, Sully teared up a little, as they looked so much like Jack's.

The warm moment passed. Sully tensed, and for an instant, it seemed as if not even the strong wind could unfreeze him. He was positive Muraco was going to change like Rowan.

Muraco walked on and did not change.

Sully gradually drifted to Muraco's side, trying to get a better view. He heard Koda and Twiggy start as Muraco noticed him staring and stopped to ask him brightly, "What is it? Tell me why you're curious."

"You're a totem," Sully said.

"Yes," Muraco said simply. "Is that so odd?"

Odd! "You're a hare!"

"Well, yes. I'm more relatable this way, right?"

"I guess so."

"I appear to you in this form because I'm a Critter at heart." Again, the smile. "And a Trickster."

Twiggy's expression showed distrust.

"I mean that in the nonliteral sense," Muraco said.

Koda nudged Sully to walk away from Muraco. "Do you have sharp teeth? Or horns?' Sully asked.

"Not any sharper than your teeth. And I don't have any horns, I promise."

"As long as you don't have horns."

"I can be more spectacular, but there's no reason for that now."

"But we need your help," Koda said quickly. "You're a totem. You can defeat the others."

"They cannot be killed."

"Krampus said you're the one who trapped them."

"So, you've met Krampus! I'm very glad you're here, indeed. Yes, I did that. To contain the totems, they need to be all in one place within a close distance," Muraco said. "I'm sure Krampus told you I'm a big disappointment and that he curses me for life. It's the totems with a temper that are the real fun to mess with."

"He sure talks like a Trickster," Twiggy muttered.

When Muraco stopped again, the mountain pass rolled with many snow mounds. It was as if someone had made an assortment of gigantic snowballs, then set a white blanket over them. A snow garden hidden in the deep dark. Cautiously, the Critters followed Muraco to a snow mound nearest to the mountain's shoulder. Dirt paw prints trailed to a large hole in the bottom of the mound. Sully smelled various Critter scents.

"Lodges don't usually have aboveground entrances. The beavers enter from the water underneath, but they're courteous of non-swimmers," Muraco said.

Incredulous, Sully asked, "You mean there's a room inside?"

"Massive, huh? It's amazing what beavers can do if you give them the time."

I bet I could make a burrow like these if Giant gave me more bedding, Sully thought.

"Quickly," Muraco hurried.

"Wait." Twiggy glanced at Sully and Koda, dread clear on his face. "We've been in this situation before."

"This is where you must go if you want to progress. If it makes you feel any easier, I'll go first." Muraco hopped into the hole. "I hope you don't mind me being a totem. I'll say it again: I'm a Critter at heart, and like my brother says, we take care of our own."

423

Sully's heart panged at that. He tried to keep the tears out of his voice. "Muraco… There's something we need to—"

"You can tell me whatever it is you need to tell me once we're all settled," Muraco said jovially.

Without much choice, the Critters entered onto a muddied floor. Long, wet threads hung from a dirty, pulped ceiling. It was like they were inside a monster's mouth. Sully grimaced. To think Koda experienced such a thing a few hours ago.

Despite the wetness, Sully warmed the farther he went in. A tunnel curved and domed into the main cavity of the lodge. He assumed it had a high ceiling for there was the slight echo of voices. He heard what were probably beavers breaching the water and more Critters gathered around for a drink. The lodges were most likely built on a very large lake. Muraco nudged Sully from behind, and Sully wondered what the hurry was. They seemed to be walking with purpose toward something.

Someone stood in front of them. With all the animals scurrying around, their scents confusing Sully's nose, he hadn't immediately smelled the Critter. Nor had Koda or Twiggy apparently. All at once, they made a startled sound and Sully stumbled on his feet as he tried to stand, sniffing to confirm that scent.

Everything else faded. The Critters in the room. The feeling in Sully's arms and legs. He couldn't move or speak. Time seemed to slow down. He wondered if he was dreaming. He must be, for the Critter standing before them was dead.

Twiggy ran to him. "Jack!"

Sully strained to see. He paced, concerned by Twiggy's heaving cries. Twiggy might be hugging Jack with all his might.

Sully managed to ask, "Are you a ghost?"

"No, Sully," Jack said, and it *was* his voice. His voice and his scent.

Sully took a step forward. Then two, and suddenly he raced to him. Sully hugged Jack's paw. This was Jack. *Jack! Alive!* And that was all he thought about. All their problems washed away with the warmth of Jack's fur on his cheek and his scent comforting him.

Koda stood at the entrance. His voice cracked as he tried to speak, and he tried again. "How?" he asked softly.

"The Haven has its secrets," Jack said.

Sully's grip on Jack's paw loosened as he heard him ask, "Where is Rowan?"

Twiggy abruptly backed away. Immediately, Jack became alert. Sully thought maybe he might have initially been confused. Then he felt him lower a bit to the floor, and he shook a little. Sully hugged him tighter and that only made things worse because Jack tried to move away. It was Sully's hug that did it. It must have confirmed his worries.

Jack said, "He's—"

"A traitor," Twiggy spat.

The silence from Jack was heartbreaking, even more to hear his confusion. "I don't understand."

"Rowan was a totem," Koda said quietly.

Sully heard Muraco walking over to Jack.

"Are you sure?" asked Jack.

"Positive," said Twiggy.

Koda said, "He was there with you and Muraco four years ago, hiding in the trees."

Sully was afraid of Jack's silence. He felt his pulse quicken from anger or from heartache. Or both.

"What was his name?"

"Krampus," Koda said.

"Krampus? This is my fault," Muraco said. Any trace of playfulness had disappeared. "I never did get to tell you all the totems, Jack. I wasn't aware he could transform but—"

"I will not grieve over what is false," Jack said. Sully cringed at the coldness of his tone. He then remembered his own anger, felt it boiling at how Jack's once good friend could make him sound this way. The coldness was a front. The strain in his throat was a dead giveaway.

Jack said to Sully, Koda, and Twiggy, "I don't wish you do so, either."

"He's been living underground killing Critters!" Twiggy exclaimed.

Sully heard Jack's paw lift to touch him. Twiggy flinched. "Why are you here?! Why weren't you out there with us if you were still alive! Look what he's done! All this time, he's been right under our noses!"

"I wanted to be there more than anything," Jack said softly.

"Why weren't you?" Twiggy sobbed.

Sully cried.

"It's not his fault," Muraco said. "He insisted that he go, but I told him not to. It wouldn't have been safe."

Twiggy demanded, "How are you here? How is it possible?"

"No matter what the totem has done," Jack said, and it seemed he was trying very hard to continue, "there is wonderful news. Twiggy... our family made it."

"What?"

"They're alive. They're in the other lodges."

Twiggy stammered, trying to form a word. "H-how? My pup, too?"

"Yes. The Haven is more than we thought it was. Critters come here every day without entering the opening," Jack said. "But only if they have died."

Sully released Jack's paw to look up at him. It was one miracle to have Jack alive. A million, maybe even billions, of resurrected Critters?!

"It is paradise," Jack said.

"Living here for so many years…" Muraco said. "Krampus knew."

"*He knew?*" Twiggy cried.

"The devil knew."

Jack bent his head over Sully and Twiggy. "I'm sorry."

Koda came over, and Sully felt him laying on Jack's paw. He heard him breathing, a kind of worried breath. Koda waited a while, then said, "Jack, he gave two relics to the chimera. He took them from me."

"They want to use them to invade the giant world," Sully said tearfully.

"We know," said Jack.

"That is my fault, too. It certainly isn't yours, Koda," Muraco said. "I can release a lot of power when I want to, but I don't know how things always work or how they will get twisted around when the world starts falling apart. You did something, though. The Trickster in the sky stopped opening its mouth."

Koda stayed by Jack. "We found out where the last relic was. Bastet had it," he said.

Jack lifted his head. "How did you do that?"

"Jack, we went to see the fox Trickster."

"You did?"

"She read the cards to us and gave us a riddle to find the last relic. And she told us Muraco was in the mountains."

"She gave us hoodies, so we would be warm in the snow," Sully said.

"A generous Trickster," said Muraco with amusement.

"What else has she helped you with?" asked Jack.

"There's much you need to catch up on," Muraco said. "Let's go somewhere more private." In Sully's excitement, he hadn't noticed a group of Critters wandering close to their group.

"Do they know... what you are?" Sully whispered to Muraco.

"No, they don't."

Muraco moved them to a private "room" in the lodge. While Twiggy went to see his family (he couldn't wait), Sully and Koda didn't immediately start their story. They simply enjoyed Jack's company. But the Cracker Jack was still in the sky, and every now and then they could still hear the totems, so they were reminded of their troubles.

They updated Jack on everything that had occurred since the collapse. They started with Krampus leading them to the nutcracker room, the horrors there, and how Krampus had discovered Sully's possession of the relic from the catacombs, of which Koda admitted, guilt-ridden. Sully knew more had been revealed in the nutcracker room; he felt small remembering his cowardly secret, though it hadn't been mentioned.

All through that part of the story Jack said not a word. It was with great consideration from Koda that he skipped telling him about Twiggy's injury. Sully could tell that Jack was making an effort to hear all of this. Once he thought he heard him sniffle and soon afterward grind his nails on the floor, chittering. It had been a terrible blow to Sully's heart when he learned about Rowan. He couldn't imagine how much worse it was for Jack.

"Are you going to be okay?" Sully asked him.

"We need to move on," Jack said.

Sometime after Twiggy returned—sniffling but obviously from overwhelming joy—they also discussed their rescue made possible by Drooler, Shebari's fortunes, and Bozo's assistance in fighting Bastet.

"Resourceful, that Bozo. We'll need him, I'm sure," said Muraco.

"For what? Another battle?" Twiggy had seated himself right next to Jack. He asked him, "This *is* your brother, right?"

Muraco chuckled.

"Yes, he is," answered Jack.

"Just making sure."

"We won't ask that you participate," Jack said. "Going after the relics was extremely courageous. You saved us some time, my friends."

"It's not a battle, per se," said Muraco. "In fact, it's more like an ambush."

"Have you come up with anything?" Twiggy asked eagerly.

"We don't have anything set in stone..."

"We want to hear it."

Muraco sounded as if he were smiling at Twiggy's boldness. "Well, get ready, 'cause I have lots to say."

Everyone moved closer into the circle.

"We've anticipated a disaster would happen," Muraco said. "We've hidden the Critters that we could, including the baby dinosaurs." Sully perked up. "They're hidden in the bigger lodges. As far as the totems, unfortunately, circumstances change, and we cannot estimate where the enemy will be positioned so far in the future. I've had four years to plan, though. I'm assuming Krampus told you how I ended up in the Haven?"

"He wouldn't shut up about it," Twiggy said.

"As expected. He's the conceited type. When he threw me into the opening, I passed through the Trickster world. It wasn't in disarray then, Jack's filled me in on the details, and I was able to arrive here in the mountains."

"We found your skeleton in the catacombs," Koda said.

"And I don't understand why," said Twiggy. "You're here."

"Those bones were no good to me anymore." Sully wondered at Muraco's frankness. "Think of it like a spider's molt. It resembles the spider exactly, but it's really just dead skin."

Jack shifted uncomfortably. "I told him how the aptrgangr led us to the site," he said.

"I'm the one who summoned him," Muraco said. "I've been around for an extremely long time and so have aptrgangrs. They're created when a person kills one of them, and then that person becomes an aptrgangr when they die. Or when a corpse is set in a sitting position."

Sully shuddered.

"Who really knows how this happened, but when I 'died,' the aptrgangr sort of appeared as a separate being. From myself, I think, probably caused by how my bones were discarded, or it could be a weird defense mechanism of mine. Who knows with magic. Anyway, I digress. I realize it's an understatement to say he wasn't exactly the best guide for Critters, but I thought he could help you in place of myself. I apologize he went rogue.

"You know, sometimes the best thing about being a totem is you discover new things about yourself all the time." Muraco laughed.

No one else laughed. Muraco coughed self-consciously.

"Is he dead?" Koda asked.

"That depends. Was his head decapitated?"

Koda seemed to pause at Muraco's frankness. "Yes, I think so. I saw his shadow."

"Then he is dead. You say the chimera attacked Bastet. There won't be much left of her, so we're left to assume she's sinking into the sea along with the aptrgangr. For some reason— don't ask me, ask mythology—that's how you get rid of aptrgangrs."

"Couldn't you summon another creature?" Sully asked. "Something that could beat up the totems?"

"Unless you desire Friar's Lantern or the Mare?"

"A lantern? What are those creatures?"

"Friar's Lantern is the aptrgangr's opposite, in which it leads you into being lost forever, and the Mare is a female horse that sits on you and gives you nightmares—get it?"

"Uh-uh," Sully said.

"We don't wish to summon more creatures," said Jack. "As you have stated, the aptrgangr quickly turned defective, and we can't afford any more creatures like him. Our focus is getting all the totems together so Muraco can place the enchantment."

"Why do they all need to be together?" Koda asked.

"Because once my power is unleashed, that is it. I'm trapped inside a totem head along with them," Muraco said. "If there is to be one I've missed, you would have to risk releasing another totem in the chance that I would be the one to escape. I highly discourage you do that."

Our traitor didn't go free. He was trapped like the rest of us, Krampus had said. What if Koda were in Muraco's situation? To never see Koda again except in some carving of him? Sully gave Jack his paw.

"The main factor that is going to aid us in winning this, is to use the totems' powers against them. Those powers can be weaknesses. There's a Native American saying for that," Muraco continued. "'The weakness of the enemy is our strength.' We're doing this in the mountains because the one totem I'm sure is the key element to bringing down at least a few of them is here."

"Which one?" Sully asked.

"Gashadokuro."

"*That* one?!"

"Naturally, because of his inability to see and that he will attack anything that moves, he was first on my list. Totems will attack each other from time to time—they're an easily aggravated bunch—but they're not exactly interested in killing each other. What's the fun in killing something that can't die?"

431

What about Krampus? Sully thought. But he assumed Krampus was a special kind of evil.

"Gashadokuro is a unique case. He won't notice the difference between a totem or a Critter or a Trickster. Maybe he doesn't care. The problem is, he's very visible on the plains. We need to lure him elsewhere, so the totems will be caught off guard," Muraco said.

"You want to lure that thing?" Twiggy said in disbelief. "With what?"

"Bozo could possess a Critter," Sully offered.

"Then if Bozo will cooperate, he'll attract Gashadokuro to our hidden location. We'll place a fallen Critter, which he'll pick up while our volunteer runs away," Muraco said.

The Critters fell quiet.

"Someone needs to cross the plains to tell Bozo," Koda said gravely.

"You're not going to do it, are you?" Twiggy asked Jack apprehensively.

"We won't use someone who has already died." Jack's tone of voice hinted he had already volunteered but had been declined. "Muraco tells me that if you die again, you will *remain* dead."

Twiggy said, "I'll go."

"No!" Sully cried.

Jack stood. "Twiggy, you—"

"I won't be the bait. I'll just be the one who tells Bozo."

"He is small and fast..." Muraco said.

"There's a likely chance you could die twice," Jack protested.

"I'm going out there, Jack. Don't try to stop me."

"I caution you this, Twiggy—and I mention it because Jack told me the younger ones wish to return home," said Muraco. "If you die, you cannot leave the Haven."

432

Sully sensed Koda tense up.

"Not a problem," Twiggy said.

Sully worried, but he thought he himself knew Twiggy's intentions the best. It was incredibly frustrating when you wanted to help, and no one wanted you to do it. They'd just had so much bad luck lately…

Jack started to protest again, and Sully interrupted him. He didn't want Jack and Twiggy to get into an argument so soon after they'd been brought back together again. "How many," Sully asked, "do you think Gashaduke— Geishaduck—"

"Gash-a-do-ku-ro," Muraco said good naturedly. "There are two other totems on the plains last time I heard. Gashadokuro won't be interested in their bodies once he's drained their blood. They're smaller in size, and we'll incapacitate them any way we can while they're 'dead.'"

Sully said, "Won't that be dangerous? How are you going to do it?"

"If we don't incapacitate them, they'll regroup," Muraco said. He smiled. "Just wait. I have something pretty clever planned."

Koda said, "That's three totems. What about the rest?"

"Four, actually, if all goes according to plan. It would be a miracle we don't have, getting everyone to Gashadokuro."

"What is the fourth?" Sully asked.

"The banshee. It's an Irish totem that sounds like a woman screaming. The humans assume it's a woman because they've never seen it. *I* have."

"What is she?" Sully asked.

"I'm all about surprises, Sully. It'll be more exciting for you to see her yourself."

Sully pouted. "Why couldn't we get a nice leprechaun?"

Muraco laughed. "I agree."

"What's a leprechaun?" asked Twiggy.

"The scream signals the forthcoming doom of a family member," Jack explained. "In this case, the family being the totems."

"The banshee arrived last when the totems had surrounded me," Muraco said.

"Why are you the only good totem?" Sully asked. "Why aren't there thirteen more like you?"

"Because at the time, one of me was all it took," Muraco said. "The totems weren't meant to have a second chance."

A kind of vengeful determination overcame Koda. Sully could sense it in him, and he didn't blame him one bit. "Tell us everything about them," Koda said. "Powers and weaknesses."

Muraco chuckled. "I haven't lost my love for storytelling."

The Critters listened intently, for their lives depended on it. Each totem was fiercer than the one before it, and each of the Critters came up with unique ways to deal with them. Sully was proud to give his ideas alongside Koda's. Together with Jack, Muraco, and Twiggy, they devised a plan.

Twiggy reminded them, "Where's the chimera in all this?"

Muraco said self-assuredly, "There's something I can deal with. Hototo is not a wise owl, but he's managed to make the smarter totems listen to him. The totems on the top of the pole are more intelligent." Muraco said with a possible smirk, "Hototo was on the bottom of our pole. I guess that says something about me."

"I bet that makes him furious," said Twiggy.

"Sure does."

Muraco sounded confident, but Sully couldn't stop worrying about Krampus. *He* had been at the top.

29

GASHADOKURO

TOTEM CALLS drew the Critters outside. They had been in the lodge for about an hour and had had plenty of time to exaggerate the Cracker Jack's size in their heads. But as they gazed at the sky, they found it was even worse than they'd thought. The Cracker Jack was *twice* the size it had been during the battle and growing fast. No longer a pucker, the lips spread out slightly as if smiling around a kiss, but as the constellation had grown vast, the mouth had widened enough to fit a totem as large as Bastet.

They may only have a few hours left.

Unusually enthusiastic, Muraco spoke above the blizzard's powerful moans. "It's time to put our spectacular plan into motion," he said.

Twiggy started. "But we haven't figured out everything! We still don't know how we're going to bring the chimera here."

"We'll be alright," Muraco shrugged him off. "We've got enough to get started. Are you ready to begin your task?"

Everyone's eyes fell on Twiggy. Sully and Koda stood inside the entrance of the lodge in their human sweaters. A dusting of flurries coated their noses, and they stepped farther in. Twiggy avoided their worrisome gaze and Jack's. His lifelong friend stood

435

too still in the cold, the snow burying his paws. He had walked fine, without a limp, and there was no ugly red spot in his side.

Twiggy would never wish Jack hurt in any way but now, at least, there would be no thought of Jack returning to the human world. After all this was over, he would be safe in the Haven forever, as Twiggy had always wished.

Jack stepped forward and the snow fell off his paws. "I could go," he said.

"Your ears would be spotted for sure," said Twiggy.

Sully pleaded, "Twiggy, don't go."

"You all act like *I'm* the one who's gonna be chased. I'm just telling Bozo what to do, then I'll come back." Twiggy was content with his tone of voice. Unfazed. Confident. Entirely opposite of how he felt.

Muraco laughed. "Your friend reminds me of myself! Bold!" He leaned in close to Twiggy's face with a mischievous air. "Be warned: that's what gets animals like us into trouble."

Muraco turned to the others. "I'm off! See *you* at the location," he told Twiggy and ran for the farther mountains.

Twiggy finally looked everyone in the eye. They watched him as if he were a mouse entering a bird's nest. It wasn't that far from the truth. "I'm off, too, I guess," Twiggy said. He wanted to say more, something like "thanks for keeping my head in the right place" to Koda or a simple "keep safe," but either one sounded like he was admitting defeat.

He said to Jack, "When that thing shot you and you were gone, I thought it was too terrible to really be happening."

Jack stood there, his eyes smaller and gentler looking.

"I'm just very glad I was right."

Twiggy darted away into the storm. Secretly, he knew there was a chance he might not make it back. Apparently, if he died once, he would return like Jack, but with so many totems out there… it was very likely he could die twice. And he needed to say what he felt to Jack, even if it was obvious. He knew how painful it was not to, in some way, say goodbye.

Before returning to the main lodge, Twiggy had hugged his pup tight. *I can't leave her. So, I have to make sure. I have to make sure this plan works* exactly *as it's supposed to.*

It took Twiggy longer than before to traverse the mountains. The wind pushed against him, pressing under his chest, threatening to lift him off the ground. He ignored the iciness in his blood as he stopped to align the deceased in a line toward Muraco's "hidden location." Muraco would do the rest. With forage in his stomach and revenge in his heart, sick of Krampus's peppermint wind, Twiggy couldn't get to the plains fast enough, never had he felt so sure, and he fought Krampus's storm all the way onto Gashadokuro territory.

He hid at the base of a snowdrift. Ice particles blew in his face and scattered toward a small mountain behind him. Peaked like the spines of some snow-buried creature, the nearby mountains, shortened by the snow piling up, mapped his course. Straight ahead in the middle of them, a disappearing-reappearing gray line marked the lip of the trench where, if he knew what was good for him, Bozo would be with Drooler.

Your joker self better be there.

Resisting the wind, Twiggy crawled a few feet sideways from the mountain and began to dig a hole out in the open. He recoiled. It felt as if he had thrust his paws into iceberg water! He resisted the pain and dug.

The ground shook with thundering gallops. Twiggy let the wind wrench him back to the mountain. He stilled. Stilled for a while, listening in terror to a Critter's scream, the clunk of Gashadokuro's jaw as the scream silenced, then the hollow ringing and groans. Snow fell heavier upon Twiggy's back.

The bounce in his feet acted up. *Don't be stupid. Get it under control, or you'll blow the whole thing.*

He relaxed his feet...

...and made a beeline for the trench. He was positive the blizzard noise would cover him. But Krampus must have been toying with him, for there came a pause in the wind as if the blizzard were holding its breath. The galloping thuds returned, closing in on him. They had been over a couple hundred yards away, but in a matter of seconds, Gashadokuro thundered out of the mountains into Twiggy's path ahead. The skull hovered in mist and was made even more terrible by the fact that the totem was *glaring*. The eye sockets squinted dramatically.

While the Critters had planned in the lodge, Sully had said, "If Gashi— Gashadope— If the totem hears you, go really still, and he won't be able to see you. Just like a T-Rex." Twiggy didn't know what a T-Rex was, but he stopped and made himself small, as if lowering his heart onto the snow could dull it. It was beating loud enough in his own skull that he was sure it would reach inside the totem's. Like a pendulum. Twiggy counted the seconds.

Thump. Thump. Gashadokuro turned straight onto the path. The ground crashed as the totem lay his bones into the snow, laying there like a fossilized sphinx. Twiggy shuddered, terrified as well as infuriated that it would lay there like a stone, without any sign of moving, playing the staring game until the bounce in Twiggy's feet got the best of him.

If he ran now, would the distance between them be enough to give him time?

The wind breathed quietly.

He decided to chance it.

Twiggy let his Critter feet run wild and gasped in utter terror at the thuds and sound of crushing snow becoming a roar in his ears. He tucked in his tail... and fell into the hole he had dug. It darkened in shadow. In three bounds, Gashadokuro was above him. The totem jerked its skull downward and blood splashed the snow.

A deceased horse's body hung by the neck in Gasha-dokuro's jaws. As the totem feasted, Twiggy cringed violently.

The feast ended quickly. The horse dropped onto the snow with a thud. Gashadokuro's ribs scaled above him as the totem thudded away, down a trail of deceased Critters, plucking up bodies by their heads as a cow chews on tufts of grass, coursing in a widely spaced line into the mountains. Twiggy didn't crawl out of the hole until the larger mountains closed the totem in.

It had been Sully's idea to dig the hole. Good ol' Sully. Bozo (who's job this *should* have been) was to be "the tiny lizard at Giant's nest" just as it dug in the bedding to hide from the dragon.

There were perks to being a house rodent, Twiggy realized. It was strange. He had never seen a pair of Critters so eager, so determined, to find their way back to a human. He had always just assumed Sully simply hadn't been around them long enough. The small Critter probably watched this human of his from the safety of the holes he had made in the walls, and as he was a friendly hamster, had fantasies they could be friends. That thought changed slightly when Twiggy saw the brothers' cages. The human knew they were there and hadn't gotten rid of them. Hadn't *killed* them. So what, then?

With Koda, ever since Sully's brother had woken in the burrows, Twiggy had disliked him. Not only for his treatment of Critters, but the absolute blind obsession he had with humans. At least, it had seemed blind and obsessive at the time. This dislike only fueled Twiggy's anger, made him more stubborn, and he used it as proof, to back up his hatred for the humans. But through their worst moments, he could see there was a soft side to Koda. Especially when Jack had been gone, and Twiggy had had to depend on him. Now that the dislike was gone, Twiggy could see past it, like clouds revealing the sun. He had been fighting himself with it for a while until he just couldn't use Koda as an excuse anymore, to ask himself the important questions.

How *could* two Critters insist on being brought back to a human if they were abused? Twiggy realized that somehow, he had been refusing to believe it. That there could be a good side he hadn't seen to the... to the humans.

Sully and Koda would be brought back to their home; Twiggy would see to that. The totem wouldn't win.

He still had to tell Bozo and Drooler the rest of the plan. Twiggy kept his pawsteps light and quick to the trench. When he found them, both Tricksters were sitting on the crocodiles, shivering slightly. Apparently, the worst of the cold was in the trench.

"Did you hear that up there? That was meant to be *your* job," Twiggy grudgingly told Bozo.

"Not my fault," Bozo said, and his teeth chattered.

Twiggy frowned at him. "We want you to bring five totems to the trench."

The clown made a harsh, startled sound. Before he could interrupt, Twiggy gave them the totems' descriptions. The Yeti and Bastet were included in the five. Muraco insisted the cat totem be brought, even in the condition they expected her to be in after the chimera. *All* totems were to be imprisoned, and Twiggy didn't say so much as a word against him for it. As he described the rest of the totems, Twiggy was utterly aware of the overwhelming power they possessed. Maybe he did feel a little bad. For Drooler.

The yellow Trickster scrunched his face in worry. He wrung his hands, glancing up at Bozo as the clown cried protests.

"Five totems!" Bozo said in angered disbelief. "Squirrel, you're not just nutty. You're suicidal! On our behalf!"

"Bastet has got to be in poor shape," Twiggy said. He hadn't sounded confident even to himself. "Bring them to the trench and be intelligent about it. Try to hide them somehow. We don't want the other totems wising up to the plan."

"And what else? I can see it in your face there's more, so just say it."

"Lure the chimera here when we're ready."

Bozo leaned back into his shoulders. He exploded. "Are you out of your *NUTTY MIND?*"

The exclamation coursed lightly in the chasm. Drooler clasped his hands on top of his head.

"Quiet!" Twiggy snapped. "I'll tell you when, so make sure you're around. You better do it, *Bozo.*"

He climbed onto the trench wall and paused. "Wait. You're supposed to lure the totem that makes those circular bite marks, the chupacabra, here, too. It won't scavenge like the vulture one, the harpy."

"I've got enough to do!" Bozo said.

Twiggy thought. For once, the clown was right. And they needed the job done fast.

"*Five* totems. Make sure you remember that," Twiggy said, leaving both Tricksters a lighter shade of green.

To think our lives are in the hands of Tricksters!

***

Jack waited until Twiggy wasn't even a speck in the snowfall. He didn't want him knowing what he was about to do.

"What's wrong?" Sully asked. The brothers were still pocketed in the lodge entrance. Jack felt more protective of them, seeing them this close to the snow. *They should be warm and at home.*

"I'm going with Muraco," Jack said.

Sully started, stepping forward outside. "You won't come back if you die!"

441

Jack gently pushed him back into the safety of the lodge. "Stay where it's warmer. The storm is worsening," he said. "I'm sorry. My brother needs me." *The guilt of having to do this to them again....*

Before Jack left, Koda had given him such a deep look of understanding that it hurt in some ways more than Jack had ever felt pain. Someone else knew what was going to happen to Muraco if they should succeed. And Koda was feeling sorry for him.

Somehow, he felt... better than he would have thought about that. Since dying, it seemed there were worse things than having Critters you cared about show they care about you as well. After he had died in the desert, he had woken in the mountains in a different body. It was identical on the outside, but inside, Jack felt younger. He possessed more energy, and his wounds had disappeared. In his delirium, he had almost mistaken Muraco for a hallucination and could not express his happiness when he found he was wrong. He had cried like a leveret.

Before all this was over, Jack intended to be with Muraco every chance he could get.

To arrive at the hidden location, Jack cut through a narrow belt of mountain. No one was in sight, and he couldn't smell anyone besides the deceased. He found Muraco aligning the nearby fallen Critters in a line that connected to Twiggy's around the curve of the nearest mountain. His brother nodded at him without so much as a trace of surprise that Jack had joined him.

Jack aided him, and together they trailed the rest of the Critters inside a mountain circle, a bowl of snow about sixty yards in circumference. They stopped at its center and from there collected the deceased in the area (over three dozen), which they scattered widely at the end of the trail. Seeing their faces, the image of Twiggy dead in Gashadokuro's jaws was made stronger in Jack's mind. *I shouldn't have let him do this.* He said a prayer.

The constant dull thuds he had been hearing harshened to vibrations in his feet. He and Muraco raced away from the trail. Many yards apart, the two stood entirely exposed. Jack lowered his head, even as he remembered the totem couldn't see. Muraco stood straight.

Gashadokuro crawled in where the mountain rim broadened to a raised wall. Critters slipped out the back of his bloody jaw. He feasted hungrily, though never able to fulfill that hunger, and still he drank down the trail with disturbing enthusiasm. The tremendous bony hands vaulted into the snow, each time sending up snow dust. Jack cringed at a sharp cracking sound as Gashadokuro landed his fists like giant hammers about a dozen Critters from the end of the trail.

The totem lifted his skull, alerted.

Not far enough. Come on, last us a little longer. Please!

It was a strange feeling, wanting the totem to pick the rest off the trail, to go faster, to hurry, so the Cracker Jack in the sky would not seem so harrowing.

Gashadokuro stared at the ground and bit at the snow, aggravated. He continued to feast until reaching the end of the trail.

Beneath the snow, the cracking exploded in a massive shatter. Even though he had prepared himself for it, Jack started as the ground gave under the totem, all in a gigantic splash of water, frost, and snow. Gashadokuro sank into the hidden lake. While at first the totem jerked about angrily, once everything calmed, Jack could hear Critter bones snapping as Gashadokuro continued to drain blood from those who had died in the water. Ice thickened on the lake, and the snow began its work to cover it.

"Success!" Muraco exclaimed in a hushed voice. "Sully is an intelligent one."

Sully had been careful while suggesting his idea. Jack soon found out the plan was a human's way of trapping animals. Sully called it "a lion pit with water."

As with most everything they had planned, they were relying heavily on timing. The deceased Critters must last Gashadokuro until the other totems arrived. When they did, the snow must cover the lake completely. The trail would serve them only once more, to feed the harpy, as, unlike Gashadokuro, she wouldn't leave anything but bones behind. The chupacabra, the goat-sucker, sucked blood like Gashadokuro, and would need to be lured by live prey. That was Bozo's task.

Still so many steps. In the sky, the inside of the Cracker Jack's mouth shined like a galaxy from moonlight in the human world. Totems like the harpy, though she could fly, were content enough to feed in the Haven so long as the supply of Critters lasted. But totems like Hototo, Camazotz, Shui Gui, and Krampus... they would never be content.

Jack brushed the snowflakes off his face. "If we don't bring all of them," he began, "say one or two is missing, will you place the enchantment?"

"If I must," Muraco said. He made no move to brush the snowflakes away. "But any of the totems that remain will be even angrier than before."

"We could try again."

"You mean to try placing a Critter like this Sydney character between the poles, hoping I'm the one released?"

Muraco had asked him respectively and yet Jack felt foolish.

"To trick the totems twice is good fortune. To trick them thrice is a miracle we don't have," Muraco said.

Jack set a paw forward in his self-consciousness. He expected such a reply.

Muraco said lightheartedly, "Hey, you know me. I only need one shot. They cheated the first time, so that doesn't count."

He looked at Jack for a reaction, maybe a smile. Jack turned his head to him but that was all.

Muraco changed the subject. "Well… I guess it's an understatement to say it's always been more fun to *talk* about totems than to see them in person. But no story about the Haven is complete without them. Even before you, as I am so old, I was telling others about it during my time on Earth. I knew about it even before coming here, isn't that odd?" Muraco seemed to reminisce. "Critters wouldn't have known about the Haven otherwise, and it's good to have something to look forward to. You remember when I told you the stories? One totem tale a night, wasn't it?"

"Yes," Jack said.

"Sometimes you'd try to get me to tell two or three." Muraco chuckled. "I'd say 'Isn't one nightmare enough for tonight?' But you liked hearing them so much, I'd at least tell you one more." He paused, reflecting. "It never crossed my mind you'd get to *see* any of them. I'm surprised you remembered everything I told you about them, even after all these years."

Jack said, "I remember you stole carrots from the farmers, so we'd have them to eat while you told the stories."

"Correct!"

"I told you it was dangerous and one day you might not come back."

Muraco bowed his head as if wincing. He smiled wanly at Jack. "Maybe I did go a little overboard sometimes…"

"I'd never wish you to be harmed. But if I would have known… what you are… it would have made it less unbearable, knowing you were alive somewhere."

Muraco looked at Jack then turned to the flurrying white bed over the lake. "You're upset I didn't tell you."

"I am."

"Jack, I didn't *want* to be a totem, that's the truth," Muraco said gently. "So, I pretended I was a hare. Seemed appropriate because hares got into trouble all the time with farmers, and I could just see myself doing that. I mean, after all they've done to those that got caught stealing."

"You've been holding a grudge?"

"Don't get me wrong. I like to think I search for the good in anyone; that's why I showed you what I did, for both you and myself. But I'm not ignorant. I know good isn't always there, and doing stupid stuff like challenging the farmers was my small way of getting back at them."

Muraco finally shook the snow off his head. "Totems and most humans are so much alike, you know? They'd soon see that everything dies if they live. That's what this is all about. To conquer because nothing else could be as important as themselves. Even with the destruction they do to themselves and the earth. The truth is, neither human nor totem would be here without Critters. You realize that, don't you, Jack? Critters help the earth in everything they do. Even now you are saving the humans and every other living thing on Earth. You keep it *alive*. So, should this not mean you are not most important?"

Jack considered him.

"But you are seen as worthless, a dime a dozen to be killed," Muraco said. "What I like about Critters, Jack, is that they live without any menace to their kind or otherwise. I sympathized with you. I thought you deserved more respect. That is why I choose to appear as I do."

As Muraco paused, there was an opportunity in which Jack could confess something of his own. But he never would. He had, at one time, felt more hatred than Twiggy had ever had toward the humans. He'd let the hatred consume him after Muraco had gone. While Jack didn't think this would happen now, he would always be afraid of letting himself dwell on the dark side in human nature, since when he had years ago, he had lost himself. A Critter should never feel they would be better off hunted, but in those long days before Twiggy came along, Jack had wanted to be gone. He wouldn't confess this to Muraco because even now, even after all that had happened and all the things that had changed within him, Jack didn't think he would ever be healed enough to allow others to see the weakness in him.

Muraco settled back into his lightheartedness. "There now. That's the most serious you'll ever see me. And I'll get off my soapbox. Jack, I didn't tell you because, well, I guess I was ashamed of being a totem."

"You aren't like them. You shouldn't have been ashamed," Jack said.

"Well, I didn't know you'd feel that way. Here's another cheesy answer: I thought a leveret should live a fairly normal life. Didn't last long. Not with the mess we're in now. I really should have told you. And about Krampus sooner, just in case I didn't get to tell you all the legends. I'm very sorry."

Jack longed to know. "Why help me at all? Why take me with you when there was so much at stake?"

"To have a companion. It's lonely being a totem. And you seemed like you needed someone." After a thoughtful pause, Muraco said, "We had fun, didn't we?"

"Y-yes." Jack lowered his head. He swallowed his tears.

"Don't mourn for me when I leave. Being under the enchantment is not like dying at all. Dying is… something I've never known and will never know. The enchantment is a constant state of dreaming. For the other totems, it may be nightmares, but for me, it is good dreams. You'll be there to make sure they are."

Jack forced himself to look out at the lake. *This is something I must accept.*

***

The ringing could no longer be heard on the plains. As it glistened so attractively of blood, there should have been feast left for the taking. The "Shaggy Beast," Peluda, climbed out of the chasm, past the Trickster hiding at the bottom, and saw nothing but red slush before the snowfall rapidly covered it.

Peluda's snake-like head, as muscular as a raptor's, thrust over the snow. As he walked like the largest alligator, the wind frosted his scales to ice chips and the green quills upon his back to icicles. Everywhere else, he was the color of fire. He breathed a hot breath. Below and around him in the air, the snow turned black.

Catching scent of him, the scent of acid, like vomit in its mouth, the harpy sitting nearby gave a warning shriek as if to run him away. She seemed to realize it was she who should flee and flew over a mountain shoulder. The chupacabra, huddled a dozen yards away, increased its distance four-fold.

Some totems were better left alone.

Peluda scrunched his quills. They flicked the seawater out onto the ground like rows of jabbing shark teeth. He held a grudge against floods. Flood exposure to his ears and decades of fumes puffing up into his nose had left him nearly deaf and incapable of smell. However, he could see extremely well and detect the faintest movement miles away.

A small shape—a Critter—darting into the mountain pass caught his eye. Peluda crushed the snow and any bodies in his path. He didn't care for spoiled prey, anyhow. The blizzard hindered him none on his way to the mountains.

The chupacabra was glad when he left.

***

Jack felt the ache to run more and more as he stared at the Cracker Jack. The strange figure had grown drastically in the past twenty minutes; it was the size of an incoming asteroid! A little more and the opening of its mouth could swallow *two* chimeras, or so it seemed. Gashadokuro had yet to drain blood from any totems.

The ringing had become an ache in Jack's ears, and he longed to be rid of it. Heavy clunking made by Gashadokuro's jaw sounded from the lake. The Critters in the water couldn't last the totem much longer.

"Patience, suku'un!" Muraco admonished, noticing the strain on Jack's face even though he had tried to hide it. "It's too late in the game to get nervous."

Jack heard an odd whistling in the wind from the raised wall, the kind which was made coursing through bird feathers. Large ones. Muraco and Jack hid in the shrubbery. In his brother's eyes, Jack saw something completely alien: a predatory look. A Hunter look, just as one prepares to catch a Critter. *I keep forgetting what he is*, Jack thought. Though the expression unnerved him (he thought he knew Muraco completely), he didn't think less of him.

The harpy entered. For the past hour, Jack had watched the increasing snowfall bury the Critters. The bird totem unburied them. They flopped as limply as ragdolls in her beak, then as lumps in her throat as she swallowed them. She flew farther up the trail. On the hidden lake, everything was still save for the clunking sounds. Jack hoped they wouldn't be a deterrent.

Chirping contentedly, the harpy ate the last Critter and flapped her wings, lifting in the direction of the entrance. Jack stepped forward, intending to lure her back to the lake, but stopped upon Muraco's restraining paw.

Gashadokuro's arm swung out of the lake. The harpy turned her head at the gigantic hand zooming into her face then seizing her by the neck. The shriek in her throat stuttered as Gashadokuro yanked her headfirst below the ice. Flailing wings and body slid violently in after.

"Would you like to hear why we don't need to retrieve the totems out of the lake?" Muraco asked conversationally as Gashadokuro cut short the harpy's last earsplitting shriek.

Jack glanced at Muraco from the corner of his eye.

"It's because the harpy's blood is poisonous."

"Poisonous?" Jack strained to split his attention from the feasting noises.

"Extremely. There are poisonous non-totem birds in the human world as well," Muraco said. "I debated how we were going to remove the totems from the lake without provoking Gashadokuro—as your friends were eager to learn and I was secretive, so I could see your surprise." Muraco beamed.

Always the surprise with him, Jack thought fondly, and then with a tightness in his heart.

"This way, she spreads the poison in the water, therefore poisoning the lake and any unfortunate totem we happen to catch."

The lake quieted. "And the harpy? Would it not be immune to its own poison?" asked Jack.

"That's exactly right! Gashadokuro also has nothing to worry about. He has no throat to swallow the poison. Unlucky for us he won't bother with prey; he's already drained. It will be a little while until the harpy replaces that blood—I speak from experience," Muraco said. "I'm hoping the loss of blood will make it slow to react, at least long enough for us to have the upper paw."

"Muraco, the clown Trickster hasn't lured in the chupacabra," Jack said, letting worry inch into his voice.

Muraco opened his mouth as if to say something carefree. He changed his mind. "You're correct."

"Something isn't right. I'm retrieving the totem myself."

Jack hopped forward, adrenaline pumping into his legs. Muraco did the same. As they were about to run, the chupacabra loped past the mountain entrance.

Gangly legs. Sweeping backbone of long spines. The totem moved with the agility of a deer. The sucker was like an anteater's nose with teeth pulled forward ahead of its face. The bug-like eyes were trained on a hurrying Critter in front.

Twiggy.

Twiggy reached the end of the blood trail. He bolted off the lake and stumbled chin-first onto the snow. The chupacabra swerved, the sucker widening to reveal more teeth.

Jack nearly screamed. Just missing Twiggy by a claw's reach, the chupacabra was taken below the ice. The spine snapped as loudly as a knee popping out of place and raked the snow. There were clunking sounds in the water, and Gashadokuro thrummed as if in appreciation.

Twiggy raced to Jack and Muraco. Windswept, he collapsed upon the snow. "Jack, what are you doing? You're supposed to be at the lodges!"

"And you, as well! Where is the clown?"

"It was going to take too much time. Bozo and Drooler have to find the totems. I figure—" He took a gulp of breath. "I did it once. May as well lure the chupacabra, too."

"Too?"

"Fine job, Twiggy!" Muraco praised. "Now, if I may ask you for another favor, deliver the message to the Tricksters."

Muraco paused in front of Jack with the solemnest expression Jack had ever seen from him.

I'm saying goodbye to him for the second time in my life.

"I'll be leaving to find my place. Somewhere in the middle, between here and the chasm, should do it," Muraco said. "I'm sorry. Should the harpy escape, don't let it fly off this island."

"How's he supposed to do that?" Twiggy cried.

"What prey others kill is better to her than what she could hunt on her own. She shouldn't harm you, Jack. Stall for us if you can." Another pause. "And keep hold of those happy memories."

Muraco ran for the entrance.

"Jack, you can't—" Twiggy hesitated and, seeing Jack's face, must have realized what had just passed between him and Muraco. He gave Jack and the lake a fearful glance, then hurried after Muraco.

Jack feared that would be the last time he saw them. His friend and his brother. Both Critters at heart no matter how he looked at it.

***

Bozo skid on the snow, his knees bent and his legs spread while he tugged against the puppet strings attached to his gloves. At the end of the strings tugged two dinosaur-sized bird feet. Green feathers and hard plated scales covered the totem's underside. Like a match flame, they turned orangish-red upon its back. Bozo ducked as a whip-like tail swung at his head and caught briefly in his hair. The half-bird, half-reptilian totem ruffled its feathers and made a muffled squawking sound. The strings wrapping its beak kept it from cock-a-doodle-dooing. What a hairy situation that had been. If he'd had time for anything else, Bozo would have bound its wings as well.

"Stupid business, tracking totems. I ought to be making puppets," Bozo complained and ducked as the totem whirled around, swerving him on the ice, and attempted plucking at his head. Yellow zombie-like eyes glowed in a large rooster's skull.

It had tried to attack him before. Too bad, Bozo had friends. He placed himself between the two snarling crocodiles. They were good about jumping out of the water. The cockatrice flapped back to the wall, kicking with a leg wounded by crocodile teeth.

Bozo tried for the umpteenth time to wring the strings around a boulder-sized chunk sticking out of the chasm wall. And for the umpteenth time, in doing so, the totem sensed what he was doing and plucked at him again. Bozo wasn't sure how much longer he could hang on. It wasn't like he had help. He had parted with Drooler to find the totems, and the dead Critters didn't have apposable thumbs and were too fragile to take on any of the burden.

Bozo griped over the cold. His arm tiring, it felt as if ice cubes were weighing him down in the cuffs and folds of his clothes. Grumbling, he lifted his skull to the chasm wall. He had placed a dead Critter at the top to mark his position.

The annoying squirrel appeared but too far to the left this time. The squirrel saw Bozo, scurried over and slipped part of the way down on the slated ice. Out of breath, he scolded, "What are you doing?! I told you to hide the totems!"

"Does this look easy to you?" Bozo snapped.

The cockatrice curved off the trench wall, raking its claws down at the squirrel. He ran for the chasm platforms, still followed by the totem. It jerked, making another muffled squawk, and flapped wildly midair. Bozo struggled against the strings as if *he* were the puppet. The cockatrice flung its body backward, and Bozo slipped onto his bottom. It stung full of ice-cold needles.

Stumbling with the pull of the strings, he stood up. "Get out of here! You're making it crazy!"

"Tie it up and get the chimera! It's gonna fly out of here!"

"I'm not restraining a pigeon, you obnoxious Critter!"

The strings pulled Bozo back to the wall where the cockatrice resumed its tantrum. The squirrel walked cautiously forward and stared with frightened revulsion at Bastet's head lying far apart from her body. Snow piled over the scattered limbs—the squirrel had been adamant about bringing all of them. Something about "the enchantment won't trap her if you don't." Bastet's purple eyes retracted in rage as she tried to wrench her jaws free of Bozo's strings.

"How many more totems do you have?" the squirrel asked, darting a look at the cockatrice.

"Use your beady eyes and count them! Ooone. Twooo."

"You're telling me you've only captured two totems?" the squirrel said very unappreciatively.

"Well, I don't know what Drooler's got! What did you think it was going to be like getting these totems? A walk through the carnival? A stroll on stage?"

The cockatrice's tail swung. Bozo ducked and managed to save his hair. "Oh, and yeah. Peluda. There. That's one more that might make you less squirrelly."

"Where is it?"

"Somewhere up there," Bozo answered irritably. "The totem was leaving a trail. See, look." He jerked his skull at a line of blackened snow trailing out of the chasm platforms to the trench wall. "There's probably a trail up there if it hasn't already been covered up."

The squirrel seemed to have a worried thought and climbed back up the trench wall. Bozo huffed.

Sometime later, the squirrel cried loudly, "He went to the lodges!"

"What? I got it here! You don't know what you want."

No answer. The squirrel had left.

"Nothing we can do about that, right, crocodiles?" Bozo grunted and yanked on the strings. The totem squawked. "They wanted the demons to come to them. Well, they come, sooner rather than later."

30

THE FINAL BATTLE

T HE LODGE SHUDDERED under the storm's assault, worsening Sully's energy as he paced in a corner. He and Koda had moved to the main area because Sully hadn't been able to stand being alone in the quiet. It just made him more nervous.

"We should be helping. We have the sweaters and everything," Sully said.

Koda drooped on the floor, his eyes tired. He had napped for a little while but like Sully, couldn't sleep long through their worries. "Don't get excited. The rest is for the others to do."

"How anticlimactic is *that?*"

Sully continued to pace. He stopped every few feet, tried climbing the wall to expel some of his energy, and slid down it to restart in the opposite direction.

"Giant told the dragon that never does anything. You're just 'scraping glass,'" Koda said mutedly.

The mention of the dragon turned Sully away from the wall. "You didn't ask Jack or Muraco how we're going to get home."

Koda paused longer than Sully would have liked. "Do you want to go back, Sully?"

The question brought Sully back to the flood.

If we don't go now, we'll never get to.

Why wouldn't you want to go home?

At the time, Koda had yelled. It threw Sully off a little to be asked so calmly now. He slumped to the floor. "I'll get to come back to the Haven someday. If I don't go home today, Giant won't know I'm alright. I guess I didn't really think about that before."

Koda looked at him fixedly.

"What about you?" Sully asked.

"I'll always want to go home. But if you decided to stay here, I couldn't leave."

"It's not as much as a nice place as I thought it was. Maybe in a year, after all the totems are gone," Sully said.

Koda nodded solemnly.

Something isn't right.

Sully pawed the floor close to him. "I really *do* want to go home."

Koda smiled faintly. "That's good."

Sully smiled, too. "We could still make it home in time for Christmas," he said brightly. "We never got to open our presents."

"It's been six nights. Or at least I think it has. I've wondered about it over and over again, but I wonder what Giant is doing right now."

Sully focused on Koda's dreary tone of voice. It was like he was thinking how terrible it would be if Giant never found them.

"You don't think we're going to beat the totems."

"No, Sully, I'm not thinking that."

"Why didn't you ask, though? About getting home?"

"I'm afraid of the answer," Koda said. "I've been thinking of the Cracker Jack in the sky. How are we going to reach it? It's not that I don't think we could do it…"

Sully thought. He had been thinking that if they beat the totems, everything else would sort itself out. A happy ending. *I guess*

I've watched too many of those.

"It is kind of miraculous, huh?"

"Miraculous things have happened," Koda said.

Loud trampling drew the brothers' attention. It was too dark to tell, but Sully sensed the Critters in the lodge becoming alert. Frantic pawsteps sounded in the entrance tunnel. Someone raced into the room and cried, "Totem! It's headed straight for us!"

A wail coursed through the lodge. Critters could be heard forming around the arrival. Sully and Koda raced over.

"What were you doing out there?" a Critter asked in a shrill voice.

"I thought I wouldn't be seen! I'm a lemming! My fur turns white in the winter. I look just like any snowball out there!"

"Apparently not!"

"Which totem is it?" Koda asked but went unheard as someone asked on the verge of shouting, "Did you *lead* it here?"

"You can't blame me!" The crowd gasped. "There's nowhere else to go!"

"That's true!" someone else shouted. "Listen to it out there! We'd never make it far in that storm!"

The exclamation riled the crowd. A few tried unsuccessfully to hush them.

"Shh! Quiet! I see something outside!"

The startled warning came from the entrance to the tunnel. The Critters instantly quieted to frightened murmurs, whispers, and hushes, while a small group of braver Critters gravitated to the tunnel with the brothers.

Sully bumped into someone with prickly fur. Possibly a porcupine. She panted as, apparently, she had run from farther down the tunnel. "There's a totem in the sky!" she said in a startled whisper.

The brothers moved carefully past the porcupine's quills.

"What're you doing? Hey!"

"Don't go out there! It's not safe!" someone cried.

At the end of the tunnel, in the snow's bright reflective glimmer, Sully's vision blurred again. *Not right now!* He rubbed his eyes and squinted. At first, all he could see was the sheen of gray starlight over the snowy mountains. Between two of them, toward the trench, a black and white smudge flapped awkwardly in place about thirty feet above the trench wall.

The cockatrice yanked its legs where two thin shining lines were attached to them. It must have been how badly Sully was seeing the totem, that he thought it looked like a scene from one of those black and white movies. The kind with old movie monsters controlled by wires to make it seem like they were flying. These wires, however, trailed into the trench instead of the sky.

Sully's heart skipped a beat. "They're puppet strings! Bozo's got to be holding it."

"What is he doing? He's going to give us away!" Koda exclaimed.

"Koda, what if Bozo can't hold onto the cockatrice?"

"He *has* to."

Sully worried. He knew *exactly* what would happen if the cockatrice were to escape through the Cracker Jack. By now, the cockatrice must know Muraco was planning on trapping the totems again, and that's why it was fighting Bozo so hard. Sully wondered at their bad luck. Muraco had been adamant about the cockatrice.

"If by any chance, you think you cannot contain all of the totems, and you have to choose," he had said, "make absolutely sure the cockatrice does not escape."

The totem had a personal hatred for humans, though no one knew exactly why, and had, by some power like Hototo's, caused the black plague back in the middle ages. The cockatrice could kill animals, giants, and the environment much faster than

Hototo. With that kind of power, it took years to recharge. Muraco thought it was due time the totem could unleash its power again and was probably saving it for the giant world.

Sully's vision blurred again—he wondered if it worsened with stress—and he rubbed his knuckles into his eyes. Opening them, he glanced inadvertently to one of the lodges and saw a hulking reptilian head peeking over it. Sully's vision refocused, bringing the totem into startling color. Purple saliva, like venom from a rattlesnake's fangs, dripped onto the snow with a sizzling hiss, turning it black and sending trails of steam into the air.

Sully pawed Koda back, and they slipped deeper into the tunnel, watching as Peluda stepped into view.

The totem didn't seem to take notice. His long neck snapped at the mounds of snow like a cobra rearing for the attack. Corrosive spit sprayed. He appeared to listen with his head cocked, a motion which reminded Sully of the dragon tilting her head, then, leaving a smoking trail, it walked slowly on, farther into the camp, to linger around the lodges.

Koda breathed in large gasps as if readying himself for a bad situation. "The chimera's going to see the cockatrice for sure." He whispered to Sully, "Stay safe. Take my relic and keep both of ours safe, even though they're probably not much good to us now." Koda prodded the relic out of his cheek and handed it to Sully.

Sully stood with it in his paws. "Wha—? Wait, what are you going to do?"

"I'm going to lure Peluda away from here."

"N-no way! He'll leave. Just wait."

"He knows a Critter entered here. And you know the totems. They don't like to let anyone get away," Koda said. "Peluda will stay here until he finds them and that will be soon as frightened as the Critters are. Someone might bolt."

Sully pleaded, "Why does it have to be you?"

"No one else here is going to. But I'm not going out there without a plan. I have one, and maybe it will help the others."

Knowing full well what Koda was going to say, Sully said, "I'll go with you."

"No, I'll go alone. I'm proud of you, Sully, I am, but the one thing that's never going to change about me is that I'll never stop protecting you."

To hear him say he was *proud*... Sully couldn't remember ever feeling so happy. They had talked over the misunderstanding at Giant's nest, but it wasn't until now that he truly felt it was behind them.

Koda backed away, casting tortured glances outside and at Sully. "Will you be okay?"

"That's a strange question. *I'm* the one who's going to be hiding." Sully sniffled.

"I'll make it." Koda stepped outside. For one terrible second, his front paws lifted off the ground. He brought them down again, and Sully could see from the strain on his face, he was using every bit of strength he had against the raging wind. He turned around, anyway, to say goodbye.

"You're my brother, Sully."

"I love you," Sully said.

"I love you, too."

Koda ran into the wind. The outside glow blinded him from Sully's view as somewhere beyond, in the white, Peluda growled sharply and charged.

***

Drooler blew into his hands. His breath formed into vapor so thick it may have formed into a ball of ice. A sheet of ice already covered his coat; he heard it crackle with each step he took. He tucked his fingers into his coat pockets, still feeling the cold on his knuckles and the ice on his fingernails. Through the fabric, the warmth from a wound below his collar bone chased some of the chill away. Drooler whimpered. He had returned to the trench once already, though not where Bozo was. He didn't look forward to finding another totem.

Stepping forward, his foot fell through the ice. Drooler sank up to his neck in water. Crying out from both surprise and the freezing cold, he drooled copiously. He quickly wiped his mouth, wincing as the little bits of ice cut his lips. Drooler looked straight ahead to see if anyone had heard him and saw a gash in the snow going an unmeasurable distance. It had to have been made recently, for the frost worked rapidly to cover it. By now, Drooler was used to seeing platforms in an assortment of disarray, though how they were collapsed around the gash was peculiar. They sank into the sea, most pointing in his direction as if something very big had swum into them beneath the surface.

His body felt numb. Drooler dragged himself out of the sea onto the snow. Shaking terribly, he crushed the ice crystalizing his clothes and his body. On the last throw of his fist, he jumped at a deep shattering sound.

Behind him, the frozen top of the sea erupted. Hail rained on him. Drooler twisted around to see a neck rising out of the water into the sky. The monster made a chilling sound, both deep like an organ pipe and as shrill as a beluga whale's call.

Squealing, Drooler covered his ears. He tried to run and stumbled. One leg was still covered in ice. Drooler slammed his fist on it. It had hardened completely in the last minute, and he may as well have hit stone. So Drooler crawled flat on his stomach, chased by the ever-loudening crash of frozen water. He backed up against a platform, turning to find that the head of the monster had lowered down at him.

Drooler shrank away and screamed louder. He stared, petrified, at the complete lack of facial features. Blackness filled its form, a pure silhouette, as it would always be in a photograph. The black at the bottom of the head stretched downward; the monster may have been opening its jaws. And still, even the inside of it remained as dark as a bottomless pit.

Drooler froze in shock, his attention now focused on another head curving around the platform. It filled the space like a freighter. A large fiery eye blinked at him. The nictitating membranes were as thick as plastic curtains. The ice on Drooler's leg melted from an intense heat. He inhaled smoke.

The Loch Ness Monster snorted and seemed almost intimidated by the new being with larger teeth. Both creatures snarled as the two stared each other down.

***

The chimera raised all four of its heads out of the chasm. Each expressed their own amusement in yaps, hums, screeches, and whooshing sounds at the cockatrice flying but caught by strings.

Krampus's thunderous voice blasted, "What's this, Muraco? You plan to deceive us with old tricks?" At the mention of Muraco, Camazotz and Shui Gui snapped their jaws. Hototo bit Krampus's ear in anger of him speaking first.

Somewhere in the mountains, Muraco was silent. At the mountain pass, Sully cried in fear, and on his way to the lodges, Twiggy screamed in frustration. Jack hopped away from the Harpy frozen in place on the shore of the lake. And at the foot of the mountain with Peluda on his trail, Koda had no time to think of how terribly hopeless everything had become.

Krampus grinned. "It will be forever before you have the chance."

All at once it seemed that Krampus was just turning his head, preparing to fly toward the Cracker Jack—now just large enough for them to pass through—when a series of platforms crashed one over the other in a line far into the chasm. Something thundered past them with a force not even the chimera could comprehend. A roar as sharp as a million squawking birds flickered Krampus's ears. It was louder than Camazotz's bats. Louder than the totem calls put together. Nearby Critters and Tricksters cowered.

The beast had made itself known.

A living jade statue raised high over the platforms. Starlight flickered on a million scales like an emerald flame. The veins in its wings were like trails of glittered strings. The spiny tail snapped like a whip and a scaly head crowned with horns snaked upward. Below, running in its glittering green shadow, Drooler ran for his life. He fell upon the snow, covering his head as the dragon flapped high. The wind cast out from its wings destroyed the surrounding ice stuck to the platforms like the falling of glass. The dragon dove directly at the chimera.

Camazotz's and Hototo's wings flapped them backward, snarling and screeching. Several platforms crashed into the sea. There was a brilliant spark of orange light, so bright it overcame the face constellations' glow and shone like a beacon in the center of a storm. It sounded as if a volcano erupted and was jetting steam. The chimera flared in the light of the dragon's fire.

***

"They didn't tell us about a dragon!" Bozo exclaimed.

He wrangled the strings and tried shifting more weight to one arm. His arms felt more like rubber than bone at this point. He tugged once more, the strength slipped out of him, and he skidded into the wall where his shoes were shoved into a crevasse.

"Get down here, you stupid kite!"

Bozo turned his skull at a crunching of snow. Drooler ran up to him. He tripped on one of the crocodile's tails and face-planted in the snow.

"About time! Get yourself up and help me!" Bozo demanded.

Drooler stood up. His fishbowl eyes were crazed with trepidation. "The Loch Ness Monster. It's back there."

"Never mind Nessie! This one's going to escape!"

Bozo let go of the strings and felt the sudden release from the totem's weight as the glove slipped off his hand to dangle in the air by the string. "Take it!" Bozo shouted. Drooler jumped to grab it and slipped his fingers through the glove.

Bozo said, "Help me tie the strings to the wall!" He positioned himself on one side of the chunk sticking out of the wall. Drooler did the same on the other side. With the totem's weight divided between them, they took turns tying their strings around the chunk.

The cockatrice flapped harder and viciously yanked its leg once more. Bozo heard a sound like a saw slicing wood. The string attached to Drooler's hand unwound around the chuck and jerked him forward into the rock. He fell back, his head bleeding, and lay limp.

"Hey, get up!" Bozo reached for the loose glove and shouted in frustration as the string attached to it snapped.

Now restraining the cockatrice by only one foot, Bozo caught movement in the corner of his eye socket. A familiar rabbit hopped down into the trench from where one of the platforms had caused a landslide in the wall.

People popping up everywhere!

"Where did *you* come from?" Bozo snapped.

The rabbit glanced at him then to Drooler. "What happened? Where are the other totems?"

"Another one." If Bozo had eyes, he would have rolled them. "Drooler said he found the Loch Ness Monster. I don't know what else he got."

"Where?"

"Back there." Bozo motioned with his skull. "Straight ahead. Can't you see I'm busy? It's a wonder with this thing flying around that I haven't been killed by that goat head and his accomplices!"

A strange, dark look came over the rabbit's face. "He won't be killing anyone anymore," he said in a low voice. The rabbit leapt across the snow in the direction Bozo had pointed.

"Hey! Gnaw on Drooler or something to wake him up!" Bozo stomped his bulbous shoes. "Curse you all! You'll never work in this world again!"

***

Twiggy scolded himself for not passing into the mountains fast enough. By now every fur follicle nipped, and his ears panged as if from a bee sting. Still, nothing stopped him.

He entered the camp with his paws burning from the cold. He shook the snow off his fur. The black trail wove faintly in and out of the lodges then curved out of the camp until Twiggy lost sight of it in the storm. He searched for the lodge with his family. One of them, a fellow squirrel, cowered in the tunnel entrance.

"Is everyone okay? My pup?" Twiggy panted.

"Yes, she is alright."

"Thank you." Twiggy turned away to run.

"Wait! What's going on?! Did you succeed?"

"If we win, there will be plenty of time to explain later. I'm looking for my friends," Twiggy said impatiently.

"The hamsters? One of them left."

Twiggy spun to face the squirrel. "Why? Where did he go?" he cried.

"He took the totem up the mountain."

"He *what?*"

***

Frost glued Koda's eyes shut. The wind gusted into his face like shooting icicles. Yet through it all, the sweater kept his body warm. He could do this.

Koda forced his eyes open but didn't dare to pause and see how much farther he had to the mountain's peak. He probably wouldn't have been able to tell anyway. Sugared in snowy mist, the never-ending steep, rugged slope was a strain on his legs, arms, and in his chest. Koda could feel it pulling him backward. He could do this, right?

He had never been a great climber. Koda supposed—he *knew*—Sully would have been better for the job.

I'm not losing my brother in this. At least one of us is making it back to Giant.

Ten feet behind him, maybe less, Koda heard the sizzling splash of acid spraying onto the snow. He bit down hard on his teeth to prevent a scream, and a cold ache shot into his gums. It was all for naught for Peluda sprang forward. Close to Koda's back, the totem's teeth ground snow instead of his bones. Koda squeaked. He scurried over a slate rock and slipped. On his tumble down, his claws caught in brush sticking out of the snow. He swung, jerking to a stop, and suddenly it felt as if the last of his breath had been knocked out of him.

His arms trembled. He pulled himself up and froze upon

seeing Peluda's dark shape just a few feet above him. The totem held awkwardly to the mountain face like a bat snarling upon a wall, his body curved sideways with his snake-like neck dipping slowly. The head shook like a rattle as the acid bubbled in his throat.

Peluda abruptly drew back his head with a snarl at something small and silver scurrying in. He arched his body away from them, and the movement wrenched him from his hold. His front half lunged forward, pulling the rest of him sideways toward Koda. Koda gasped and ducked as the totem's sharp quills passed just above, barely missing him. Peluda fell down the slope in a chaotic tumble of rocks and snapping brush.

Sully called into the wind, "Koda, up here!"

The something silver. Sully. His hoodie had blown back from his head. Koda was sure now that it was his brother who the totem had lunged at. Sully had saved him.

Peluda clung to the mountain, hissing and stabbing the snow with his claws. Koda heaved himself over the brush and ran to Sully. "You were supposed to stay at camp!"

"I'm glad I didn't listen!"

***

Explosions of fire blazed like a ball of lightning. Snowflakes disintegrated in the flames, and the fur seared off Camazotz's face. The bat totem screamed forth his bats. They tried to aid him, but their wings caught fire, and they plummeted like small burning planes into the sea.

The water rolled from the weight of the creatures heaving about and the wind gusting under thrashing wings. Shui Gui's watery form wavered from the force of it. The water ghost snapped at the dragon's flanks, both the chimera's tail and the dragon's beating the columns. Rubble crunched under their feet. In a flying torrent, Shui Gui aimed for the dragon's nostrils but quailed from the flames shooting out and drying any drop of moisture.

As if in retaliation, the jade dragon slammed into the chimera with crushing force. They flapped back onto their feet, a look of indignation that seemed to Krampus like the look of offended children. The dragon did not slow. Its head darted between their necks and ripped into their shoulder with its teeth. The chimera finally lost balance. But as the dragon was about to pull away, Krampus hooked his horn around its neck and plunged them both into the sea.

Always the screeching with Hototo. So loud and irritating, Krampus thought. On his back with the dragon clawing on top of them, Hototo plucked at the dragon's hard-plated face. His beak bent at the tip. Infuriated, screeching louder, he and Camazotz came at the dragon from both sides, biting and clawing as if that hadn't already been proven not to work.

Krampus wasn't so desperate as to make such a feeble attempt. He blew almost gently into the dragon's face. Ice crystalized on its scales and into its eyes, and he took pleasure from the sparkling sight. The dragon roared in pain, shrinking away to shake its head. Hototo and Camazotz kicked it back into a platform.

Krampus laughed. "There! Now that I've done all the work for you."

The lesser totems cowered as fire ignited. Out of the blaze, wearing it like a mane of fire, the dragon leapt forward with its claws raised. Between blows, it plunged its teeth into the nearest totem's neck. Camazotz and the dragon battled fangs.

The pleasure of fighting diminished into irritation. "Know when to go down!" Krampus growled and fiercely blew his icy breath at the dragon's legs. Frost hardened them to the ice forming in the sea. He swung the wave of frost over its body and to its wings. In the few seconds before melting free, the frozen scales on

468

the dragon's side chipped and clattered onto the ice, revealing the soft flesh underneath.

Camazotz and Hototo stupidly drove them into the dragon before Krampus could inflict more damage. He was beginning to think becoming a part of the chimera was more a liability than an advantage. *Fine. So be it.* Krampus jerked his head, jabbing his horn into the dragon's wound. As it roared, he jabbed again and released his ice breath to keep it grounded in the water. He pulled away too late, and the dragon sliced its teeth down the back of his neck. One claw shoved into Hototo's face.

Growing mad with rage, Hototo wrestled his head to the side and tried to bite its wing. The dragon spit more fire. The tail whipped and sent up a flaming rock. The fire ball sailed to the plains and destroyed part of the trench wall. As he tried to fly backward, Hototo's wing slammed into a platform. Falling rock pinned him.

Hototo screeched, "BLASTED OVERSIZED LIZARD!"

The dragon reared back and, with overwhelming strength, plowed into the chimera, backing them right through a platform, then another and another, until all four totems fell on their back. Water and icicles exploded upward.

Growling, the dragon shook the ice off its frostbitten wings. "I'm not a lizard! I'm a bearded dragon!"

***

Bozo's jaw clunked open. "I can't believe it! That stuck-up Critter is alive!"

The fireball the dragon had flung had broken apart the snow and ice. Forced to stand on the crocodiles as if they were skis, Bozo gripped his one arm with his other hand, trying to relieve some of the strain as the cockatrice yanked on the string.

"Bring them to the plains!" Bozo shouted at the top of his

voice. "Hey! Over here! Bring them here!" He paused. "Wait a minute. *I'm* at the plains!" The chimera would crush him flat.

The dragon didn't seem to have heard him anyway. She was still too far away.

Bozo's arm yanked backwards, and his shoulder cracked. The cockatrice flew for the chasm, dragging Bozo and his shoes out of the rock, and flapped high toward the mountains with Bozo dangling. The totem had removed him from the wall to escape.

One of the crocodiles jumped at Bozo with its jaws wide open and bit his legs. Bozo cried out and pulled between it and the totem midair. "You're scratchin' my bones!"

He huffed as the crocodile tore his pants (his very expensive pants!), while the cockatrice flapped up and down just fast enough that it would soon yank Bozo's arm out of its socket.

"Forget it!"

Bozo gazed at the dead Critters in the water. As always when he was about to perform, the energy of his glow divided, and he weakened just slightly, enough to feel as if he had finished a set of jumping jacks. What he estimated was over two hundred dead Critters were reanimated by his glow. Bozo brought them out of the depths to fill the trench with light.

Together, perfectly in sync, the Critters shouted, "Hey, dragon!" Then they chanted, "To the mountains! To the mountains!"

The dragon had a hold of the owl's face again. She swung his head into the bat and goat totems' heads. Bozo could practically hear the classic cartoon sound effect *KLONK* two times in a row.

"I'm having fun just where I am," she said.

One of Bozo's legs slipped out of the crocodile's mouth. He expected his shoulder and his wrist to dislocate at any second. "Confound it, dragon!"

The Critters yelled, "WE'RE NOT KIDDING. BRING

THEM TO THE MOUNTAINS."

"Fine." The dragon roared, her mouth pulled back in a snarl, and spit sprayed past her teeth. She punched her head into the chimera's stomach, ramming them toward the mountains, and wrenched her neck upward to throw them sprawling into more platforms. The sea divided around them in an even huger splash.

"Ooh, gotta make it all dramatic!" Bozo said.

The water creature writhed in the sea, unattached itself from the chimera, and glided atop the water away from the trench. The dragon spun heavily to attack it and flung her head back at the goat totem who had stabbed her. He pulled her with his horn in her side as the bat totem caught her snout. The chimera pounced on her and pushed her into the chasm's floor.

Laughing triumphantly, the goat totem mocked, "Muraco! What will you do now?"

Bozo cursed. "It's getting away!"

Out of nowhere in front of the water creature, a reptilian head popped out of the ice with its jaws wide open. The water totem didn't have time to react, and its watery body splashed into its mouth. The Loch Ness Monster swallowed it, raising its neck farther out of the sea.

A few feet ahead, the rabbit breached from the wave. He paddled quickly away and appeared to fling a challenging stare at the chimera.

The goat totem gaped as if at a loss for words. He lunged past the dragon, completely ignoring her, and was slapped in the face by her wing. He shouted in fury, "JACK! YOU INCOMPITENT—"

The dragon snatched his horn with her jaws and jerked, snapping his horn in two. With an even greater expression of shock, Krampus opened his mouth to blow frost, but her claw grabbed him around the muzzle. She replaced her claw with her teeth and

471

dragged the chimera by the goat totem's head as if she meant to tear it from their body.

Cringing against the wind, Bozo made the Critters cheer. He didn't like the goat, either. "Most satisfying thing I've seen all day!" he said.

Enraged, the owl totem pecked at the dragon, his beak bending like a scrunched tin can and not seeming to care. His maddened eyes darted to the cockatrice and to Bastet, who was a long, scattered form beneath the snow. "Leave the mountains, you FOOLS! Do you wish to be imprisoned for eternity?"

The rabbit, Jack, swam to the trench. "Shui Gui won't be able to drown the Loch Ness Monster," he said and caught his breath. "What's the totem count? The Monster is my catch."

"Three." Bozo grunted. The ache in his arms was making a comeback. "Drooler, what's your count?"

Drooler had woken up and was slowly floating up straight in the water. He touched the wound on his head. "One," he said dazedly.

"Pssh. I did all the work!"

"That's five," Jack said. "That's it! They're all here!"

The chasm thundered. The sea rocked from incredibly powerful gusts of wind. Coming in fast, as vast as two continents, the dragon wrestled with the chimera.

"Run!" Bozo released the strings and fell into the water. As the cockatrice flew free, he splashed frantically away from the trench wall, pulling Drooler along by the collar of his sweater. Seconds later, the wall obliterated in a shattering implosion of rock. Crust and sea exploded in the chasm. Both chimera and dragon roared.

I'll be deaf by the time this is all over, Bozo thought.

***

Koda and Sully stood upon the mountain precipice with the face constellations behind them and the Cracker Jack above. Peluda's hisses and grinding stomps alone came through the snowy haze.

What have I done in bringing it here? Koda backed up and somehow, as if to scare him, he was able to hear pebbles skipping down the cliff face over the storm. "I'm stopping," Koda said.

Sully didn't ask questions. He shuffled close to him, fidgeting. "I'm staying with you."

The last few crunches of snow came far apart. Koda waited. His heart pumped fast and accelerated as Peluda's head appeared in the snowfall. The totem hovered in the white, breathing angrily—a hissy, deep rattle. The slitted eyes found their target. Acid bubbled on Peluda's tongue.

Koda thought of home. He held the faces of Sully, Giant, Jack, and Twiggy in his mind.

His vision blackened. Drowning in panic, Koda couldn't believe this was really happening. He couldn't see! He shook his head, dunked his head in the snow, anything to bring his vision back! But it did not return. He needed to see! He *had* to, to know when the totem was going to attack. Timing was everything, *sight* was everything, and he couldn't see!

Sully stayed by his side. "Koda!"

The scream pierced him, bringing Koda to tears. He knew then Sully trusted him completely, that he wouldn't leave him, no matter what.

Peluda lunged forward, to propel the hissing acid…

…and Koda's sight returned.

Through a panicked blur, he glimpsed what he had been waiting for. On the side of the mountain, about five feet from the precipice, the cockatrice's snow-misted shape flew for the Cracker Jack.

"Jump!" Koda screamed.

Peluda spit his acid.

Part of the spray hit the snow where Koda and Sully had just been standing while the rest flew into the air… and, as it passed by, the cockatrice's wings. Screaming, the totem went down, thudding into the side of the cliffs.

Koda hung by his nails on the edge. Higher up, Sully gripped a crack in the rock. Peluda clung to the mountainside, agitated by a high shrieking call like a herald of death.

It sounded like a woman's scream.

***

Standing on the plains with the world in front of him, Muraco smiled. What clever Critters would be living there someday. *Yes, you will be going home, Sully and Koda. You two hamsters and your friends, the most unlikely of all to have won.*

He grinned wider. *How very humbling for the totems.*

Hearing Krampus call Jack's name in such utter contempt, that was a memory Muraco would think of every day with the utmost satisfaction.

Pushed by the dragon, the chimera obliterated the plains in Muraco's bright heavenly light. He saw himself from far above as if he were flying. This was already so much like a dream. A premonition of what was to come. He had already begun to separate from his body as a tall, Native American spirit. Muraco shone like white sunrays, lighting everything on the island. The air hummed with his energy.

A violent, scratchy growl rose in Krampus's throat and became a scream of rage. "MURACO! YOU AND YOUR CRITTERS WILL SUFFER! WE'LL GUT YOU ALLLL! ONE DAY!"

Muraco knew his eyes were glowing white as he viewed Krampus centered in a bright vignette. "I do this for my brother and all the Critters you've wronged. May you never escape again."

His Critter body fell limp. It was a feeling of calmness as he released all the light in his spirit. Everyone but himself squinted against his brilliance. Within the rising hum and the rage-filled totem calls, there was a loud hardening sound of growing wood. How satisfying, that sound. Muraco wanted to laugh but found his lips had woodened.

He could still see. For a few seconds more, through a forming layer of bark, he saw he was at the top of a totem pole surrounded by angry wooden faces.

He could relax now. Muraco felt himself tiring, and he began to slip into a dream.

Goodbye, Jack. Have fun.

31

GOODBYE

T HE SNOWFALL evaporated, and snowbanks fell in chunks from the mountains' shoulders. The pathways showed evergreen without black trails as grass grew across the plains to where five totem poles stood at the edge of a colossal rift. In the chasm beyond them, sleet melted on the Haven's crust, and the peppermint fragrance faded from the air. Krampus's power was already fading. The Cracker Jack remained in a bright, still starry-faced sky, though the constellations now displayed relief instead of anger amongst the false sunshine.

And it was all so very silent below, amongst the Critters, who had just begun emerging from the lodges.

Seeing the world this way, from so high up on the mountain, it was enough to make any Critter feel tinier than they were. To Koda, he simply felt alive.

Down in the pass, Koda heard Twiggy shout, "We've won!" His laugh, hoarse with joy, echoed to the precipice. "They're gone! We've WON!"

Sully laughed, too. "Koda, we did it!"

Smiling tiredly, Koda started to respond but stopped as he heard frightened exclamations from the crowd. The dragon, Sydney, tossed rock and water as she crawled out of the rift onto the plains.

The hundreds of Critters who had been hiding deep in the snow scattered in all directions, screaming. Sydney merely watched them go with a smirk. She laid herself down on the ground with a purposeful quake, sending the Critters into even greater panic.

"Everyone, it's alright! She's not a totem!" Twiggy shouted and proceeded to try and convince the crowd. Most continued panicking while others appeared too stunned to move. Twiggy gave up and, seeing Koda and Sully on the mountain, ran to them.

The two brothers climbed carefully down from the mountain shoulder onto dry grass—another blessing. No slush remained, and not a single snowflake fell on them. Everything had become green.

Twiggy didn't slow, and Koda didn't flinch in the slightest, as Twiggy ran into Sully at full speed, embracing him with a hug that seemed both joyful and full of relief.

"I saw the cockatrice. And this weird, flying shape in the sky I couldn't see well through the storm. I think it was the banshee." Twiggy panted. He looked at Sully. "You were up there, too? They told me Koda—"

"It was Koda's idea," Sully said proudly.

"That explains why it was crazy," said Twiggy. "But you're awesome for it."

"Thanks," Koda said.

Twiggy smiled and started as he remembered something. "Jack!"

Sydney's new booming voice startled them. "If you're looking for the rabbit and his friends, Skullduggery and Drools-A-Lot, they're over here."

The Critters raced to the trench past the crowd who had, for the most part, hid in the lodges. Their happiness lessened once they stepped onto the plains. Victims of Gashadokuro and the chupacabra lay fallen in the grass as a sad reminder. More and more

Critters appeared as the snow melted. It became even more apparent to Koda how much the Haven had lost. He passed them silently. As they came up to the totem poles, Twiggy darted around it in a wide path.

At the trench, Jack appeared distracted as he waited for the Tricksters to climb out of the chasm. Bozo heaved Drooler out onto the ground. The yellow Trickster muttered frantically.

"Something's wrong," Koda said and hurried.

The smaller Critters ran up to the group as Bozo was scolding Drooler. "He just keeps babbling on! What is it? Spit it out!"

"He drools enough already!" Sydney thundered above. Being this close to her took Koda's breath away. She sat on the edge of the rift—all her spine scales climbing up and down her body like a series of small mountains—with her tail hanging down into the chasm. A section without scales on her side bled lightly from a sizeable hole. It didn't seem to be bothering her, and the wound appeared to be shrinking.

Drooler scrambled to his feet. "The totem!"

"No, the dragon isn't a totem," Twiggy said.

"I thought it was!" Drooler shrieked.

Koda's heart clenched in worry. The Critters huddled around Drooler. "What are you saying?" Koda asked.

"You got five totems, didn't you?" Twiggy pressed.

"*I* got the most. I captured three," Bozo bragged.

"Bozo, not right now!" Twiggy snapped. "Jack, what happened?"

"I brought one totem and Drooler brought one," Jack said, confused. He glanced worriedly at the Tricksters. "What totems did you capture exactly? Bozo, I saw you had two, but I assumed the third was farther down the trench."

"No, the third went to the mountains," Bozo corrected

defensively, as if someone might try to pin blame on him.

"That's Peluda," Sully chimed in quickly. "Koda took him away from the lodges so it could attack the cockatrice on the mountain."

"Still counts as my catch," Bozo insisted.

"No! NO!" Drooler cried. "Peluda was supposed to be *my* catch!"

Bozo snapped at him. "What does it matter?"

"Shh. Let him talk," Jack said.

Drooler talked fast. "I tried taking the cockatrice to the trench, but it hurt me. It got away. When I went back to find it, I found the dragon." Drooler pointed at Sydney. "I thought I brought Peluda! 'A reptile that spits a burning substance' is what you said. They sound the same!"

"He counted Sydney..." Koda turned behind him to look at the totem poles. He had been so anxious on their way to the trench. Now, as he faced them, he gasped.

One of the totem poles was shorter by a head.

"Jack, we're missing a totem!"

Koda jumped and Sully squeaked beside him as a roar from the chasm pierced the air. A totem stood atop a far-off platform. The last Koda had seen it was as a wooden face in the mountain pass. The ugliest thing he'd ever seen had long since been surpassed by others, but now, in the flesh, it was still a repulsive sight.

The Yeti pounded on his chest, the silver of his apish face turned dark in his rage. Grime from the sea and wet, ground rock turned his winter coat brown. The Yeti roared.

The Critters of the Haven screamed.

The Yeti's third roar abruptly cut short with the sound of the platform collapsing. Sydney's tail sliced into it, struck upward at the Yeti, and threw the totem into the sea. Once again, he became trapped under rock.

Sydney turned her head back to the Critters. They gawked at her with stunned faces. "That was getting annoying," Sydney said.

Jack hopped forward to Bozo and Drooler. "Neither one of you contained the Yeti?" he confronted them.

Bozo hesitated, then shoved Drooler. "You idiot! Why would they say 'burning substance' instead of fire? You brought zero totems. I did all the work!"

Drooler cowered.

"I knew it! I knew you were going to mess everything up!" Twiggy lunged at Bozo. "I bet you did it on purpose!"

"Me?!"

The Critters throughout the plains scurried about in a chaotic jumble. "Everyone, the totem has been dealt with. We are alright," Jack calmed them.

"That's right," Sydney said. "What are all you Critters worried about? I got it covered."

"She can't stay here," Koda told Jack. "She's doing as much damage to the Haven as the totems."

"What are we going to do?" Sully whined.

Jack nervously pawed the grass, stuck for an answer. He glanced at the lodges, the chasm, then Sydney.

"Take it up with you," Jack said. "Both of them. The Yeti isn't anywhere near as unmanageable as the chimera or Peluda. The humans will find something to do with the Yeti," Jack assured.

Koda worried. But Jack was right. If any totem had to be left behind, the Yeti seemed to be the best choice.

"Yeah... That's a great idea!" Twiggy held his paws tightly and wiped them over his face in relief. "Wow, I really thought we were done for."

Sully asked Jack, pleading in his voice, "You mean, we can go home?"

Jack looked at Sydney. She examined her claws and looked

very smug. "I think you have your ride home," Jack said.

Sully spun to Koda. "Koda, we can go *home!*"

"Now you have *two* things to thank me for," Sydney said. The Critters stumbled as she lowered off the plains, taking a chunk out of the rift with her. She sifted through the rubble for the Yeti.

"I don't think Sydney's going to fit in Giant's nest." Sully beamed at Koda.

Koda shared in his happiness, but it was bittersweet as he looked around at their companions. They were going home, and yet...

Jack said, "Please forgive me. I must break my promise. I can't take you myself."

"It's okay. Without you, I would never have made it this far," Koda said.

Twiggy's twitching movements slowed. "The totems are gone or will be soon. Are you sure... you don't want to stay?"

"The other half of my life is up there," Koda said, looking up at the sky before glancing at Sully. His brother's eyes had wetted.

Suddenly, Twiggy leaned forward and hugged Koda. Caught a little off guard but not at all bothered, Koda hugged him back.

Twiggy released him. "Everything's going to be okay."

Koda nodded. "Thank you." He met everyone's eyes. "For helping us."

"You'll return one day," Jack said. "It'll be a better world then."

Sully hugged Jack's paw tightly. "I'll think about you every day."

"I as well," Jack's ears covered Sully as he rested his head over him.

"Bye, Jack," Koda said.

"You are remarkable Critters, Sully and Koda. Have good days."

Koda smiled, and he teared up a little. He would miss Jack's guidance and comfort.

Sully held onto Jack's paw a while longer, then let go to hug Twiggy. He didn't seem able to talk through his tears. Twiggy tightened their hug. "You'll be back, pika."

Drooler shambled over and bent down to pat them on the head. Twiggy gave him a funny look, but he smiled. Sully hugged Drooler's hand.

"Well, if that'll be all…" Bozo said.

"Actually, we could use your help gathering the fallen. They deserve a proper burial." Jack gazed softly at them. "If they have died before, perhaps they will go to another paradise."

Bozo said simply, "I can do that."

As he began to walk away toward the chasm, Sully called to him. "Goodbye, Bozo."

Bozo turned.

"Thank you for your help," Jack said.

"We're sorry we blasted a cannonball at you," Twiggy mumbled.

Bozo grunted. As soon as his back was turned, Drooler stood up and hurried after him. He poked the clown's shoulder and jumped sideways as Bozo turned to look. His voice becoming faint, Bozo scolded him, but as the yellow Trickster stuck with him, Bozo could clearly be heard asking, "You like plays, don't you? Well, I've got the best theater in this whole world. You'll see. I've got everything planned…" And Drooler listened to him with apparent curiosity.

Watching them go, Koda asked, "Will the Tricksters and Critters get along?"

"I think so," Jack said. "Tricksters don't kill. They'll eat what the Critters eat."

His gaze wandered to the totem poles. A brighter sheen

from the face constellations cast Muraco, at the top above the owl, in a radiant glow. The white hare remained white even in wooden form, and the Trickster in him showed in the smiling carved eyes. Koda realized that his body was nowhere to be seen anywhere on the plains.

"Our world will never be the same. But there's good to be found in most everyone, no matter what species," Jack murmured.

Sully went over to Jack. He stood by him and unpouched the two relics. The last pieces in existence. Sully set them in front of Jack, who stared at them. After a bit of silence, he laid a paw over the relics.

The ground quaked. Sydney held the Yeti wrapped in her tail and slammed the unconscious totem onto the plains.

Jack woke as if from a dream. He pawed Sully affectionately and looked up at Sydney. "Your dragon and the smoking creature must have merged with each other somehow," he said.

"I remembered what that fox scaleless said," said Sydney. "All that complicated stuff about reacting from things around it. When this thing showed up, I wasn't even thinking about it. I was thinking about those stupid bunch of heads you call totems. I thought how great it would be if I were bigger than them and could put them in their place. I always did like green. So, that was pretty cool, I guess, when I turned into a flying dragon and all." Sydney looked smugly down at Twiggy. "Probably what the fox scaleless meant when she said I'd be useful, huh?"

Twiggy frowned at her. He walked over to Jack and touched his arm as he looked at the totem poles. "Are the Critters going to be safe? From the totems?"

"I could burn them," Sydney offered.

"No!" Jack exclaimed. "No. We don't know what will happen if you do. It's safe now. This is a paradise place, and no unique Critters like Sydney will enter the circle."

"I keep telling you, I'm not a Critter," Sydney snarled. She curved her neck at the sky. "Now hurry up and wrap up this lovefest. That Halloween thing is closing."

The Cracker Jack's mouth was shrinking along with its entire head as the pumpkin skin faded into the sky, the ridges becoming stars. Koda's anxiety returned.

"How are we going to get up there?" Sully asked. He stood, pointing worriedly at the sky. "We'd fall off the dragon's back!"

Sydney displayed her new pillar-sized teeth, which gleamed in the false sunshine. She rested her head on the grass and opened her mouth.

Jack said, "I think she'll have to carry you inside her mouth."

"She's gonna eat them!" Twiggy cried.

"Stop being such rodents," said Sydney. "Come on! Before the pumpkin turns into stars or whatever. You think, after saving your Haven, I'd wreck your happy ending like that?"

"You better not," said Twiggy.

Koda climbed the beveled scales into the dragon's mouth. Sully hurried in behind. The two looked unsurely around at the cavernous mouth, smelling smoke.

Sydney's tongue moved under Koda and Sully. "Maybe..." she said.

Sully gulped.

Her teeth slowly closed over their view of Jack and Twiggy, concerned but hopeful expressions on their faces. Just before her teeth fully closed, something fell—possibly from the sky. Something flashed red before Koda's blurring vision turned it white.

Sydney's tongue rolled massively under them again and slipped out onto the grass. As the tongue slipped back inside, it brought in the third red tarot card facing right-side up. On it was an image of Sydney in her dragon form, laying on the grass, with Sully and Koda as two small specks in the cave of her mouth.

The text on the bottom spelled GOODBYE.

Sully said, "I think we passed the test."

Sydney's wings wildly batted the wind as she lifted off the plains. Koda worried they would fall to the back of her throat and be swallowed, but she kept them level. Could her wings fit through the Cracker Jack? What size was it now? He hadn't checked before they ran inside.

He held on as, with a great uplift, Sydney raised them into bright sunlight shining into her mouth. Koda heard birds squawking. There was the sound of small flapping wings as Sydney's wings tucked in with a *FWUMP*. A hard thump as they landed sent Sully and Koda rocking on her tongue, and they scrambled to look out through her teeth. The sunlight flared everything from sight.

"Koda, can you see anything?" Sully asked excitedly.

Koda bobbed around him, too excited to speak.

Sydney said, "Come on out, you two. I think I'm changing out here."

Sydney opened her mouth, and they jumped off her jaw to the ground. What Koda most clearly noticed was the air. It was denser, not as fresh as the Haven, and it smelled of winter. But it was a normal winter air, without a hint of snow or peppermint. He sniffed trees, pinecones, and giant smells. They were in a forest. Was it the national forest? If it was, he smelled not a trace of spoiled grass or decaying bark. It was healthy. Koda could just see, somewhere far off, a clearing marked with small buildings and buzzing with giant life, and a road opposite it striped in parts by thick firs.

He inhaled all the joy of seeing everything before his vision started to fade. The road disappeared in an irregularity of light, trees blurred to random bold streaks of black, and the color... The color was gone. What Koda could see was no farther than three inches in front of his nose. Nothing more.

"We can't see like a giant anymore," Sully said softly.

Koda sympathized with his sadness. *I've seen mountains. And skies and snow and more color than I ever thought existed. Even if it was only for a few days, we've seen more than any hamster has.* Losing the giant sight here in this forest was like the final gear moving into place that would make his life normal again.

A giant's scream forced Koda out of his thoughts.

Sydney shouted to the clearing, "That's right! Fear me!" The sharp explosive sound of her voice prompted more screams.

She was a massive black shape with only her eyes and glittering wings standing out like twinkling stars. Smoke waved around her crazily as some change took place. Koda could hear the crisp shifting sound of her scales as if they were leaves rustling. Sydney growled. The most prevalent features of her dragon self, including her horns and wings, shrank into her form as she herself shrank. Finally, with all the smoke gone—and likely the Smoking Beast as well—she was the dragon they knew. A bearded dragon, once again.

Sydney looked herself over. "Not a scratch. It was fun while it lasted." She sighed. "I'm gonna miss having those big teeth."

"Why did you help us?" Koda asked.

"I was itching to take a bite out of Yellow Eyes."

"You didn't have to fly us here," Sully said.

"Yeah, and I coulda ate you, too. Maybe I'll do it right now," Sydney said angrily.

Sully stood perfectly calm by Koda.

Sydney grumbled. "See a couple'a monsters and you're impervious to fear. Well, we'll see about that later. Insect-Giver likes you. That's the *only* reason you're not coming home in my stomach."

Sully smiled. "Thank you, Sydney."

She was about to speak again, possibly with another come-back, when footsteps sped up to the grove. Something clattered onto the ground. There was an exclamation of surprise as a little way from them, a giant faltered out of the bushes and fell back against a tree. Koda remembered the Yeti. To him, the totem resembled a rather large, oddly shaped bush.

Sydney bared her teeth. "Poacher!"

"Poacher?" Koda said. She acted as if she knew him.

And him, too, apparently. The stocky giant leaned forward at Sydney. "You!"

"Yeah, it's me, you dope. How's your car?"

His attention returned to the Yeti, and he snapped back against the tree. More bushes rustled. A crowd gathered in the grove, their voices excited.

"It's a Sasquatch!" someone cried.

"Who ever heard of a white Sasquatch?" said another.

"It's not a Sasquatch. It's just some guy in a hokey costume." One of the giants stepped boldly up to the Yeti.

"I wouldn't do that…" said Sydney.

The giant poked the totem.

And with a violent, rugged growl, the Yeti stirred. The crowd screamed as the totem swung at the giant, and he lunged away, barely missing the attack. Koda, Sully, and even Sydney jolted. The Yeti towered above the giants, stomping forward and jerking his head at those running away for the clearing.

A loud *POP!* went off like a cork firing from a bottle. The Yeti turned around and roared at the stocky giant who now held a long gun. Koda would forever remember how the hunter's gun had glinted silver in false sunlight. This gun did the same. It was likely what he had heard clatter in the bushes. Another pop went off, and the totem staggered. He fell with a thud, his breathing deep as puffs through his nose.

The stocky giant panted. "I saw something big. Glad I had that thing with me."

"Did you kill it?" someone called out. A few giants stood a safe distance away in the foliage, their postures tense and ready to run.

"No, he's tranquilized," he called back.

Sydney looked at the Yeti. "Guy's not having a good day. Let's get out of here."

She started to walk the two brothers toward the road and drew back, mouth agape, as the stocky giant lunged from the tree. "No, not this time! You're coming with me!"

He bent down to her. Sydney snapped at his fingers and turned to run too late as he grabbed her tail. Dangling, Sydney began spitting the worst of names.

"Ha! Gotcha! You car-wrecking bearded dragon!"

"Finally, someone gets it right!" Sydney shouted, but she continued to swear.

The stocky giant saw Koda and Sully and cautiously stepped forward.

Koda paused, unsure of what to do. If this had happened before, he would have thought it unthinkable for a giant to harm them. He knew better now, but he would always see his Giant first in every human.

The stocky giant grabbed the two brothers and held them up to the light, seeming to take interest in their sweaters. "Are these made of cobwebs?"

He walked them to the road as more murmuring giants entered the grove to gawk at the Yeti.

"Where's he taking us?" Sully wiggled in his hand. "We have to go home!"

They arrived at a truck parked on the side of the road. Sydney made some comment about "destroying the other one pretty good." The stocky giant opened the back hatch, placed Sully and Koda in an open carrier, and locked it. With Sydney, he was much more careful. He placed her in a carrier and hastily pulled his hand away before she could bite him again. Then he closed the hatch and jogged back to the excitement in the grove.

The wait was long with nothing for Koda and Sully to do but worry. Sometime later vans carrying strange mechanical equipment on top drove up behind the truck. Giants with cameras hurried out of them, one tripping and almost face-planting on the pavement.

"It's working," said Sydney. "I almost feel sorry for the snowman."

The dragon wouldn't stop talking about how the poacher was going to stuff them or make little bags out of her scales. She worried Koda and Sully for a bit, but Koda soon wondered otherwise. He didn't *feel* uneasy, or likely he was too tired to worry after all that had already happened.

What seemed like hours later, the stocky giant returned. The car's tires grated pebbles on the concrete. Wind hummed outside. Still another hour later, Sydney complained about not being given anything to eat and gave snide comments about the "poacher" while he talked vigorously on the phone. The word "sasquatch" was mentioned several times. Whoever he was talking to, Koda heard them constantly bursting out in laughter.

The gravel shifted as the tires turned. A seatbelt unclasped, a door then the trunk opened. The stocky giant took their carriers out of the car. Feeling a rise in anxiety, Koda got a hold of himself. He would trust everything would be alright.

All Koda could see past the barred door was sunlight as the stocky giant walked them outside. Sydney had stopped making insults and that seemed strange. Sully called to her to ask what she could see. After a pause, Sydney grunted. There was something like amusement in that grunt.

A door creaked. Someone cried out. It was a happy cry, and

it sounded familiar.

Sydney's carrier floated out of the sunlight, and gentle hands removed the dragon from it. Both forms were blurry and dark, but as Sydney was taken inside the doorway, and Koda and Sully were raised out of their carriers, he saw a clear warm smile. She smelled like someone they knew.

Sully stood and almost fell over. His nose and whiskers twitched, and he bobbed up and down. Crying, overwhelmed with happiness, Koda rested his head on her palm and grasped her finger with his left paw.

"I've got you." She spilled a laugh through her tears.

She was their Giant.

EPILOGUE

I N THE DEAD of night, a grandfather clock played the
Westminster Chimes. Insect-Giver and the rodents were
asleep. The only one awake in the house was Sydney.

The TV was still on, providing Sydney plenty of enter-
tainment as reporters chattered on about the Yeti. An interviewee
called it "a legend brought back to life." Sydney couldn't understand, of course, but she was able to figure out most of what
followed. The poacher had his fifteen minutes of fame, and after all
the reporters were done pouring all over him, scaleless in fancy suits
and glasses (scientists, probably) joined in on the talk. When a video
of the State Zoo was shown, Sydney assumed that after the
scientists were done with the Yeti, the totem would soon be
Oregon's main attraction.

Poor snowman, indeed.

Sydney had been given a satisfactory welcome: crickets,
mealworms, and no nasty greens. She felt fuller than she had in
days, and she licked her nose in pleasure. The air tasted of brown
sugar ham. Gift wrapping cluttered the rug. A new one had been
placed on the floor, as well as a new Christmas tree where Insect-
Giver had hung the cobweb sweaters as ornaments. For presents,
the rodents had been gifted their yogurt drops and cheese wedges

491

and for Sydney, a nice chunky hornworm.

She ignored the Christmas lights and, tilting her head, peered out of her dwelling at the rodent's homes. Sydney tapped her nails slowly and creepily on the glass. The rodents didn't stir. For once, Sully hadn't escaped.

"Hmph."

Sydney looked to the window. Insect-Giver had put up curtains over the glass, though Sydney expected it was snowflake-covered. Already she could feel a small chill, then a rise of warmth in her stomach. That was odd since her basking light was turned off.

Sydney's tail twitched. She writhed upon the driftwood, bending at her stomach. Something hot was coming up. It didn't hurt. Just peculiar. Her eyes dilated, and she opened her mouth wide.

The glass of her home alighted as she spit a tremendous flame. It sputtered and threw ash, then winked out under her tongue.

She burped.

"Excuse me," Sydney said, and grinned.

THE END

GLOSSARY

Queretaro Otomi and Yucatec Maya are unique languages mainly spoken in Mexico. I apologize for any errors in translation that may have occurred.

Tx'utho bicho: (Queretaro Otomi) little critter

Nahiossi: (Cheyenne) has three fingers

Duende: a goblin-like creature from Latin America folklore.

Ga bendiga. Dí t'olo ne yá ts'edi.: (Queretaro Otomi): Bless us. We are small and weak.

T'u'ul: (Yucatec Maya) rabbit

Muraco: (Native American) White moon

Yān. Yān sǐ bìng chéngwéi shuǐ de yībùfèn.: (Chinese) Drown. Drown and become a part of the water.

Willkommen: (German) Welcome

Nussknacker: (German) Nutcracker

Backpfeifengesicht: (German) a face badly in need of a punch.

Handi ko ngeki Ante ir colillas ar congelen.: (Queretaro Otomi) Come with me before your butts freeze.

Suku'un: (Yucatec Maya) brother

ACKNOWLEDGEMENTS

About three years ago, *Critter Haven* began as an idea for a series called *The Great Cheese Adventure*, which featured my pets as the main characters. I have a YouTube channel dedicated to small animals, and when I asked viewers if they were interested in the idea, most said "yes." If not for them, I likely wouldn't have made the series (even for myself). But I did, and by the time the final episode came around, I started thinking I wanted to turn *The Great Cheese Adventure* into a novel.

It's been a long process, and I'm very grateful to those who supported me along the way. Thank you very much to my beta readers, E.B. Roland and Frances Fitzgerald, for helping make my novel the best it could be. A big thank you goes to my copy editor, Katherine Gale-Han, for being so kind in her support and feedback. I consider my beta readers and Katherine as good friends.

I'd like to credit Sam Cooke's *Twistin' the Night Away* for the inspiration for Bozo's performance on stage and Bobby Lake-Thom for his book, *Spirits of the Earth*, which gave me a better understanding of Native American culture and their connection with animals. Thank you so much, Alexey, for the stunning book cover (I can't stop looking at it!) and I'd also like to thank my mom for listening to me whenever I had doubts about my writing. She's always been there for me.

Critter Haven is dedicated to my animals, Sully, Koda, and Sydney. Sully and Koda passed away while I was writing their story. I miss them very much. I like to think they are happy eating yogurt drops and cheese wedges somewhere. Maybe in a critter haven.

ANGELINA MORETTI lives in Arizona but would prefer to live somewhere snowy. Besides writing, she loves to read, create papier-mâché creatures, and spend time with her ball python, Hannibal, and two bearded dragons, Sydney and Link. *Critter Haven* is her debut novel.

Learn more about *Critter Haven* and the author at
www.angelinamoretti.com

Made in the USA
Monee, IL
03 October 2022

15185901R00298